The Poetical Works of
CHRISTOPHER SMART

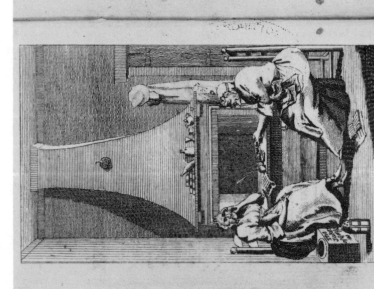

The Midwife;

OR THE

OLD WOMAN'S MAGAZINE.

Containing all the WIT, *and all the*
HUMOUR, *and all the* LEARNING, *and*
all the JUDGEMENT, *that has ever been,*
or ever will be inserted in all the other
Magazines, or the Magazine of Magazines,
or the Grand Magazine of Magazines, *or*
any other Book whatever: so that
those who buy this Book will want
—————— *no other.* —————

Publish'd pursuant to several Acts
of Parliament, and by the Permission
of their most Christian and most Catholic
MAJESTIES, *the* GREAT MOGUL *and the*
——————— STATES GENERAL.———————

Embellish'd with CUTS *according to* CUSTOM.

LONDON.

Printed for MARY MIDNIGHT *and sold by*
T. CARNAN *in S*t *Pauls Church Yard.*
Price Three Pence.

16. of October 1750.

De la Barriere Inv*t.*   F. Garden Sculp*t.*

Title-page and frontispiece from *The Midwife*, Vol. i (1751).

The Poetical Works of
CHRISTOPHER SMART

IV

Miscellaneous Poems
English and Latin

EDITED BY

Karina Williamson

CLARENDON PRESS · OXFORD

1987

Oxford University Press, Walton Street, Oxford OX2 6DP

Oxford New York Toronto
Delhi Bombay Calcutta Madras Karachi
Petaling Jaya Singapore Hong Kong Tokyo
Nairobi Dar es Salaam Cape Town
Melbourne Auckland

and associated companies in
Beirut Berlin Ibadan Nicosia

Oxford is a trade mark of Oxford University Press

Published in the United States
by Oxford University Press, New York

British Library Cataloguing in Publication Data
Smart, Christopher
The poetical works of Christopher Smart.
Vol. 4: Miscellaneous poems, English and
Latin
I. Title   II. Williamson, Karina
821'.6   PR3687.S7
ISBN 0-19-812768-5
0195118694
Library of Congress Cataloging in Publication Data
(Revised for vol. 4)
Smart, Christopher, 1722–1771.
The poetical works of Christopher Smart.
Includes indexes.
Bibliography: p.
Contents: v. 1. Jubilate agno—v. 2. Religious
poetry, 1763–1771— —v. 4. Miscellaneous poems,
English and Latin.
I. Williamson, Karina.   II. Title.
PR3687.S7A6 .980 821'.6 79-41319
ISBN 0-19-811869-4 (v. 1)

Set by Latimer Trend & Company Ltd, Plymouth
Printed and bound in Great Britain by
Biddles Ltd, Guildford and King's Lynn

ACKNOWLEDGEMENTS

MY greatest debt with this volume is to Betty Rizzo and Robert Mahony, who put their vast stores of information about Smart's writings and publications unstintingly at my disposal. I have been generously helped too by scholars outside my own field, who have patiently answered inquiries which must often have appeared ignorant or trivial from their point of view. I am grateful particularly to John Griffith for spending long and uncomplaining hours over Smart's Latin verse, and for supplying the translations of *Arion, Christopherus Smart Samueli Saunders, On St. David's Day 1753,* and *Faber Acicularius* printed in this edition; to Peter Ward Jones and Robert Bruce of the Bodleian Music Room, Harry Johnstone and J. R. Goodall (whose thesis on "English Chamber Cantata and Through-composed Solo Song 1660–*c.*1785" was a mine of information), for guidance in the field of eighteenth-century music; and to Kenneth Garlick and John Kerslake for advice about paintings. For other help, advice, or fruitful suggestions I should like to thank Donald Eddy, David Fleeman, Richard Larschan, Roger Lonsdale, Angus McIntosh, Geoffrey Nuttall, John Platt, George Rousseau, Arthur Sherbo, Leo Sides, my colleague Doreen Innes, and my former pupils Robin Dix, Elaine Henderson, and Philip Lewin. The staff of the Bodleian Library have, once again, proved unfailingly courteous and helpful, and I am thankful also for the services of the British Library, the Folger Shakespeare Library, Pembroke College Library, Cambridge, Wellesley College Library, the Berg Collection, New York Public Library, and the Osborn Collection, Yale University Library.

I should like finally to record a deep sense of gratitude to my husband Colin who, though he did not live to see the publication of these volumes, lightened the task of completing them by his patience and understanding.

K.W.

St Hilda's College
Oxford

CONTENTS

CONTENTS

CONTENTS

CONTENTS

CONTENTS

xi

CONTENTS

LIST OF ILLUSTRATIONS

ABBREVIATIONS AND REFERENCES

A. *Abbreviations used in Introduction and Commentary*

For classical references, the abbreviations are those used in the *Oxford Classical Dictionary*. Translations from Horace by Smart are from his prose translation (1756). Works cited are published in London unless otherwise indicated.

Ainsworth	Robert Ainsworth, *Thesaurus Linguæ Latinæ compendiarius*, 1736.
Ainsworth and Noyes	E. G. Ainsworth and C. E. Noyes, *Christopher Smart: a biographical and critical study*, University of Missouri Studies xviii, 1943.
AV	Authorized Version of the Bible (King James Version).
BL	The British Library, London.
BNYPL	*Bulletin of the New York Public Library*.
Bodl.	The Bodleian Library, Oxford.
Boswell's Life	*Boswell's Life of Johnson*, ed. G. B. Hill, revised L. F. Powell, 6 vols., 1934–50.
Botting	Roland B. Botting, "Christopher Smart in London", *Research Studies of the State College of Washington* vii (1939), 3–54.
Brittain	*Poems by Christopher Smart*, ed. Robert Brittain, Princeton 1950.
Callan	*The Collected Poems of Christopher Smart*, ed. Norman Callan, 2 vols., 1949.
Carr	Harry Carr, *The Freemason at Work*, 1976.
CC	*The Cambridge Chronicle and Journal*, 1762–1848.
Chambers	Ephraim Chambers, *Cyclopædia, or an Universal Dictionary of Arts and Sciences*, 2 vols., 1728.
CJ	*The Cambridge Journal*, 1744–62.
CM	*The Christian's Magazine*, 1760–7.
CP6	*A Collection of Pretty Poems for the amusement of children six foot high*, 1756.
Critical Rev.	*The Critical Review*, 1756–1817.
Dearnley	Moira Dearnley, *The Poetry of Christopher Smart*, 1968.
Devlin	Christopher Devlin, *Poor Kit Smart*, 1961.
DNB	*Dictionary of National Biography*.

ELH	*Journal of English Literary History.*
Eternity	Smart, *On the Eternity of the Supreme Being*, 1750.
GJ	*Gray's-Inn Journal*, 1752–4.
GM	*The Gentleman's Magazine*, 1731–1907.
Goodness	Smart, *On the Goodness of the Supreme Being*, 1756.
Gray, *Corresp.*	*Correspondence of Thomas Gray*, ed. P. Toynbee and L. Whibley, 3 vols., 1935.
Gray's *Bibliography*	G. J. Gray, "A Bibliography of the Writings of Christopher Smart", *Transactions of the Bibliographical Society* 6 (1903), 269–305.
Hunter	*The Poems of the late Christopher Smart* (with account of his life by Christopher Hunter), 2 vols., Reading, 1791.
Hymns	Smart, *Hymns and Spiritual Songs for the Fasts and Festivals of the Church of England*, 1765.
Hymns (1771)	Smart, *Hymns for the Amusement of Children*, 1771.
JA	Smart, *Jubilate Agno.*
Jones	Claude E. Jones, "Christopher Smart, Richard Rolt and *The Universal Visiter*", *The Library*, 4th ser. 18 (1937), 212–14.
Immensity	Smart, *On the Immensity of the Supreme Being*, 1751.
LB	William Boyce, *Lyra Britannica*, [1747].
LH	Thomas Arne, *Lyric Harmony*, [1746].
LM	*The London Magazine*, 1732–85.
London Stage	*The London Stage 1660–1800*, Part 3: 1729–47, ed. A. Scouten, 2 vols. Part 4: 1747–76, ed. G. Stone, Jr., 3 vols. Carbondale, Ill., 1961–2.
LTM	*The Literary Magazine*, 1756–8.
Mahony and Rizzo	R. Mahony and B. W. Rizzo, *Christopher Smart: an annotated bibliography 1743–1983*, New York, 1984.
MB	*The Muses Banquet*, Reading, 1752.
MLR	*Modern Language Review.*
MM	*The Monthly Magazine; or, British Register*, 1796–1843.
Monthly Rev.	*The Monthly Review*, 1749–1845.
MW	*The Midwife; or, The Old Woman's Magazine*, 3 vols., 1751–3.
N&Q	*Notes and Queries.*
NT	New Testament.
ODCC	*Oxford Dictionary of the Christian Church.*
OED	*Oxford English Dictionary.*
Omniscience	Smart, *On the Omniscience of the Supreme Being*, 1752.
OT	Old Testament.

Parables	Smart, *The Parables of Our Lord and Saviour Jesus Christ*, 1768.
PBSA	*Publications of the Bibliographical Society of America.*
Power	Smart, *On the Power of the Supreme Being*, 1754.
Phædrus	Smart, *A Poetical Translation of the Fables of Phædrus*, 1765.
PQ	*Philological Quarterly.*
RES	*Review of English Studies.*
Sherbo	Arthur Sherbo, *Christopher Smart: Scholar of the University*, Michigan, 1967.
ST	*The Student, or, the Oxford and Cambridge Miscellany*, 2 vols., 1750–1.
UV	*The Universal Visiter*, 1756.
VM	Thomas Arne, *Vocal Melody*, [1750].
Walpole, *Corresp.*	*The Yale Edition of Horace Walpole's Correspondence*, ed. W. S. Lewis, New Haven, 48 vols., 1937–83.
Williamson (1973)	"Christopher Smart: problems of attribution reconsidered", *The Library*, 5th ser. 28 (1973), 116–23.
—— (1974)	"Christopher Smart in the Songbooks", *RES*, NS 25 (1974), 410–21.
—— (1979)	"Smart's *Principia*: science and anti-science in *Jubilate Agno*", *RES*, NS 30 (1979), 409–22.

B. *Additional abbreviations used in the textual notes*

[For collections and separate editions, see below, pp. 000–000]

MO	*Mrs. Midnight's Orations.*
MU	*The Museum.*
PA	*The Public Advertiser.*
PC	Smart MSS in Pembroke College Library, Cambridge.
RM	*The Reading Mercury.*
SS	Song-sheets.
UM	*The Universal Magazine of Knowledge and Pleasure.*
UMU	*The Universal Museum.*

C. *Editions quoted*

Samuel Butler, *Hudibras*, ed. J. Wilders, Oxford, 1967.

John Milton, *Poetical Works*, ed. D. Bush, Oxford Standard Authors, 1966.

The Twickenham Edition of the Poems of Alexander Pope, gen. ed. John Butt, 6 vols., 1939–67.

ABBREVIATIONS AND REFERENCES

William Shakespeare: the complete works, ed. P. Alexander, 1951.

Jonathan Swift, *Poetical Works,* ed. H. Davis, Oxford Standard Authors, 1967.

James Thomson, *The Seasons and The Castle of Indolence,* ed. J. Sambrook, Oxford Paperback English Texts, 1972.

Quotations from the Bible are from the Authorized Version (King James Version).

INTRODUCTION

(i) *General*

THE works in this volume are arranged in chronological order, according to date of composition as far as determinable, or, failing that, by date of first publication. This arrangement highlights the sheer diversity of Smart's output: there is hardly a genre current in the eighteenth century that he did not attempt at one time or another in his career, from epigram to mock-epic, ballad to georgic. His register is correspondingly wide, ranging from the familiar to the religious sublime, from low comedy to Pindaric afflatus. Nevertheless, the broad outline of his evolution from an academic and popular versifier into an ardent and dedicated Christian poet remains clear.

The turning-point, as Smart himself reports it in *Hymn to the Supreme Being*, was a dangerous illness which he suffered sometime during or before 1756. Reduced by fever to a state of physical and mental collapse ('My mind lay open to the powers of night'), he was rescued from perdition by divine grace:

> He pitying did a second birth bestow
> A birth of joy—not like the first of tears and woe
>
> (71–2)

His powers as man and poet were thereafter to be consecrated to the service and glorification of God:

> Ye strengthen'd feet, forth to his altar move;
> Quicken, ye new-strung nerves, th'enraptur'd lyre;
> Ye heav'n directed eyes, o'erflow with love;
> Glow, glow, my soul, with pure seraphic fire;
> Deeds, thoughts, and words no more his mandates break,
> But to his endless glory work, conceive, and speak.
>
> (73–8)

The miscellaneity of Smart's poetry before 1756 is an accurate reflection of his unstable and often rackety existence in the first period of his career. Most of it was written for particular occasions or popular consumption, or both, and in compliance with current conventions of language and genre. If this limits its individuality as poetry, it does not deprive it of extrinsic interest; the epistles and addresses to friends and benefactors, the love poems, epitaphs, and invitations, yield useful glimpses of Smart's personal life. One group in particular, the poems concerning Harriote Pratt, for whom his nephew, Christopher Hunter, tells us Smart 'entertained a long and unsuccessful passion', are almost all the evidence that survives of this episode. Since the details of Harriote's personal history, as far as they can be traced, have not hitherto been assembled, it may be helpful to supply them here.[1]

Harriote came from an old Norfolk family, the Pratts of Ryston, whose most distinguished representative was the architect Sir Roger Pratt (1620–84). Sir Roger built Ryston Hall, the family seat near Downham Market, to classical designs in 1669–72 (the house was remodelled beyond recognition in the 1780s). Harriote was the younger daughter of another Roger Pratt (d. 1771), High Sheriff of Norfolk from 1727, who had been a member of Pembroke College, Cambridge, Smart's own college. His two sons, Edward and Jermyn, were sent to Caius College, however, in 1735 and 1741 respectively. Edward Pratt (1717–84), a fellow of Caius during Smart's time at Cambridge, commanded a company in the Norfolk Militia in the 1756–63 war. Jermyn Pratt (1723–91) took orders in 1749 and held the livings of Marlingford and Watlington in Norfolk. Both brothers married into Norfolk families, the Astleys of Melton Constable and Stanforths of Salthouse, whose names figure in the subscription lists for Smart's poems and psalms. Harriote herself was married on 18 September 1752 to Thurlow Stafford, whose family was already closely linked by marriage to the Pratts. He too was up at Cambridge, entering Magdalene College in 1739, the same year as Smart was admitted to Pembroke. Like Edward Pratt, Stafford was a captain in the Norfolk Militia, but died in 1760. Harriote did

---

[1] The spelling *Harriote* is Smart's, both in his letter (quoted below) and in *JA*, B31. Hunter's brief reference to her is in *1791*, I, p. xxxiii. For other information about the family, I am indebted to Mr E. R. M. Pratt, of Ryston; Burke's *Commoners*; Venn's *Alumni Cantabrigienses; The History and Antiquities of the County of Norfolk* (1781); Norfolk Record Society, *Index of Wills* (1969); *GM* (1760); *DNB*.

not remarry. At the time she subscribed to Smart's psalms (1765), she was living at Crow Hall, a house situated near Ryston, between Denver and Downham Market, where she appears to have remained until her death in 1779.

Smart presumably came to know Harriote through friendship with her brothers. Jermyn is mentioned by name in *Jubilate Agno* (B531), but both brothers subscribed to Smart's poems and psalms. The first poem about Harriote, *On seeing Miss H——— P—t, in an Apothecary's Shop*, was published in 1746, but the one piece of first-hand evidence of Smart's 'long and unsuccessful passion' for her is a letter addressed to Charles Burney from Downham Market three years later, in which Smart writes:

You must know I am situated within a mile of my Harriote & Love has robd Friendship of her just dues; but you know the force of the passion too well to be angry at its effect. . . . I am as much a stranger as you to what is going on at Vaux Hall, for we are so wrapt up in our own snugness at this part of the kingdom, that we know little what's doing in the rest of the world. There was a great musical crash at Cambridge, which was greatly admired, but I was not there, being much better pleased with hearing my Harriote on her spinnet & organ at her ancient mansion.[2]

Smart's retreat to the snug seclusion of Cambridge and Norfolk did not last long. By Michaelmas Term 1749 he had effectively left Cambridge for good and moved to London, where he was soon engaged as writer and editor for the publisher, John Newbery, and in August 1751 he announced the transference of his heart from Harriote to a new charmer in *The Lass with the Golden Locks*, the first of a number of poems about Newbery's stepdaughter, Anna Maria ('Nancy') Carnan, whom Smart married in 1752.

The crisis of 1756 did not produce an instantaneous transformation of Smart's poetry, but rather precipitated a change for which he had long been preparing. Success as an academic versifier, Grub-street hack, and writer for the theatres and pleasure-gardens, was never the summit of his ambition, however exuberantly he entered into these roles. Even as a

---

[2] Houghton Library, Harvard, dated 29 July 1749. The letter is printed in full in R. Lonsdale's *Dr. Charles Burney* (Oxford, 1965), p. 26.

young man he had higher goals in view. The earliest indication comes in *The Hop-Garden,* which he must have begun at Cambridge not later than 1743 (see commentary). Although a georgic of over 700 lines in 'verse Miltonian' was in itself ambitious enough as a venture for a twenty-one-year-old, Smart acknowledges its subordinate rank in the hierarchy of genres. While hoping for success in the chosen mode ('Smile the muse'), he nevertheless wishes he were capable of a loftier enterprise, but feels himself disqualified by his youthfulness:

> Oh! cou'd I emulate Dan Sydney's muse,
> Thy Sydney, Cantium . . .
>
> Had I such pow'r, no peasants toil, no hops
> Shou'd e'er debase my lay: far nobler themes,
> The high atchievements of thy warrior kings
> Shou'd raise my thoughts, and dignify my song.
> But I, young rustic, dare not leave my cot,
> For so enlarg'd a sphere . . .

(i. 11–27)

The choice of Sidney's *Arcadia* (to which Smart evidently refers) as a model for the epic poet is unexpected. Sidney is clearly appropriate because of his Kentish origins, but Smart also has some justification for thinking of the *Arcadia* as an heroic poem, in Sidney's own declaration in the *Defence of Poetry* that 'it is not rhyming and versing that maketh a poet', and his classification of Xenophon's *Cyropaedia* as 'an absolute heroical poem'.[3]

A more significant anticipation of Smart's future development comes in the preface to his *Ode for Music* (1746), when he speaks of the suggestion made to him by a friend that 'David's playing to King Saul when he was troubled with the evil Spirit' would be a good subject for an ode on St Cecilia's Day. Although 'much pleased with the hint at first', he was deterred from taking it up by 'the greatness of the subject', in the belief that the 'chusing too high subjects has been the ruin of many a tolerable Genius'. Once again the poet presents himself as incapable of, or unprepared for (the phraseology is ambiguous, perhaps deliberately so) the highest flights. But the gratuitous

---

[3] *Miscellaneous Prose*, ed. K. Duncan-Jones and J. van Dorsten (Oxford, 1973), p. 81.

introduction of the subject of David is in itself a telling sign of the direction of Smart's thinking. The ambition revealed in the *Hop-Garden* to enlarge the sphere of his poetry is now focused on a particular (and by hindsight particularly significant) religious theme. As Allan Gedalof has shown, the evolution of Smart's poetics can in fact be charted with some precision in terms of his references to David.[4]

The real change in Smart's poetry, both in conception and in practice, did not however begin until 1750 with the first of his poems written for the Seatonian Prize at Cambridge. This award, offered annually from 1750 under the will of Thomas Seaton, was for the best 'Poem, or Ode, or Copy of Verses' written by a Master of Arts of the University of Cambridge on the subject of 'one or other of the Perfections or Attributes of the Supreme Being'.[5] Smart entered for and won the prize every year from 1750–55 (except for 1754,[6] when he did not compete), and these Seatonian poems are among the most ambitious of his original compositions before 1756. Although they may have been undertaken at first as an academic exercise, the religious theme evidently released imaginative energies of a new kind. In form and subject-matter, it is true, Smart's Seatonian poems are conventional enough. Subtitled 'A Poetical Essay', each of them conforms to the model of loosely integrated discourse on a general topic, usually in iambic pentameters, set by Pope's well-known 'Essays' in verse. The practice of using the 'poetical essay' for disquisitions on religion and science was well-established by 1750, and the divine attributes had become a popular theme. In 1737, for example, the *Gentleman's Magazine* ran a competition for the best poem on this subject, the winning entries for which were published in April and June. The subject was taken up with particular enthusiasm by the physico-theologians, whose object was to reconcile religion with the new science by demonstrating that scientific study of the physical world revealed (in Addison's words) 'that Design in all the Works of Nature, which

---

[4] 'The Rise and Fall of Smart's David', *PQ* 60 (1981), 369–86.

[5] See Sherbo, p. 62, for the terms of the competition in full.

[6] The 1753 prize was not awarded until Dec., so Smart's poem was published in 1754. The award for 1754 went to George Bally for a poem *On the Justice of the Supreme Being*. See *Musæ Seatonianæ* (1772), 41–60.

necessarily leads us to the Knowledge of its first Cause' (*Spectator*, No. 339). Smart's themes are mostly drawn from the common stock of physico-theological ideas which had been popularized in prose by Addison's essays and Derham's *Physico-Theology* (1713), and in verse by Blackmore's much-acclaimed *Creation* (1712). The argument for God's existence based on the artful contrivances of Nature (*Immensity*), the limitations of human knowledge contrasted with the instinctive sagacity of brutes (*Omniscience*), the benevolence of the Creator manifested in the order and beauty of the world (*Goodness*): these are standard themes in a tradition of poetry going back to the beginning of the century.[7]

The Seatonian poems are nevertheless of the first significance in Smart's development. In them he realizes with peculiar intensity, and with a Christian emphasis unusual in the tradition, the physico-theological commonplace that the study of nature reveals a creation wonderfully designed and co-ordinated in itself and the source of inexhaustible benefits for mankind. Already in these poems he sees gratitude and praise—central themes in his poetry after 1756—as the reflexive activity of nature and the prime obligation of man and the poet. Where the tendency of physico-theology was towards natural religion, Smart goes out of his way to insist that the *two* 'prime Pillars' of the universe are Creation and Redemption (*Eternity*, 54–5); it was not uncommon for poems on the divine attributes to point to redemption as the supreme example of God's goodness, but Smart makes it the 'crown' and confirmation of God's power (*Power*, 110–11). But above all, it is in this period, and in these poems especially, that Smart begins to work out his role as poet, striving for a way of reconciling personal ambition with an increasingly imperious religious faith.

In the first of his Seatonian poems, Smart resumes the posture of the diffident young acolyte, 'the youthful uninspired Bard' (he was actually twenty-eight by this time), daring to 'hymn th' Eternal' only when God condescends to elevate his song (*Eternity*, 13–21). This time it is not youthfulness alone

[7] See W. P. Jones, *The Rhetoric of Science* (1966); D. B. Morris, *The Religious Sublime: Christian Poetry and Critical Tradition in Eighteenth-Century Poetry* (Lexington, 1972).

that hampers the poet, but the inadequacy of language itself:

> —O what can words
> The weak interpreters of mortal thoughts,
> Or what can thoughts . . .
>
> If to the Heav'n of Heavens they'd wing their way
> Advent'rous, like the birds of night they're lost,
> And delug'd in the flood of dazling day.—
>
> (6–12)

The failure to complete the verb in the first clause dramatizes the poet's incapacity, unaided, to master the divine syntax. Only God, the 'Great Poet of the Universe' (21), can enable him to transcend human limitations: then indeed he may hope to 'soar' to heaven and add his 'feeble voice' to the 'grand Chorus' of seraphim and cherubim. Behind the grandiose rhetoric of this passage lurks an even more ambitious conception: if God the Creator is a *Poet* then the human poet too may aspire to god-like powers of creation. This implication is reinforced in the lines which follow, referring to the creation of light through 'th' inspiring word', an anticipation of Smart's concern with the concept of the creative *Logos* in the religious poems of his later years. Smart does not pursue that idea here, but returns eventually to the image of flight. In the final passage of *Eternity*, the conflict between Christian faith, which calls for humility and self-abnegation, and the desire of the poet to be something more than a 'feeble voice', comes into the open. Only after death, Smart concludes, can 'the human tongue new-tun'd' utter praise commensurate with its great subject, for

> Tho' gratitude were bless'd with all the pow'rs
> Her bursting heart cou'd long for, tho' the swift,
> The firey-wing'd imagination soar'd
> Beyond ambition's wish—yet all were vain
> To speak Him as he is, who is INEFFABLE.
>
> (136–40)

The musical metaphor of the human tongue *new-tun'd* is significant. Smart's favourite figure for poetry and poetic inspiration is the lyre or harp. The image itself is of course traditional, even hackneyed, but he uses it with particular emphasis and precision. It supplies the opening flourish in his second Seatonian poem, *Immensity* (1751):

> Once more I dare to rouse the sounding string
> *The Poet of my God*—Awake my glory,
> Awake my lute and harp—
>
> (1–3)

The latter phrases are borrowed from the Psalter: already Smart is beginning to adopt David's singing robes and to write with increasing confidence as God's poet. But the harp/lyre image occurs in other poems also at this time. *Inscriptions on an Æolian Harp*, first published in 1750, uses the then novel image of the Æolian harp as a paradigm of spontaneous art, like the music of birds or 'the untaught virgin's song'. This may not appear to have a direct bearing on poetry, but by 1754, when the *Inscriptions* were published in the *Gentleman's Magazine*, they had acquired a new epigraph from Horace which underlines the connection. The quotation, *Fingent Æolio carmine nobilem* ('shall make him distinguished for Æolian verse'), is from Horace's ode to Melpomene, *Odes* IV. iii, in which he attributes to that Muse his success as a lyrical poet (*Romanæ fidicen lyæ*, 'player of the Roman lyre'). Again, in a poem written in 1751, *On the sudden Death of a Clergyman*, the reference to Orpheus' harp ('If, like th' Orphean lyre, my song could charm') might seem like a mere rhetorical trope, but in context it points even more significantly than the previous poem to Smart's developing conception of his poetic role. The phrase *th' Orphean lyre* comes from the invocation to Book III of *Paradise Lost*, where it stands for pagan poetry, rejected by Milton in favour of 'the Heav'nly Muse'. Smart similarly disclaims the art of Orpheus, but ostensibly for different reasons. Orpheus, he reminds us, was able to bring the dead back to life by the power of his music, but his (Smart's) 'artless muse' cannot hope to achieve any such miracle:

> 'Tis impotence of frantic love,
> Th' enthusiastic flight of wild despair,
> To hope the Thracian's magic power to prove.
> Alas! thy slender vein,
> Nor mighty is to move, nor forgetive to feign . . .
>
> (8–12)

This is something more complicated than conventional self-disparagement: only a madman or an 'enthusiast' (Smart was later to become both), it implies, would want to emulate Orpheus, whose 'magic power' is pejoratively equated with the 'forgetive' and 'feigning' craft of the poet. *Forgetive* (inventive) is the quality of mind induced by good sherris-sack, according to Falstaff (*2 Henry IV*, IV. iii. 107). The product of an 'artless muse' may, after all, be more trustworthy than the inventions of an intoxicated brain; for higher than any form of art is the perfect integration of life and utterance in the service of God, as Smart concludes:

> Better than what the pencil's daub can give,
>   Better than all that Phidias ever wrought,
> Is this—that what he taught shall live,
>   And what he liv'd for ever shall be taught.
>
> (43–6)

The contrasts between art and nature implicit in these two poems, and the ideal of spontaneous and artless utterance, form the main theme of *Immensity*. The architecture of Vitruvius and Palladio is compared adversely with the artistry of the ant and the bee (121–2), the paintings of Claude and Poussin cannot rival the 'living landskip' (79–81), and the colours of Correggio and Titian are put into the shade by the bloom of hawthorn and cherry (123–5). God's presence within all forms of creation ensures that simply by acting out their own nature they utter his due praise:

> conspicuous in the linnet's throat
> Is his unbounded goodness—Thee her Maker,
> Thee her Preserver chants she in her song . . .
>
> (99–101)

The function of the poet is now more firmly and unambiguously defined. His aspiration is no longer to join the angelic choir, but rather to participate in the 'grand thanksgiving' of nature with her 'ten thousand tongues':

> Hail, all hail,
> Ye tenants of the forest and the field!
> My fellow subjects of th' eternal King,
> I gladly join your Mattins, and with you
> Confess his presence, and report his praise.
>
> (6–10)

His song derives immediately from God: 'The tongue which thou hast tun'd, shall chant thy praise' (144). Like the Æolian harp, he emits music almost involuntarily when rightly 'tun'd'. For Smart, as for Herbert earlier, *tuning* means more than merely the tempering of language: it is a matter of setting the whole spirit in harmony with God's purpose and the symphony of nature. When Orpheus reappears in Smart's poetry, identified this time with David, in the fifth Seatonian poem, *Goodness* (1755), he is invoked for exactly this purpose. Smart acknowledges again in Orpheus/David the power to influence nature by music, but as if admonishing his own presumption in *On the sudden Death of a Clergyman* he now insists that this was David's power alone (1–5); but 'greater yet', he continues, was that 'divinest skill' which enabled David to restore Saul to spiritual health by his 'tuneful touch'. This is the grace he asks for himself:

> —in this breast
> Some portion of thy genuine spirit breathe,
> And lift me from myself, each thought impure
> Banish; each low idea raise, refine,
> Enlarge, and sanctify;—so shall the muse
> Above the stars aspire, and aim to praise
> Her God on earth, as he is prais'd in heaven.
>
> (11–17)

The Miltonic echoes (see commentary) reinforce the point: like Milton, Smart asks to be made worthy of his high task.

Smart's vision of a universal chorus of praise and thanksgiving is at last consummated in *Goodness*: to the 'ten thousand tongues' of nature spontaneously returning their thanks to the Creator are now added the 'ten thousand temples' of Christian Europe pouring forth his praise:

xxx

> Then join the general chorus of all worlds,
> And let the song of charity begin
> In strains seraphic and melodious pray'r.
>
> (116–26)

(The repetition of the phrase *melodious pray'r* in the first of Smart's *Hymns and Spiritual Songs* is not fortuitous: Hymn 1 restates with lyrical compression the central theme of *Goodness*).

It is now evident that the phrases used in the *Hymn to the Supreme Being* to describe the poet's anticipated reformation are not empty rhetoric; the 'new-strung nerves' and 'enraptur'd lyre' signify his new conception of poetry as an organic function of the whole personality. Attuned to the harmony of God's creation, the poet can aspire through conscious self-dedication to that unity of being and expression that the lower creatures instinctively possess:

> Deeds, thoughts, and words no more his mandates break,
> But to his endless glory work, conceive, and speak.
>
> (*Hymn to the Supreme Being*, 77–8)

> Take ye therefore what ye give him,
>   Of his fulness grace for grace,
> Strive to think him, speak him, live him,
>   Till you find him face to face.
>
> (*Hymns and Spiritual Songs*, Hymn 1. 33–6)

In the writing of religious poetry, Smart's poetic ambition and Christian faith were thus happily reconciled. In the years of astonishing creativity following his 'second birth' in 1756, he was buoyed up by the confident assurance that inspiration, in the sense of a gift of 'invention' transmitted directly to the poet from God, was possible. As Elkanah asks Hannah rhetorically,

> Is not Genius heav'nly Fire,
>   Thoughts so great and Words so free,
> Heighten'd on the living Lyre
>   Giv'n from God and giv'n to Thee?
>
> (*Hannah* 1. ii. 20–3)

In *Hymns and Spiritual Songs* he appeals to the 'Muse, through Christ the Word, inventive' (Hymn 3), 'For there is no invention but the gift of God', as he declares in *Jubilate Agno*

(B82). As long as motive and subject matter were sanctified there could be no clash between the poet and the Christian:

> The muse at length, no more perplext
>   In search of human wit,
> Shall kneel her down, and take her text
>   From lore of sacred writ.

(Hymns and Spiritual Songs, Hymn 11. 5–8)

The perplexity so joyfully resolved by the abandonment of 'human wit' in favour of divine poetry reappears in the secular poetry published after Smart's release from the asylum, where different solutions are tried. The three small volumes of verse published in 1763–4 seem at first sight to be a reversion to the miscellaneous writing of Smart's early years. Odes, epitaphs, songs, a fable, complimentary addresses and translations of minor classical poems: they look very much like the mixture as before. At least one poem, *Disertissime Romuli nepotum*, must indeed have been written before 1756, on internal evidence, and it has been inferred—not unreasonably on the face of it— that the epitaphs on the Duchess of Cleveland, who died in 1742, the Duke of Argyll (d. 1743), and Henry Fielding (d. 1754) are also early work. But there is clear evidence that the epitaph on Fielding must have been written after 1758, and both this poem and the epitaph on the Duchess of Cleveland are more pervasively Christian than the epitaphs published before 1756. It looks as if Smart was commemorating an old friend and an old patron in the same spirit as he blessed and rejoiced in the memory of the dead in *Jubilate Agno*. In fact the semblance of a regression in 1763–4 to earlier secular models quickly dissolves on closer examination. As Marcus Walsh observes, 'in an important sense almost all the poetry Smart wrote after 1759 is religious poetry',[8] and it cannot be fully understood unless it is read in the context of Smart's overtly religious verse of this period. Smart seems to have been experimenting with a new kind of poetry. Just as his translation of the psalms was 'attempted in the spirit of Christianity'[9] (reinterpreting Old Testament texts in the light of New

---

[8] *Christopher Smart: Selected Poems* (revised edn., Manchester, 1979), p. 18.

[9] Title-page of *Psalms*: the process had already begun in the version of the 42nd Psalm published in 1756.

Testament theology), so, in the ostensibly non-religious verse of this later period, he attempted to integrate the secular within a framework of Christian belief.

Reason and Imagination, standing at the head of Smart's first collection of secular verse to be published in 1763, can be seen as a sort of manifesto. At the beginning, his 'doubtful Muse' is shown in suspended flight while the forces of those hoary antipodes, Reason and Imagination, fight it out between themselves; their debate, cast in the form of a fable, forms the main content of the poem. In style and dialectic structure, the fable proper is similar to some of Smart's earlier fables, particularly *Care and Generosity*, and may indeed be an old piece refurbished as has been suggested (see commentary), but the refurbishing, if such it is, goes beyond a mere lick of paint and the importation of new furniture. The framework within which the fable is set not only adds a specifically Christian moral but significantly affects the way in which the tale itself has to be read (the deliberate omission of the framing passages by Newbery and Hunter in 1791 suggests that they recognized this well enough). The poem is addressed to William Kenrick, an old rival from the days of the paper war of the seventeen-fifties[10], but Smart is now bent on burying the hatchet. The immediate occasion was probably the publication of Kenrick's *Epistles Philosophical and Moral*, 1759 (see commentary), to which Smart replies with a friendly rebuke, affirming the supremacy of scriptural truth and Christian action over human learning and poetry itself (139–60). But the poem has another target in view. Recent years had seen a spate of books focusing on the nature of poetical genius and the function of the imagination. Thomas Warton's *Observations on the Fairy Queen* had appeared in 1754 (the second edition, corrected and enlarged, was published in 1762), the first volume of Joseph Warton's *Essay on the Writings and Genius of Pope* in 1756, Young's *Conjectures on Original Composition* in 1759, and Hurd's *Letters on Chivalry and Romance* in 1762. In different ways these works all promote the view of the imagination as a creative faculty by which the true poet is distinguished from the

---

[10] See Ainsworth and Noyes, pp. 40–7; Botting, pp. 15–21; Brittain, pp. 24–6; Sherbo, pp. 71–2.

moralist or man of wit, as opposed to reason which chills and represses this vital power. Truth and morality are consigned to the sphere of philosophy, while the peculiar glory of poetry is seen as its capacity to create fictions more sublime and animating than reality. Hence the appeal of chivalric romance:

such are their Terrible Graces of magic and enchantment, so magnificently marvellous are their fictions and fablings, that they contribute, in a wonderful degree, to rouse and invigorate all the powers of imagination: to store the fancy with those sublime and alarming images, which true poetry best delights to display.[11]

In the context of these ideas, Smart's seemingly tame reconciliation of Imagination and Reason looks like a reactionary gesture, but it is something more than that. The setting of the fable in Horace's Sabine grove but at the time of the Incarnation ('Just at the coming of the WORD') suggests that Smart is aiming at a syncretic kind of poetry, combining classical and Christian ideals. The classical concept of imitation (truth to nature) is reinterpreted as Christian truth, which transcends fictions, however beguiling, as the object of poetry. He seeks to discredit the notion of imagination as the hallmark of the poet by accentuating its wanton, lawless, and fantastic aspects, and portraying reason, by contrast, as a pious, hermit-like figure, 'reading to the Eastern light', devoutly kneeling and poring over the Book of Wisdom (69–76, 121–2). Whether the 'Book of Wisdom' refers specifically to the Wisdom of Solomon in the Apocrypha (a book of profound influence on Christian theology), or more generally to the widom of God, as in *Omniscience* (179), the implication is the same: reason is the faculty of divine understanding ('that reason thou inspir'dst', as Smart had called it in *Omniscience*, 26). Imagination carries a wand which 'Magick's utmost pow'r excell'd' (56), but has to exchange it in the end for Reason's compass and rule (135), the instruments with which the carpenter keeps his work true. Once again, as in *On the sudden Death of a Clergyman*, the idea of a magic power in poetic art is rejected in favour of Christian truth and sincerity. The final exhortation to 'let Invention reason right' by attending to the

---

[11] T. Warton, op. cit., 2nd edn., ii. 268.

Word of God ('truth to full perfection brought') is surely intended as much for the 'doubtful Muse' as for Kenrick.

Smart put his new-found principles into practice in 1763-4 mainly by writing panegyrical poems in honour of national heroes or men and women of exemplary virtue. This too represents a reconciliation of classical and Christian ideals, for Smart asserts that Horace ('the *Heathen Psalmist*', as he calls him) 'well knew that the business of poetry is to express gratitude, reward merit, and promote moral edification'.[12] Secular and divine meet in the concept of the 'Christian Hero', who by virtuous life or patriotic service qualifies for 'God's applause' (*Ode to General Draper*, 37–40), a mark of approbation which unites the soldiers, sailors, and benefactors of Smart's own day with heroic Christians of every age. Admiral Pocock, General Draper, Mrs Draper, John Sherratt, Lady Hussey Delaval, and General Kingsley are each in turn given the accolade of 'God's applause' and so join the saints and martyrs of the early church:

> Heroes of the Christian cause,
> Candidates for God's applause.
>
> (*Hymns and Spiritual Songs*, 18. 19–20)

Praise of Christian heroes is praise of God himself: the rationale of this is provided by Hymn 17 in the *Hymns and Spiritual Songs*, in which Christ himself is described as the

> . . . sole original and cause
> Of all heroic actions past,
> The God of patriot deeds and gracious laws.
>
> (2–4)

This explains the seemingly bizarre logic of the opening stanza of *Ode to Admiral Sir George Pocock*, in which Pocock's naval successes are linked to Christ's feat as a pilot on the sea of Galilee related in John vi:

> We therefore first to him the song renew,
> Then sing of POCOCK's praise, and make the point in view.
>
> (5–6)

---

[12] *The Works of Horace, translated into verse* (1767), Preface, I, pp. x, xxii.

Poetry is thus vindicated once again by the sacredness of its subject; by celebrating the deeds of heroes (particularly English heroes) it 'humbles' itself only to 'rise',

> Seeks to the temple of th' Angelic choir,
> And hoists the ENGLISH FLAG upon the topmost spire.
>
> ... built upon thy deeds my song shall tow'r,
> And swell, as it ascends, in spirit and in pow'r.

(11–12, 23–4)

The strangest and most radical of Smart's experiments in Christian-secular poetry is *Munificence and Modesty*, which combines moral and religious allegory in a way which challenges, perhaps deliberately, the view of Thomas Warton that 'the mixture of divine truth and profane invention' is a 'capital fault' in poetry.[13]

Allegory is defined in a contemporary handbook as

> a fable or story, in which, under the disguise of imaginary persons or things, some real action, or instructive moral is conveyed to the mind. Every *allegory* therefore has two senses, the one literal, and the other mystical; the first has been aptly enough compared to a dream or vision, of which the last is the true meaning or interpretation.[14]

Smart's story can be interpreted in terms of both *moral* and *real action*. In the moral sense, Modesty represents Christian humility and self-abnegation, which involves the recognition of fallen man's worthlessness and the surrender of personal desires to the will of God. Munificence is the grace of God in granting redemption and eternal life to those who humble themselves in this way (ll. 82–3). The story in the moral sense precisely enacts the Christian paradox already exploited in the ode to Pocock, that humility exalts (see Luke 14: 11). In terms of 'action', the allegory is a disguised representation of the Assumption of the Blessed Virgin Mary.[15] This strictly Roman doctrine (defined in a papal decree of 1950 interestingly titled *Munificentissimus*

---

[13] Op. cit., 2nd edn., ii. 97–101.

[14] *The Art of Poetry on a New Plan* (1762), ii. 3.

[15] The suggestion that Mary was the hidden subject of this poem was first made, but not elaborated, by Devlin (p. 157). It was challenged by Dearnley (p. 207), but without counter-argument, except over the identity of the painting to which Smart refers in the subtitle (see commentary).

Deus) is based on apocryphal New Testament narratives, the best known of which is ascribed to St John the Evangelist. In this narrative, Mary confesses her lowliness, whereupon the archangel Gabriel descends and announces the promise of her assumption; subsequently Christ himself, riding on a throne or chariot of cherubim, comes down to transport her to heaven where she is promised everlasting life (see commentary). Smart's celebration, even in disguised form, of a 'popish' doctrine is hard to reconcile with the sometimes virulent expression of anti-Romanist feeling in his religious poetry at this time, and in the *Ode to the Earl of Northumberland* shortly afterwards. But his reverence for the Virgin Mary seems to have cut across sectarian allegiances. He rejoices in the Immaculate Conception, for example, in *Jubilate Agno* (B139), and addresses the Virgin with un-Protestant ardour in the hymn on the Annunciation in *Hymns and Spiritual Songs*. Hunter, who excluded *Munificence and Modesty* from the 1791 collection, may well have done so because of its Marian flavour, though he no doubt objected to it on the grounds of obscurity and excessive enthusiasm also.

Munificence and Modesty is interesting from another point of view. Previously, in the *Ode to General Draper* and *Epistle to John Sherratt*, Smart had written disparagingly of painting as a medium inferior to poetry for honouring Christian virtue. Now, by basing his poem on a painting by Guido Reni (as the subtitle informs us), he seems to be harnessing the two arts. The concept of a pictorial poetry, realising the Horatian tag *ut pictura poesis*, was of course not new.[16] What is remarkable about Smart's poem is its baroque emotionalism. It was presumably this that led Christopher Devlin to assume that the painting Smart was imitating was Reni's *Coronation of the Virgin*; his guess was mistaken, as Moira Dearnley later showed (see commentary), but not his perception of the quality of the poem. Its florid and exuberant imagery and high-pitched religious emotion do indeed mimic in verbal terms the art of the High Baroque. To find examples of this ecstatic quality in pictorial poetry, one has to go back to Crashaw, or to Dryden's *Ode to Mrs. Anne Killigrew*.

[16] See J. G. Hagstrum, *The Sister Arts: the tradition of literary pictorialism from Dryden to Gray* (Chicago, 1958).

Smart's reputation in the eighteenth century rested almost entirely on the poems written before his confinement. His versatility is recognized in the tributes paid to him on the occasion of the benefit performance of *Merope* (1759), which unite in lauding his 'wit', his 'wisdom', and his 'elevated genius' (see Appendix C). His odes were judged by Hunter to be generally 'spirited and poetical' though not always notable for 'perspicuity'; in *Idleness* Hunter found 'the elegance of Sappho, and in *To Ethelinda* 'the sprightliness of Anacreon', while the *Morning Piece* he thought 'uniformly beautiful' (I, pp. xxx–xxxiii). Smart's fables were among the most successful of his miscellaneous poems. Burney rated him after Gay as 'the most agreeable metrical Fabulist in our language':

his versification is less polished, and his apologues in general perhaps less correct, than those of Gay and Moore: but in originality, in wit, in humour, the preference seems due to Smart.[17]

But it was the Seatonian poems, above all, that made his name and established him, in Burney's words, as 'the pride of Cambridge and the chief poetical ornament of that university'.[18] Contemporary critics admired them particularly for their 'enthusiasm'. Hunter's assessment, though written twenty years after Smart's death, sums up accurately enough the eighteenth-century verdict:

The five Poems on the Divine Attributes are written with the sublimest energies of religion, and the true enthusiasm of poetry; and had the pen of their author stopped with these compositions, they alone would have given him a very distinguished rank among the writers of verse. (I, pp. xxxiii–xxxiv).

George Dyer, the friend of Charles Lamb, praised them in similar terms, saying the poems 'are characterized by a religious enthusiasm quite natural to the writer, and are still further replete with the enthusiasm of poetry'.[19] They were frequently reprinted in eighteenth-century anthologies, four of the five poems were published in a German translation in 1768, and an oratorio was composed from selected passages of

---

[17] *Monthly Rev.* (Jan. 1792), p. 40.
[18] Ibid., p. 37.
[19] *MM.* (1803), p. 426.

Smart's Seatonian poems and set to music by Joseph Fisher.[20]

The poems of 1763–4 had a poor press on the whole, partly because Smart alienated the reviewers by responding intemperately to criticism of *A Song to David*, which was published a few months before the first of the three small collections. But even without this provocation, it is unlikely that the obscurity and religious fervour of these poems would have been to the taste of the majority of readers of the time. John Langhorne, reviewing *Ode to the Earl of Northumberland* (1764), commented that,

there is in the later productions of Mr. Smart a *tour* of expression, which we many times are at a loss to understand; and it often seems to us, that his words as well as his sentiments, are rather too much under the influence of his imagination.[21]

William Mason, who concluded from *A Song to David* that Smart was 'as mad as ever',[22] was not alone in attributing his new manner to his insanity. Boswell read *Poems* (1763) as soon as they were published, and commented:

His *Genius and Imagination* [i.e. *Reason and Imagination*] is very pretty. The other pieces have shivers of genius here and there, but are often ludicrously low. Poor man, he has been released from his confinement, but not from his unhappy disorder.[23]

Smart's religious enthusiasm found a champion, however, even in 1763. A review by his old friend, Bonnell Thornton, had this to say about *Reason and Imagination*:

The world has been so often entertained with the ingenious productions of Mr. Smart, that any thing from his hand must awaken our attention; and this little Fable will at the same time gratify and reward their curiosity. Poets indeed are often termed Enthusiasts and that rather from the extravagance and rant of folly, than from any impulsory feelings of real Genius. It may perhaps in this immoral and irreligious age do Mr. Smart small credit that he appears as an advocate for Christianity; the Coxcomb and the Fool, who laugh at

[20] See Betty Rizzo, 'Christopher Smart's Posthumous Reputation and the Oratorio "Providence"', *N&Q* 224 (1979), 45–6.

[21] *Monthly Rev.* (Sept. 1764), p. 231.

[22] Gray, *Corresp.* ii. 802.

[23] Letter to Sir David Dalrymple, 30 July 1763: *Letters*, ed. C. B. Tinker (Oxford, 1924), i. 39.

what they do not understand, may deride such unfashionable attempts; while the Man of Wit, who often too fatally misemploys it, and the Man of Parts, who scandalously betrays them, ought to blush.[24]

The reviewer's fears were realized, for Smart's poems found little favour with the public, judging by the infrequency with which they were reprinted. Their lack of popularity doubtless contributed to the rapid extinction of Smart's reputation after his death. Only twelve years later, in 1783, a correspondent in the *Gentleman's Magazine* numbers him among forgotten authors ('I could wish also to see some memorials of Smart the poet'),[25] and in spite of the publication of his collected poems in 1791, a proposal to reprint his verse translation of Phaedrus in 1800 apparently failed the test of commercial prudence.[26] Like many an artist and writer before and after him, Smart paid the price of originality. His old friend, Charles Burney, epitomized the mixture of exasperation and admiration which Smart's work aroused among even sympathetic contemporaries when he summed up at the end of his review of the 1791 collection:

Some of his defects may be fairly ascribed to redundant genius, and to impatience of labor; others to fanaticism, generated perhaps by the awful subjects which he undertook to treat in the prize poems ... His errors are those of a bold and daring spirit, which bravely hazards what a vulgar mind could never suggest.[27]

(ii) *Sources and the Canon*

AUTHORITATIVE manuscript sources of Smart's minor poems are few. There are holographs of *On Gratitude* (once in the possession of the poet, Robert Browning, now in the Berg Collection, New York Public Library) and *Epistle to Dr. Nares* (a postcard pasted into a copy of Smart's *Poems*, 1791, in Pembroke College Library, Cambridge). The manuscripts of *On St. David's Day*, in Richard Morris's *Miscellaneous Collections*,

---

[24] *CC*, 23 July 1763, reprinted from *St. James's Chronicle*, 16–19 July 1763.
[25] *GM* (1783), p. 488.
[26] See K. Williamson, 'Charles Burney, Francis Newbery and Smart: Two New Letters', *N&Q* 220 (1975), 360–2.
[27] Loc. cit., p. 43.

relating to British history,[28] and of *The Bite*[29] (both in the British Library) may also be in Smart's hand. Pembroke College Library holds manuscript copies of six other pieces by Smart, which were published at different times from 1744 to 1752: *Idleness*; *To Miss A—n* (titled *Sonnet*); *The Silent Fair*; *Audivere, Lyce*; *Epithalamium*; part of *Hudibras*, Canto I, translated in to Latin. The copies are in an eighteenth-century hand, perhaps that of 'Lawman, the mad Attorney' who is named as Smart's copyist in 1747.[30] The translation from *Hudibras* has the superscription, 'by a Freshman of Pembroke—Christopher Smart', which dates it 1739–40. The others describe the author merely as 'Mr Smart of Pembroke Hall', which could imply that they were written before he became a Fellow in 1745, but is not sufficiently firm evidence of date to be used as such. Two other poems depend on manuscript sources: '*Madam if you please*' and *Lines with a pocket book*, both transcribed by Smart's daughter, Elizabeth Le Noir, in a letter to E. H. Barker, *c*. 1825, in the Bodleian Library.

The authoritative printed sources are the collections and separate editions listed below, with the sigla used for them in the present edition (for fuller details, see Robert Mahony and Betty W. Rizzo, *Christopher Smart: an annotated bibliography 1743–1983*).

Collections

1752   Poems on Several Occasions. By Christopher Smart, . . . London: Printed for the Author by W. Strahan; and sold by J. Newbery . . . MDCCLII.

Prefaced by a dedication to the Earl of Middlesex, list of subscribers, and table of errata, to which a quotation from Horace's *Ars Poetica* is disarmingly attached: *aut incuria fudit | Aut humana parum cavit Natura*

---

[28] See Moira Dearnley, 'Christopher Smart: "Some Young Cymro in Cambridge"', *RES*, NS 19 (1968), 54–6. The MS is signed 'Christopher Smart' and is in a hand similar to his, but several differences in letter formation suggest that it is a copy rather than a holograph.

[29] Recently discovered by Betty Rizzo (see p. 448). It is signed 'Kitty Smart' and looks remarkably like his autograph, but the brevity of the fragment makes positive identification risky.

[30] Gray, *Corresp.* i. 274.

('either shed by negligence, or too little guarded against by human frailty'). The quotation on the title-page, from the same source, *nonumque prematur in annum* ('let [your manuscript] be kept back for nine years') looks like a hint that the poems are early work, but this is not always a safe inference. While certainly true of some (the last set of Tripos Verses, for example, was written precisely nine years before publication) it is manifestly untrue of others such as the Prologue and Epilogue to *Othello*, which is dated 1751. The poems are arranged by kind, viz: pp. 1–32 'Odes'; pp. 33–193 longer poems; pp. 195–219 'Ballads, Fables, and other Miscellaneous Pieces', to which Smart attached a quotation from Phaedrus, *Adhuc supersunt multa, quae possim loqui, / Et copiosa abundat rerum varietas* ('Many themes that I might speak of still remain, and an abundant variety of subjects'); pp. 221–30 *The Judgment of Midas. A Masque.*

1763   Poems by Mr. Smart. Viz. Reason and Imagination a Fable. Ode to Admiral Sir George Pocock. Ode to General Draper. An Epistle to John Sherratt, Esq. ... London ... [n.d.]
          Published July 1763.

1763B   Poems on several Occasions. Viz. Munificence and Modesty. Female Dignity ... Verses from Catullus ... Epitaphs ... By Mr. Smart ... London ... [n.d.]
          Published November 1763.

1764   Ode to the Right Honourable the Earl of Northumberland ... With some other Pieces. By Christopher Smart, A.M. ... London ... MDCCLXIV.

1791   The Poems, of the late Christopher Smart, ... Consisting of his prize poems, odes, sonnets, and fables, Latin and English translations; together with many original compositions, not included in the Quarto Edition. To which is prefixed, an account of his life and writings, never before published. In two volumes. ... Reading: Printed and sold by Smart and Cowslade; and sold by F. Power and Co. ... MDCCXCI.

          This was very much a family affair. 'Smart and Cowslade' were the poet's widow and son-in-law respectively. Francis Power was John Newbery's grandson.

The editor was Francis Newbery, assisted by Smart's nephew Christopher Hunter, who according to Nichols 'sedulously revised' the text as well as supplying the account of Smart's life and writings.[31] It included all the poems from *1752* ('the Quarto Edition'), a few from the 1763–4 collections, the separate works listed below with the exception of the *Solemn Dirge*, and fifty-five shorter poems, all but five of which have been traced to earlier publications. The most notable feature of this edition is its omission of the bulk of Smart's later poetry: the psalms, hymns, and *Song to David*, verse translations of Phaedrus and Horace, versified parables, and three-quarters of the poems from the 1763–4 collections. Hunter's justification for his policy was that these works 'were written after his confinement, and bear for the most part melancholy proofs of the estrangement of his mind. Such poems however have been selected from his pamphlets [i.e. the 1763–4 volumes] and inserted in the present work, as were likely to be acceptable to the Reader' (I, p. xlii *n*).

As in *1752*, the poems are arranged according to kind, with numbered series of Odes, Fables, Ballads, and Epigrams (see Appendix C), and other divisions not specified but clearly discernible: complimentary addresses, Seatonian prize poems, translations, epitaphs, etc. (see Mahony and Rizzo, Item 178).

Separate Editions

1743   Carmen Cl. Alexandri Pope in S. Cæciliam Latine redditum a Christophero Smart, ... Cantabrigiæ ... MDCCXLIII.

1746   Carmen Cl. Alexandri Pope in S. Cæciliam ... Editio Altera. To which is added Ode for Musick on Saint Cecilia's Day, by Christopher Smart, ... Cambridge ... MDCCXLVI.

1750   The Horatian Canons of Friendship. Being the Third Satire of the First Book of Horace Imitated. ... By Ebenezer Pentweazle, ... London ... 1750. (The

[31] See Mahony and Rizzo, Item 178.

second 'edition', published in the same year, is a reissue).

E　　On the Eternity of the Supreme Being. A Poetical Essay. By Christopher Smart, ... Cambridge ... M.DCC.L.

E2　——Second Edition, Cambridge, 1752.

E3　——Third Edition, Cambridge, 1756.

OP　An Occasional Prologue and Epilogue to Othello, ... Written by Christopher Smart, ... London [1751].

OP2　——Second Edition, London [1751].

OP3　——Third Edition, London [1751].

A Solemn Dirge, sacred to the memory of His Royal Highness Frederic Prince of Wales, ... Written by Mr Smart. ... London ... M.DCC.LI. (The second and third 'editions', published in 1751, are reissues).

IM　On the Immensity of the Supreme Being. A Poetical Essay. By Christopher Smart, ... Cambridge ... MDCCLI.

IM2　——Second Edition, Cambridge, 1753.

IM3　——Third Edition, London, 1757.

O　　On the Omniscience of the Supreme Being. A Poetical Essay. By Christopher Smart, ... Cambridge ... M.DCC.LII.

O2　　——Second Edition, Cambridge, 1756.

1753　The Hilliad: An Epic Poem. By C. Smart, ... London ... MDCCLIII.

1753D　——Dublin ... M,DCC,LIII.

P　　On the Power of the Supreme Being. A Poetical Essay. By Christopher Smart, ... Cambridge ... MDCCLIV.

P2　　——Second Edition, London, 1758.

G　　On the Goodness of the Supreme Being. A Poetical Essay. By Christopher Smart, ... Cambridge ... M.DCC.LVI.

G2　　——Second Edition, Cambridge, 1756.

1756　Hymn to the Supreme Being, ... By Christopher Smart, ... London ... MDCCLVI.

1761　Poems on the Attributes of the Supreme Being, By Christopher Smart, ... Dublin ... M,DCC,LXI.

(Smart's five Seatonian Prize poems, probably reprinted without his knowledge).

The 1791 collection, which remained the source of all collections of Smart's poetry for the following century, laid the foundations of the Smart canon but left a considerable number of his miscellaneous poems still to be recovered. It was not until G. J. Gray compiled his *Bibliography of the Writings of Christopher Smart* in 1903 that the task of sifting Smart's uncollected pieces from the mass of eighteenth-century ephemera was systematically resumed.

Research in this century, from Gray's pioneering effort onwards, has resulted in a substantial extension of the canon, but it has also given rise to many doubtful or erroneous attributions, and the major task now is to establish sound criteria for distinguishing between the authentic and the spurious. Internal evidence, uncorroborated by other kinds, has repeatedly shown itself to be an undependable guide to authorship in the eighteenth century, but the problem of authentication is complicated in Smart's case by two other factors: uncertainty about the extent of his contribution to publications for which he is known or believed to have had editorial responsibility; and his habit of signing contributions with pseudonyms or initials.

Smart was sole or part editor of at least three periodicals. The first of these, *The Student, or, the Oxford and Cambridge Miscellany*, was started by Bonnell Thornton in January 1750. Smart joined the venture presumably in June 1750 (when 'Cambridge' was added to the title) and seems to have shared editorial responsibility with Thornton until the magazine closed in July 1751. Meanwhile Smart had been engaged by Newbery (publisher of the *Student*) as editor and principal writer of another monthly magazine, *The Midwife, or the Old Woman's Magazine*, which ran from October 1750 to June 1753. An unsubstantiated tradition credits him with responsibility for yet another Newbery production in this period: the short-lived *Lilliputian Magazine,* three issues of which appeared in 1751.[32] In 1755, Smart and his friend Richard Rolt signed the

[32] See Roland B. Botting, 'Christopher Smart and the *Lilliputian Magazine*', *ELH* 9 (1942), 286–7.

notorious 99-year contract with Thomas Gardner to supply material for a new periodical, *The Universal Visiter and Monthly Memorialist*, which ran from January to December, 1756.[33] Smart was released by illness from editorial responsibility early in the year, but contributions from him continued to appear, though with diminishing frequency, up to October 1756. A great deal of Smart's miscellaneous verse (authenticated by its inclusion in one of his own collections or by reliable testimony) made its first appearance in these periodicals, sometimes under his own name but more often anonymously or with pen-name or initial, the most common of which were Mrs (Mary) Midnight, Ebenezer Pentweazle, Nelly Pentweazle, Mr Lun, C.S., and S. We know also that Smart used these and other sobriquets for his contributions to periodicals *not* edited by himself.

Clearly, any unassigned poem in a periodical edited by Smart, and any poem published elsewhere that bears one of his known signatures, *may* be by him. Many previously unattributed poems have been recovered by scholars working on this assumption. But consideration of potential attributions based on provenance and signature without further corroboration always needs to take account of the fact that, even in the *Midwife* for which Smart was the principal supplier of material, there were other contributors; and that pseudonyms and initials are liable to expropriation of confusion.[34] Smart's contributions to the *Universal Visiter* are a somewhat different matter, in that here there is independent evidence for his authorship. Handwritten annotations in a copy of this work formerly in the British Library (but unfortunately destroyed in the 1939–45 war) identified Smart as the author of most of the poems signed 'S'. The copy bore the signature of 'Ann Gardner', probably the daughter of the publisher, and the notes were presumably hers or her father's.[35]

Further difficulty in establishing the canon arises from the fact that a number of Smart's newly attributed poems came out of his involvement in paper wars with rival journalists, the

---

[33] See *Boswell's Life* ii. 345; but the contract was not as oppressive as Johnson made it appear, see Mahony and Rizzo, Item 551.

[34] See Williamson (1973), p. 123.

[35] See Jones, and Mahony and Rizzo, Item 551.

theatre war between Garrick and Rich, and above all the *Old Woman's Oratory*,[36] which opens up the possibility that others too are by Smart.

The story of the *Old Woman's Oratory*, a feature of the London stage at intervals from 1751 to 1760, and of the provincial theatre to an unexplored extent,[37] has yet to be unravelled. The *Oratory* was a cross between vaudeville, comic concert, and circus, featuring *inter alia* songs, recitations, dances, performing animals, and infant musicians. A typical performance is described in graphic (if hostile) terms by Horace Walpole:

I was t' other night to see what is now grown the fashion, Mother Midnight's Oratory—it appeared the lowest buffoonery in the world ... There is a bad oration to ridicule, what it is too like, Orator Henley: all the rest is perverted music. There is a man who plays so nimbly on the kettle drum, that he has reduced that noisy instrument to be an object of sight, for if you don't see the tricks with his hands, it is no better than ordinary. Another plays on a violin and a trumpet together; another mimics a bagpipe with a German flute, and makes it full as disagreeable. There is an admired dulcimer, a favourite saltbox, and a really curious Jew's harp. Two or three men intend to persuade you that they play on a broomstick, which is drolly brought in, carefully shrouded in a case, so as to be mistaken for a bassoon or base viol, but they succeed in nothing but the action. The last fellow imitates farting and curtseying to a French horn. There are twenty medley overtures, and a man who speaks a prologue and epilogue, in which he counterfeits all the actors and singers upon earth ...[38]

That Smart played a principal role as entrepreneur, writer, and sometimes performer, is now well known, but how much of the verse associated with the *Oratory* performances was written by him, and how much was the work of other known and unknown contributors remains a problem. It is no surprise that in writing his life, Christopher Hunter, anxious for his uncle's reputation, should pass over in silence this undignified aspect of Smart's career, or that the 1791 collection should exclude all

---

[36] See G. E. Jensen (ed.), *The Covent-Garden Journal* (New Haven, 1915), i. 29–98; Botting, pp. 15–21; Sherbo, pp. 71–81, 88–91.

[37] See Betty Rizzo, 'Enter the Epilogue on an Ass—By Christopher Smart', *PBSA* 73 (1979), 340–4.

[38] Letter to Montagu, 12 May 1752, *Corresp.* ix. 131.

the verse identifiably associated with it; but by the same token, omission from *1791* is not evidence against Smart's authorship.

In preparing this volume I have chosen to err, if need be, on the side of caution. My working principle has been to admit into the canon only those attributions that rest on at least two kinds of evidence—provenance, signature, contemporary testimony, or internal evidence—unless the evidence of one kind is peculiarly strong. The poems connected with the *Oratory* that seem most likely to be by Smart are printed in Appendix A. Even under this conservative policy, however, the canon includes over thirty pieces not published in any previous collection of Smart's verse, and over fifty not included in collections before this century.

(iii) *The Text*

COPY-TEXT for works published separately in Smart's lifetime is the first edition. Holograph poems are printed from manuscript. For the remaining poems, choice of copy-text was more difficult, the multiplicity of sources making the relative order and authority of texts indeterminate or at least doubtful. Each poem has had to be treated as a separate case, but some guidelines were discoverable, and have been followed. The collected editions published in Smart's lifetime (with the exception of *1761*) are well-printed, accurate, and faithful to his idiosyncrasies in spelling, punctuation, and use of capitals. These editions have been used as copy-text wherever possible. The periodicals with which Smart was closely associated vary in dependability. The *Midwife*, though carelessly printed, has Smart's known editorship as guarantee of textual authenticity. The *Student* is better printed and can also be regarded as textually authoritative. It is extremely unlikely that Smart had anything to do with seeing his work in the *Universal Visiter* through the press after the first issue or two, but this is in fact the only source for the majority of poems by him which appear in it. I have preferred these three periodicals to *1791* because of the danger of editorial interference in the latter; but I have usually preferred *1791* to other periodicals and collections. *1791* draws not only on a variety of printed sources (as the title-page indicates) but also on manuscript material. 'Of the *Fables* and *lighter Poems*,' Hunter writes, 'the greater part are either printed for the first time, or collected by the diligence of friends from books now scarcely to be found' (I, p. xxxvi). Only four fables and the epistle to Mrs Tyler had not in fact been previously printed, but Francis Newbery had probably inherited manuscript copies of most if not all of Smart's fables from his father, who had advertized a collection of *Tales and Fables in Verse* by Smart in 1755–6.[39] He must also have had authorial copy of other poems, including at least some of those published in *1752*: although most of the *1752* poems are printed literatim, variants in a few appear to be authorial. *1791* therefore must always be treated with respect, but also with caution: traces of Hunter's 'sedulous' revision are sometimes unmistakeable (see, e.g., *The Hop-Garden* i. 72, 254; ii. 129) and on several other occasions the *1791* variants look suspiciously like editorial 'improvements' or corrections. There also remains the important but unanswered question of the copy used by Newbery when not clearly one of the known printed sources. I have been unable to determine from collation in these cases whether the *1791* copy was earlier or later than previously printed texts, Smart's original, or a transcription of some untraced printed version.

The variety of sources poses questions not only about textual authority but also about choice of printing style. While editions of Smart's work published in his lifetime are broadly consistent typographically (although printed by different houses, and over a period of change in printing conventions), there are conspicuous divergences of style between these and *1791*, and between the *Midwife*, the *Student*, and the *Universal Visiter*; not to mention the diversity of styles found among other printed sources. The choice lay between standardization and reproduction of copy-text regardless of typographical consistency. The first alternative was chosen because the confusion of styles resulting from the second would have been misleading as well as aesthetically objectionable. It is evident from Smart's manuscripts that he habitually used both capitals and italics for rhetorical effect, and his intentions seem to have been

---

[39] See Mahony and Rizzo, Item 6. This publication has never been traced and presumably did not materialize, although it continued to be advertised up to 1773 in the *London Catalogue*.

faithfully fulfilled in the typography of his own editions. These typographical indicators of tone and meaning are obscured in publications such as the *Midwife* and other London magazines, in which typography is mainly determined by the house style. I have therefore taken *1752* as typographical model for all the miscellaneous poems except those printed from Smart's holograph.[40] I have not, however, attempted to standardize the spelling, since *1752*, like the manuscript of *Jubilate Agno*, is not itself wholly consistent in this respect.

I have been sparing in emendation of copy-text. Where necessary, it has been based as far as possible on the authority of another text, and for the purpose of (*a*) supplying material which had been omitted apparently inadvertently, (*b*) correcting manifest errors, (*c*) incorporating authorial alterations, (*d*) clarifying the intention of copy-text where it has been obscured by punctuation. Misprints have been silently corrected in copy-text and ignored in collated texts. Corrections from the Errata printed in *1752* have been silently incorporated when they involved simple misprints, but when they indicated change of intention the alteration has been recorded in the textual notes. The forms *ere* and *e'er* were used interchangeably by eighteenth-century printers to mean *before*, but to avoid confusion *e'er* in this sense has been changed to *ere* throughout; *its* and *it's*, however, have been left untouched. Ampersands and Latin contractions, such as *q:* for *que*, have been expanded, but because of the notorious inconsistency of authors and printers alike, diacritical marks have been omitted entirely. Stanza numbers have also been omitted from monostrophic poems.

Minor variants of spelling and punctuation, not affecting meaning, sound or metre, and rearrangement of stanzas (e.g. combination of four-line stanzas into eight-liners, repetition of lines or half-lines as refrains) have not normally been recorded in the textual notes.

---

[40] *1752* itself, however, is occasionally erratic, as in the seemingly arbitrary sprinkling of capitals in *A Morning Piece* and *A Noon-Piece*, which I have not attempted to normalize.

MISCELLANEOUS POEMS
LATIN AND ENGLISH

"Madam if you please"

Madam if you please
To hear such things as these.
Madam, I have a rival sad
And if you don't take my part it will made me mad.
He says he will send his son;
But if he does I will get me a gun.
Madam if you please to pity,
O poor Kitty, O poor Kitty!

To Ethelinda,

On her doing my Verses the honour of wearing them in her bosom.
Written at Thirteen.

Happy verses! that were prest
In fair Ethelinda's breast!
Happy muse, that didst embrace
The sweet, the heav'nly-fragrant place!
Tell me, is the omen true,   5
Shall the bard arrive there too?

Oft thro' my eyes my soul has flown,
And wanton'd on that ivory throne:
There with extatic transport burn'd,
And thought it was to heav'n return'd.   10
Tell me, is the omen true,
Shall the body follow too?

When first at nature's early birth,
Heav'n sent a man upon the earth,
Ev'n Eden was more fruitful found,   15
When Adam came to till the ground:
Shall then those breasts be fair in vain,
And only rise to fall again?

MADAM IF YOU PLEASE. Text: Letter from Elizabeth Le Noir to E. H. Barker
(c.1825), Bodl. MS 1006, fo. 245.
TO ETHELINDA. First published in *1752*. Text: *1752*. Collated: *1791*.

3

No, no, fair nymph—for no such end
Did heav'n to thee its bounty lend;   20
That breast was ne'er design'd by fate,
For verse, or things inanimate;
Then throw them from that downy bed,
And take the poet in their stead.

Arion.

Nautarum jussu se præcipitavit Arion
  In mare cantator funeris ipse sui:
Delapsum recipit gelidis amplexibus æquor,
  Fatorumque ferax undaque et unda tumet.
Sed Delphinus adest,—sed adest secumque salutem   5
  Attulit et vati et squamea terga dedit.
O hominum feritas! O mollia corda ferarum,
  Blanda mage humanis omnia monstra feris.

Translation
By the sailors' command Arion hurled himself into the sea, himself
the chanter of his own obsequies. As he dived in, the sea received him
in its chilly embrace, and wave upon wave, fertile with doom, swelled
up. But the dolphin was there to help: he was there indeed, and by his
presence brought safety and offered his scaly back to the bard.
O beastliness of men! O gentle heart of beasts! All the monsters that
exist are more kindly than beasts in human shape.

Fanny, blooming fair.

Translated into Latin, in the manner of Mr. Bourne.

> *When Fanny, blooming fair,*
>   *First caught my ravish'd sight,*
> *Pleas'd with her shape and air,*
>   *I felt a strange delight:*

ARION. Text: *UV* (Jan. 1756), p. 42.
5 salutem] salutem, *UV*
FANNY, BLOOMING FAIR. First published in *GM* (Apr. 1754), p. 185. Text: *1791.*
Collated: *GM.*

Whilst eagerly I gaz'd,   5
   Admiring every part,
And ev'ry feature prais'd,
   She stole into my heart.

In her bewitching eyes
   Ten thousand loves appear;   10
There Cupid basking lies,
   His shafts are hoarded there.
Her blooming cheeks are dy'd
   With colour all her own,
Excelling far the pride   15
   Of roses newly blown.

Her well-turn'd limbs confess
   The lucky hand of Jove;
Her features all express
   The beauteous queen of love.   20
What flames my nerves invade
   When I behold the breast
Of that too charming maid
   Rise suing to be prest!

Venus round Fanny's waist   25
   Has her own cestus bound,
There guardian Cupids grace,
   And dance the circle round.
How happy must he be,
   Who shall her zone unloose!   30
That bliss to all but me,
   May heav'n and she refuse.

Cum primum ante oculos, viridi lasciva juventa,
   Non temere attonitos Fannia pulchra stetit,
Ut mihi se gratus calor insinuavit in ossa
   Miranti speciem, virgineumque decus!
Dum partes meditor varias, et amabile—quid non?   5
   Lustrandique acies magna libido capit,
Prodigus et laudum dum formam ad sidera tollo,
   Subdolus en! furtim labitur intus amor.

6 capit,] capit; *GM, 1791*

5

Idalii pueri, Venerisque exercitus omnis
    Exornat multo lumina fœta dolo;   10
Hic currus, hic tela jacent, hic arcus Amoris,
    Cypri posthabitis hic manet ipse jugis.
Nativis gena pulchra rosis vestita superbit,
    Invalidam artificis spernere nata manum;
Non tantas jactat veneres suavissimus horti   15
    Incola, quando novis spirat amoma comis.

Concinnis membris patet immortalis origo,
    Illa Jovis monstrant quid potuere manus;
Reginamque Cnidi, formosam Cyprida, reddit,
    Quicunque egregio ludit in ore decor!   20
Quanta mihi nervos, heu, quanta est flamma medullas,
    Pectoris ut video luxuriantis ebur—
Pectoris eximiæ nymphæ—jam dulce tumentis
    Jam subsidentis—sed cupit ante premi.

Circumdat mediam cestus (mihi credite) nympham   25
    Insignis cestus, quem dedit ipsa Venus:
Dulce satellitium circa illam ludit amorum,
    Atque hilares ducit turba jocosa choros.
Felix ante homines istius cingula zonæ
    Qui solvas, felix, quisquis es, ante Deos!   30
Omnes tanta, omnes, nisi me, contingere posse
    Gaudia, vosque Dii, tuque puella neges.

Part of the first Canto of *Hudibras*

translated into Latin Doggrel.

When civil dudgeon first grew high,
And men fell out they knew not why, &c.   [I. i. 1–104]

---

27 illam] illum *GM*   31 Omnes tanta,] Omnes, tanta *GM, 1791*
PART OF HUDIBRAS. MS: *PC.* Ll. 1–91 first published in *ST* (Sept.–Oct. 1750), i.
358–60, ii. 39–40. First published in full in Zachary Grey's *Critical, Historical, and
Explanatory Notes upon Hudibras* (1752), Appendix, pp. 57–60 (*Z*). Text: *ST* (1–91), *PC*
(92–119). Collated: *PC, Z.*

Cum arsit civica phrenesis,
Pacis hominibus pertæsis;
Nec cuiquam nota fuit causa,
Tam dira quæ produxit ausa;
Cum tristes iræ, et furores,   5
Multum elicerent cruoris;
Et, velut qui sunt mente capti,
Præ mero ire parum apti;
Sic hi pugnabant, dum pro more
Religio cuique est in ore;   10
Hanc coluit quisque nomen tenus,
Sed nemo novit quodnam genus:
Cum præco alta e testudine,
Aurita stante multitudine,
Hanc dedit exhortationem,   15
Ut foveant seditionem;
Et manu tusum ecclesiastica
Pulvinar movit vi elastica:
Tunc ivit foras noster Heros,
Ut vinceret gigantes feros.   20
   Aspectum si quis observaret,
Hunc florem equitum juraret;
Nam nusquam genu flexum dedit,
Nisi cum titulum accepit;
Nec ictum æqua tulit mente,   25
Nisi ab honorario ente.
Duplicem scivit usum chartæ,
Tanta, ut nullus alter, arte,
Mercurio doctus tam, quam Marte.
Clarus in bello, in pace quoque,   30
Et jure Cæsar ex utroque.
(Sic victum sorices, ut ferunt,
Utroque elemento quærunt)
Sed multus author litem gerat,

1 arsit civica] gliscens circa *PC*   gliscens civica *Z*   2 pertæsis] prætesis
PC   3–4 *omitted*, *PC*, *Z*   6 elicerent] elicient *PC*   8 ∧ 9 Amoris
altercantur vice, / Et totum hoc pro meretrice, *PC*, *Z*   9 pugnabant] pugnarant
PC, *Z*   12 quodnam] quoddam *PC*   13 e] ex *PC*   17 tusum] tunsum
Z   26 ente] ense *PC*, *Z*   29 ∧ 30 Pugnavit nemo fortius, neque / Conscripsit
breviter quisquam æque. *PC*, *Z*   34 author litem] authoritatem *PC*   auctor
litem *Z*

An fortior, an prudentior erat,   35
Hi illud, illi hoc defendant;
Sed, licet acriter contendant,
Tam parva fuit differentia,
Vix, et ne vix vicit prudentia.
Hinc habuerunt illum multi   40
Aptum perfungi vice stulti.
Nam sic Montagnus vacans otio,
Omnique liber a negotio,
Dum lusit molliter cum fele,
Fudisse fertur hoc querelæ;   45
"Quis scit, quin felis hæc (proh facinus!)
Si putat, putat quod sum asinus."
Sed quid mehercule censeret,
Thrasonem nostrum si videret,
(Nam sic se noster appellavit,   50
In martem siquis provocavit)
Sed sic qui putant, putant male,
Nam noster erat nihil tale.
Quid, si ingenio fuit lautus,
De usu fuit perquam cautus.   55
Perraro quidem secum ferat,
Nam metuit, ne forsan terat,
Sic multi pictas induunt vestes,
Nonnisi in diebus festis.
Præterea Græce bene scivit,   60
Sed nemo eum erudivit:
Sic facultate naturali
Grunitum faciunt porcelli.
Latine nemo scivit melius
Vix aves concinunt facilius: 65
Utroque dives, cuique egeno
Diffudit copiam cornu pleno.
Hebræas etiam radices
In solo sterili felices.

---

36 defendant] defendunt *PC*, *Z*   37 contendant] contendunt *PC*, *Z*
38 Tam] Iam *PC*   42–7 Montaignum etiam sic ludentem / Cum fele tempus
conterentem, / Ferunt putasse et vereri / Se Feli asinum videri. *PC*, *Z*   48 Sed] At
PC, *Z*   52 male] mali *PC*   54 Quid] Quod *PC*, *Z*   66 dives] pollens
PC, *Z*

Tot habuit ut plerique eum   70
Curtum crediderint Judæum,
Et forsan fuit, Veneris ergo,
Judæus factus a chirurgo.
   In logica emunctæ naris
In analytica præclarus,   75
Ingenio fuit tam subtili
Discerneret ut situm pili,
Et si qua hora disputaret,
Cui parti magis inclinaret;
Utramque tueretur, quæque   80
Affirmat, mox infirmat æque.
Ostendit, cum suscepit litem.
Quod vir et equus non sint idem.
Avem non esse buteonem,
Et esse satrapam bubonem,   85
Et anseres justiciarios,
Cornices fidei commissarios,
Deberet disputatione,
Et solveret—solutione—
Hæc omnia faceret, et plura,   90
Perfecto modo et figura.
   Rhetorica si fuit opus,
Dictis occurrit frequens tropus.
Et medium rupit si sermonem
Tussis exagitans pulmonem,   95
Ampullas protulit monstrare
Qua fecit regula, et quare.
Nam metuit ne fors putetur
Quod plebis phrasi uteretur,
Et strenue cavet, ne credatur   100
Se loqui ut intelligatur.
Rhetorices nam documenta
Nil docent nisi instrumenta.
Oratio fuit nunc si voluit
Suavis, nunc gravide quiddam sonuit.   105

77 Discrevit positionem pili, *PC*, *Z*   78 Et] Ut *PC*, *Z*   83 sint] sunt
PC, *Z*   85 Et esse] Probat, & *PC*   Probet, et *Z*   86 Et anserum
justiciarium *PC*   Et anserem justiciarium *Z*   87 Cornicem ... commissarium.
PC, *Z*   89 solutione] cum ratione *PC*, *Z*

Locutio fuit perturbata,
Dum Babel stetit, usurpata.
Sublimes perquam erant logi
Quales affectant pedagogi.
Anglo-Latino-Græca fuit   110
Lingua, quæ tanta copia fluit,
Et tam promiscue, fu distinguas
In uno ore trinas linguas.
Hinc quoties voluit effutire
Putaret quisque se audire   115
Tres Babylonios colonos
Confusos edidisse sonos,
Aut ipsum Cerberum quam clare
Ex ore triplici latrare.

108 perquam] quidem *Z*   112 fu] fere *Z*   115 quisque *Z*] quisquam *PC*
116 Babylonios *Z*] Babylonicos *PC*

[TRIPOS VERSES I]

Datur Mundorum Pluralitas.

Unde labor novus hic menti? Quæ cura quietam
Sollicitat, rapiensque extra confinia terræ,
Cœlestes sine more jubet volitare per ignes?
Scilicet impatiens angusto hoc orbe teneri,
Fontinelle, tuos audax imitarier ausus   5
Gestio, et insolitas spirant præcordia flammas.

   Fallor, an ipse venit? Delapsus ab æthere summo
Pegason urget eques, laterique flagellifer instat:
Me vocat; et duris desiste laboribus, inquit,
"Me duce, carpe viam facilem, tibi singula clare   10
Expediam, tibi cernere erit, quos sidera norunt,
Indigenas cultusque virum, moresque docebo."
Nec mora, pennipedem conscendo jussus, ovansque
(Quanquam animus secum volvens exempla priorum
Bellerophonteæ pallet dispendia famæ)   15
Post equitem sedeo, liquidumque per aera labor.
—Mercurium petimus primum: Dux talibus infit,
"Aspicias vanæ malesana negotia gentis,
Quam mens destituit Titane exusta propinquo.
Stramineis viden'? Hic velatus tempora sertis   20
Emicat, et solos reges crepat atque tetrarchas.
Ille suam carbone Chloen depingit amator
Infelix, ægram rudia indigestaque mentem
Carmina demulcent, indoctaque tibia musas.
En! sedet incomptus crines barbataque menta   25
Astrologus, nova qui venatur sidera, solus
Semper in obscuro penetrali; multaque muros
Linea nigrantes, et multa triangula pingunt.
Ecce! sed interea curru flamante propinquat
Titan.—Clamo, O me! gelida sub rupe, sub umbra   30
Siste precor: tantos nequeo perferre calores."

DATUR MUNDORUM. First published in *1752*. Text: *1752*. Collated: *1791*.

Pegason inde tuo genius felicior astro
Appulit, alma Venus. Spirant quam molliter auræ!
Ridet ager, frugum facilis, lascivaque florum
Nutrix; non Euri ruit hic per dulcia Tempe   35
Vis fera, non Boreæ; sed blandior aura Favoni,
Lenis agens tremulo nutantes vertice sylvas,
Usque fovet teneros, quos usque resuscitat, ignes.
Hic lætis animata sonis Saltatio vivit:
Hic jam voce ciet cantum, jam pectine, dulces   40
Musica docta modos: pulchræ longo ordine nymphæ
Festivas ducunt choreas, dilecta juventus
Certatim stipant comites: late halat amomo
Omne nemus, varioque æterni veris odore:
Cura procul: circumvolitant risusque jocique: 45
Atque amor est, quodcunque vides. Venus ipsa volentes
Imperio regit indigenas, hic innuba Phœbe,
Innuba Pallas amet, cupiant servire Catones.

   Jamque datum molimur iter, sedesque beatas
Multa gemens linquo; et lugubre rubentia Martis   50
Arva, ubi sanguineæ dominantur in omnia rixæ,
Advehimur, ferro riget horrida turba, geritque
Spiculaque, gladiosque, ferosque in bella dolones.
Pro chorea, et dulci modulamine, Pyrrhicus illis
Saltus, et horribiles placet ære ciere sonores.   55
Hic conjux viduata viro longo effera luctu
Flet noctem, solumque torum sterilesque Hymenæos
Deplorans, lacerat crines, et pectora plangit:
Nequicquam—sponsus ni forte appareat, hospes
Heu! brevis, in somnis, et ludicra fallat imago.   60
Immemor ille tori interea ruit acer in hostem:
Horrendum strepit armorum fragor undique campis;
Atque immortales durant in sæcula pugnæ.

   Hinc Jovis immensum delati accedimus orbem.
Illic mille locis exercet sæva tyrannus   65
Imperia in totidem servos, totidemque rebelles:
Sed brevis exercet: parat illi fata veneno
Perjurus, populosque premit novus ipse tyrannus.
Hi decies pacem figunt pretio atque refigunt:
Tum demum arma parant: longe lateque cohortes   70

12

Extenduntur agris; simul æquora tota teguntur
Classibus, et ficti celebrantur utrinque triumphi.
Fœdera mox ineunt nunquam violanda; brevique
Belli iterum simulacra cient; referuntur in altum
Classes, pacificoque replentur milite campi.   75
Filius hic patri meditatur, sponsa marito,
Servus hero insidias. Has leges scilicet illis
Imposuit natura locis, quo tempore patrem
Jupiter ipse suum solio detrusit avito.
Inde venena viris, perjuria, munera, fraudes   80
Suadet opum sitis, et regnandi dira cupido.

   Saturni tandem nos illætabilis ora
Accipit: ignavum pecus hic per opaca locorum
Pinguescunt de more, gravi torpentque veterno.
Vivitur in specubus: quis enim tam sedulus, arces   85
Qui struat ingentes, operosaque mœnia condat?
Idem omnes stupor altus habet, sub pectore fixus.
Non studia ambitiosa Jovis, variosque labores
Mercurii, non Martis opus, non Cyprida norunt.
Post obitum, ut perhibent, sedes glomerantur in istas   90
Qui longam nullas vitam excoluere per artes;
Sed Cerere et Baccho pleni, somnoque sepulti
Cunctarum duxere æterna oblivia rerum.
Non avium auditur cantus, non murmur aquarum,
Mugitusve boum, aut pecorum balatus in agris: 95
Nudos non decorant segetes, non gramina campos.
Sylva, usquam si sylva, latet sub monte nivali,
Et canet viduata comis: hic noctua tantum
Glisque habitat, bufoque et cum testudine, talpa.
Flumina dum tarde subterlabentia terras   100
Pigram undam volvunt, et sola papavera pascunt:
Quorum lentus odor, lethæaque pocula somnos
Suadent perpetuos, circumfusæque tenebræ.

   Horrendo visu obstupui: quin Pegason ipsum
Defecere animi; sensit dux, terque flagello   105
Insonuit clarum, terque alta voce morantem
Increpuit: secat ille cito pede lævia campi
Ætherei, terræque secunda allabitur aura.

                      Cantabr. in Comitiis prioribus 1740–1

Translation
Say, what uncommon cares disturb my rest,
And kindle raptures foreign to my breast?
From earth's low confines lift my mind on high,
To trace new worlds revolving in the sky?
Yes—I'm impatient of this orb of clay,   5
And boldly dare to mediate my way,
Where Fontinelle first saw the planets roll,
And all the God tumultuous shakes my soul.

  'Tis He! He comes! and thro' the sun-bright skies
Drives foaming Pegasus, and thus he cries: 10
"Cease, cease, dear youth, too studiously employ'd,
And wing with me the unresisting void;
'Tis thine with me round other worlds to soar,
And visit kingdoms never known before;
While I succinctly shew each various race,   15
The manners and the genius of the place."
I (tho' my mind with lively horror fraught,
Thinks on Bellerophon, and shudders at the thought)
Mount quick the winged steed; he springs, he flies,
Shoots thro' the yielding air, and cleaves the liquid skies!   20
—First, swift Cyllenius, circling round the sun,
We reach, when thus my friendly guide begun:
"Mark well the genius of this fiery place,
The wild amusements of the brainsick race,
Whose minds the beams of Titan, too intense,   25
Affect with frenzy, and distract the sense.
A monarch here gives subject princes law,
A mighty monarch, with a crown of straw.
There sits a lover, sad in pensive air,
And like the dismal image of despair,   30
With charcoal paints his Chloe heav'nly fair.
In sadly-soothing strain rude notes he sings,
And strikes harsh numbers from the jarring strings.
Lo! an astrologer, with filth besmear'd,
Rough and neglected, with a length of beard,   35
Pores round his cell for undiscover'd stars,
And decks the wall with triangles and squares.
Lo!—But the radiant car of Phœbus nigh
Glows with red ardour, and inflames the sky—
Oh! waft me, hide me in some cool retreat;   40
I faint, I sicken with the fervent heat."

Thence to that milder orb we wing our way,
Where Venus governs with an easy sway.
Soft breathes the air; fair Flora paints the ground,
And laughing Ceres deals her gifts around.   45
This blissful *Tempe* no rough blasts molest,
Of blust'ring Boreas, or the baleful East;
But gentle Zephyrs o'er the woodlands stray,
Court the tall trees, and round the branches play,
Ætherial gales dispensing as they flow,   50
To fan those passions which they teach to glow.
Here the gay youth in measur'd steps advance,
While sprightly music animates the dance;
There the sweet melody of sound admire,
Sigh with the song, or languish to the lyre: 55
Fair nymphs and amorous youths, a lovely band,
Blend in the dance, light-bounding hand in hand.
From ev'ry grove the buxom Zephyrs bring
The rich ambrosia of eternal spring.
Care dwells not here, their pleasures to destroy,   60
But Laughter, Jest, and universal joy:
All, all is love; for Venus reigns confest
The sole sultana of each captive breast:
Cold Cynthia here wou'd Cupid's victim prove, ⎫
Or the chaste daughter of imperial Jove,   ⎬   65
And Cato's virtue be the slave of love.   ⎭

But now thro' destin'd fields of air we fly,
And leave those mansions, not without a sigh:
Thence the dire coast we reach, the dreary plains,
Where Mars, grim god, and bloody discord reigns.   70
The host in arms embattled sternly stands,
The sword, the dart, the dagger, in their hands.
Here no fair nymphs to silver sounds advance,
But buskin'd heroes form the Pyrrhic dance.
And brazen trumpets, terrible from far,   75
With martial music fire the soul to war.
Here the lone bride bewails her absent lord,
The sterile nuptials, the deserted board,
Sighs the long nights, and, frantic with despair,
Beats her bare breast, and rends her flowing hair: 80
In vain she sighs, in vain dissolves in tears—
In sleep, perhaps, the warrior lord appears,

A fleeting form that glides before her sight,
A momentary vision of the night.
Meanwhile, regardless of her anxious pray'r,   85
The hardy husband sternly stalks to war;
Our ears the clang of ringing armour rends,
And the immortal battle never ends.

   Hence thro' the boundless void we nimbly move,
And reach the wide-extended plains of Jove.   90
Here the stern tyrant sways an iron rod;
A thousand vassals tremble at his nod.
How short the period of a tyrant's date!
The pois'nous phial speeds the work of fate:
Scarce is the proud, imperious tyrant dead,   95
But, lo! a second lords it in his stead.
Here peace, as common merchandize, is sold,
Heav'n's first best blessing for pernicious gold:
War soon succeeds, the sturdy squadrons stand
Wide o'er the fields a formidable band;   100
With num'rous fleets they croud the groaning main,
And triumph for the victories they feign:
Again in strict alliances unite,
Till discord raise again the phantom of a fight;
Again they sail; again the troops prepare   105
Their falchions for the mockery of war.
The son inhuman seeks his father's life,
The slave his master's, and her lord's the wife.
With vengeance thus their kindling bosoms fire,
Since Jove usurp'd the sceptre of his sire.   110
Thence poisons, perjuries, and bribes betray; ⎫
Nor other passions do their souls obey   ⎬
Than thirst of gold, and avarice of sway.   ⎭

   At length we land, vast fields of æther crost,
On Saturn's cold uncomfortable coast;   115
Here in the gloom the pamper'd sluggards lull
The lazy hours, lethargically dull.
In caves they live; for who was ever known
So wise, so sedulous to build a town?
The same stupidity infects the whole,
Fix'd in the breast, and center'd in the soul.   120
These never feel th' ambitious fires of Jove, ⎫
To Industry not Mercury can move,   ⎬
Mars cannot spur to war, nor Venus woo to love. ⎭

Here rove those souls, 'tis said, when life departs,   125
Who never cultivated useful arts;
But stupify'd with plenty and repose,
Dreamt out long life in one continued dose!
No feather'd songsters, with sweet-warbled strains
Attune to melting melody the plains,   130
No flocks wide-past'ring bleat, nor oxen low,
No fountains musically murm'ring flow;
Th' ungenial waste no tender herbage yields,
No harvests wave luxuriant in the fields.
Low lie the groves, if groves this land can boast, ⎫   135
Chain'd in the fetters of eternal frost,   ⎬
Their beauty wither'd, and their verdure lost. ⎭
Dull animals inhabit this abode,
The owl, mole, dormouse, tortoise, and the toad.
Dull rivers deep within their channels glide,   140
And slow roll on their tributary tide:
Nor aught th' unvegetative waters feed,
But sleepy poppy and the slimy reed;
Whose lazy fogs, like Lethe's cups, dispense
Eternal slumbers of dull indolence.   145

   Agast I stood, the drowsy vapours lull
My soul in gloom, ev'n Pegasus grew dull.
My guide observ'd, and thrice he urg'd his speed,
Thrice the loud lash resounded from the steed;
Fir'd at the strokes, he flies with slacken'd rein ⎫   150
Swift o'er the level of the liquid plain,   ⎬
Glides with the gentle gale, and lights on earth again. ⎭

The pretty Bar-Keeper of the Mitre

Written at College, 1741

"Relax, sweet girl, your wearied mind,
    And to hear the poet talk,
Gentlest creature of your kind,
    Lay aside your spunge and chalk;
Cease, cease the bar-bell, nor refuse   5
To hear the jingle of the Muse.

Hear your numerous vot'ries prayers,
    Come, O come and bring with thee
Giddy whimsies, wanton airs,
    And all love's soft artillery;   10
Smiles and throbs, and frowns, and tears,
With all the little hopes and fears."

She heard—she came—and ere she spoke,
    Not unravish'd you might see,
Her wanton eyes that wink'd the joke,   15
    Ere her tongue could set it free.
While her forc'd blush her cheeks inflam'd,
And seem'd to say she was asham'd.

No handkerchief her bosom hid,
    No tippet from our sight debars   20
Her heaving breasts with moles o'erspread,
    Markt, little hemispheres, with stars;
While on them all our eyes we move,
Our eyes that meant immoderate love.

In every gesture, every air,   25
    Th' imperfect lisp, the languid eye,

THE PRETTY BAR-KEEPER. MS: Bodl. Eng. misc. e. 241, fos. 80–81. First published
in *ST* (Jan. 1751), ii. 150–1. Text: *ST*. Collated: *MS*, *1791*. *Title*. To the Barkeeper
of the Mitre Cambridge. *MS*
3 Gentlest of the gentle kind *MS*   7 your] thy *MS*   14 you might] might
you *MS*   17 her forc'd] the forc'd *MS*   a forc'd *1791*   19–24 *omitted, MS*

In every motion of the fair
   We awkward imitators vie,
And forming our own from her face,
Strive to look pretty, as we gaze.   30

If e'er she sneez'd, the mimic crowd
   Sneez'd too, and all their pipes laid down;
If she but stoopt, we lowly bow'd,
   And sullen, if she 'gan to frown,
In solemn silence sat profound—   35
But did she laugh?—the laugh went round.

Her snuff-box if the nymph pull'd out,
   Each JOHNIAN in responsive airs,
Fed with the tickling dust his snout,
   With all the politesse of bears.   40
Dropt she her fan benath her hoop?
Ev'n stake-stuck CLARIANS *strove* to stoop.

The sons of culinary KAY's
   Smoaking from the eternal treat,
Lost in ecstatic transport gaze,   45
   As tho' the fair was good to eat;
Ev'n gloomiest KING's-MEN, pleas'd awhile,
"Grin horribly a ghastly smile."

But hark; she cries, "my mamma calls,"
   And strait, she's vanish'd from our sight;   50
'Twas then we saw the empty bowls,
   'Twas then we first perceiv'd it night;
While all, sad synod, silent moan,
Both that she went—and went alone.

29 our own from her] from her our own *MS*   31 sneez'd] sneer'd *1791*
32 Sneez'd and their pipes at once laid down *MS*   Sneer'd too, and all their pipes
laid down; *1791*   34 And sullen sate did she but frown, *MS*   35 Sigh'd she,
we hove the sigh profound *MS*   37 nymph] fair *MS*   44 Smoaking] Still
smoaking *MS*   45 transport] rapture *MS*   46 was] were *MS*   49 But
hark! my mother calls she cried, *MS*   50 And quickly vanish'd from our sight
MS   51 'Twas then the empty bowls we spied *MS*   53 Whilst all sad silent
synod moan *MS*

[TRIPOS VERSES II]

Materies gaudet vi Inertiæ.

Vervecum in patria, qua late Hibernica squalent
Arva inarata, palus horrenda voragine crebra
Ante oculos jacet; haud illic impune viator
Per tenebras iter instituat; tremit undique tellus
Sub pedibus malefida, vapores undique densos   5
Sudat humus, nebulisque amicitur tristibus herba.

  Huc fato infelix si quando agiteris iniquo,
Et tuto in medium liceat penetrare, videbis
Attonitus, nigra de nube emergere templum,
Templum ingens, immane, altum penetrale Stuporis.   10
Plumbea stat turris, plumbum sinuatur in arcus,
Et solido limosa tument fundamina plumbo.
Hanc, pia Materies, Divo ædem extruxit inerti,
Stultitiæ impulsu—quid enim? Lethargica semper
Sponte sua nihil aggreditur, dormitat in horas,   15
Et, sine vi, nullo gaudet Dea languida motu.

  Hic ea monstra habitant, quæ olim sub luminis auras
Materies peperit somno patre, lividus iste
Zoilus, et Bavio non impar Mævius; audax
Spinoza, et Pyrrho, cumque Hobbesio Epicurus.   20
Ast omnes valeat quæ musa referre? frequentes
Usque adeo videas Hebetes properare?—nec adfert
Quidquam opis Anglorum doctæ vicinia gentis.
Sic quondam, ut perhibent, stupuit Bœotica tellus
Vicina licet Antycira, nihil inde salutis,   25
Nil tulit hellebori Zephyrus, cum sæpe per æquor
Felicem ad Lesbon levibus volitaverit alis,
Indigenæ mellita ferens suspiria Floræ.

  Porticus illa vides? Gothicis suffulta columnis,
Templi aditus, quam laxa patet! custodia qualis   30
Ante fores! quatuor formæ sua tollere miris

MATERIES GAUDET. First published in *1752*. Text: *1752*. Collated: *1791*.

Ora modis! en! torva tuens stat limine in ipso
Personam Logices induta Sophistica, denis
Cincta Categoriis, matrem quæ maxima natu
Filia materiem agnoscit—quantum instar in ipsa est!   35
Grande caput, tenues oculi, cutis arida produnt
Fallacem: rete una manus tenet, altera fustem.
Vestis arachneis sordet circumdata telis,
Queis gaudet labyrinthæos Dea callida nodos.
Aspicias jam funereo gradientem incessu—   40
Quam lente cælo Saturni volvitur astrum,
Quam lente, saltaverunt post Orphea montes,
Quam lente, Oxonii, solennis pondera cænæ
Gestant tergeminorum abdomina bedellorum.

Proxima deinde tenet loca sorte insana Mathesis,   45
Nuda pedes, chlamydem discincta, incompta capillos,
Immemor externi, punctoque innixa reclinat.
Ante pedes vario inscriptam diagrammate arenam
Cernas, rectis curva, atque intertexta rotunda
Schemata quadratis—queis scilicet abdita rerum   50
Pandere se jactat solam, doctasque sorores
Fastidit, propriæque nihil non arrogat arti.
Illàm olim, duce Neutono, tum tendit ad astra,
Ætheriasque domos superum, indignata volantem
Turba mathematicum retrahit, pœnasque reposcens   55
Detinet in terris, nugisque exercet ineptis.

Tertia Microphile, proles furtiva parentis
Divinæ; produxit enim commixta furenti
Diva viro Physice—muscas et papiliones
Lustrat inexpletum, collumque et tempora rident   60
Floribus, et fungis, totaque propagine veris.
Rara oculis nugarum avidis animalia quærit
Omne genus, seu serpit humi, seu ludit in undis,
Seu volitans tremulis liquidum secat aera pennis.
O! ubi littoribus nostris felicior aura   65
Polypon appulerit, quanto cava templa Stuporis
Mugitu concussa trement, reboabit et ingens
Pulsa palus! Plausu excipiet Dea blanda secundo

38 sordet *1752 Errata*] sordit *1752, 1791*

Microphile ante omnes; jam non crocodilon adorat;
Non bombyx, conchæve juvant: sed Polypon ardet,   70
Solum Polypon ardet,—et ecce! faceta feraci
Falce novos creat assidue, pascitque creatos,
Ah! modo dilectis pascit nove gaudia muscis.

Quartam Materies peperit conjuncta Stupori,
Nomen Atheia illi, monstrum cui lumen ademptum,   75
Atque aures; cui sensus abest; sed mille trisulcæ
Ore micant linguæ, refugas quibus inficit auras.
Hanc Stupor ipse parens odit, vicina nefandos
Horret sylva sonos, neque surda repercutit Echo
Mendacem natura redarguit ipsa, Deumque   80
Et cœlum, et terræ, veraciaque Astra fatentur.
Se simul agglomerans surgit chorus omnis aquarum,
Et puro sublime sonat grave fulmen olympo.

Fonte ortus Lethæo, ipsius ad ostia templi,
Ire soporifero tendit cum murmure rivus,   85
Huc potum Stolidos Deus evocat agmine magno:
Crebri adsunt, largisque sitim restinguere gaudent
Haustibus, atque iterant calices, certantque stupendo.
Me, me etiam, clamo, occurrens;—sed vellicat aurem
Calliope, nocuasque vetat contingere lymphas.

Translation
In Ireland's wild, uncultivated plains,
Where torpid sloth, and foggy dulness reigns,
Full many a fen infests the putrid shore,
And many a gulph the melancholy moor.
Let not the stranger in these regions stray,   5
Dark is the sky, and perilous the way;
Beneath his foot-steps shakes the trembling ground, ⎫
Dense fogs and exhalations hover round,   ⎬
And with black clouds the tender turf is crown'd.   ⎭

Here shou'd'st thou rove, by Fate's severe command,   10
And safely reach the center of the land;
Thine eyes shall view, with horror and surprize, ⎫
The fane of Dulness, of enormous size,   ⎬
Emerging from the sable cloud arise.   ⎭

A leaden tow'r upheaves its heavy head, ⎫ 15
Vast leaden arches press the slimy bed, ⎬
The soft soil swells beneath the load of lead. ⎭
Old Matter here erected this abode,
At Folly's impulse, to the Slothful God.
And here the drone lethargic loves to stay, 20
Slumb'ring the dull, inactive hours away;
For still, unless by foreign force imprest,
The languid Goddess holds her state of rest.

Their habitation here those monsters keep,
Whom Matter father'd on the God of Sleep: 25
Here Zoilus, with cank'ring envy pale,
Here Mævius bids his brother Bavius, hail;
Spinoza, Epicure, and all those mobs
Of wicked wits, from Pyrrho down to Hobbes.
How can the Muse recount the numerous crew 30
Of frequent fools that crowd upon the view?
Nor can learn'd Albion's sun that burns so clear,
Disperse the dulness that involves them here.
Bœotia thus remain'd, in days of yore, ⎫
Senseless and stupid, tho' the neighb'ring shore ⎬ 35
Afforded salutary hellebore: ⎭
No cure exhal'd from Zephyr's buxom breeze,
That gently brush'd the bosom of the seas,
As oft to Lesbian fields he wing'd his way, ⎫
Fanning fair Flora, and in airy play ⎬ 40
Breath'd balmy sighs, that melt the soul away. ⎭

Behold that portico! how vast, how wide!
The pillars Gothic, wrought with barb'rous pride:
Four monstrous shapes before the portal wait,
Of horrid aspect, centry to the gate: 45
Lo! in the entrance, with disdainful eye,
In Logick's dark disguise, stands Sophistry:
Her very front would common sense confound,
Encompass'd with ten categories round:
She from Old Matter, the great mother, came, 50
By birth the eldest—and how like the dame!
Her shrivel'd skin, small eyes, prodigious pate,
Denote her shrewd, and subtle in debate:
This hand a net, and that sustains a club,
T' entangle her antagonist, or drub. 55

23

The spider's toils, all o'er her garment spread,
Imply the mazy errors of her head.
Behold her marching with funereal pace,
Slow as old Saturn rolls thro' boundless space,
Slow as the mighty mountains mov'd along,   60
When Orpheus rais'd the lyre-attended song:
Or, as at Oxford, on some Gaudy day,
Fat Beadles, in magnificent array,
With big round bellies bear the pond'rous treat,
And heavily lag on, with the vast load of meat.   65

    The next, mad Mathesis; her feet all bare,
Ungirt, untrim'd, with dissoluted hair:
No foreign object can her thoughts disjoint;
Reclin'd she sits, and ponders o'er a point.
Before her, lo! inscrib'd upon the ground,   70
Strange diagrams th' astonish'd sight confound,
Right lines and curves, with figures square and round.
With these the monster, arrogant and vain,
Boasts that she can all mysteries explain,
And treats the sacred Sisters with disdain.   75
She, when great Newton sought his kindred skies,
Sprung high in air, and strove with him to rise,
In vain—the mathematic mob restrains
Her flight, indignant, and on earth detains;
E'er since the captive wretch her brains employs   80
On trifling trinkets, and on gewgaw toys.

    Microphile is station'd next in place,
The spurious issue of celestial race;
From heav'nly Physice she took her birth,
Her sire a madman of the sons of earth;   85
On flies she pores with keen, unwearied sight,
And moths and butterflies, her dear delight;
Mushrooms and flow'rs, collected on a string,
Around her neck, around her temples cling,
With all the strange production of the spring.   90
With greedy eyes she'll search the world to find
Rare, uncouth animals of every kind;
Whether along the humble ground they stray,
Or nimbly sportive in the waters play,
Or thro' the light expanse of æther fly,   95
And with fleet pinions cleave the liquid sky.

Ye gales, that gently breathe upon our shore,
O! let the Polypus be wafted o'er;
How will the hollow dome of Dulness ring,
With what loud joy receive the wond'rous thing?   100
Applause will rend the skies, and all around
The quivering quagmires bellow back the sound;
How will Microphile her joy attest,
And glow with warmer raptures than the rest?
This will the curious crocodile excell,   105
The weaving worm, and silver-shining shell;
No object e'er will wake her wonder thus
As Polypus, her darling Polypus.
Lo! by the wounds of her creating knife,
New Polypusses wriggle into life,   110
Fast as they rise, she feeds with ample store
Of once rare flies, but now esteem'd no more.

 The fourth dire shape from mother Matter came,
Dulness her sire, and Atheism is her name;
In her no glimpse of sacred Sense appears,   115
Depriv'd of eyes, and destitute of ears:
And yet she brandishes a thousand tongues,
And blasts the world with air-infecting lungs.
Curs'd by her sire, her very words are wounds,
No grove re-ecchoes the detested sounds.   120
Whate'er she speaks all nature proves a lye, ⎫
The earth, the heav'ns, the starry-spangled sky ⎬
Proclaim the wise, eternal Deity: ⎭
The congregated waves in mountains driven
Roar in grand chorus to the Lord of Heaven;   125
Thro' skies serene the glorious thunders roll,
Loudly pronounce the God, and shake the sounding Pole.

 A river, murmuring from Lethæan source,
Full to the fane directs its sleepy course;
The Pow'r of Dulness, leaning on the brink,   130
Here calls the multitude of fools to drink.
Swarming they crowd to stupify the skull,
With frequent cups contending to be dull.
Me, let me taste the sacred stream, I cry'd, ⎫
With out-stretch'd arm—the Muse my boon deny'd, ⎬ 135
And sav'd me from the sense-intoxicating tide. ⎭

[TRIPOS VERSES III]

Mutua Oscitationum Propagatio Solvi Potest Mechanicé.

Momus, scurra, procax superum, quo tempore Pallas
Exiluit cerebro Jovis, est pro more jocatus
Nescio quid stultum de partu: excanduit ira
Jupiter, asper, acerba tuens; "et tu quoque," dixit,
"Garrule, concipies, fætumque ex ore profundes:"⠀⠀⠀⠀⠀5
Haud mora, jamque supinus in aula extenditur ingens
Derisor; dubia velantur lumina nocte;
Stertit hians immane; —e naso Gallica clangunt
Classica, Germanique, simul sermonis amaror:

⠀⠀Edita vix tandem est monstrum Polychasmia, proles⠀⠀10
Tanto digna parente, aviæque simillima Nocti.
Illa oculos tentat nequicquam aperire, veterno
Torpida, et horrendo vultum distorta cachinno.
Æmulus hanc Jovis aspiciens, qui fictile vulgus
Fecerat infelix, imitarier arte Prometheus⠀⠀⠀⠀⠀15
Audet—nec flammis opus est cœlestibus: auræ
Tres Stygiæ flatus, nigræ tria pocula Lethes
Miscet, et innuptæ suspiria longa puellæ,
His adipem suis et guttur conjungit aselli,
Tensaque cum gemitu somnisque sequacibus ora.⠀⠀20
Sic etiam in terris Dea, quæ mortalibus ægris
Ferret opem, inque hebetes dominarier apta, creata est.

⠀⠀Nonne vides, ut præcipiti petit oppida cursu
Rustica plebs, stipatque forum? sublime tribunal
Armigerique equitesque premunt, de more parati⠀⠀25
Justitiæ lances proferre fideliter æquas,
Grande capillitium induti, frontemque minacem.
Non temere attoniti caupones, turbaque furum
Aufugiunt, gravidæque timent trucia ora puellæ.
At mox fida comes Polychasmia, matutinis⠀⠀⠀⠀⠀30
Quæ se miscuerat poc'lis Cerealibus, ipsum

MUTUA OSCITATIONUM. First published in *1752*. Text: *1752*. Collated: *1791*.

Judicis in cerebrum scandit—jamque unus et alter
Cæperunt longas in hiatum ducere voces:
Donec per cunctos Dea jam solenne, profundum
Sparserit Hum—nutant taciti, tum brachia magno   35
Extendunt nisu, patulis et faucibus hiscunt.
Interea legum Caupones jurgia miscent,
Queis nil Rhetorice est, nisi copia major hiandi:
Vocibus ambiguis certant, nugasque strophasque
Alternis jaculantur, et irascuntur amice,   40
Donantque accipiuntque stuporis missile plumbum.

    Vos, Fanatica turba, nequit pia musa tacere.
Majoremne aliunde potest diducere rictum?
Ascendit gravis Orator, miseraque loquela
Expromit thesin; in partes quam deinde minutas   45
Distrahit, ut connectat, et explicat obscurando:
Spargitur heu! pigris verborum somnus ab alis,
Grex circum gemit, et plausum declarat hiando.

    Nec vos, qui falso matrem jactatis Hygeian
Patremque Hippocratem, taceam—Polychasmia, vestros   50
Agnosco natos: tumidas sine pondere voces
In vulgum eructant; emuncto quisque bacillum
Applicat auratum naso, graviterque facetus
Totum se in vultum cogit, medicamina pandens—
Rusticus haurit amara, atque insanabile dormit;   55
Nec sensus revocare queant fomenta, nec herbæ,
Non ars, non miræ magicus sonus ABRACADABRÆ.

    Ante alios summa es, Polychasmia, cura Sophistæ:
Ille Tui cæcas vires, causamque latentem
Sedulus exquirit—quo scilicet impete fauces   60
Invitæ disjungantur; quo vortice aquosæ
Particulæ fluitent, comitesque ut fulminis imbres,
Cum strepitu erumpant; ut deinde vaporet ocellos
Materies subtilis; ut in cutis insinuet se
Retia; tum, si forte datur contingere nervos   65
Concordes, cunctorum ora expanduntur hiulca.
Sic ubi, Phœbe pater, sumis chelyn, harmoniamque
Abstrusam in chordis simul elicis, altera, siquam

Æqualis tenor aptavit, tremit æmula cantus,
Memnoniamque imitata lyram sine pollicis ictu   70
Divinum resonat proprio modulamine carmen.

    Me quoque, mene tuum tetigisti, ingrata, Poetam?
Hei mihi! totus hio tibi jam stupefactus; in ipso
Parnasso captus longe longeque remotas
Prospecto Musas, sitioque, ut Tantalus alter,   75
Castalias situs inter aquas, inhiantis ab ore
Nectarei fugiunt latices—hos Popius urna
Excipit undanti, et fontem sibi vendicat omnem.

    Haud aliter Socium esuriens Sizator edacem
Dum videt, appositusque cibus frustratur hiantem,   80
Dentibus infrendens nequicquam lumine torvo
Sæpius exprobrat; nequicquam brachia tendit
Sedulus officiosa, dapes removere paratus.
Olli nunquam exempta fames, quin frusta suprema
Devoret, et peritura immani ingurgitet ore: 85
Tum demum jubet auferri; nudata capaci
Ossa sonant, lugubre sonant, allisa catino.

Translation
When Pallas issued from the brain of Jove,
Momus, the Mimic of the Gods above,
In his mock mood impertinently spoke,
About the birth, some low, ridiculous joke:
Jove, sternly frowning, glow'd with vengeful ire,   5
And thus indignant said th' Almighty Sire,
"Loquacious Slave, that laugh'st without a cause,
Thou shalt conceive, and bring forth at thy jaws."
He spoke—stretch'd in the hall the Mimic lies,
Supinely dull, thick vapours dim his eyes: 10
And as his jaws a horrid chasm disclose,
It seem'd he made a trumpet of his nose;
Tho' harsh the strain, and horrible to hear,
Like German jargon grating on the ear.

    At length was Polychasmia brought to light, ⎤   15
Worthy her sire, a monster of a sight,   ⎥
Resembling her great grandmother, Old Night. ⎦

28

Her eyes to open oft in vain she try'd,
Lock'd were the lids, her mouth distended wide.
Her when Prometheus happen'd to survey   20
(Rival of Jove, that made mankind of clay)
He form'd without the aid of heav'nly ray.
To three Lethæan cups he learnt to mix
Deep sighs of virgins, with three blasts from Styx,
The bray of asses, with the fat of brawn,   25
The sleep-preceding groan, and hideous yawn.
Thus Polychasmia took her wond'rous birth,
A Goddess helpful to the sons of earth.

  Lo! how the rustic multitude from far
Haste to the town, and crowd the clam'rous bar.   30
The prest bench groans with many a squire and knight,
Who weigh out justice, and distribute right:
Severe they seem, and formidably big,
With front important, and huge periwig.
The little villains skulk aloof dismay'd,   35
And panic terrors seize the pregnant maid.
But soon friend Polychasm', who always near,
Herself had mingled with their morning beer,
Steals to the judges brain, and centers there.
Then in the court the horrid yawn began,   40
And Hum, profound and solemn, went from man to man:
Silent they nod, and with prodigious strain
Stretch out their arms, then listless yawn again:
For all the flow'rs of rhetoric they can boast,
Amidst their wranglings, is to gape the most: 45
Ambiguous quirks, and friendly wrath they vent,
And give and take the leaden argument.

  Ye too, Fanaticks, never shall escape
The faithful muse; for who so greatly gape?
Mounted on high, with serious care perplext,   50
The miserable preacher takes his text;
Then into parts minute, with wondrous pain,
Divides, connects, and then divides again,
And does with grave obscurity explain:
While from his lips lean periods lingring creep,   55
And not one meaning interrupts their sleep,
The drowsy hearers stretch their weary jaws
With lamentable groan, and yawning gape applause.

The Quacks of Physic next provoke my ire,
Who falsely boast Hippocrates their sire: 60
Goddess! thy sons I ken—verbose and loud,
They puff their windy bubbles on the crowd:
With look important, critical, and vain,
Each to his nose applies the gilded cane;
And as he nods, and ponders o'er the case,   65
Gravely collects himself into his face,
Explains his med'cines—which the rustic buys,
Drinks the dire draught, and of the doctor dies;
No pills, no potions can to life restore;   ⎞
ABRACADABRA, necromantic pow'r   ⎟   70
Can charm, and conjure up from death no more.   ⎠

But more than aught that's marvellous and rare,
The studious Soph makes Polychasm' his care;
Explores what secret spring, what hidden cause,
Distends with hideous chasm th' unwilling jaws,   75
What latent ducts the dewy moisture pour
With sound tremendous, like a thunder-show'r:
How subtile matter, exquisitely thin,
Pervades the curious net-work of the skin,
Affects th' accordant nerve—all eyes are drown'd   80
In drowsy vapours, and the yawn goes round.
When Phœbus thus his flying fingers flings
Across the chords, and sweeps the trembling strings;
If e'er a lyre at unison there be,
It swells with emulating harmony,   85
Like Memnon's harp, in ancient times renown'd,
Breathing, untouch'd, sweet-modulated sound.

But oh! ungrateful! to thy own true bard,
Oh! Polychasm', is this my just reward?
Thy drowsy dews upon my head distill,   90
Just at the entrance of th' Aonian hill;
Listless I gape, unactive, and supine,
And at vast distance view the sacred Nine:
Wistful I view—the streams increase my thirst,
In vain—like Tantalus, with plenty curst,   95
No draughts nectareous to my portion fall,
These godlike Pope exhausts, and greatly claims them all.

Thus the lean Sizar views, with gaze agast,
The hungry Tutor at his noon's repast;
In vain he grinds his teeth—his grudging eye,   100
And visage sharp, keen appetite imply;
Oft he attempts, officious, to convey
The lessening relicks of the meal away—
In vain—no morsel 'scapes the greedy jaw,
All, all is gorg'd in magisterial maw;   105
Till at the last, observant of his word,
The lamentable waiter clears the board,
And inly-murmuring miserably groans,
To see the empty dish, and hear the sounding bones.

CARMEN CL. *ALEXANDRI POPE* IN
S. CÆCILIAM
LATINE REDDITUM

——τὸ πόρσω
Δ' ἔστι σοφοῖς ἄβατον,
Κἀσόφοις. οὐ μὴν διώξω. κεινὸς εἴην.

PINDAR

I.

Descende cœlo, spiritu quæ melleo
    Imples, Camœna, tibias;
Descende, pulsas quæ lyram volucri manu,
    Nervumque sopitum excita:
        Discat fundere suaviter severas   5
        Testudo numerosa cantilenas:
            Cava classica clangoribus auras
            Repleant, resonent tremebundarum
            Laquearia convulsa domorum:
Inque vicem lenta gravia organa majestate   10
Spirent, augustoque sonore inflata tumescant.
        Ut clare, ut placidi molliter auribus
        Se furtim bibulis insinuant modi!
        Mox tollunt violentum altius altius
            Auditum Superis sonum!   15
Jamque exultantes numeri atque audacia turgent
Carmina, jam tremulus fractis fluitat furor auris;
        Donec minutatim remota,
            Jam liquefacta,
            Jam moritura,   20
            Murmura languent,
            Murmura dulci
        Leniter attenuata casu.

CARMEN IN S. CAECILIAM. First published, separately, in 1743. Text: *1743*. Collated: *1746*; *1767*; *1791*.

II.

Æquas ut servat moderatrix Musica mentes!
  Ut premit, aut laxat mollibus imperiis!   25
    Seu gaudiorum turbida pectora
    Tumultuosis fluctibus æstuant,
      Tranquillat; urget seu malorum
      Pondus, humo levat Illa voce,
Gestit bellantes animoso accendere cantu;   30
Blandaque amatori medicamina sufficit ægro:
    Languens ecce! caput Mœstitia erigit,
    Morpheus molliculis prosilit e toris,
    Ulnas implicitas pandit Inertia,
      Audit deciduis Invidia anguibus: 35
Intestina animi cessant bella; applicat aures
Seditio, nec præcipites reminiscitur iras.

III.

Ast ubi dulcis amor patriæ pia mittit in arma,
O! quanto accendunt mavortia tympana pulsu!
Sic, cum prima viam navis tentaret inausam,   40
Thrax cecinit, puppique lyrum tractavit in alta,
    Dum vidit Argo Pelion arduum
    Pinus sorores deserere impigras,
      Et turba circumfusa muto
      Semideum stupuere plausu: 45
Incedit heros, quisquis audiit sonum,
    Amore flagrans gloriæ;
Dux seminudum quisque rapit manu
Ensem, et coruscat multiplicem ægida:
    Ad arma sylvæ, ad arma montes,   50
      Terra, mare, astra sonant ad arma!

IV.

Sed, cum per Orci limites cavernosi,
Amplexibus quos igneis obit fumans
Phlegethon, Poetam, Morte non minus pollens,

28–31 Tranquillat; urgeantve curæ, / Attonitas levat illa mentes. / Belligeris animosos inspirat pectora cantu, / Vulneribus facilem præbet Amoris opem. *1767*
47 Flagratque vasta gloriæ lubidine; *1767*

Adire jussit pallidos Amor manes,   55
    Quæ miracl'a sonorum!
  Quæ feralia monstra videri,
    Diras per oras dissita!
      Horrida fulgura,
      Vox penetrabilis   60
      Sæva querentium,
      Et picei ignis
      Triste crepusculum,
      Diri ululatus,
      Et gemitus gravis   65
      Mœsta profunditas,
    Dumque luunt pœnas animæ, tremuli singultus.
Sed audin'! audin'! auream ferit chelyn,
    Miserisque fecit otium:
En! tenue ut patulis auribus agmen adest!   70
Quiescit ingens Sisyphi saxum, et suæ
    Acclinis Ixion rotæ;
    Atque leves ineunt pallida spectra choros!
Ferratis sua membra toris collapsa reclinant
Oblitæ irarum Eumenides, et lurida circum   75
Colla auscultantes sese explicuere colubri!

v.

  Per fluentorum vada, quæ perenni
  Rore delibant sinuosa ripas;
  Per levem, siqua Elysii vireta
    Ventilat aura;   80
  Per beatorum Genios colentes
  Arva, qua passim asphodelis renidet
  Gramen auratis, amarinthinæve um-
    bracula frondis;
  Per duces, si quis dubiam per umbram   85
  Splendidis late loca lustrat armis;
  Myrteæ et quisquis querulus vagatur
    Incola sylvæ;
Reddite (vos rapuistis enim) mihi reddite sponsam,
Obtestor, parilive adjungite me quoque fato!   90

83–4 Gramen auratis, amarinthinive / Tegmina prati; *1767*

Canit, canenti Dis ferus annuit,
Ceditque blandarum harmoniæ precum,
   Et victa mansuescunt severæ
   Persephones sine more corda.
O decus egregium! Mortemque Orcumque Poeta   95
   Flectit, et infernis faucibus exit ovans!
Fata obstant—novies Styx circumfusa coercet—
   Nequicquam—vincit musica, vincit amor.

VI.

Sed nimium, heu! nimium impatiens respexit amator:
Ah! cecidit, cecidit, subitoque elapsa refugit!   100
Qua prece jam surdas flectes, temerarie, Parcas?
   At tu, si crimen, crimen amantis habes.
    Nunc pendulis sub antris,
    Jugesve propter undas,
    Ubi callibus reductis   105
    Temere vagatur Hebrus,
      Heu! solus, neque
      Auditus, neque
      Cognitus ulli,
      Fletus integrat,   110
    Teque gemens vocat, Eurydice,
      Perdita, perdita,
      Heu! omne in ævum perdita!
   Nunc totum Eumenides exagitant, jugis
   En! canæ Rhodopes in gelidis tremit,   115
Ardescens tremit, insanit, spemque abjicit omnem.
Ecce! per avia lustra furens fugit ocyor Euro;
Evoe! perstrepit, audin', ut Hæmus, et ingemit evoe!—
      —Ah! perit!—
Eurydicen tamen extrema cum voce profundit,   120
   Eurydicen tremulo murmure lingua canit,
      Eurydicen nemus,
      Eurydicen aquæ,
Eurydicen montes, gemebundaque saxa retorquent.

95–6 Io Triumphe! Mors et Orcus Orpheo / Lætantur domitore domari, / Vatemque mira insigniunt victoria! *1746, 1767, 1791*

VII.

Luctus musica temperat feroces,   125
Et fati levat ingruentis ictus:
Dulcis musica molliter dolorem
Mutat lætitia; sonante plectro
Spes aversa redit, Furor recumbit:
Nobis illa eadem breves adauget   130
Terræ delicias, opesque cœli
Præsentire docet remotiores.
Hinc solum cecinit Numen, memor, unde beatam
Ceperat harmoniam et modulamina non sua, Virgo.
Organa plena choris ubi magnifico concentu   135
    Miscentur, aurem ætherei inclinant incolæ;
Terrestres animæ tolluntur in astra tumenti
Carmine, divinoque alitur sacra flamma furore;
    Dum prona cœlo pendet angelum cohors.
        Orpheum jam taceant Pierides suum,   140
        Major Cæciliæ vis datur inclytæ.
            Ille vix umbram revocavit Orco;
            Illa sublatas super astra mentes
            Inserit coelo, superisque miscet
                Carmine Divis.   145

FINIS.

136 Miscentur, aures applicantur cælitum; *1767*   140–5 Orpheum, Pierides
tandem tacuisse licebit, / Cæciliam a vobis nobiliora manent; / Vix ille Eurydicen sine
fruge reduxit ab umbris; / Illa animam e terris, et super astra vehit. *1767*

SECULAR ODE.

On the Jubilee at Pembroke-College*, Cambridge, in 1743.

I.

God of science, light divine,
O'er all the world of learning shine;
Shine fav'ring from th' etherial way:
But here with tenfold influence dwell,
Here all thy various rays compell   5
    To dignify this joyful day.
Nor thou, Melpomene, thy aid refuse,
Nor leave behind the comic muse;
    Mirthful mild, and gravely gay,
    Hither from your thrones away.   10
And thou, jolly Bacchus, shalt haste to come down,
While the full-flowing † cup with fresh flow'rets we crown;
    But boast not here thy madding influence,
        For close beside thee Pallas' self shall stand,
        And hold thy temerarious hand,   15
    Forbidding rage to triumph over sense.
        And ye, illustrious-sacred shades,
Who whilom in these muse-resounding glades,
        High in rapture wont to stray,
    Or trim the learned lamp, till dawn of day,   20
        Ye blessed sons of happier fates,
        Deign to look down from heav'n and see
        How lasting sweet the memory,
    Which to eternal fame fair virtue consecrates.
See, still fresh bloom your names thro' every age,   25
Still greatly live along the speaking page.

---

  * Founded by Maria de Valentia countess of Pembroke, whose lord was unfortunately killed in a tournament on his wedding-day, upon which his wife devoted herself solely to works of religion.
  † A golden cup, called the foundress's cup, and supposed to be as old as the college. It is only used upon very particular occasions.

SECULAR ODE. Text: *UV* (Jan. 1756), pp. 39–41.

II.

But chiefly thou, Dan Spencer, peerless bard,
  Sith in these pleasaunt groves you 'gan devise,
Of Red-cross knight, and virtue's high reward,
  And here first plann'd thy works of vast emprize,   30
Descend! nor thy inferior sons despise,
  Chaunting her praises on this festal day,
Who taught us, where the road to honour lies,
  Her steps still marking out the arduous way:
Blest is the theme I ween, and blessed be the lay.   35

III.

  Behold, in virtue, and in beauty's pride,
  Behold, at once, a widow and a bride!
  See all the nuptial revels at a stand,
  And Hymen's torch in Libitina's hand.
O what a scene!————————   40
    But, yonder, from on high, descend
  Religion, orphan-virtue's firmest friend,
    And laurell'd learning, mistress of the muse,
  Who, o'er the arts, sits on an eminence,
  By genius erected, and by sense,   45
    And with unbounded prospect all things views.
  With gentle hands they raise her drooping head,
And bid her trust in heav'n, nor wail the happy dead.
  All that is great and good she now pursues;
  She meditates a mansion for the muse,   50
  Nor will she lose a day;
To you, religion, wisdom and to you
She gives that prime, which pleasure calls her due,
  And folly wastes in wantonness away.
She, by no specious flow'rs beguil'd,   55
That deck *imagination's wild*,
  And witless youth decoy,
Chose learning's *cultivated* glades,
And virtue's *ever-blooming* shades,
  That give alone true joy.   60

IV.

To Granta now, where gentle Camus laves
The reedy shore, and rolls his silver waves,
    She flies, and executes, with bounteous hand,
    The work her mighty soul had plann'd,
And unborn minds she forms, and future souls she saves. 65
And to ensure that work to endless fame,
Left what can never die, her own illustrious name.
    Let others, with enthusiasm fill'd,
    Nunneries and convents build;
Where, decay'd with fasts and years,   70
    Melancholy loves to dwell,
    Moaping in her midnight cell,
And counts her beads, and mumbles o'er th' unmeaning
    pray'rs.
    Religious joy, and sober pleasure,
    Virtuous ease, and learned leisure,   75
    Society and books, that give
    Th' important lesson how to live:
    These are gifts, are gifts divine,
    For, fair Pembroke, these were thine.

On taking a Batchelor's Degree.

In allusion to Horace, Book iii. Ode 30.

Exegi monumentum aere perennius, &c.

'Tis done:—I tow'r to that degree,
    And catch such heav'nly fire,
That HORACE ne'er could rant like me,
    Nor is (*a*) King's-chapel higher.
My name in sure recording page   5
    (*b*) Shall time itself o'erpow'r,

(*a*) *Regali situ pyramidum altius—*
(*b*) *Quod non innumerabilis*
    Annorum series, &c.

---

61 Camus laves] Comus laves, *UV*
ON TAKING A BATCHELOR'S DEGREE. First published in *ST* (Sept. 1750), i. 348–9.
Text: *ST.* Collated: *1791.*

If no rude mice with envious rage
  The buttery books devour.
A * title too, with added grace,
  My name shall now attend,   10
(c) Till to the church with silent pace
  A nymph and priest ascend.
Ev'n in the schools I now rejoice,
  Where late I shook with fear,
Nor heed the (d) Moderator's voice   15
 Loud thund'ring in my ear.
Then with (e) Æolian flute I blow
  A soft Italian lay,
Or where (f) Cam's scanty waters flow,
  Releas'd from lectures, stray.   20
Meanwhile, friend † BANKS, my merits claim
  Their just reward from you,
For HORACE bids us (g) challenge fame,
  When once that fame's our due.
Invest me with a graduate's gown,   25
  Midst shouts of all beholders,
(h) My head with ample square-cap crown,
  And deck with hood my shoulders.

* BATCHELOR.
† A celebrated taylor.

(c) ——dum Capitolium
  Scandet cum tacita virgine pontifex.
(d) —qua violens obstrepit Aufidus
(e) ——Æolium carmen ad Italos
Deduxisse modos.
(f) —qua pauper aquæ Daunus, &c.
(g) ——Sume superbiam
Quæsitam meritis—
(h) ——mihi Delphica
Lauro cinge volens—comam.

THE
HOP-GARDEN
A
GEORGIC.

In Two BOOKS.

Me quoque Parnassi per lubrica culmina raptat
Laudis amor: studium sequor insanabile vatis,
Ausus non operam, non formidare poetæ
Nomen, adoratum quondam, nunc pæne procaci
Monstratum digito.——

Van. Præd. Rust.

THE HOP-GARDEN. First published in *1752*. Text: *1752*. Collated: *1791*.

BOOK the FIRST.

The land that answers best the farmer's care,
And silvers to maturity the Hop:
When to inhume the plants; to turn the glebe;
And wed the tendrils to th' aspiring poles:
Under what sign to pluck the crop, and how   5
To cure, and in capacious sacks infold,
I teach in verse Miltonian. Smile the muse,
And meditate an honour to that land
Where first I breath'd, and struggled into life
Impatient, Cantium, to be call'd thy son.   10

Oh! cou'd I emulate Dan Sydney's muse,
Thy Sydney, Cantium—He from court retir'd
In Penshurst's sweet elysium sung delight,
Sung transport to the soft-responding streams
Of Medway, and enliven'd all her groves: 15
While ever near him, goddess of the green,
Fair * Pembroke sat, and smil'd immense applause.
With vocal fascination charm'd the † Hours
Unguarded left Heav'ns adamantine gate,
And to his lyre, swift as the winged sounds   20
That skim the air, danc'd unperceiv'd away.
Had I such pow'r, no peasants toil, no hops
Shou'd e'er debase my lay: far nobler themes,
The high atchievements of thy warrior kings
Shou'd raise my thoughts, and dignify my song.   25
But I, young rustic, dare not leave my cot,
For so enlarg'd a sphere—ah! muse beware,
Lest the loud larums of the braying trump,
Lest the deep drum shou'd drown thy tender reed,
And mar its puny joints: me, lowly swain,   30
Every unshaven arboret, me the lawns,

* Sister to Sir Philip Sydney.
† —Πυλαι μυκον ουρανου ᾱς εχον Ωραι. HOM.E.

i. 11 Dan] skilled *1791*   22 toil, no hops] humble toil *1791*

Me the voluminous Medway's silver wave,
‡ Content inglorious, and the hopland shades!

Yeomen, and countrymen attend my song:
Whether you shiver in the marshy § Weald,   35
Egregious shepherds of unnumber'd flocks,
Whose fleeces, poison'd into purple, deck
All Europe's kings: or in fair * Madum's vale
Imparadis'd, blest denizons, ye dwell;
Or † Dorovernia's awful tow'rs ye love: 40
Or plough Tunbridgia's salutiferous hills
Industrious, and with draughts chalybiate heal'd,
Confess divine Hygeia's blissful seat;
The muse demands your presence, ere she tune
Her monitory voice; observe her well,   45
And catch the wholesome dictates as they fall.

    'Midst thy paternal acres, Farmer, say
Has gracious heav'n bestow'd one field, that basks
Its loamy bosom in the mid-day sun,
Emerging gently from the abject vale,   50
Nor yet obnoxious to the wind, secure
There shall thou plant thy hop. This soil, perhaps,
Thou'lt say, will fill my garners. Be it so.
But Ceres, rural goddess, at the best
Meanly supports her vot'ry', enough for her,   55
If ill-persuading hunger she repell,
And keep the soul from fainting: to enlarge,
To glad the heart, to sublimate the mind,
And wing the flagging spirits to the sky,
Require th' united influence and aid   60
Of Bacchus, God of hops, with Ceres join'd:
'Tis he shall generate the buxom beer.

‡ Rura mihi, et rigui placeant in vallibus amnes,
  Flumina amem, sylvasque in glorius! VIRG. GEORG. 2.
§ Commonly, but improperly call'd, the Wild.
* Maidstone.
† Canterbury.

61 join'd:] join'd *1752*, *1791*

Then on one pedestal, and hand in hand,
Sculptur'd in Parian stone (so gratitude
Indites) let the divine co-part'ners rise. 65
Stands eastward in thy field a wood? 'tis well.
Esteem it as a bulwark of thy wealth,
And cherish all its branches; tho' we'll grant,
Its leaves umbrageous may intercept
The morning rays, and envy some small share 70
Of Sol's beneficence to the infant germ.
Yet grutch not that: when whistling Eurus comes,
With all his worlds of insects in thy lands
To hyemate, and monarchize o'er all
Thy vegetable riches, then thy wood 75
Shall ope it's arms expansive, and embrace
The storm reluctant, and divert its rage.
Armies of animalc'les urge their way
In vain: the ventilating trees oppose
Their airy march. They blacken distant plains. 80

 This site for thy young nursery obtain'd,
Thou hast begun auspicious, if the soil
(As sung before) be loamy; this the hop
Loves above others, this is rich, is deep,
Is viscous, and tenacious of the pole. 85
Yet maugre all its native worth, it may
Be meliorated with warm compost. See!
* Yon craggy mountain, whose fastidious head,
Divides the star-set hemisphere above,
And Cantium's plains beneath; the Appennine 90
Of a free Italy, whose chalky sides
With verdant shrubs dissimilarly gay,
Still captivate the eye, while at his feet
The silver Medway glides, and in her breast
Views the reflected landskip, charm'd she views 95
And murmurs louder ectasy below.
Here let us rest awhile, pleas'd to behold
Th' all-beautiful horizon's wide expanse,

* Boxley-Hill, which extends through great part of Kent.

---

72 grutch] grudge *1791* 87 warm] warmth *1791*

Far as the eagle's ken. Here tow'ring spires
First catch the eye, and turn the thoughts to heav'n.   100
The lofty elms in humble majesty
Bend with the breeze to shade the solemn groves;
And spread an holy darkness; Ceres there
Shines in her golden vesture. Here the meads
Enrich'd by Flora's dædal hand, with pride   105
Expose their spotted verdure. Nor are you
Pomona absent; you 'midst th' hoary leaves
Swell the vermilion cherry; and on yon trees
Suspend the pippen's palatable gold.
There old Sylvanus in that moss-grown grot   110
Dwells with his wood-nymphs: they with chaplets green
And russet mantles oft bedight, aloft
From yon bent oaks, in Medway's bosom fair
Wonder at silver bleak, and prickly pearch,
That swiftly thro' their floating forests glide.   115
Yet not even these—these ever-varied scenes
Of wealth and pleasure can engage my eyes
T' o'erlook the lowly hawthorn, if from thence
The thrush, sweet warbler, chants th'unstudied lays
Which Phœbus' self vaulting from yonder cloud   120
Refulgent, with enliv'ning ray inspires.
But neither tow'ring spires, nor lofty elms,
Nor golden Ceres, nor the meadows green,
Nor orchats, nor the russet-mantled nymphs,
Which to the murmurs of the Medway dance,   125
Nor sweetly warbling thrush, with half those charms
Attract my eyes, as yonder hop-land close,
Joint-work of art and nature, which reminds
The muse, and to her theme the wand'rer calls.

   Here then with pond'rous vehicles and teams   130
Thy rustics send, and from the caverns deep
Command them bring the chalk: thence to the kiln
Convey, and temper with Vulcanian fires.
Soon as 'tis form'd, thy lime with bounteous hand
O'er all thy lands disseminate; thy lands   135
Which first have felt the soft'ning spade, and drank
The strength'ning vapours from nutricious marl.

45

This done, select the choicest hop, t'insert
Fresh in the opening glebe. Say then, my muse,
Its various kinds, and from th' effete and vile,   140
The eligible separate with care.
The noblest species is by Kentish wights
The Master-hop yclep'd. Nature to him
Has giv'n a stouter stalk, patient of cold,
Or Phœbus ev'n in youth, his verdant blood   145
In brisk saltation circulates and flows
Indesinently vigorous: the next
Is arid, fetid, infecund, and gross
Significantly styl'd the Fryar: the last
Is call'd the Savage, who in ev'ry wood,   150
And ev'ry hedge unintroduc'd intrudes.
When such the merit of the candidates,
Easy is the election; but, my friend
Would'st thou ne'er fail, to Kent direct thy way,
Where no one shall be frustrated that seeks   155
Ought that is great or good. * Hail, Cantium, hail!
Illustrious parent of the finest fruits,
Illustrious parent of the best of men!
For thee Antiquity's thrice sacred springs
Placidly stagnant at their fountain head,   160
I rashly dare to trouble (if from thence,
If ought for thy util'ty I can drain)
And in thy towns adopt th' Ascræan muse.
Hail heroes, hail invaluable gems,
Splendidly rough within your native mines,   165
To luxury unrefined, better far
To shake with unbought agues in your weald,
Than dwell a slave to passion and to wealth,
Politely paralytic in the town!
Fav'rites of heav'n! to whom the general doom   170
Is all remitted, who alone possess

---

* Salve magna parens frugum, Saturnia tellus
   Magna virum; tibi res antiquæ laudis et artis
   Ingredior, sanctos ausus recludere fontes,
   Ascræumque cano Romana per oppida carmen.   VIRG. GEORG. 2.

---

162 I ought for thy utility can drain) *1791*   165-9 *omitted, 1791*

Of Adam's sons fair Eden—rest ye here,
Nor seek an earthly good above the hop;
A good! untasted by your ancient kings,
And almost to your very sires unknown.   175

 In those blest days when great Eliza reign'd
O'er the adoring nation, when fair peace
Or spread an unstain'd olive round the land,
Or laurell'd war did teach our winged fleets
To lord it o'er the world, when our brave sires   180
Drank valour from uncauponated beer;
Then th' hop (before an interdicted plant,
Shun'd like fell aconite) began to hang
Its folded floscles from the golden vine,
And bloom'd a shade to Cantium's sunny shores   185
Delightsome, and in chearful goblets laught
Potent, what time Aquarius' urn impends
To kill the dulsome day—potent to quench
The Syrian ardour, and autumnal ills
To heal with mild potations; sweeter far   190
Than those which erst the subtile * Hengist mix'd
T' inthral voluptuous Vortigern. He, with love
Emasculate and wine, the toils of war,
Neglected, and to dalliance vile and sloth
Emancipated, saw th' incroaching Saxons   195
With unaffected eyes; his hand which ought
T' have shook the spear of justice, soft and smooth,
Play'd ravishing divisions on the lyre:
This Hengist mark'd, and (for curs'd insolence
Soon fattens on impunity! and becomes   200
Briareus from a dwarf) fair Thanet gain'd.
Nor stopt he here; but to immense attempts
Ambition sky-aspiring led him on
Adventrous. He an only daughter rear'd,
Roxena, matchless maid! nor rear'd in vain.   205
Her eagle-ey'd callidity, grave deceit,

* See the following story told at large in Lambarde's perambulation of
Kent.

<hr>

182 Then th'] The *1791*   200 becomes] rises *1791*   206 grave *omitted, 1791*

And fairy fiction rais'd above her sex,
And furnish'd her with thousand various wiles
Preposterous, more than female; wondrous fair
She was, and docile, which her pious nurse   210
Observ'd, and early in each female fraud
Her 'gan initiate: well she knew to smile,
Whene'er vexation gall'd her; did she weep?
'Twas not sincere, the fountains of her eyes
Play'd artifical streams, yet so well forc'd   215
They look'd like nature; for ev'n art to her
Was natural, and contrarieties
Seem'd in Roxena congruous and allied.
Such was she, when brisk Vortigern beheld,
Ill-fated prince! and lov'd her. She perceiv'd,   220
Soon she perceiv'd her conquest; soon she told,
With hasty joy transported, her old sire,
The Saxon inly smil'd, and to his isle
The willing prince invited, but first bad
The nymph prepare the potions; such as fire   225
The blood's meand'ring rivulets, and depress
To love the soul. Lo! at the noon of night
Thrice Hecate invok'd the maid—and thrice
The goddess stoop'd assent; forth from a cloud
She stoop'd, and gave the philters pow'r to charm.   230
These in a splendid cup of burnish'd gold
The lovely sorceress mix'd, and to the prince
Health, peace, and joy propin'd, but to herself
Mutter'd dire exorcisms, and wish'd effect
To th' love-creating draught: lowly she bow'd   235
Fawning insinuation bland, that might
Deceive Laertes' son; her lucid orbs
Shed copiously the oblique rays; her face
Like modest Luna's shone, but not so pale,
And with no borrow'd lustre; on her brow   240
Smil'd Fallacy, while summoning each grace,
Kneeling she gave the cup. The prince (for who!
Who cou'd have spurn'd a suppliant so divine?)
Drank eager, and in ecstasy devour'd

208 her with] with a *1791*

Th' ambrosial perturbation; mad with love 245
He clasp'd her, and in Hymeneal bands
At once the nymph demanded and obtain'd.
Now Hengist, all his ample wish fulfill'd,
Exulted; and from Kent th' uxorious prince
Exterminated, and usurp'd his seat. 250
Long did he reign; but all-devouring time
Has raz'd his palace walls—Perchance on them
Grows the green hop, and o'er his crumbled bust
In spiral twines ascends the scancile pole.—
But now to plant, to dig, to dung, to weed; 255
Tasks how indelicate? demand the muse.

Come, fair magician, sportive Fancy come,
With thy unbounded imagery; child of thought,
From thy aerial citadel descend,
And (for thou canst) assist me. Bring with thee 260
Thy all-creative Talisman; with thee
The active spirits ideal, tow'ring flights,
That hover o'er the muse-resounding groves,
And all thy colourings, all thy shapes display.
Thou too be here, Experience, so shall I 265
My rules nor in low prose jejunely *say*,
Nor in smooth numbers musically err;
But vain is Fancy and Experience vain,
If thou, O Hesiod! Virgil of our land,
Or hear'st thou rather, Milton, bard divine, 270
Whose greatness who shall imitate, save thee?
If thou O * Philips fav'ring dost not hear
Me, inexpert of verse; with gentle hand
Uprear the unpinion'd muse, high on the top
Of that immeasurable mount, that far 275
Exceeds thine own Plinlimmon, where thou tun'st
With Phœbus' self thy lyre. Give me to turn
Th' unwieldly subject with thy graceful ease,

* Mr. John Philips, author of Cyder, a poem.

---

254 scancile] scantile *1791*   256 Tasks humble, but important, ask the muse.
1791   258 With thy unbounded imagery;] With wildest imagery; thou *1791*

Extol its baseness with thy art; but chief
Illumine, and invigorate with thy fire.   280

When Phœbus looks thro' Aries on the spring,
And vernal flow'rs promise the dulcet fruit,
Autumnal pride! delay not then thy setts
In Tellus' facile bosom to depose
Timely: if thou art wise the bulkiest chuse: 285
To every root three joints indulge, and form
The Quincunx with well regulated hills.
Soon from the dung-enriched earth, their heads
Thy young plants will uplift, their virgin arms
They'll stretch, and marriageable claim the pole.   290
Nor frustrate thou their wishes, so thou may'st
Expect an hopeful issue, jolly Mirth,
Sister of taleful Jocus, tuneful Song,
And fat Good-nature with her honest face.
But yet in the novitiate of their love,   295
And tenderness of youth suffice small shoots
Cut from the widow'd willow, nor provide
Poles insurmountable as yet. 'Tis then
When twice bright Phœbus' vivifying ray,
Twice the cold touch of winter's icy hand,   300
They've felt; 'tis then we fell sublimer props.
'Tis then the sturdy woodman's axe from far
Resounds, resounds, and hark! with hollow groans
Down tumble the big trees, and rushing roll
O'er the crush'd crackling brake, while in his cave   305
Forlorn, dejected, 'midst the weeping dryads
Laments Sylvanus for his verdant care.
The ash, or willow for thy use select,
Or storm-enduring chesnut; but the oak
Unfit for this employ, for nobler ends   310
Reserve untouch'd; she when by time matur'd,
Capacious, of some British demi-god,
Vernon, or Warren, shall with rapid wing
Infuriate, like Jove's armour-bearing bird,

Fly on thy foes; They, like the parted waves, 315
Which to the brazen beak murmuring give way
Amaz'd, and roaring from the sight recede.—
In that sweet month, when to the list'ning swains
Fair Philomel sings love, and every cot
With garlands blooms bedight, with bandage meet 320
The tendrils bind, and to the tall pole tie,
Else soon, too soon their meretricious arms
Round each ignoble clod they'll fold, and leave
Averse the lordly prop. Thus, have I heard
Where there's no mutual tye, no strong connection 325
Of love-conspiring hearts, oft the young bride
Has prostituted to her slaves her charms,
While the infatuated lord admires
* Fresh-budding sprouts, and issue not his own.
Now turn the glebe: soon with correcting hand 330
When smiling June in jocund dance leads on
Long days and happy hours, from ev'ry vine
Dock the redundant branches, and once more
With the sharp spade thy numerous acres till.
The shovel next must lend its aid, enlarge 335
The little hillocks, and erase the weeds.
This in that month its title which derives
From great Augustus' ever sacred name!
Sovereign of Science! master of the Muse!
Neglected Genius' firm ally! Of worth 340
Best judge, and best rewarder, whose applause
To bards was fame and fortune! O! 'twas well,
Well did you too in this, all glorious heroes!
Ye Romans!—on Time's wing you've stamp'd his praise,
And time shall bear it to eternity. 345

Now are our labours crown'd with their reward,
Now bloom the florid hops, and in the stream
Shine in their floating silver, while above
T'embow'ring branches culminate, and form

* Miraturque novas frondes, et non sua poma. VIRG.

329 -budding] -butting *1791* 346 labours *1752 Errata*] lab'rours *1752*, *1791*

A walk impervious to the sun; the poles   350
In comely order stand; and while you cleave
With the small skiff the Medway's lucid wave,
In comely order still their ranks preserve,
And seem to march along th' extensive plain:
In neat arrangement thus the men of Kent,   355
With native oak at once adorn'd and arm'd,
Intrepid march'd; for well they knew the cries
Of dying Liberty, and Astræa's voice,
Who as she fled, to echoing woods complain'd
Of tyranny, and William; like a god,   360
Refulgent stood the conqueror, on his troops
He sent his looks enliv'ning as the sun's,
But on his foes frown'd agony, frown'd death.
On his left side in bright emblazonry
His falchion burn'd; forth from his sevenfold shield   365
A basilisk shot adamant; his brow
Wore clouds of fury!—on that with plumage crown'd
Of various hue sat a tremendous cone:
Thus sits high-canopied above the clouds,
Terrific beauty of nocturnal skies,   370
* Northern Aurora; she thro' th' azure air
Shoots, shoots her trem'lous rays in painted streaks
Continual, while waving to the wind
O'er Night's dark veil her lucid tresses flow.
The trav'ler views th' unseasonable day   375
Astound, the proud bend lowly to the earth,
The pious matrons tremble for the world.
But what can daunt th' insuperable souls
Of Cantium's matchless sons? On they proceed,
All innocent of fear; each face express'd   380
Contemptuous admiration, while they view'd
The well-fed brigades of embroider'd slaves
That drew the sword for gain. First of the van,
With an enormous bough, a shepherd swain

* Aurora Borealis, or lights in the air; a phœnomenon which of late years
has been very frequent here, and in all the more northern countries.

358 Liberty] Freedom *1791*   363 agony, frown'd] agony, and *1791*   366 brow]
bow *1791*

Whistled with rustic notes; but such as show'd   385
A heart magnanimous: The men of Kent
Follow the tuneful swain, while o'er their heads
The green leaves whisper, and the big boughs bend.
'Twas thus the Thracian, whose all-quick'ning lyre
The floods inspir'd, and taught the rocks to feel,   390
Play'd before dancing Hæmus, to the tune,
The lute's soft tune! The flutt'ring branches wave,
The rocks enjoy it, and the rivulets hear,
The hillocks skip, emerge the humble vales,
And all the mighty mountain nods applause.   395
The conqueror view'd them, and as one that sees
The vast abrupt of Scylla, or as one
That from th' oblivious Lethæan streams
Has drank eternal apathy, he stood.
His host an universal panic seiz'd   400
Prodigious, inopine; their armour shook,
And clatter'd to the trembling of their limbs;
Some to the walking wilderness gan run
Confus'd, and in th' inhospitable shade
For shelter sought—Wretches! they shelter find,   405
Eternal shelter in the arms of death!
Thus when Aquarius pours out all his urn
Down on some lonesome heath, the traveller
That wanders o'er the wint'ry waste, accepts
The invitation of some spreading beech   410
Joyous; but soon the treach'rous gloom betrays
Th' unwary visitor, while on his head
Th' inlarging drops in double show'rs descend.

    And now no longer in disguise the men
Of Kent appear; down they all drop their boughs,   415
And shine in brazen panoply divine.
Enough—Great William (for full well he knew
How vain would be the contest) to the sons
Of glorious Cantium, gave their lives, and laws,
And liberties secure, and to the prowess   420
Of Kentish wights, like Cæsar, deign'd to yield.

391 Play'd before] Enchanted *1791*   398 Lethæan streams] streams of Lethe's
pool *1791*   421 Kentish wights] Cantium's sons *1791*

Cæsar and William! Hail immortal worthies,
Illustrious vanquish'd! Cantium, if to them,
Posterity with all her chiefs unborn,
Ought similar, ought second has to boast,   425
Once more (so prophecies the Muse) thy sons
Shall triumph, emulous of their sires—till then
With olive, and with hop-land garlands crown'd,
O'er all thy land reign Plenty, reign fair Peace.

424 with *1752 Errata*] will *1752*   425 boast, *1752 Errata*] boast. *1752, 1791*

BOOK the SECOND.

Omnia quæ multo ante memor provisa repones,
Si te digna manet divini gloria ruris.

VIRG. Georg. lib. I.

At length the Muse her destin'd task resumes
With joy; agen o'er all her hop-land groves
She longs t' expatiate free of wing. Long while
For a much-loving, much-lov'd youth she wept,
And sorrow'd silence o'er th' untimely urn.   5
Hush then, effeminate sobs; and thou, my heart,
Rebel to grief no more—And yet a while,
A little while, indulge the friendly tears.
O'er the wild world, like Noah's dove, in vain
I seek the olive peace, around me wide   10
See! see! the wat'ry waste—In vain, forlorn
I call the Phœnix fair Sincerity;
Alas!—extinguish'd to the skies she fled,
And left no heir behind her. Where is now
Th' eternal smile of goodness? Where is now   15
That all-extensive charity of soul,
So rich in sweetness, that the classic sounds
In elegance Augustan cloath'd, the wit
That flow'd perennial, hardly were observ'd,
Or, if observ'd, set off a brighter gem.   20
How oft, and yet how seldom did it seem!
Have I enjoy'd his converse?—When we met,
The hours how swift they sweetly fled, and till
Agen I saw him, how they loiter'd. Oh!
* THEOPHILUS, thou dear departed soul,   25
What flattering tales thou told'st me? How thou'dst hail
My Muse, and took'st imaginary walks
All in my hopland groves! Stay yet, oh stay!

* Mr. Theophilus Wheeler of Christ-College, Cambridge.

ii. 3 longs] seeks *1791*   5 And sorrow'd] Sorrowing in *1791*   20 a] that *1791*

Thou dear deluder, thou hast seen but half—
He's gone! and ought that's equal to his praise   30
Fame has not for me, tho' she prove most kind.
Howe'er this verse be sacred to thy name,
These tears, the last sad duty of a friend.
Oft I'll indulge the pleasurable pain
Of recollection; oft on Medway's banks   35
I'll muse on thee full pensive; while her streams
Regardful ever of my grief, shall flow
In sullen silence silverly along
The weeping shores—or else accordant with
My loud laments, shall ever and anon   40
Make melancholy music to the shades,
The hopland shades, that on her banks expose
Serpentine vines and flowing locks of gold.

    Ye smiling nymphs, th' inseparable train
Of saffron Ceres; ye, that gamesome dance,   45
And sing to jolly Autumn, while he stands
With his right hand poizing the scales of heav'n,
And with his left grasps Amalthea's horn:
Young chorus of fair bacchanals, descend,
And leave a while the sickle; yonder hill,   50
Where stand the loaded hop-poles, claims your care.
There mighty Bacchus stradling cross the bin,
Waits your attendance—There he glad reviews
His paunch, approaching to immensity
Still nearer, and with pride of heart surveys   55
Obedient mortals, and the world his own.
See! from the great metropolis they rush,
Th' industrious vulgar. They, like prudent bees,
In Kent's wide garden roam, expert to crop
The flow'ry hop, and provident to work,   60
Ere winter numb their sunburnt hands, and winds
Engaol them, murmuring in their gloomy cells.
From these, such as appear the rest t' excell
In strength and young agility, select.
These shall support with vigour and address   65

52 stradling] seated *1791*

56

The bin-man's weighty office; now extract
From the sequacious earth the pole, and now
Unmarry from the closely clinging vine.
O'er twice three pickers, and no more, extend
The bin-man's sway; unless thy ears can bear   70
The crack of poles continual, and thine eyes
Behold unmoved the hurrying peasant tear
Thy wealth, and throw it on the thankless ground.
But first the careful planter will consult
His quantity of acres, and his crop,   75
How many and how large his kilns; and then
Proportion'd to his wants the hands provide.
But yet, of greater consequence and cost,
One thing remains unsung, a man of faith
And long experience, in whose thund'ring voice   80
Lives hoarse authority, potent to quell
The frequent frays of the tumultuous crew.
He shall preside o'er all thy hop-land store,
Severe dictator! His unerring hand,
And eye inquisitive, in heedful guise,   85
Shall to the brink the measure fill, and fair
On the twin registers the work record.
And yet I've known them own a female reign,
And gentle * Marianne's soft Orphean voice
Has hymn'd sweet lessons of humanity   90
To the wild brutal crew. Oft her command
Has sav'd the pillars of the hopland state,
The lofty poles from ruin, and sustain'd,
Like ANNA, or ELIZA, her domain,
With more than manly dignity. Oft I've seen,   95
Ev'n at her frown the boist'rous uproar cease,
And the mad pickers, tam'd to diligence,
Cull from the bin the sprawling sprigs, and leaves
That stain the sample, and its worth debase.
All things thus settled and prepared, what now   100
Can let the planters purposes? Unless
The Heavens frown dissent, and ominous winds

* The Author's youngest Sister.

101 let] stop *1791*   102 Heavens] Heav'ns *1752, 1791*

57

Howl thro' the concave of the troubled sky.
And oft, alas! the long experienc'd wights
(Oh! could they too prevent them) storms foresee.   105
* For, as the storm rides on the rising clouds,
Fly the fleet wild-geese far away, or else
The heifer towards the zenith rears her head,
And with expanded nostrils snuffs the air:
The swallows too their airy circuits weave,   110
And screaming skim the brook; and fen-bred frogs
Forth from their hoarse throats their old grutch recite:
Or from her earthly coverlets the ant
Heaves her huge eggs along the narrow way:
Or bends Thaumantia's variegated bow   115
Athwart the cope of heav'n: or sable crows
Obstreperous of wing, in crouds combine:
Besides, unnumber'd troops of birds marine,
And Asia's feather'd flocks, that in the muds
Of flow'ry-edg'd Cayster wont to prey,   120
Now in the shallows duck their speckled heads,

* Numquam imprudentibus imber
Obfuit. Aut illum surgentem vallibus imis
Aëriæ fugere grues: aut bucula cœlum
Suspiciens, patulis captavit naribus auras:
Aut arguta lacus circumvolitavit hirundo:
Et veterem in limo ranæ cecinere querelam.
Sæpius et tectis penetralibus extulit ova
Angustum formica terens iter, et bibit ingens
Arcus et e pastu decedens agmine magno
Corvorum increpuit densis exercitus alis.
Jam varias pelagi volucres, et quæ Asia circum
Dulcibus in stagnis rimantur prata Caystri,
Certatim largos humeris infundere rores;
Nunc caput objectare fretis, nunc currere in undas,
Et studio incassum videas gestire lavandi.
Tum cornix plena pluviam vocat improba voce,
Et sola in sicca secum spatiatur arena.
Nec nocturna quidem carpentes pensa puellæ
Nescivere hyemem.

VIRG. Georg. i.

112 grutch] grudge *1791*   117 crouds] clouds *1791*

58

And lust to lave in vain, their unctious plumes
Repulsive baffle their efforts: Next hark
How the curs'd raven, with her harmful voice,
Invokes the rain, and croaking to herself,   125
Struts on some spacious solitary shore.
Nor want thy servants and thy wife at home
Signs to presage the show'r; for in the hall
Sheds Niobe her prescious tears, and warns
Beneath thy leaden tubes to fix the vase,   130
And catch the falling dew-drops, which supply
Soft water and salubrious, far the best
To soak thy hops, and brew thy generous beer.
But tho' bright Phœbus smile, and in the skies
The purple-rob'd serenity appear;   135
Tho' every cloud be fled, yet if the rage
Of Boreas, or the blasting East prevail,
The planter has enough to check his hopes,
And in due bounds confine his joy; for see
The ruffian winds, in their abrupt career,   140
Leave not a hop behind, or at the best
Mangle the circling vine, and intercept
The juice nutricious: Fatal means, alas!
Their colour and condition to destroy.
Haste then, ye peasants; pull the poles, the hops;   145
Where are the bins? Run, run, ye nimble maids,
Move ev'ry muscle, ev'ry nerve extend,
To save our crop from ruin, and ourselves.

Soon as bright Chanticleer explodes the night
With flutt'ring wings, and hymns the new-born day,   150
The bugle-horn inspire, whose clam'rous bray
Shall rouse from sleep the rebel rout, and tune
To temper for the labours of the day.
Wisely the several stations of the bins
By lot determine. Justice this, and this   155
Fair Prudence does demand; for not without
A certain method cou'dst thou rule the mob
Irrational, nor every where alike
Fair hangs the hop to tempt the picker's hand.

123 Next hark] hearken next *1791*   129 prescious] prescient *1791*

59

Now see the crew mechanic might and main   160
Labour with lively diligence, inspir'd
By appetite of gain and lust of praise:
What mind so petty, servile, and debas'd,
As not to know ambition? Her great sway
From *Colin Clout* to Emperors she exerts.   165
To err is human, human to be vain.
'Tis vanity, and mock desire of fame,
That prompts the rustic, on the steeple top
Sublime, to mark the outlines of his shoe,
And in the area to engrave his name.   170
With pride of heart the churchwarden surveys,
High o'er the bellfry, girt with birds and flow'rs,
His story wrote in capitals: "'Twas I
That bought the font; and I repair'd the pews."
With pride like this the emulating mob   175
Strive for the mastery—who first may fill
The bellying bin, and cleanest cull the hops.
Nor ought retards, unless invited out
By Sol's declining, and the evening's calm,
Leander leads Lætitia to the scene   180
Of shade and fragrance—Then th' exulting band
Of pickers male and female, seize the fair
Reluctant, and with boist'rous force and brute,
By cries unmov'd, they bury her in the bin.
Nor does the youth escape—him too they seize,   185
And in such posture place as best may serve
To hide his charmer's blushes. Then with shouts
They rend the echoing air, and from them both
(So custom has ordain'd) a largess claim.

Thus much be sung of picking—next succeeds   190
Th' important care of curing—Quit the field,
And at the kiln th' instructive muse attend.

On your hair-cloth eight inches deep, nor more,
Let the green hops lie lightly; next expand
The smoothest surface with the toothy rake.   195

163 and] so *1791*   169 outlines] area *1791*   170 area] outline *1791*

Frontispiece by Francis Hayman to *Poems on Several Occasions*, 1752, illustrating *The Hop Garden*, Book II, lines 181–4.

61

Thus far is just above; but more it boots
That charcoal flames burn equably below,
The charcoal flames, which from thy corded wood,
Or antiquated poles, with wond'rous skill,
The sable priests of Vulcan shall prepare.   200
Constant and moderate let the heat ascend;
Which to effect, there are, who with success
Place in the kiln the ventilating fan.
Hail, learned, useful * man! whose head and heart
Conspire to make us happy, deign t'accept   205
One honest verse; and if thy industry
Has serv'd the hopland cause, the Muse forebodes
This sole invention, both in use and fame,
The † mystic fan of Bacchus shall exceed.

  When the fourth hour expires, with careful hand   210
The half-bak'd hops turn over. Soon as time
Has well exhausted twice two glasses more,
They'll leap and crackle with their bursting seeds,
For use domestic, or for sale mature.

  There are, who in the choice of cloth t'enfold   215
Their wealthy crop, the viler, coarser sort,
With prodigal œconomy prefer:
All that is good is cheap, all dear that's base.
Besides, the planter shou'd a bait prepare,
T' intrap the chapman's notice, and divert   220
Shrewd Observation from her busy pry.

  When in the bag thy hops the rustic treads,
Let him wear heel-less sandals; nor presume
Their fragrancy barefooted to defile:
Such filthy ways for slaves in Malaga   225
Leave we to practise—Whence I've often seen,
When beautiful Dorinda's iv'ry hands
Had built the pastry-fabric (food divine

* Dr. Hales.
† Mystica Vannus Iacchi. VIRG. GEOR. I.
_____

223 sandals] sandal *1791* 228 Had] Has *1791*

For Christmas gambols and the hour of mirth)
As the dry'd foreign fruit, with piercing eye,   230
She cull'd suspicious—lo! she starts, she frowns
With indignation at a negro's nail.

    Should'st thou thy harvest for the mart design,
Be thine own factor; nor employ those drones
Who've stings, but make no honey, selfish slaves!   235
That thrive and fatten on the planter's toil.

    What then remains unsung? unless the care
To stack thy poles oblique in comely cones,
Lest rot or rain destroy them—'Tis a sight
Most seemly to behold, and gives, O Winter!   240
A landskip not unpleasing ev'n to thee.

    And now, ye rivals of the hopland state,
Madum and Dorovernia rejoice,
How great amidst such rivals to excel!
Let * Grenovicum boast (for boast she may)   245
The birth of great Eliza.—Hail, my queen!
And yet I'll call thee by a dearer name,
My countrywoman, hail! Thy worth alone
Gives fame to worlds, and makes whole ages glorious!

    Let Sevenoaks vaunt the hospitable seat   250
Of † Knoll most ancient: Awefully, my Muse,
These social scenes of grandeur and delight,
Of love and veneration, let me tread.
How oft beneath yon oak has amorous Prior
Awaken'd Echo with sweet Chloe's name!   255
While noble Sackville heard, hearing approv'd,
Approving, greatly recompens'd. But he,
Alas! has number'd with th' illustrious dead,
And orphan merit has no guardian now!

* Greenwich, where Q. Elizabeth was born.
† The seat of the Duke of Dorset.

---

231 cull'd] culls *1791*   243 Dorovernia rejoice] Dorovernia now rejoice
1791   258 has] is *1791*

Next Shipbourne, tho' her precincts are confin'd   260
To narrow limits, yet can shew a train
Of village beauties, pastorally sweet,
And rurally magnificent. Here * Fairlawn
Opes her delightful prospects: Dear Fairlawn
There, where at once at variance and agreed,   265
Nature and art hold dalliance. There where rills
Kiss the green drooping herbage, there where trees,
The tall trees tremble at th' approach of heav'n,
And bow their salutation to the sun,
Who fosters all their foliage—These are thine,   270
Yes, little Shipbourne, boast that these are thine—
And if—But oh!—and if 'tis no disgrace,
The birth of him who now records thy praise.

Nor shalt thou, Mereworth, remain unsung,
Where noble Westmoreland, his country's friend,   275
Bids British greatness love the silent shade,
Where piles superb, in classic elegance,
Arise, and all is Roman, like his heart.

Nor Chatham, tho' it is not thine to shew
The lofty forest or the verdant lawns,   280
Yet niggard silence shall not grutch thee praise.
The lofty forests by thy sons prepar'd
Becomes the warlike navy, braves the floods,
And gives Sylvanus empire in the main.
Oh that Britannia, in the day of war,   285
Wou'd not alone Minerva's valour trust,
But also hear her wisdom! Then her oaks
Shap'd by her own mechanics, wou'd alone
Her island fortify, and fix her fame;
Nor wou'd she weep, like Rachael, for her sons,   290
Whose glorious blood, in mad profusion,
In foreign lands is shed—and shed in vain.

Now on fair Dover's topmost cliff I'll stand,

* The seat of Lord Vane.

---

281 grutch] grudge *1791*   293–304 *omitted, 1791*

And look with scorn and triumph on proud France.
Of yore an isthmus jutting from this coast,   295
Join'd the Britannic to the Gallic shore;
But Neptune on a day, with fury fir'd,
Rear'd his tremendous trident, smote the earth,
And broke th' unnatural union at a blow.—
"'Twixt you and you, my servants and my sons,   300
Be there (he cried) eternal discord—France
Shall bow the neck to Cantium's peerless offspring,
And as the oak reigns lordly o'er the shrub,
So shall the hop have homage from the vine."

DE
ARTE CRITICA.
A
LATIN VERSION
OF
Mr. POPE's Essay on CRITICISM.

Nec me animi fallit—
Difficile illustrare Latinis versibus esse
(Multa novis verbis præsertim cum sit agendum)
Propter egestatem linguæ, et rerum novitatem.   Lucret.

Dictu difficile est, an sit dementia major
Egisse invita vatem criticumne Minerva;
Ille tamen certe venia tibi dignior errat
Qui lassat, quam qui seducit in avia, sensus.
Sunt, qui absurda canunt; sed enim stultissima stultos   5
Quam longe exuperat criticorum natio vates;
Se solum exhibuit quondam, melioribus annis
Natus hebes, ridendum; at nunc musa improba prolem
Innumeram gignit, quæ mox sermone soluto
Æquiparet stolidos versus, certetque stupendo.   10

    Nobis judicium, veluti quæ dividit horas
Machina, construitur, motus non omnibus idem,
Non pretium, regit usque tamen sua quemque. Poetas
Divite perpaucos vena donavit Apollo,
Et criticis recte sapere est rarissima virtus;   15
Arte in utraque nitent felices indole soli,
Musaque quos placido nascentes lumine vidit.
Ille alios melius, qui inclaruit ipse, docebit,
Jureque quam meruit, poterit tribuisse coronam.
Scriptores (fateor) fidunt propriæ nimis arti,   20
Nonne autem criticos pravus favor urget ibidem?

DE ARTE CRITICA. First published in *1752*. Ll. 385–94 quoted apparently from Smart's MS in John Holliday's *Life of William late Earl of Mansfield* (1797), p. 26 (*JH*). Text: *1752*. Collated: *JH, 1791.*

At vero propius si stemus, cuique fatendum est,
Judicium quoddam natura inseverit olim:
Illa diem certe dubiam diffundere callet
Et, strictim descripta licet, sibi linea constat.   25
Sed minimum ut specimen, quod pictor doctus adumbrat,
Deterius tibi fiat eo mage, quo mage vilem
Inducas isti fucum, sic mentis honestæ
Doctrina effigiem maculabit prava decoram.
His inter cæcas mens illaqueata scholarum   30
Ambages errat, stolidisque supervenit *illis*
(Dis aliter visum est) petulantia. Perdere sensum
Communem hi sudant, dum frustra ascendere Pindum
Conantur, mox, ut se defensoribus ipsis
Utantur, critici quoque fiunt: omnibus idem   35
Ardor scribendi, studio hi rivalis aguntur,
Illis invalida eunuchi violentia gliscit.
Ridendi proprium est fatuis cacoethes, amantque
Turbæ perpetuo sese immiscere jocosæ.
Mævius invito dum sudat Apolline, multi   40
Pingue opus exuperant (si dis placet) emendando.

Sunt qui belli homines primo, tum deinde poetæ,
Mox critici evasere, meri tum denique stulti.
Est, qui nec criticum nec vatem reddit, inersque
Ut mulus, medium quoddam est asinum inter equumque.
Bellula semihominum vix pœne elementa scientum   46
Primula gens horum est, premitur quibus Anglia, quantum
Imperfecta scatent ripis animalcula Nili,
Futile, abortivum genus, et prope nominis expers,
Usque adeo æquivoca est, e qua generantur, origo.   50
Hos centum nequent linguæ numerare, nec una
Unius ex ipsis, quæ centum sola fatiget.

At tu qui famam simul exigis atque redonas
Pro meritis, criticique affectas nobile nomen,
Metitor te ipsum, prudensque expendito quæ sit   55
Judicii, ingenii tibi, doctrinæque facultas;
Si qua profunda nimis cauto vitentor, et ista

54 nomen,] nomen. *1752*, *1791*

Linea, qua coeunt stupor ingeniumque, notator.
Qi finem imposuit rebus Deus omnibus aptum,
Humani vanum ingenii restrinxit acumen.   60
Qualis ubi oceani vis nostra irrumpit in arva
Tunc desolatas alibi denudat arenas;
Sic animæ reminiscendi dum copia restat,
Consilii gravioris abest plerumque potestas;
Ast ubi Phantasiæ fulgent radiantia tela,   65
Mnemosyne teneris cum formis victa liquescit.
Ingenio tantum Musa uni sufficit una,
Tanta ars est, tantilla scientia nostra videtur:
Non solum ad certas artes astricta sequendas,
Sæpe has non nisi quadam in simplice parte sequatur.   70
Deperdas partos utcunque labore triumphos,
Dum plures, regum instar, aves acquirere lauros;
Sed sua tractatu facilis provincia cuique est,
Si non, quæ pulchre sciat, ut vulgaria, temnat.

Naturam sequere imprimis, atque illius æqua   75
Judicium ex norma fingas, quæ nescia flecti:
Illa etenim, sine labe micans, ab origine diva,
Clara, constanti, lustrantique omnia luce,
Vitamque, speciemque, et vires omnibus addat,
Et fons, et finis simul, atque criterion artis.   80
Quærit opes ex hoc thesauro ars, et sine pompa
Præsidet, et nullas turbas facit inter agendum.
Talis vivida vis formoso in corpore mentis,
Lætitiam toti inspirans et robora massæ,
Ordinat et motus, et nervos sustinet omnes,   85
Inter opus varium tamen ipsa abscondita fallit.
Sæpe is, cui magnum ingenium Deus addidit, idem
Indigus est majoris, ut hoc bene calleat uti;
Ingenium nam judicio velut uxor habendum est
Atque viro, cui fas ut pareat, usque repugnat.   90
Musæ quadrupedem labor est inhibere capistro,
Præcipites regere, at non irritare volatus.
Pegasos, instar equi generosi, grandior ardet
Cum sentit retinacula, nobiliorque tuetur.

72 lauros *1791*] laurus *1752*

Regula quæque vetus tantum observata peritis   95
Non inventa fuit criticis, debetque profecto
Naturæ ascribi, sed enim quam lima polivit;
Nullas naturæ divina monarchia leges,
Exceptis solum quas sanxerit ipsa, veretur.

Qualibus, audistin' resonat celeberrima normis   100
Græcia, seu doctum premit, indulgetve furorem?
Illa suos sistit Parnassi in vertice natos,
Et, quibus ascendere docet, salebrosa viarum,
Sublimique manu dona immortalia monstrat,
Atque æquis reliquos procedere passibus urget.   105
Sic magnis doctrina ex exemplaribus hausta,
Sumit ab hisce, quod hæc duxerunt ab Jove summo.
Ingenuus judex musarum ventilat ignes,
Et fretus ratione docet præcepta placendi.
Ars critica officiosa Camœnæ servit, et ornat   110
Egregias veneres, pluresque irretit amantes.
Nunc vero docti longe diversa sequentes,
Contempti dominæ, vilem petiere ministram;
Propriaque in miseros verterunt tela poetas,
Discipulique suos pro more odere magistros.   115
Haud aliter sane nostrates pharmacopolæ
Ex medicum crevit quibus ars plagiaria chartis,
Audaces errorum adhibent sine mente medelas,
Et veræ Hippocratis jactant convicia proli.
Hi veterum authorum scriptis vescuntur, et ipsos   120
Vermiculos, et tempus edax vicere vorando.
Stultitia simplex *ille*, et sine divite vena,
Carmina quo fiant pacto miserabile narrat.
Doctrinam ostentans, mentem alter perdidit omnem,
Atque alter nodis vafer implicat enodando.   125

Tu quicunque cupis judex procedere recte,
Fac verteris cujusque stylus discatur ad unguem;
Fabula, materies, quo tendat pagina quævis;
Patria, religio quæ sint, queis moribus ævum:
Si non intuitu cuncta hæc complecteris uno,   130
Scurra, cavillator—criticus mihi non eris unquam.
Ilias esto tibi studium, tibi sola voluptas,

Perque diem lege, per noctes meditare serenas;
Hinc tibi judicium, hinc ortum sententia ducat,
Musarumque undas fontem bibe lætus ad ipsum.   135
Ipse suorum operum sit commentator, et author,
Mæonidisve legas interprete scripta Marone.

Cum caneret primum parvus Maro bella virosque,
Nec monitor Phœbus tremulas jam velleret aures,
Legibus immunem criticis se forte putabat,   140
Nil nisi naturam archetypam dignatus adire:
Sed simul ac caute mentem per singula volvit,
Naturam invenit, quacunque invenit Homerum.
Victus, et attonitus, male sani desinit ausi,
Jamque laboratum in numerum vigil omnia cogit,   145
Cultaque Aristotelis metitur carmina norma.
Hinc veterum discas præcepta vererier, illos
Sectator, sic naturam sectaberis ipsam.

At vero virtus restat jam plurima, nullo
Describenda modo, nullaque parabilis arte,   150
Nam felix tam fortuna est, quam cura canendi.
Musicam in hoc reddit divina poesis, utramque
Multæ ornant veneres, quas verbis pingere non est,
Quasque attingere nil nisi summa peritia possit.
Regula quandocunque minus diffusa videtur   155
(Quum tantum ad propriam collinet singula metam)
Si modo consiliis inserviat ulla juvandis
Apta licentia, lex enim ista licentia fiat.
Atque ita quo citius procedat, calle relicto
Communi musæ sonipes bene devius erret.   160
Accidit interdum, ut scriptores ingenium ingens
Evehat ad culpam egregiam, maculasque micantes
Quas nemo criticorum audet detergere figat;
Accidit ut linquat vulgaria claustra furore
Magnanimo, rapiatque solutum lege decorem,   165
Qui, quum judicium non intercedat, ad ipsum
Cor properat, finesque illic simul obtinet omnes.
Haud aliter si forte jugo speculamur aprico,
Luminibus res arrident, quas Dædala tellus
Parcior ostentare solet, velut ardua montis   170

Asperitas, scopulive exesi pendulus horror.
Cura tamen semper magna est adhibenda poesi,
Atque hic cum ratione insaniat author, oportet:
Et, quamvis veteres pro tempore jura refigunt,
Et leges violare suas regaliter audent,   175
Tu caveas, moneo, quisquis nunc scribis, et ipsam
Si legem frangas, memor ejus respice finem.
Hoc semper tamen evites, nisi te gravis urget
Nodus, præmonstrantque authorum exempla priorum.
Ni facias, criticus totam implacabilis iram   180
Exercet, turpique nota tibi nomen inurit.

Sed non me latuere, quibus sua liberiores
Has veterum veneres vitio dementia vertit.
Et quædam tibi signa quidem monstrosa videntur,
Si per se vel perpendas, propiorave lustres,   185
Quæ recta cum constituas in luce locoque,
Formam conciliat distantia justa venustam.
Non aciem semper belli dux callidus artis
Instruit æquali serie ordinibusque decoris,
Sed se temporibusque locoque accomodat, agmen   190
Celando jam, jamque fugæ simulachra ciendo.
Mentitur speciem erroris sæpe astus, et ipse
Somniat emunctus judex, non dormit Homerus.

Aspice, laurus adhuc antiquis vernat in aris,
Quas rabidæ violare manus non amplius audent;   195
Flammarum a rabie tutas, Stygiæque veneno
Invidiæ, Martisque minis et morsibus ævi.
Docta caterva, viden! fert ut fragrantia thura;
Audin ut omnigenis resonant præconia linguis!
Laudes usque adeo meritas vox quæque rependat,   200
Humanique simul generis chorus omnis adesto.
Salvete, O vates! nati melioribus annis,
Munus et immortale æternæ laudis adepti!
Queis juvenescit honos longo maturior ævo,
Ditior ut diffundit aquas, dum defluit amnis!   205
Vos populi mundique canent, sacra nomina, quos jam
Inventrix (sic dis visum est) non contigit ætas!
Pars aliqua, o utinam! sacro scintillet ab igne

Illi, qui vestra est extrema et humillima proles!
(Qui longe sequitur vos debilioribus alis   210
Lector magnanimus, sed enim, sed scriptor inaudax)
Sic critici vani, me præcipiente, priores
Mirari, arbitrioque suo diffidere discant.

Omnibus ex causis, quæ animum corrumpere junctis
Viribus, humanumque solent obtundere acumen,   215
Pingue caput solita est momento impellere summo
Stultitiæ semper cognata superbia; quantum
Mentis nascenti fata invidere, profuso
Tantum subsidio fastus superaddere gaudent;
Nam veluti in membris, sic sæpe animabus, inanes   220
Exundant vice * spirituum, vice sanguinis auræ
Suppetias inopi venit alma superbia menti,
Atque per immensum capitis se extendit inane!
Quod si recta valet ratio hanc dispergere nubem
Naturæ verique dies sincera refulget.   225
Cuicunque est animus penitus cognoscere culpas,
Nec sibi, nec sociis credat, verum omnibus aurem
Commodet, apponatque inimica opprobria lucro.

Ne musæ invigiles mediocriter, aut fuge fontem
Castalium omnino, aut haustu te prolue pleno: 230
Istius laticis tibi mens abstemia torpet
Ebria, sobrietasque redit revocata bibendo.
Intuitu musæ primo, novitateque capta
Aspirat doctrinæ ad culmina summa juventus
Intrepida, et quoniam tunc mens est arcta, suoque   235
Omnia metitur modulo, male lippa labores
Pone secuturos oculis non aspicit æquis:
Mox autem attonitæ jam jamque scientia menti
Crebrescit variata modis sine limite miris!
Sic ubi desertis conscendere vallibus Alpes   240
Aggredimur, nubesque humiles calcare videmur,
Protinus æternas superasse nives, et in ipso
Invenisse viæ lætamur limine finem:
His vero exactis tacito terrore stupemus

* Animalium scilicet.

72

Durum crescentem magis et magis usque laborem,　　245
Jam longus tandem prospectus læsa fatigat
Lumina, dum colles assurgunt undique fæti
Collibus, impositæque emergunt Alpibus Alpes.

　Ingeniosa leget judex perfectus eadem
Qua vates scripsit studiosus opuscula cura,　　250
Totum perpendet, censorque est parcus, ubi ardor
Exagitat naturæ animos et concitat œstrum;
Nec tam servili generosa libidine mutet
Gaudia, quæ bibulæ menti catus ingerit author.
Verum stagnantis mediocria carmina musæ,　　255
Quæ reptant sub lima et certa lege stupescunt,
Quæ torpent uno erroris secura tenore,
Hæc equidem nequeo culpare—et dormio tantum.
Ingenii, veluti naturæ, non tibi constant
Illecebræ forma, quæ certis partibus insit;　　260
Nam te non reddit labiumve oculusve venustum,
Sed charitum cumulus, collectaque tela decoris.
Sic ubi lustramus perfectam insigniter ædem,
(Quæ Romam splendore, ipsumque ita perculit orbem)
Læta diu non ulla in simplice parte morantur　　265
Lumina, sed sese per totum errantia pascunt;
Nil longum latumve nimis, nil altius æquo
Cernitur, illustris nitor omnibus, omnibus ordo.

　Quod consummatum est opus omni ex parte, nec usquam
Nunc exstat, nec erat, nec erit labentibus annis.
Quas sibi proponat metas adverte, poeta
Ultra aliquid sperare, illas si absolvat, iniquum est;
Si recta ratione utatur, consilioque
Perfecto, missis maculis, vos plaudite clamo.　　275
Accidit, ut vates, veluti vafer Aulicus, erret
Sæpius errorem, ut vitet graviora, minorem.
Neglige, quas criticus, verborum futilis auceps,
Leges edicit: nugas nescire decorum est.
Artis cujusdam tantum auxiliaris amantes　　280
Partem aliquam plerique colunt vice totius; illi
Multa crepant de judicio, nihilominus istam
Stultitiam, sua quam sententia laudat, adorant.

Quixotus quondam, si vera est fabula, cuidam
Occurrens vati, criticum certamen inivit   285
Docta citans, graviterque tuens, tanquam arbiter alter
Dennisius, *Graii* moderatus fræna theatri;
Acriter id dein asseruit, stultum esse hebetemque,
Quisquis Aristotelis posset contemnere leges.
Quid?—talem comitem nactus feliciter author,   290
Mox tragicum, quod composuit, proferre poema
Incipit, et critici scitari oracula tanti.
Jam μυθον, τα παθη, ἡ ἡθη προβλημα, λυσιν que et
Cætera de genere hoc equiti describat hianti,
Quæ cuncta ad normam quadrarent, inter agendum   295
Si tantum prudens certamen omitteret author.
"Quid vero certamen omittes?" excipit heros;
Sic veneranda Sophi suadent documenta. "Quid ergo,
Armigerumque equitumque cohors scenam intret, oportet,"
Forsan, at ipsa capax non tantæ scena catervæ est: 300
"Ædificave aliam—vel apertis utere campis."

Sic ubi supposito morosa superbia regnat
Judicio, criticæque tenent fastidia curæ
Vana locum, curto modulo æstimat omnia censor,
Atque modo perversus in artibus errat eodem,   305
Moribus ac multi, dum parte laborat in una.

Sunt, qui nil sapiant, salibus nisi quæque redundat
Pagina, perpetuoque nitet distincta lepore,
Nil aptum soliti justumve requirere, late
Si micet ingenii chaos, indiscretaque moles.   310
Nudas naturæ veneres, vivumque decorem
Fingere, qui nequeunt, quorundam exempla secuti
Pictorum, haud gemmis parcunt, haud sumptibus auri,
Ut sese abscondat rutilis inscitia velis.
Vis veri ingenii, natura est cultior, id quod   315
Senserunt multi, sed jam scite exprimit unus,
Quod primo pulchrum intuitu, rectumque videtur
Et mentis menti simulachra repercutit ipsi.
Haud secus ac lucem commendant suaviter umbræ,

307 redundat *1752 Errata*] redundet *1752, 1791*

74

Ingenio sic simplicitas superaddit honorem: 320
Nam fieri possit musa ingeniosior æquo,
Et pereant tumidæ nimio tibi sanguine venæ.

   Nonnulli vero verborum in cortice ludunt,
Ornatusque libri solos muliebriter ardent.
Egregium ecce! stylum clamant! sed semper ocellis 325
Prætereunt male, si quid inest rationis, inunctis.
Verba, velut frondes, nimio cum tegmine opacant
Ramos, torpescunt mentis sine germine. Prava
Rhetorice, vitri late radiantis ad instar
Prismatici, rutilos diffundit ubique colores; 330
Non tibi naturæ licet amplius ora tueri,
At male discretis scintillant omnia flammis:
Sed contra veluti jubar immutabile solis,
Quicquid contrectat facundia, lustrat et auget,
Nil variat, sed cuncta oculo splendoris inaurat. 335
Eloquium mentis nostræ quasi vestis habenda est,
Quæ si sit satis apta, decentior inde videtur;
Scommata magnificis ornata procacia verbis
Indutos referunt regalia syrmata faunos;
Diversis etenim diversa vocabula rebus 340
Appingi fas est, aulæ velut aulica vestis,
Alteraque agricolis, atque altera congruit urbi.
Quidam scriptores, antiquis vocibus usi,
Gloriolam affectant, veterum æmula turba sonorum,
Si mentem spectes juvenentur more recentum. 345
Tantula nugamenta styloque operosa vetusto,
Docti derident soli placitura popello.
Hi nihilo mage felices quam comicus iste
FUNGOSO, ostentant absurdo pepla tumore,
Qualia nescio quis gestavit nobilis olim; 350
Atque modo veteres doctos imitantur eodem,
Ac hominem veteri in tunica dum simia ludit.
Verba, velut mores, a justis legibus errant,
Si nimium antiquæ fuerint, nimiumve novatæ;
Tu cave ne tentes insueta vocabula primus, 355
Nec vetera abjicias postremus nomina rerum.

Lævis an asper eat versus plerique requirunt
Censores, solosque sonos damnantve probantve;
Mille licet veneres formosam Pierin ornent,
Stultitia vox arguta celebrabitur una: 360
Hi juga Parnassi non ut mala corda repurgent;
Auribus ut placeant, visunt: sic sæpe profanos
Impulit ad resonum pietas aurita sacellum.
His solum criticis semper par syllaba cordi est,
Vasto etsi usque omnis pateat vocalis hiatu;   365
Expletivaque sæpe suas quoque suppetias dent,
Ac versum unum oneret levium heu! decas en! pigra vocum;
Dum non mutato resonant male cymbala planctu,
Atque augur miser usque scio, quid deinde sequatur.
Quacunque aspirat *clementior aura Favoni*,   370
Mox (nullus dubito) *graciles vibrantur aristæ*
Rivulus ut *molli serpit per lævia lapsu*,
Lector, non temere expectes, *post murmura, somnos*.
Tum demum qua late extremum ad distichon, ipsa
Magnificum sine mente nihil, Sententia splendet,   375
Segnis Hypermeter, audin? adest, et claudicat, instar
Anguis saucia terga trahentis, prorepentisque.
Hi proprias stupeant nugas, tu discere tentes,
Quæ tereti properant vena, vel amabile languent.
Istaque fac laudes, ubi vivida Denhamii vis   380
Walleriæ condita fluit dulcedine musæ.
Scribendi numerosa facultas provenit arte,
Ut soli incessu faciles fluitare videntur,
Plectro morigeros qui callent fingere gressus.
Non solum asperitas teneras cave verberet aures,   385
Sed vox quæque expressa tuæ sit mentis imago.
Lene edat Zephyrus suspiria blanda, politis
Lævius in numeris labatur læve fluentum;
At reboat, furit, æstuat æmula musa, sonoris
Littoribus cum rauca horrendum impingitur unda.   390
Quando est saxum Ajax vasta vi volvere adortus,
Tarde incedat versus, multum perque laborem.

---

361 Hi *1752 Errata*] Qui *1752*, 1791   365 Vasto *1791*] Vasta *1752*
387 suspiria] suspirans *JH*   blanda,] blanda *JH*   388 labatur] labatur, *JH*
389 musa] Musa *JH*   390 impingitur] vapulat *JH*

Non ita sive Camilla cito salis æquora rasit,
Sive levis leviterque terit, neque flectit aristas.
Audin! Timothei cœlestia carmina, menti   395
Dulcibus alloquiis varios suadentia motus!
Audin! ut alternis Lybici Jovis inclyta proles
Nunc ardet famam, solos nunc spirat amores,
Lumina nunc vivis radiantia volvere flammis,
Mox furtim suspiria, mox effundere fletum!   400
Dum Persæ, Græcique pares sentire tumultus
Discunt, victricemque lyram rex orbis adorat.
Musica quid poterit corda ipsa fatentur, et audit
Timotheus nostras merita cum laude Drydenus.

Tu servare modum studeas bene cautus, et istos   405
Queis aut nil placuisse potest, aut omnia, vites.
Exiguas naso maculas suspendere noli,
Namque patent nullo stupor atque superbia mentis
Clarius indicio; neque mens est optima certe,
Non secus ac stomachus, quæcunque recusat et odit   410
Omnia, difficilisque nihil tibi concoquit unquam.
Non tamen idcirco vegeti vis ulla leporis
Te tibi surripiat; mirari mentis ineptæ est,
Prudentis vero tantum optima quæque probare.
Majores res apparent per nubila visæ,   415
Atque ita luminibus stupor ampliat omnia densis.

His Galli minus arrident, illisque poetæ
Nostrates, hodierni aliis, aliisque vetusti.
Sic * fidei simile, ingenium sectæ arrogat uni
Quisque suæ; solis patet illis janua cœli   420
Scilicet, inque malam rem cætera turba jubentur.
Frustra autem immensis cupiunt imponere metam
Muneribus Divum, atque illius tela coarctant
Solis, hyperboreas etiam qui temperat auras,
Non solum australes genios fœcundat et auget.   425
Qui primis late sua lumina sparsit ab annis,

* Christianæ scilicet.

---

393 Non ita, sive Camilla salis viridaria rasit *JH*   394 Sive levis, leviturque volat
sine fraude per arvum. *JH*

Illustrat præsens, summumque accenderit ævum.
(Cuique vices variæ tamen; et jam sæcula sæclis
Succedunt pejora, et jam meliora peractis)
Pro meritis musam laudare memento, nec unquam   430
Neglige quod novitas distinguit, quodve vetustas.

    Sunt qui nil proprium in medium proferre fuerunt,
Judiciumque suum credunt popularibus auris;
Tum vulgi quo exempla trahunt retrahuntque sequuntur,
Tolluntque expositas late per compita nugas.   435
Turba alia authorum titulos et nomina discit
Scriptoresque ipsos, non scripta examinat. Horum
Pessimus iste cluet, si quem serviliter ipsos
Visere magnates stupor ambitiosus adegit.
Qui critice ad mensam domino ancillatur inepto,   440
Futilis ardelio, semper referensque ferensque
Nuntia nugarum. Quam pinguia, quam male nata
Carmina censentur, quæcunque ego forte vel ullus
Pangere Apollineæ tentat faber improbus artis!
At siquis vero, siquis vir magnus adoptet   445
Felicem musam, quantus nitor ecce! venusque
Ingenio accedunt! quam prodigialiter acer
Fit subito stylus! omnigenam venerabile nomen
Prætexit sacris culpam radiis, et ubique
Carmina culta nitent, et pagina parturit omnis.   450

    Stultula plebs doctos studiosa imitarier errat,
Ut docti nullos imitando sæpius ipsi;
Qui, si forte unquam plebs rectum viderit, (illis
Tanto turba odio est) consulto lumina claudunt.
Talis schismaticus Christi, grege sæpe relicto,   455
Cœlos ingenii pro laude paciscitur ipsos.

    Non desunt quibus incertum mutatur in horas
Judicium, sed semper eos sententia ducit
Ultima palantes. Illis miseranda camæna
More meretricis tractatur, nunc Dea certe,   460
Nunc audit vilis lupa: dum præpingue cerebrum,
Debilis et male munitæ stationis ad instar,
Jam recti, jam stultitiæ pro partibus astat.

Si causam rogites, aliquis tibi decat eundo
Quisque dies teneræ præbet nova pabula menti,   465
Et sapimus magis atque magis. Nos docta propago
Scilicet et sapiens proavos contemnimus omnes,
Heu! pariter nostris temnenda nepotibus olim.
Quondam per nostros dum turba scholastica fines
Regnavit, si cui quam plurima clausula semper   470
In promptu, ille inter doctissimus audiit omnes;
Religiosa fides simul ac sacra omnia nasci
Sunt visa in litem; sapuit sat nemo refelli
Ut se sit passus. Jam gens insulsa Scotistæ,
Intactique abaci Thomistæ pace fruentes   475
Inter araneolos pandunt sua retia fratres.
Ipsa fides igitur cum sit variata, quid ergo,
Quid mirum ingenium quoque si varia induat ora?
Naturæ verique relictis finibus amens
Sæpius insanire parat populariter author,   480
Expectatque sibi vitalem hoc nomine famam,
Suppetit usque suus plebi quia risus ineptæ.

   Hic solitus propria metirier omnia norma,
Solos, qui secum sunt mente et partibus iisdem
Approbat, at vanos virtuti reddit honores,   485
Cui tantum sibi sic larvata superbia plaudit.
Partium in ingenio studium quoque regnat, ut aula,
Seditioque auget privatas publica rixas.
DRYDENO obstabant odium atque superbia nuper
Et stupor omnigenæ latitans sub imagine formæ,   490
Nunc criticus, nunc bellus homo, mox deinde sacerdos;
Attamen ingenium, joca cum siluere, superstes
Vivit adhuc, namque olim utcunque sepulta profundis
Pulchrior emerget tenebris tamen inclyta virtus.
Milbourni, rursus si fas foret ora tueri,   495
Blackmorique novi reducem insequerentur; HOMERUS
Ipse etiam erigeret vultus si forte verendos
ZOILUS ex orco gressus revocaret. Ubique
Virtuti malus, umbra velut nigra, livor adhæret,
Sed verum ex vana corpus cognoscitur umbra.   500

485 at] ac *1791*

Ingenium, solis jam deficientis ad instar
Invisum, oppositi tenebras tantum arguit orbis,
Dum claro intemerata manent sua lumina divo.
Sol prodit cum primum, atque intolerabile fulget
Attrahit obscuros flamma magnete vapores;   505
Mox vero pingunt etiam invida nubila callem
Multa coloratum, et crescentia nubila spargunt
Uberius, geminoque die viridaria donant.

　　Tu primus meritis plaudas, nihil ipse meretur,
Qui serus laudator adest. Brevis, heu! brevis ævi   510
Participes nostri vates celebrantur, et æquum est
Angustam quam primum assuescant degere vitam.
Aurea nimirum jamdudum evanuit ætas,
Cum vates patriarchæ extabant mille per annos:
Jam spes deperiit, nobis vita altera, famæ,   515
Nostraque marcescit sexagenaria laurus!
Aspicimus nati patriæ dispendia linguæ,
Et vestis CHAUCERI olim gestanda DRYDENO est.
Sic ubi parturuit mens dives imagine multa
Pictori, calamoque interprete cœpit acuti   520
Concilium cerebri narrare coloribus aptis,
Protinus ad nutum novus emicat orbis, et ipsa
Evolvit manui sese natura disertæ;
Dulcia cum molles coeunt in fœdera fuci
Tandem maturi, liquidamque decenter obumbrant   525
Admistis lucem tenebris, et euntibus annis,
Quando opus ad summum perductum est culmen, et audent
E viva formæ extantes spirare tabella:
Perfidus heu! pulchram color ævo prodidit artem,
Egregiusque decor jam nunc fuit omnis, et urbes,   530
Et fluvii, pictique homines, terræque fuerunt!

　　Heu! dos ingenii, veluti quodcunque furore
Cæco prosequimur, nihil unquam muneris adfert,
Quod redimat comitem invidiam! juvenilibus annis
Nil nisi inane sophos jactamus, et ista voluptas   535
Vana, brevis, momento evanuit alitis horæ!
Flos veluti veris peperit quem prima juventus,
Ille viret, periitque virens sine falce caducus.

Quid vero ingenium est quæso? Quid ut illius ergo
Tantum insudemus? nonne est tibi perfida conjux   540
Quam dominus vestis, vicinia tota potita est;
Quo placuisse magis nobis fors obtigit, inde
Nata magis cura est. Quid enim? crescentibus almæ
Musæ muneribus populi spes crescit avari.
Laus ipsa acquiri est operosa, et lubrica labi;   545
Quin quosdam irritare necesse est; omnibus autem
Nequaquam fecisse satis datur; ingeniumque
Expallet vitium, devitat conscia virtus,
Stulti omnes odere, scelesti perdere gaudent.

Quando adeo infestam sese ignorantia præstet,   550
Absit, ut ingenium bello doctrina lacessat!
Præmia proposuit meritis olim æqua vetustas,
Et sua laus etiam conatos magna secuta est;
Quanquam etenim fortis dux solus ovabat, at ipsis
Militibus crines pulchræ impediere corollæ.   555
At nunc qui bifidi superarunt improba montis
Culmina, certatim socios detrudere tentant;
Scriptorem, quid enim! dum quemque philautia ducit
Zelotypum, instaurant certamina mutua vates,
Et sese alterni stultis ludibria præbent.   560
Fert ægre alterius, qui pessimus audit honores,
Improbus improbuli vice fungitur author amici;
En fædis quam fæda viis mortalia corda
Cogit persequier famæ malesuada libido!
Ah! ne gloriolæ usque adeo sitis impia regnet,   565
Nec critici affectans, hominis simul exue nomen;
Sed candor cum judicio conjuret amice,
Peccare est hominum, peccanti ignoscere, divum.

At vero si cui ingenuo præcordia bilis
Non despumatæ satis acri fæce laborant,   570
In scelera accensas pejora exerceat iras,
Nil dubitet, segetem præbent hæc tempora largam.
Obscæno detur nulla indulgentia vati,
Ars licet ingenio superaddita cerea flecti

556 nunc] tunc *1791*

Pectora pelliciat. Verum, hercule, juncta stupori 575
Scripta impura pari vano molimine prorsus
Invalidam æquiparant eunuchi turpis amorem.
Tunc ubi regnavit dives cum pace voluptas
In nostris flos iste malus caput extulit oris.
Tunc ubi rex facilis viguit, qui semper amore, 580
Consiliis raro, nunquam se exercuit armis:
Scripserunt mimos proceres, meretricibus aulæ
Successit regimen; nec non magnatibus ipsis
Affuit ingenium, stipendiaque ingeniosis.
Patriciæ in scenis spectavit opuscula musæ 585
Multa nurus, lasciva tuens, atque auribus hausit
Omnia larvato secura modestia vultu.
Machina, virginibus quæ ventilat ora, pudicum
Dedidicit clausa officium, ad ludicra cachinnus
Increpuit, rubor ingenuus nihil amplius arsit. 590
Deinde ex externo traducta licentia regno
Audacis fæces Socini absorbuit imas,
Sacrilegique sacerdotes tum quemque docebant
Conati efficere, ut gratis paradison adiret;
Ut populus patria cum libertate sacratis 595
Asserent sua jura locis, ne scilicet unquam
(Crediderim) Omnipotens foret ipse potentior æquo.
Templa sacram satiram jam tum violata silebant:
Et laudes vitii, vitio mirante, sonabant!
Accensi hinc musæ Titanes ad astra ruerunt, 600
Legeque sancitum quassit blasphemia prælum.—
Hæc monstra, O critici, contra hæc convertite telum,
Huc fulmen, tonitruque styli torquete severi,
Et penitus totum obnixi exonerate furorem!
At tales fugias, qui, non sine fraude severi, 605
Scripta malam in partem, livore interprete, vertunt;
Pravis omnia prava videntur, ut omnia passim
Ictericus propria ferrugine tingit ocellus.

   Jam mores critici proprios, adverte, docebo;
Dimidiata etenim est tibi sola scientia virtus. 610
Non satis est ars, ingenium, doctrinaque vires,
Quæque suas jungant, si non quoque candor honestis,
Et veri sincerus amor sermonibus insint.

Sic tibi non solum quisque amplos solvet honores,
Sed te, qui criticum probat, exoptabit amicum,   615

Mutus, quando animus dubius tibi fluctuat, esto;
Sin tibi confidis, dictis confide pudenter.
Quidam hebetes semper perstant erroribus; at tu
Præteritas lætus culpas fateare, diesque
Quisque dies redimat, criticoque examine tentet.   620

Hoc tibi non satis est, verum, quod præcipis, esse,
Veridici mala rusticitas mage sæpe molesta est
Auribus, ingenuam quam verba ferentia fraudem;
Non ut præceptor, cave des præcepta, reique
Ignaros, tanquam immemores, catus instrue: verax   625
Ipse placet, si non careat candore, nec ullos
Judicium, urbanis quod fulget moribus, urit.

Tu nulli invideas monitus, rationis avarus
Si sis, præ reliquis sordes miserandus avaris.
Ne vili obsequio criticorum jura refigas,   630
Nec fer judicium nimis officiosus iniquum;
Prudentem haud irritabis (ne finge) monendo,
Qui laude est dignus patiens culpabitur idem.

Consultum melius criticis foret, illa maneret
Si nunc culpandi libertas. Appius autem,   635
Ecce! rubet, quoties loqueris, torvoque tremendus
Intuitu, reddit fævi trucia ora gigantis
Jam picta in veteri mage formidanda tapete.
Fæc mittas tumidum tituloque et stemmate stultum,
Cui quædam est data jure licentia sæpe stupendi;   640
Tales ad libitum vates absque indole, eadem,
Qua sine doctrina doctores lege creantur.
Contemptis prudens satiris res linque tacendas,
Assentatorumque infamem exerceat artem,
Nominibus libros magnis gens gnara dicandi,   645
Quæ cum mendaci laudes effutiat ore,
Non mage credenda est, quam quando pejerat olim

628 invideas *1791*] invidias *1752*

Non iterum pingues unquam conscribere versus.
Non raro est satius bilem cohibere suescas,
Humanusque sinas hebetem sibi plaudere: prudens   650
Hic taceas moneo, nihil indignatio prodest,
Fessus eris culpando, ea gens haud fessa canendo:
Nam temnens stimulos, tardum cum murmure cursum
Continuat, donec jam tandem, turbinis instar
Vapulet in torporem, et semper eundo quiescat.   655
Talibus ex lapsu vis est reparata frequenti,
Ut tardi titubata urgent vestigia manni.
Horum pleraque pars, cui nulla amentia defit,
Tinnitu numerorum et amore senescit inani,
Perstat difficili carmen deducere vena,   660
Donec inexhausto restat fæx ulla cerebro,
Relliquias stillat vix expressæ male mentis,
Et miseram invalida exercet prurigine musam.

   Sunt nobis vates hoc de grege, sed tamen idem
Affirmo, criticorum ejusdem sortis abunde est.   665
Helluo librorum, qui sudat, hebetque legendo,
Cui mens nugarum docta farragine turget
Attentas propriæ voci male recreat aures,
Auditorque sibi solus miser ipse videtur.
Ille omnes legit authores, omnesque lacessit   670
Durfeio infestus pariter magnoque Drydeno.
Judice sub tali semper furatur, emitve
Quisque suum bonus author opus: non Garthius (illi
Si credas) proprium contexuit ipse poema.
In scenis mova si comœdia agatur, "amicus   675
Hujus scriptor (ait) meus est, cui non ego paucas
Ostendi maculas; sed mens est nulla poetis."
Non locus est tam sanctus, ut hunc expellere possit,
Nec templum in tuo est, plusquam via; quin petc sacras,
Aufugiens aras, et ad aras iste sequetur   680
Occidetque loquendo; etenim stultus ruet ultro
Nil metuens, ubi ferre pedem vix angelus audet.
Diffidit sibimet sapientia cauta, brevesque
Excursus tentans in se sua lumina vertit;
Stultitia at præceps violento vortice currit   685

Nonunquam tremefacta, nec unquam e tramite cedens,
Flumine fulmineo se totam invicta profundit.

Tu vero quisnam es monita instillare peritus,
Qui, quod scis, lætus monstras, neque scire superbis,
Non odio ductus pravove favore, nec ulli   690
Addictus sectæ, ut pecces, neque cæcus, ut erres;
Doctus, at urbanus, sincerus, at aulicus idem,
Audacterque pudens mediaque humanus in ira.
Qui nunquam dubites vel amico ostendere culpas,
Et celebres inimicum haud parca laude merentem.   695
Purgato ingenio felix, sed et infinito,
Et quod librorumque hominumque scientia ditat;
Colloquium cui come, animus summissus et ingens,
Laudandique omnes, ratio cum præcipit, ardor!

Tales extiterunt critici, quos Græcia quondam,   700
Romaque mirata est natos melioribus annis.
Primus Aristoteles est ausus solvere navem,
Atque datis velis vastum explorare profundum.
Tutus iit, longeque ignotas attigit oras
Lumina Mæoniæ observans radiantia stellæ.   705
Jam vates, gens illa, diu quæ lege soluta est,
Et sævæ capta est male libertatis amore,
Lætantes dominum accipiunt, atque omnis eodem,
Qui domuit naturam, exultat præside musa.

Nusquam non grata est incuria comis Horati,   710
Qui nec opinantes nos erudit absque magistro,
Ille suas leges, affabilis instar amici
Quam veras simul et quam claro more profundit!
Ille licet tam judicio quam divite vena
Maximus, audacem criticum, non scriptor inaudax,   715
Præstaret se jure, tamen sedatus ibidem
Censor, ubi cecinit divino concitus œstro,
Carminibusque eadem inspirat, quæ tradidit Arte.
Nostrates homines plane in contraria currunt,
Turba, stylo vehemens critico, sed frigida Phœbo;   720
Nec male vertendo Flaccum torsere poetæ
Absurdi, mage quam critici sine mente citando.

Aspice, ut expoliat numeros Dionysius ipsi
Mæonidæ, veneresque accersat ubique recentes!
Conditam ingenio jactat Petronius artem,   725
Cui doctrina scholas redolet simul et sapit aulam.

  Cum docti Fabii cumulata volumina versas,
Optima perspicua in serie documenta videre est,
Haud secus utilia ac apothecis condimus arma,
Ordine perpetuo sita juncturaque decora,   730
Non modo ut obtineat quo sese oblectet ocellus,
Verum etiam in promptu, quando venit usus, habenda.

  Te solum omnigenæ inspirant, Longine, Camænæ,
Et propriam penitus tibi mentem animumque dederunt;
En! tibi propositi criticum fideique tenacem,   735
Qui vehemens sua jura, sed omnibus æqua ministrat;
Quo probat exemplo, quas tradit acumine leges,
Semper sublimi sublimior argumento!

  Successere diu sibi tales, pulsaque fugit
Barbara præscriptas exosa licentia leges.   740
Roma perpetuo crescente scientia crevit,
Atque artes aquilarum equitare audacibus alis;
Sed tandem superata iisdem victoribus uno
Roma triumphata est musis comitantibus ævo.
Dira superstitio et comes est bacchata tyrannis,   745
Et simul illa animos, hæc corpora sub juga misit.
Credita ab omnibus omnia sunt, sed cognita nullis,
Et stupor est ausus titulo pietatis abuti!
Obruta diluvio sic est doctrina secundo,
Et Monachis finita Gothorum exorsa fuerunt.   750

  At vero tandem memorabile nomen Erasmus,
(Cuique sacerdoti jactandus, cuique pudendus)
Barbariæ obnixus torrentia tempora vincit,
Atque Gothos propriis sacros de finibus arcet.

  At Leo jam rursus viden' aurea secula condit,   755
Sertaque neglectis revirescunt laurea musis!
Antiquus Romæ Genius de pulvere sacro

Attollit sublime caput. Tunc cœpit amari
Sculptura atque artes sociæ, cælataque rupes
Vivere, et in pulchras lapides mollescere formas;   760
Divinam harmoniam surgentia templa sonabant,
Atque stylo et calamo Raphael et Vida vigebant;
Illustris vates! cui laurea serta poetæ
Intertexta hederis critici geminata refulgent:
Jamque æquat claram tibi, Mantua, Vida Cremonam, 765
Utque loci, sic semper erit vicinia famæ.

Mox autem profugæ metuentes improba musæ
Arma, Italos fines linquunt, inque Arctica migrant
Littora; sed criticam sibi Gallia vendicat artem.
Gens ullas leges, docilis servire, capessit,   770
Boiloviusque vices domini gerit acer Horati.
At fortes spernunt præcepta externa Britanni,
Moribus indomiti quoque; nam pro jure furendi
Angliacus pugnat genius, Romamque magistram,
Romanumque jugum semper contemnere pergit.   775
At vero jam tum non defuit unus et alter
Corda, licet tumefacta minus, magis alta gerentes,
Ingenii partes veri studiosa fovendi
Inque basi antiqua leges et jura locandi.
Talis, qui cecinit doctrinæ exemplar et author,   780
"Ars bene scribendi naturæ est summa potestas."
Talis Roscommon—bonus et doctissimus idem,
Nobilis ingenio mage nobilitatus honesto;
Qui Graios Latiosque authores novit ad unguem,
Dum veneres texit pudibunda industria privas.   785
Talis Walshius ille fuit—judex et amicus
Musarum, censuræ æquus laudisque minister,
Mitis peccantum censor, vehemensque merentum
Laudator, cerebrum sine mendo, et cor sine fuco!
Hæc saltem accipias, lacrymabilis umbra, licebit, 790
Hæc debet mea musa tuæ munuscula famæ,
Illa eadem, infantem cujus tu fingere vocem,
Tu monstrare viam; horridulas componere plumas
Tu sæpe es solitus—duce jam miseranda remoto
Illa breves humili excursus molimine tentat,   795
Nec jam quid sublime, quid ingens amplius audet.

Illi hoc jam satis est—si hinc turba indocta docetur,
Docta recognoscit studii vestigia prisci:
Censuram haud curat, famam mediocriter ardet,
Culpare intrepida, at laudis tamen æqua ministra;   800
Haud ulli prudens assentaturve notetve;
Se demum mendis haud immunem esse fatetur,
At neque fastidit lima, quando indiget, uti.

Idleness.

Goddess of ease, leave Lethe's brink,
    Obsequious to the Muse and me;
For once endure the pain to think,
    Oh! sweet insensibility!

Sister of peace and indolence,   5
    Bring, Muse, bring numbers soft and slow,
Elaborately void of sense,
    And sweetly thoughtless let them flow.

Near some cowslip-painted mead,
    There let me doze out the dull hours,   10
And under me let Flora spread,
    A sofa of her softest flow'rs.

Where, Philomel, your notes you breathe
    Forth from behind the neighbouring pine,
And murmurs of the stream beneath   15
    Still flow in unison with thine.

For thee, O Idleness, the woes
    Of life we patiently endure,
Thou art the source whence labour flows,
    We shun thee but to make thee sure.   20

For who'd sustain war's toil and waste,
    Or who th' hoarse thund'ring of the sea,
But to be idle at the last,
    And find a pleasing end in thee.

IDLENESS. MS: *PC*. First published in *Vocal Musical Mask* [1744], p. 8 (*VMM*). Text: *1752*. Collated: *PC*; *VMM*; *Universal Harmony* (1745), p. 66 (*UH*); *MB*, i. 11; *1791*.
Title. The Request *UH*   The Charms of Idleness *MB*   *No title in VMM*
9 Near] Near to *VMM, UH, MB*   cowslip] cowslips *VMM, UH*   10 out
the] away *VMM, UH, MB*   15 And] Whilst *VMM, UH*   While *MB*
19 whence] when *PC*   21 who'd sustain] who'd endure *PC, VMM, UH*   who
would bear *MB*   22 th'hoarse thund'ring] the thund'ring *MB*

On an Eagle confined in a College-Court.

Imperial bird, who wont to soar
　　High o'er the rolling cloud,
Where Hyperborean mountains hoar
　　Their heads in Ether shroud;—
Thou servant of almighty JOVE,　　　　　　　　　5
Who, free and swift as thought, could'st rove
　　To the bleak north's extremest goal;—
Thou, who magnanimous could'st bear
The sovereign thund'rer's arms in air,
　　And shake thy native pole!—　　　　　　　　10

Oh cruel fate! what barbarous hand,
　　What more than Gothic ire,
At some fierce tyrant's dread command,
　　To check thy daring fire,
Has plac'd thee in this servile cell,　　　　　　15
Where Discipline and Dulness dwell,
　　Where Genius ne'er was seen to roam;
Where ev'ry selfish soul's at rest,
Nor ever quits the carnal breast,
　　But lurks and sneaks at home!　　　　　　　20

Tho' dim'd thine eye, and clipt thy wing,
　　So grov'ling! once so great!
The grief-inspired Muse shall sing
　　In tend'rest lays thy fate.
What time by thee scholastic Pride　　　　　　25
Takes his precise, pedantic stride,
　　Nor on thy mis'ry casts a care,
The stream of love ne'er from his heart
Flows out, to act fair pity's part;
　　But stinks, and stagnates there.　　　　　　30

Yet useful still, hold to the throng—
　　Hold the reflecting glass,—

ON AN EAGLE. First published in *ST* (June 1751), ii. 356–7. Text: *1752*. Collated: *ST*; *1791*. *Title*. Ode to an Eagle confin'd in a College-Court *ST*

That not untutor'd at thy wrong
   The passenger may pass:
Thou type of wit and sense confin'd,   35
Cramp'd by the oppressors of the mind,
   Who study downward on the ground;
Type of the fall of Greece and Rome;
While more than mathematic gloom,
   Envelopes all around!   40

A Description of the Vacation, to a Friend in the Country.

Dear Charles,   *Camb. July* 9. 1745.
At length arrives the dull vacation,
And all around is desolation;
At noon one meets unapron'd cooks,
And leisure gyps with downcast looks.
The barber's coat from white is turning,   5
And blackens by degrees to mourning;
The cobler's hands so clean are grown,
He does not know them for his own;
The sciences neglected snore,
And all our bogs are cobweb'd o'er;   10
The whores crawl home with limbs infirm
To salivate against the term;
Each coffee-house, left in the lurch,
Is *full* as *empty*—as a church—
The widow cleans her unus'd delph,   15
And's forc'd to read the news herself;
Now boys for bitten apples squabble,
Where geese sophistic us'd to gabble;
Of hoary owls a reverend band
Have at St. Mary's took their stand,   20
Where each in solemn gibberish howls,
And gentle Athens owns her fowls.
To Johnian hogs observe, succeed
Hogs that are real hogs indeed;

37 Who study] Born to look *ST*
A DESCRIPTION. Text: *MW* (June 1751), ii. 126–8.

And pretty Master Pert of Trinity,   25
Who in lac'd waistcoat woos Divinity,
Revisits, having doft his gown,
His gay acquaintance in the town:
The barbers, butlers, taylors, panders,
Are press'd and gone to serve in Flanders;   30
Or to the realms of Ireland sail,
Or else (for cheapness) go to gaol.—
Alone the pensive black-gowns stray
Like ravens on a rainy day.
Some saunter on the drowsy dam,
Surrounded by the hum-drum Cam,   35
Who ever and anon awakes,
And grumbles at the mud he makes,
Oh how much finer than the Mall
At night to traverse thro' Clare-Hall!
And view our nymphs, like beauteous geese,
Cackling and waddling on the Piece;   40
Or near the gutters, lakes, and ponds
That stagnate round serene St. John's,
Under the trees to take my station,
And envy them their vegetation.

* * * * * * * * * * * *
  * * * * * * * * * *

Cætera desiderantur.

26 woos] woes *MW*

ODE FOR MUSICK
ON
SAINT *CECILIA*'s DAY

Hanc Vos, Pierides festis cantate calendis,
Et testudinea, Phœbe superbe, lyra
Hoc solenne sacrum multos celebretur in annos,
Dignior est vestro nulla puella choro.

TIBULLUS.

PREFACE.

The Author of the following piece has been told, that the writing an Ode
on S. Cecilia's *Day, after Mr.* Dryden *and Mr.* Pope, *would be great*
presumption; which is the reason he detains the Reader in this place to
make an apology, much against his will, he having all due contempt for
the impertinence of Prefaces. In the first place then, it will be a little hard   5
(he thinks) if he should be particularly mark'd out for censure, many
others having wrote on the same subject without any such imputations; but
they (it may be) did not live long enough to be laugh'd at, or, by some
lucky means or other, escaped those shrewd remarks, which, it seems, are
reserved for him. In the second place, this subject was not his choice, but   10
imposed upon him by a Gentleman very eminent in the science of Musick,
for whom he has a great friendship, and who is, by his good sense and
humanity, as much elevated above the generality of mankind, as by his
exquisite art he is above most of his profession. The request of a friend,
undoubtedly, will be sneer'd at by some as a stale and antiquated apology: 15
it is a very good one notwithstanding, which is manifest even from it's
triteness; for it can never be imagined, that so many excellent Authors, as
well as bad ones, would have made use of it, had they not been convinced
of it's cogency. As for the writer of this piece, he will rejoice in being
derided, not only for obliging his friends, but any honest man whatsoever,   20
so far as may be in the power of a person of his mean abilities. He does not
pretend to equal the very worst parts of the two celebrated performances
already extant on the subject; which acknowledgment alone will, with the
good-natured and judicious, acquit him of presumption; because these
pieces, however excellent upon the whole, are not without their blemishes.   25

ODE FOR MUSICK. First published with *Carmen Cl. Alexandri Pope in S. Cæciliam* (2nd
edn., 1746). Text: *1746*. Collated: *1791*.

93

There is in them both an exact unity of design, which though in compositions of another nature a beauty, is an impropriety in the Pindaric, *which should consist in the vehemence of sudden and unlook'd-for transitions: hence chiefly it derives that enthusiastic fire and wildness, which greatly distinguish it from other species of Poesy. In the first stanza of* * Dryden *and in the fifth of* † Pope *there is an air, which is so far from being adapted to the majesty of an Ode, that it would make no considerable figure in a Ballad. And lastly, they both conclude with a turn which has something too epigrammatical in it. Bating these trifles, they are incomparably beautiful and great; neither is there to be found two more finish'd pieces of Lyric Poetry in our language,* L'allegro *and* Il penseroso *of* Milton *excepted, which are the finest in any.* Dryden's *is the more sublime and magnificent; but* Pope's *is the more elegant and correct;* Dryden *has the fire and spirit of* Pindar, *and* Pope *has the terseness and purity of* Horace. Dryden's *is certainly the more elevated performance of the two, but by no means so much so as people in general will have it. There are few that will allow any sort of comparison to be made between them. This is in some measure owing to that prevailing but absurd custom which has obtain'd from* * Horace's *time even to this day,* viz. *of preferring Authors to the Bays by seniority. Had Mr.* Pope *wrote first, the mob, that judge by this rule, would have given him the preference; and the rather, because in this piece he does not deserve it.*

It would not be right to conclude, without taking notice of a fine subject

*   Happy, Happy, Happy pair,
        None but the brave,
        None but the brave,
    None but the brave deserve the fair.

†   Thus song cou'd prevail
        O'er death and o'er hell,
    A conquest how hard and how glorious!
        Tho' Fate had fast bound her
        With Styx nine times round her,
    Yet Music and Love were victorious.

* It seems to have been otherwise in *Homer's* time:
    Τὴν γὰρ αοιδην μαλλον επικλειουσ' ανθρωποι
    'Ητις ακουοντεσσι νεωτατη αμφιπεληται. Homer. Odyss.
    And *Pindar* would have it otherwise in his.
    ———αινει γὲ Παλαιον
    μεν οινον, ανθεα δ' ὑμνων
    νεωτερών——— Olymp. 9.

94

for an Ode on S. Cecilia's *Day, which was suggested to the Author by his friend the learned and ingenious. Mr.* Comber *late of* Jesus *College* 50 *in this* University; *that is* David's *playing to* King Saul *when he was troubled with the evil Spirit. He was much pleased with the hint at first, but at length was deterr'd from improving it by the greatness of the subject, and he thinks not without reason. The chusing too high subjects has been the ruin of many a tolerable Genius. There is a good rule which* 55 Fresnoy *prescribes to the Painters; which is likewise applicable to the Poets.*

Supremam in tabulis lucem captare diei
Insanus labor artificum; cum attingere tantum 60
Non pigmenta queant: auream fed Vespere lucem;
Seu modicum mane albentem; sive ætheris actam
Post hyemem nimbis transfuso sole caducam;
Seu nebulis fultam accipient, tonitruque rubentem.

Ode on S. *Cecilia*'s Day.

ARGUMENT.

Stanza I, II. *Invocation of Men and Angels to join in the praise of S.* Cecilia. *The Divine origin of Musick. Stanza* III. *Art of Musick, or it's miraculous power over the brute and inanimate Creation exemplified in* Waller *and Stanza* IV, V. *in* Arion. *Stanza* VI. *The* Nature *of Musick, or it's power over the Passions. Instances of this in it's exciting pity. Stanza* VII. *In promoting Courage and Military Virtue. Stanza* VIII. *Excellency of Church Musick. Air to the memory of Mr.* Purcell.— *praise of the Organ and it's Inventress Saint* Cecilia.

I.

From your lyre-enchanted tow'rs,
Ye musically mystic Pow'rs,
Ye, that inform the tuneful spheres,
Inaudible to mortal ears,
While each orb in Ether swims⠀⠀⠀⠀⠀⠀⠀⠀5
Accordant to th' inspiring hymns;
Hither Paradise remove
Spirits of Harmony and Love!
Thou too, divine Urania, deign t' appear,
⠀⠀And with thy sweetly-solemn lute⠀⠀⠀⠀10
⠀⠀To the grand argument the numbers suit;
⠀⠀⠀⠀Such as sublime and clear,
⠀⠀⠀⠀Replete with heavenly love,
⠀⠀Charm th' inraptur'd souls above.
Disdainful of fantastic play,⠀⠀⠀⠀⠀⠀⠀⠀15
⠀⠀Mix on your ambrosial tongue
⠀⠀Weight of sense with sound of song,
And be angelically gay.

Chorus.

Disdainful &c.

II.

And you, ye sons of Harmony below,
⠀⠀How little less than angels, when ye sing!⠀⠀20

96

With emulation's kindling warmth shall glow,
   And from your mellow-modulating throats
   The tribute of your grateful notes
In Union of Piety shall bring.
   Shall Echo from her vocal cave   25
   Repay each note, the Shepherd gave,
   And shall not we our mistress praise
   And give her back the borrow'd lays?
But farther still our praises we pursue;
    For ev'n Cecilia, mighty maid,   30
    Confess'd she had superior aid—
She did—and other rites to greater pow'rs are due.
   Higher swell the sound and higher:
    Let the winged numbers climb:
   To the heav'n of heav'ns aspire,   35
    Solemn, sacred, and sublime:
   From heav'n musick took it's rise,
   Return it to it's native skies.

Chorus
Higher swell the sound &c.

III.

Musick's a celestial art;
   Cease to wonder at it's pow'r,   40
Tho' lifeless rocks to motion start,
   Tho' trees dance lightly from the bow'r,
   Tho' rolling floods in sweet suspence
   Are held, and listen into sense.
In Penshurst's plains when Waller, sick with love,   45
Has found some silent solitary grove,
Where the vague moon-beams pour a silver flood
Of trem'lous light athwart th' unshaven wood,
   Within an hoary moss-grown cell,
He lays his careless limbs without reserve,   50
And strikes, impetuous strikes each quer'lous nerve
    Of his resounding shell.
   In all the woods, in all the plains
   Around a lively stillness reigns;
   The deer approach the secret scene,   55

And weave their way thro' labyrinths green;
While Philomela learns the lay,
And answers from the neighbouring bay.
    But Medway, melancholy mute,
       Gently on his urn reclines,   60
    And all-attentive to the lute,
       In uncomplaining anguish pines:
The crystal waters weep away,
And bear the tidings to the sea:
       Neptune in the boisterous seas   65
Spreads the placid bed of peace,
    While each blast,
    Or breathes it's last,
Or just does sigh a symphony and cease.

Chorus

Neptune &c.

IV.

Behold Arion—on the stern he stands   70
   Pall'd in theatrical attire,
To the mute strings he moves th' enliv'ning hands,
   Great in distress, and wakes the golden lyre:
While in a tender Orthian strain
He thus accosts the Mistress of the main: 75
   By the bright beams of Cynthia's eyes
   Thro' which your waves attracted rise,
     And actuate the hoary deep;
   By the secret coral cell,
Where Love, and Joy, and Nepture dwell   80
    And peaceful floods in silence sleep;
   By the sea-flow'rs, that immerge
   Their heads around the grotto's verge,
     Dependent from the stooping stem;
   By each roof-suspended drop,   85
That lightly lingers on the top,
    And hesitates into a gem;
   By thy kindred wat'ry Gods,

77 your] yours *1746, 1791*

The lakes, the riv'lets, founts and floods,
And all the pow'rs that live unseen   90
  Underneath the liquid green;
Great Amphitrite (for thou can'st bind
The storm, and regulate the wind)
Hence waft me, fair Goddess, oh waft me away,
Secure from the men and the monsters of prey!   95

CHORUS.

Great Amphitrite &c.

v.

He sung—The winds are charm'd to sleep,
Soft stillness steals along the deep,
  The Tritons and the Nereids sigh
  In soul-reflecting sympathy,
And all the audience of waters weep.   100
But Amphitrite her Dolphin sends—* the same,
Which erst to Neptune brought the nobly perjur'd Dame—
  Pleas'd to obey, the beauteous monster flies,
  And on his scales as the gilt sun-beams play,
  Ten thousand variegated dies   105
  In copious streams of lustre rise,
Rise o'er the level main and signify his way—
And now the joyous Bard, in triumph bore,
Rides the voluminous wave, and makes the wish'd-for shore.
  Come, ye festive, social throng,   110
  Who sweep the lyre, or pour the song,
    Your noblest melody employ,
    Such as becomes the mouth of joy,
    Bring the sky-aspiring thought,
    With bright expression richly wrought,   115
And hail the Muse ascending on her throne,
The main at length subdued, and all the world her own.

---

* Fabulantur Græci hanc perpetuam Deis virginitatem vovisse: sed cum a Neptuno sollicitaretur ad Atlantem confugisse, ubi a Delphino persuasa Neptuno assensit. *Lilius Gyraldus.*

CHORUS.

Come, ye festive, &c.

VI.

But o'er th' affections too she claims the sway,
Pierces the human heart, and steals the soul away;
And as attractive sounds move high or low,   120
Th' obedient ductile passions ebb and flow,
  Has any Nymph her faithful lover lost,
    And in the visions of the night,
    And all the day-dreams of the light,
  In sorrow's tempest turbulently tost—   125
    From her cheeks the roses die,
The radiations vanish from her sun-bright eye,
    And her breast, the throne of love,
    Can hardly, hardly, hardly move,
      To send th' ambrosial sigh.   130
But let the skillful bard appear,
And pour the sounds medicinal in her ear;
  Sing some sad, some plaintive ditty,
    Steept in tears, that endless flow,
  Melancholy notes of pity,   135
    Notes that mean a world of woe;
She too shall sympathize, she too shall moan,
And pitying others sorrows sigh away her own.

CHORUS.

Sing some sad, some &c.

VII.

  Wake, wake the kettle-drum, prolong
  The swelling trumpet's silver song,   140
  And let the kindred accents pass
  Thro' the horn's meandring brass.
Arise—The patriot muse invites to war,
And mounts Bellona's brazen car;
While *Harmony*, terrific Maid!   145
Appears in martial pomp array'd:
The sword, the target, and the lance
She wields, and as she moves, exalts the Pyrrhic dance.

Trembles the earth, resound the skies—
Swift o'er the fleet, the camp she flies   150
With thunder in her voice, and lightning in her eyes.
    The gallant warriours engage
    With inextinguishable rage,
        And hearts unchil'd with fear;
    Fame numbers all the chosen bands,   155
    Full in the front fair *Vict'ry* stands,
        And *Triumph* crowns the rear.

CHORUS.

The Gallant warriours &c.

VIII.

But hark the Temple's hollow'd roof resounds,
And Purcell lives along the solemn sounds—
    Mellifluous, yet manly too,   160
        He pours his strains along,
    As from the lyon Sampson slew,
        Comes sweetness from the strong.
    Not like the soft Italian swains,
        He trills the weak enervate strains,   165
            Where sense and musick are at strife;
    His vigorous notes with meaning teem,
        With fire, with force explain the theme,
            And sing the subject into life.
Attend—he sings Cecilia—matchless Dame!   170
    'Tis She—'tis She—fond to extend her fame,
        On the loud chords the notes conspire to stay,
        And sweetly swell into a long delay,
            And dwell delighted on her name.
    Blow on, ye sacred Organs, blow,   175
    In tones magnificently slow;
    Such is the musick, such the lays,
    Which suit your fair Inventress' praise:
    While round religious silence reigns,
    And loitering winds expect the strains   180
    Hail majestic mournful measure
    Source of many a pensive pleasure!

101

Blest pledge of love to mortals giv'n,
As pattern of the rest of heav'n!
And thou chief honor of the veil,   185
Hail, harmonious Virgin, hail!
When *Death* shall blot out every name,
And *Time* shall break the trump of Fame,
Angels may listen to thy lute:
Thy pow'r shall last, thy bays shall bloom,   190
When tongues shall cease, and worlds consume,
And all the tuneful spheres be mute.

GRAND CHORUS.
When Death *shall blot out every name &c.*

THE END.

A
LATIN VERSION
OF
MILTON'S L'ALLEGRO

Χρυσεα χαλκειων, ἑκατομβοι᾽ ἐννεαβοιων. HOM.

῾Ο ΠΑΙΓΝΙΩΔΗΣ

Procul hinc, O procul esto informis Ægrimonia,
    Quam janitori Obscuritas nigerrima
        Suscepit olim Cerbero,
    Desertam in cavea Stygis profunda,
Horribiles inter formas, visusque profanos,   5
        Obscœnosque ululatus,
    Incultam licet invenire sedem,
        Nox ubi parturiens
Zelotypis furtim nido superincubat alis
    Queriturque tristis noctua,   10
Sub densis illic ebenis scopulisque cavatis,
    Vestri rugosis more supercilii,
Æternum maneas Cimmeria in domo.

Sed huc propinquet comis et pulcherrima,
Quæ nympha divis audit Euphrosyne choris,   15
Patiens tamen vocatur a mortalibus
Medicina cordis hilaritas, quam candida
Venus duabus insuper cum Gratiis
Dias Lyæo patri in auras edidit:
Sive ille ventus (cæteri ut Mystæ canunt)   20
Jocundus aura qui ver implet mellea,
Zephyrus puellam amplexus est Tithoniam
Quondam calendis feriatam Maiis,
Tunc pallidis genuit super violariis,
Super et rosarum roscida lanugine,   25
Alacrem, beatam, vividamque filiam.
Agedum puella, quin pari vadant gradu
Jocus et Juventas, Scommata et Protervitas,

LATIN VERSION OF L'ALLEGRO. First published in *1752*. Text: *1752*. Collated: *1791*.

Dolusque duplex, nutus et nictatio,
Tenuisque risus huc et huc contortilis;   30
Qualis venusta pendet Hebes in gena,
Amatque jungi lævibus gelasinis;
Curæ sequatur Ludus infestus nigræ, et
Laterum Cachinnus pinguium frustra tenax.
Agite caterva ludat exultim levis,   35
Pedesque dulcis sublevet lascivia;
Dextrumque claudat alma Libertas latus,
Oreadum palantium suavissima;
Et, si tuis honoribus non defui,
Me scribe vestræ, læta Virgo, familiæ,   40
Ut illius simul et tui consortio
Liberrima juvenemur innocentia;
Ut cum volatus auspicatur concitos,
Stupidamque alauda voce noctem territat;
Levata cœlestem in pharon diluculo,   45
Priusque gilvum quam rubet crepusculum.
Tunc ad fenestras (anxii nolint, velint)
Diem precemur prosperam viciniæ,
Caput exerentes e rosis sylvestribus,
Seu vite, sive flexili cynosbato.   50
Dum Martius clamore Gallus vivido
Tenuem lacessit in fuga caliginem,
Graditurve farris ad struem, vel horreum,
Dominæ præeuns, graduque grandi glorians.
Sæpe audiamus ut canes et cornua   55
Sonore læto mane sopitum cient,
Dum qua præalti clivus albescit jugi,
Docilis canora reddit Echo murmura.
Mox, teste multo, qua virent colles, vager,
Ulmosque sepes ordinatas implicat,   60
Eoa stans apricus ante limina,
Ubi sol coruscum magnus instaurat diem
Vestitus igni, lucidoque succino,
Inter micantum mille formas nubium.
Vicinus agrum dum colonus transmeat,   65
Atque æmulatur ore fistulam rudi,
Mulctramque portat cantitans puellula,
Falcique cotem messor aptat stridulæ,

Suamque pastor quisque garrit fabulam,
Reclinis in convalle, subter arbuto.   70
Mox illecebras oculus arripuit novas,
Dum longus undiquaque prospectus patet,
Canum novale, et fusca saltus æquora,
Qua pecora gramen demetunt vagantia,
Sublimium sterilia terga montium,   75
Qui ponderosa sæpe torquent nubila,
Maculosa vernis prata passim bellibus,
Amnes vadosi, et latiora flumina.
Pinnasque murorum, atque turres cernere est
Cristata circum quas coronant robora,   80
Ubi forte quædam nympha fallit, cui decor
Viciniam (cynosura tanquam) illuminat.
Juxta duarum subter umbra quercuum,
Culmis operta fumus emicat casa,
Qua jam vocati Thyrsis et Corydon sedent,   85
Famemque odoro compriment convivio,
Herbis, cibisque rusticis, nitidissima
Quæ sufficit succincta Phillis dextera:
Mox Thestyli morem gerens jacentia
Aureis catenis cogit in fasces sata: 90
Vernisve in horis, sole tostum virgines
Fænum recenti pellicit fragrantia;
Est et serenis quando fœta gaudiis
Excelsiora perplacent magalia;
Utcunque juxta flumen in numerum sonant   95
Campanæ, et icta dulce barbitos strepit,
Dum multa nympha, multa pubes duriter
Pellunt trementes ad canorem cespites
Dubias per umbras; qua labore liberi
Juvenesque ludunt, et senes promiscui,   100
Melius nitente sole propter ferias.
Jam quando vesperascit, omnes allicit
Auro liquenti Bacchus hordiaceus,
Phyllisque narrat fabulosa facinora,
Lamia ut paratas Mabba consumpsit dapes,   105
Se vapulasse, et esse pressam ab Incubo,
Fatuoque trita ab igne seductam via;
Ut et laborem subiit Idolon gravem,

Floremque lactis meritus est stipendium;
Unius (inquit) ante noctis exitum   110
Tot grana frugis fuste trivit veneficus,
Quot expedire rustici nequeunt decem,
Quo jam peracto plumbeum monstrum cubat,
Focumque totum latere longo metiens
Crinita membra fessus igne recreat;   115
Dein, priusquam gallus evocat diem,
Tandem satur phantasma sese proripit.
Sic absolutis fabulis ineunt toros,
Atque ad susurros dormiunt favonii,
Turrita deinde perplacebunt oppida,   120
Et gentis occupatæ mixta murmura,
Equitumque turba, nobilesque splendidi,
Qui pacis ipsa vel triumphant in toga,
Nurusque, quarum lumen impetus viris
Jaculatur acres, præmiumque destinat   125
Marti aut Minervæ, quorum uterque nititur
Nymphæ probari, quæ probatur omnibus:
Hymenæus illic sæpe prætendat facem
Clarissimam, croceumque velamen trahat,
Spectac'la, mimi, pompa, commissatio,   130
Veterumque ritu nocte sint convivia,
Talesque visus, quos vident in somniis
Juvenes poetæ, dum celebris rivuli
Securi ad oram vespere æstivo jacent.
Tunc ad theatra demigrem frequentia   135
Johnsone, si tu, docte soccum proferas;
Sive * Ille musæ filius fundat sonos,
Quam dulce, quam feliciter temerarios!
Curæque carmen semper antidotos modis
Mentem relaxet involutam Lydiis;   140
Oh! sim perenni emancipatus carmini,
Quod tentet usque ad intimum cor emicans,
Auresque gratis detinens ambagibus
Pedibus ligatis suaviter nectat moras,
Dum liquida vox, labyrinthus ut, deflectitur   145

* Shakespear.

_____

144 ligatis] legatis *1791*

Dolo perita et negligenti industria,
Variaque cæcos arte nodos explicat,
Animam latentem qui coercent musices;
Adeo ut quiete expergefactus aurea
Toros relinquat ipse Thrax amarinthinos,   150
Medioque tales captet Elysio sonos,
Quales avaram suadeant Proserpinam
Nulla obligatam lege sponsam reddere.
His si redundes gaudiis, prudentis est,
Lætitia, tecum velle vitam degere.   155

The Precaution,

Moderniz'd from Chaucer, and sung by Mr. Lowe at Vaux-Hall.

From sweet, bewitching tricks of love,
    Young men, your hearts secure;
Lest from the paths of sense you rove,
    In dotage premature:
Look at each lass thro' wisdom's glass,   5
    Nor trust the naked eye;
Gallants! beware, look sharp, take care,
    The blind eat many a fly.

Not only on their hands and necks,
    The borrow'd white you'll find,   10
Some belles, where interest directs,
    Can even paint the mind:
Joy in distress they can express,
    Their very tears will lie;
Gallants! beware, &c.   15

There's not a spinster in the realm,
    But all mankind can cheat;

THE PRECAUTION. First datable publication: *RM* (4 Aug. 1746). Text: *LM* (Aug. 1746), p. 421. Collated: *RM*; *LH* [Sept. 1746], ii. 6; *MB*, i. 7; *SS* [n.d.] BL Mus. G.307 (204). *Title.* The Blind eat many a Fly *RM*   The Caution *LH*   *Refrain* Gallants] Young men *RM*
10 you'll] you *RM*   11 where] when *RM, LH, SS*   14 will] can *RM, MB, SS*   16 not a] every *SS*   17 Knows how mankind can cheat *SS*

Down to the cottage, from the helm,
    The learn'd, the brave, and great.
With lovely looks, and golden hooks,   20
    T' entangle us they try:
Gallants! beware, &c.

Could we with ink the ocean fill,
    Was earth of parchment made,
Was ev'ry single stick a quill,   25
    Each man a scribe by trade;
To write the tricks of half the sex
    Would drain the ocean dry:
Gallants! beware, &c.

On seeing Miss H——— P—t, in an Apothecary's Shop.

Fallacious nymph, who here by stealth,
Would seem to be the goddess Health!
Mask'd in that divine disguise,
Think'st thou to 'scape poetick eyes?
Back, Siren—for I know thou'st stray'd,   5
From the harmonious ambuscade;
Where many a traveller, that took
The invitation of thy look,
Has felt the coz'nage of thy charms,
Tickled to death within thy arms.   10
Know, that I saw you yester-night,
At once with horror and delight,
Drag Luna from her heavenly frame,
And out-shine her when she came.
Yes, inchantress, I can tell   15
How by the virtue of a spell,
Cloath'd like cherub-innocence,
Here you fix your residence;

19 and great] the great *RM*, *MB*   28 drain the] suck the *RM*, *LH*, *MB* suck that *SS*

ON SEEING MISS H——— P—T. First published in *MU* (27 Sept. 1746), ii. 20–1. Text: *MW* (Apr. 1751), ii. 34–5. Collated: *MU*.
5 thou'st] thou *MU*   10 thy] thine *MU*.

108

That securely you may mix
Your philters in the streams of Styx;   20
And have at hand, in every part,
Materials for your magic art,
Fossils, fungus's, and flow'rs,
With all the fascinating pow'rs.
God of the prescribing trade,   25
Doctor Phœbus, lend thine aid;
If thou'lt some antidote devise,
I'll call thee Harvey of the skies;
Or (for, at one glance, thou can'st see
All that is, or that shall be,   30
Intentions rip'ning into act,
And plans emerging up to fact)
Look in her eyes, and thence explain
All the mischief that they mean.
Say in what grove, and near what trees   35
Will she seek the Hippomanes.
There, there I'll meet her,—there I'll try
Th' asswasive pow'r of harmony.
I think I've got an amulet,
That will her rage awhile abate.   40
No—all resistance is in vain—
Charmer I yield—I hug my chain:
Alas! I see 'tis to no end
With such puissance to contend;
For since continually you dwell   45
In that apothecary's cell;
And while so studiously you pry
Into the sage dispensary,
And read so many doctors bill,
You learn infallibly to kill.—   50

[*Hudibras*, Canto I, lines 279–84, translated into Latin]

> Sic Taliacoti ars amica
> Vectoris parte de postica,
> Falsis invenit carnem nasis,
> Quæ duret tamdiu, quam *Basis*:
> Sed rostrum parili ruina
> Cum clune periit consobrina.

A Song.

Gay Florimel of noble birth,
The most engaging fair on earth
   To please a blithe gallant,
Has much of wit and much of worth,
And much of tongue to set it forth,   5
   But then she has an aunt.

How oft, alas! in vain I've try'd
To tempt her from her guardian's side,
   And trap her on love's hook;
She's like a little wanton lamb   10
That frisks about the careful dam,
   And shuns the shepherd's crook.

Like wretched Dives am I plac'd
To see the joys I cannot taste,
   Of all my hopes bereaven;   15
Her aunt's the dismal gulph betwixt,
By all the powers of malice fixt,
   To cheat me of my heav'n.

HUDIBRAS, CANTO I. First published in *MU* (27 Sept. 1746), ii. 21–2. Text: *MW* (Apr. 1751), ii. 36. Collated: *MU*.
2 Vectoris *MU*] Victoris *MW*
A SONG. First published in *LH* [Sept. 1746], ii. 19. Text: *MW* (July 1751), ii. 171–2. Collated: *LH*; *MU* (22 Nov. 1746), ii. 180; *MB*, ii. 8.
1 noble] gen'rous *MU*   2 fair] thing *LH*   3 blithe] blind *MU*   9 on] in *MU*   12 And] But *LH*   14 cannot] ne'er must *LH*   16 dismal] dreadfull *LH*

The Pretty Chambermaid:

In Imitation of Ne sit ancillæ tibi amor pudori, &c. of Horace.

Colin, oh! cease thy friend to blame,
Who entertains a servile flame.
Chide not—believe me, 'tis no more
Than great Achilles did before,
Who nobler, prouder far than he is,   5
Ador'd his chambermaid Briseis.

The thund'ring Ajax Venus lays
In love's inextricable maze:
His slave Tecmessa makes him yield,
Now mistress of the sevenfold shield.   10
Atrides with his captive play'd,
Who always shar'd the bed she made.

'Twas at the ten years siege, when all
The Trojans fell in Hector's fall,
When Helen rul'd the day and night,   15
And made them love, and made them fight:
Each hero kiss'd his maid, and why,
Tho' I'm no hero, may not I?

Who knows? Perhaps Polly may be
A piece of ruin'd royalty.   20
She has (I cannot doubt it) been
The daughter of some mighty queen;
But fate's irremeable doom
Has chang'd her sceptre for a broom.

Ah! cease to think it—how can she,   25
So generous, charming, fond, and free,
So lib'ral of her little store,
So heedless of amassing more,

THE PRETTY CHAMBERMAID. First published in *GM* (Oct. 1746), p. 552. Text: *1752*.
Collated: *GM*; *1791*.
10 Now mistress of the] Not ought avails his *GM*   16 them . . . them] 'em . . . 'em
GM   19 Who knows, but Polly too may be *GM*   Who knows? Polly perhaps may be
1791   27 lib'ral] lavish *GM*

Have one drop of plebeian blood,
In all the circulating flood?   30

But you, by carping at my fire,
Do but betray your own desire—
Howe'er proceed—made tame by years,
You'll raise in me no jealous fears.
You've not one spark of love alive,   35
For, thanks to heav'n, you're forty-five.

THE
HORATIAN CANONS
OF
FRIENDSHIP.

BEING THE
THIRD SATIRE of the FIRST BOOK OF HORACE

IMITATED.

With Two DEDICATIONS;

The FIRST to that ADMIRABLE CRITIC, the

REV. MR. WILLIAM WARBURTON,

OCCASIONED BY
HIS DUNCIAD, and HIS SHAKESPEARE;

And the SECOND to my good Friend

The TRUNK-MAKER at the Corner of *St. Paul's Church-Yard.*

By EBENEZER PENTWEAZLE,
of TRURO *in the* County *of* CORNWALL, *Esq;*

'Tis all from Horace.   POPE.

LONDON:

Printed for the AUTHOR, and Sold by J. NEWBERY, at the *Bible
and Sun* in *St. Paul's Church-Yard.* 1750.

TO THAT

ADMIRABLE CRITIC
THE
Rev. Mr. William Warburton.

Reverend Sir,

Some years have elapsed since I admired you, whom I never
saw, and your works, which I never read, by tradition: I
thought you almost infallible, and, in all submission, kiss'd
your toe with the rest of the deluded multitude. But (thanks to
hoenst, ingenious *Edwards*) I am at length convinced that your
Holiness is an old woman, a mere Pope Joan; and, as *Hudibrass*
did by *Sidrophel*,

> .., *I now perceive,*
> *You are no conjuror, by your leave.*

The other Gentleman, of Lincoln's Inn, has shewn your
picture to the publick, and the publick have acknowledged the
likeness. Your Shakespeare has given us a sample of your head,
as your Dunciad has of your heart. I say *your* Shakespear, and
your Dunciad; for neither of those excellent authors would own
their works, were they alive to see what you have made of
them.

> *Incipit esse tuum,*

Or, as Dryden expresses it,

> *You make the benefits of others studying*
> *Much like the meals of politic Jack-pudding,*
> *Whose dish to challenge no man has the courage;*
> *'Tis all his own when once h' has spit i' th' porridge.*
>
> > Prologue to Albumazar.

Your reading (it must be allow'd) has been very extensive; yet I
defy you to produce, out of all your learned lumber, one
instance parallel to this, *viz.* The making a dead man write
posthumous satyr against gentlemen, whom he either did not
know, or, if he did, he must have admired. Did you ever read
the fragments of Menander? Let me recommend the following

passage, which I think you will hardly disapprove; since it is a panegyric upon impudence.

35

$$\Omega \; \mu\epsilon\gamma\iota\sigma\tau\epsilon \; \tau\omega\nu \; \Theta\epsilon\omega\nu$$
$$N\nu\nu \; o\upsilon\sigma' \; A\nu\alpha\iota\delta\epsilon\iota', \; \epsilon\iota \; \Theta\epsilon o\nu \; \kappa\alpha\lambda\epsilon\iota\nu \; \sigma\epsilon \; \delta\epsilon\iota,$$
$$\varDelta\epsilon\iota \; \delta\epsilon, \; \tau o \; \kappa\rho\alpha\tau o\upsilon\nu \; \gamma\alpha\rho \; \nu\upsilon\nu \; \nu o\mu\iota\zeta\eta\tau\alpha\iota \; \Theta\epsilon o\varsigma,$$
$$E\phi' \; o\sigma o\nu \; \beta\alpha\delta\iota\zeta\epsilon\iota\varsigma, \; \dot\epsilon\phi' \; o\sigma o\nu \; \dot\eta\xi\epsilon\iota\nu \; \mu o\iota \; \delta o\kappa\epsilon\iota\varsigma;$$

Thou Goddess, Impudence (if without blame,   40
To thee we may attribute that high name)
Yet thou art surely of immortal line,
If to have power infinite's divine:
How vast thy force, thy influence how great,
And how stupendous thy still rising height!

45

I might take this opportunity of calling you to an account for balderdashing the English language, by introducing French words, such as Mes^{rs} *Entreme, Impuissance,* and a thousand others, when we have more significant ones of our own to express the same ideas. I might accuse you of coining such   50 words as *ming* for mixture, which you cleverly contrive by turning the *w* in wing upside down, together with *hym,* which you say is a particular kind of dog; and when your hand was in, you might as well have said a particular kind of fish, which is the constant custom of the Lexicographers, when they don't   55 understand a word in Pliny, or some other antient writers. But I shall leave matters of this sort to a gentleman much my superior, both in genius and learning, who is very hard at work for you, and who will do you noble justice; besides, I am called off from you at present to a man of much more worth and   60 utility; namely, the Trunk-maker at the corner of St Paul's Churchyard.

REVEREND SIR,
     Your Servant,
         EBENEZER PENTWEAZLE.

TO THE

TRUNK-MAKER

At the CORNER of

St. PAUL's CHURCH-YARD.

SIR,

Not many days ago, at a meeting of a club of merry fellows at the Castle, after supper was over I toasted All our friends round Paul's; *upon which Mr. Critic Catchup cry'd out,* Mr. Pentweazle, I beg you would not forget the Trunk-maker in the corner, a person to whom you are likely to furnish a great deal of lining, and who in this golden and truly Augustan age will probably be the best Patron you'll meet with. *Upon this I humbly ask'd pardon for my omission, and take this opportunity of making some amends; for it must be own'd that in these times (as Mr. Warburton says)* "so highly improv'd in true Philosophy," *the Trunk-makers are* * "not the worst judges or rewarders of merit."

However, I beg leave to be indulged a few words with regard to the degrees of merit, because I think it would be absurd to prefer Authors to the Trunk indiscriminately. As for your pastoral writers and epigramma-tists, they (it should seem) ought only to line Trunks for little Misses, but your Epic writers, your Tragedians, and your Comedians might be a proper ornament for the Trunks of persons of Condition, and the works of the incomparable Mr. Justice Fielding *might line the Trunk of an Emperor. As for the works of the Rev. Mr. W——, Mr. R——, Dr. ——, &c. &c. &c. they should line the Trunks that are intended for exportation, for they will never be read any more in this kingdom.*

I beg to conclude by expressing the utmost esteem for you and your profession, and declaring that I sincerely believe Merit would not go so

---

* This is Mr. *Warburton*'s complement to his booksellers.

totally unrewarded had some of our modern Mæcenas's *half the generosity and abilities of the* T R U N K - M A K E R *at the Corner of St. Paul's Church.*

I am Your Obedient

And expect to be

Your Obliged Humble Servant,

E B E N E Z E R   P E N T W E A Z L E.

N.B. I think it proper to declare that nothing in the above Dedication is intended to ridicule or reflect upon Mr Nickless, who is an excellent artist in his way, and a very sensible worthy man.

THE

HORATIAN CANONS

OF

FRIENDSHIP.

¹ Nay, 'tis the same with all th' affected crew
Of singing men and singing women too:
Do they not set their catcalls up of course?
The King himself may ask them till he's hoarse;
But wou'd you crack their windpipes and their lungs,   5
The certain way's to bid them hold their tongues.
'Twas thus with *Minum,—Minum* one wou'd think,
My Lord Mayor might have govern'd with a wink.
Yet did the Magistrate e'er condescend
To ask a song as kinsman or as friend,   10
The urchin coin'd excuses to get off,
'Twas—hem—the devil take this whoreson cough.
But wait awhile, and catch him in the glee, ⎫
He'd roar the * Lion in the lowest key, ⎬
Or strain the † morning Lark quite up to G. ⎭   15

* *The Lion's Song, in Pyramus and Thisbe.*
† *A song in one of Mr Handel's Oratorios.*

---

¹ Omnibus hoc vitium est cantoribus, inter amicos
Ut nunquam inducant animum cantare rogati:
Injussi nunquam desistant. Sardus habebat
Ille Tigellius hoc. Cæsar, qui cogere posset,
Si peteret per amicitiam partis, atque suam, non
Quidquam proficeret: si collibusset, ab ovo
Usque ad mala citaret, Io Bacche, modo summa
Voce, modo hac resonat quæ chordis quatuor ima.

THE HORATIAN CANONS. First published, separately, in 1750. Text: *1750*. Collated:
MW (July 1751), ii. 170 (ll. 79–117); *MW* (Aug. 1752), iii. 108 (ll. 1–6); *1791*.
1 th' affected] the coxcomb *MW*   5 crack] split *MW*   6 certain] surest
MW

Act Beard, or Lowe, and shew his tuneful art
From the plumb-pudding down to the desert.
² Never on earth was such a various elf,
He every day possess'd a diff'rent self;
Sometimes he'd scowr along the streets like wind,⁣   20
As if some fifty bailiffs were behind;
At other times he'd sadly, saunt'ring crawl,
As tho' he led the hearse, or held the sable pall.
³ Now for promotion he was all on flame,
And ev'ry sentence from St James's came.   25
He'd brag how Sir John —— met him in the Strand,
And how his Grace of —— took him by the hand;
How the Prince saw him at the last review,
And ask'd who was that pretty youth in blue?
Now wou'd he praise the peaceful sylvan scene,   30
The healthful cottage, and the golden mean.
Now wou'd he cry, contented let me dwell
Safe in the harbour of my college cell;
No foreign cooks, nor livry'd servants nigh,
Let me with comfort eat my mutton-pye;   35
While my pint-bottle, op'd by help of fork,
With wine enough to navigate a cork,
My sober solitary meal shall crown,
To study edge the mind, and drive the vapours down.
Yet, strange to tell, this wond'rous student lay   40
Snoring in bed for all the livelong day;
Night was his time for labour—in a word,
Never was man so cleverly absurd.

² Nil æquale homini fuit illi: sæpe velut qui
Currebat fugiens hostem: persæpe velut qui
Junonis sacra ferret. Habebat sæpe ducentos,
Sæpe decem servos: modo reges, atque tetrarchas.
³ Omnia magna loquens. Modo, Sit mihi mensa tripes, et
Concha salis puri, et toga, quæ defendere frigus,
Quamvis crassa, queat. decies centena dedisses
Huic parco paucis contento: quinque diebus
Nil erat in loculis. noctes vigilabat ad ipsum
Mane: diem totum stertebat. nil fuit unquam
Sic impar sibi. nunc aliquis dicat mihi: quid tu?

⁴ But here a friend of mine turns up his nose,
And you (he cries) are perfect, I suppose: 45
Perfect! not I (pray, gentle Sir, forbear) ⎤
In this good age, when vices are so rare, ⎬
I plead humanity, and claim my share. ⎦
Who has not faults? great MARLBOROUGH had one,
Nor CHESTERFIELD is spotless, nor the SUN.   50
Grubworm was railing at his friend *Tom Queer*,
When *Witwoud* thus reproach'd him with a sneer,
Have you no flaws, who are so prone to snub,
I have—but I forgive myself, quoth *Grub*.
This is a servile selfishness, a fault   55
Which Justice scarce can punish, as she ought.
Blind as a poking, dirt-compelling mole,
To all that stains thy own polluted soul,
Yet each small failing spy'st in other men,
Spy'st with the quickness of an eagle's ken.   60
Tho' strong resentment rarely lag behind,
And all thy virulence be paid in kind.
⁵ Philander's temper's violent, nor fits
The wond'rous waggishness of modern wits;
His cap's awry, all ragged is his gown,   65
And (wicked rogue!) he wears his stockings down;

---

⁴ Nullane habes vitia? immo alia, haud fortasse minora.
Mænius absentem Novium cum carperet: heus tu,
Quidnam ait. ignoras te? an ut ignotum dare nobis
Verba putas? egomet mi ignosco, Mænius inquit.
Stultus, et improbus hic amor est, dignusque notari.
Cum tua pervideas oculis mala lippus inunctis,
Cur in amicorum vitiis tam cernis acutum.
Quam aut aquila, aut serpens Epidaurius? at tibi contra
Evenit, inquirant vitia ut tua rursus, et illi.
⁵ Iracundior est paullo, minus aptus acutis
Naribus horum hominum: rideri possit, eo quod
Rusticius tonso toga defluit, et male laxus
In pede calceus hæret. at est bonus, ut melior vir
Non alius quisquam: at tibi amicus: at ingenium ingens
Inculto latet hoc sub corpore, denique teipsum
Concute, num qua tibi vitiorum inseverit olim
Natura, aut etiam consuetudo mala. namque
Neglectis urenda filix innascitur agris.

But h'as a soul ingenuous as his face,
To you a friend, and all the human race;
Genius, that all the depths of learning sounds,
And generosity, that knows no bounds.   70
In gems like these if the good youth excel,
Let them compensate for the aukward shell.
Sift then yourself, I say, and sift again,
Glean the pernicious tares from out the grain;
And ask thy heart if Custom, Nature's heir,   75
Hath sown no undiscover'd fern-seed there.
This be our standard then, on this we rest,
Nor search the Casuists for another test.
[6] Let's be like lovers gloriously deceiv'd,
And each good man a better still believ'd;   80
E'en Celia's wart Strephon will not neglect,
But praises, kisses, loves the dear defect.
Oh! that in friendship we were thus to blame,
And ermin'd candour, tender of our fame,   84
Wou'd cloath the honest error with an honest name!
Be we then still to those we hold most dear,
Fatherly fond, and tenderly severe.
The sire, whose son squints forty thousand ways,
Finds in his features mighty room for praise:

---

[6] Illuc prævertamur: amatorem quod amicæ
Turpia decipiunt cæcum vitia, aut etiam ipsa hæc
Delectant: veluti Balbinum polypus Agnæ:
Vellem in amicitia sic erraremus; et isti
Errori nomen virtus posuisset honestum.
At, pater ut nati, sic nos debemus amici,
Si quod sit vitium, non fastidire. strabonem
Appellat pætum pater: et pullum, male parvus
Si cui filius est: ut abortivus fuit olim
Sisyphus. hunc varum, distortis cruribus, illum
Balbutit scaurum, pravis fultum male talis.
Parcius hic vivit: frugi dicatur. ineptus,
Et jactantior hic paullo est: concinnus amicis
Postulat ut videatur. at est truculentior atque
Plus æquo liber: simplex, fortisque habeatur.
Caldior est: acreis inter numeretur. opinor,
Hæc res et jungit, junctos et servat amicos.

Ah! born (he cries) to make the ladies sigh,   90
Jacky, thou hast an am'rous cast o' th' eye.
Another's child's abortive—he believes
Nature most perfect in diminutives;
And men of ev'ry rank, with one accord
Salute each crooked brachet with My Lord.   95
(For bandy legs, hump-back, and knocking knee,
Are all excessive signs of Q——ty.)
Thus let us judge our friends—if Scrub subsist
Too meanly, Scrub is an œconomist;
And if Tom Tinkle is full loud and pert,   100
He aims at wit, and does it to divert.
Largus is apt to bluster, but you'll find
'Tis owing to his magnitude of mind:
Lollius is passionate, and loves a whore,
Spirit and constitution!—nothing more—   105
Ned to a bullying peer is ty'd for life,
And in commendam holds a scolding wife;
Slave to a fool's caprice, and woman's will;
But patience, patience is a virtue still!
Ask of Chamont a kingdom for a fish,   110
He'll give you three rather than spoil a dish;
Nor pride, nor luxury, is in the case,
But Hospitality—an't please your Grace.
Should a great gen'ral give a drab a pension—   114
Meanness!—the devil—'tis perfect condescension.
Such ways make many friends, and make friends long,
Or else my good friend Horace reasons wrong.
[7] But we alas! e'en virtuous deeds invert,

[7] At nos virtutes ipsas invertimus, atque
Sincerum cupimus vas incrustare. probus quis
Nobiscum vivit: multum est demissus homo. illi
Tardo cognomen pingui damus. hic fugit omneis
Insidias, nullique malo latus obdit apertum,
Cum genus hoc inter vitæ versetur, ubi acris
Invidia, atque vigent ubi crimina: pro bene sano,
Ac non incauto, fictum, astutumque vocamus.
Simplicior si quis, qualem me sæpe libenter
Obtulerim tibi Mæcenas, ut forte legentem
Aut tacitum impellat, quovis sermone molestus,
Communi sensu plane caret, inquimus.

95 brachet] rascal 1791

And into vice misconstrue all desert.
See we a man of modesty and merit,   120
Sober and meek—we swear he has no spirit;
We call him stupid, who with caution breaks
His silence, and will think before he speaks.
Fidelio treads the path of life with care,
And eyes his footsteps; for he fears a snare.   125
His wary way still scandal misapplies,
And calls him subtle, who's no more than wise.
If any man is unconstrain'd and free,
As oft, my Lælius, I have been to thee,
When rudely to your room I chance to scowr,   130
And interrupt you in the studious hour;
From Coke and Littleton your mind unbend,
With more familiar nonsense of a friend;
Talk of my friendship, and of your desert, ⎫
Shew you my works, and candidly impart ⎬   135
At once the product of my head and heart, ⎭
Nasutus calls me fool, and clownish bear,
Nor (but for perfect candour) stops he there.
[8] Ah! what unthinking, heedless things are men,
T' enact such laws as must themselves condemn?   140
In every human soul some vices spring
(For fair perfection is no mortal thing)
Whoe'er is with the fewest faults endu'd,
Is but the best of what cannot be good.

[8] Eheu,
Quam temere in nosmet legem sancimus iniquam.
Nam vitiis nemo sine nascitur: optimus ille est,
Qui minimis urgetur. amicus dulcis, ut æquum est,
Cum mea compenset vitiis bona, pluribus hisce,
Si modo plura mihi bona sunt, inclinet; amari
Si volet: hac lege in trutina ponetur eadem.
Qui, ne tuberibus propriis offendat amicum
Postulat; ignoscat verrucis illius. æquum est,
Peccatis veniam poscentem, reddere rursus.
Denique, quatenus excidi penitus vitium iræ,
Cætera item nequeunt stultis hærentia; cur non
Ponderibus, modulisque suis ratio utitur, ac res
Ut quæque est, ita suppliciis delicta coercet?

130, 132, 134 your] thy *1791*   131, 135 you] thee *1791*

Then view me, friend, in an impartial light, 145
Survey the good and bad, the black and white;
And if you find me, Sir, upon the whole,
To be an honest and ingenuous soul,
By the same rule I'll measure you again,
And give you your allowance to a grain. 150
'Tis friendly and 'tis fair, on either hand,
To grant th' indulgence we ourselves demand.
If on your hump we cast a fav'ring eye,
You must excuse all those who are awry.
In short, since vice or folly, great or small, 155
Is more or less inherent in us all,
Whoe'er offends, our censure let us guide,
With a strong biass to the candid side;
Nor (as the stoicks did in antient times)
Rank little foibles with enormous crimes. 160
[9] If, when your butler, ere he brings a dish,
Shou'd lick his fingers, or shou'd drop a fish,
Or from the side-board filch a cup of ale,
Enrag'd you send the puny thief to gaol;
You'd be (methinks) as infamous an oaf, 165
As that immense portentous scoundrel *—
Yet worse by far (if worse at all can be)
In folly and iniquity is he;
Who, for some trivial, social, well-meant joke,
Which candour shou'd forget as soon as spoke, 170
Wou'd shun his friend, neglectful and unkind,
As if old Parson Packthread was behind:

   * *An infamous attorney.*

---

[9] Si quis eum servum, patinam qui tollere jussus,
Semesos pisceis, tepidumque ligurierit jus,
In cruce suffigat; Labeone insanior inter
Sanos dicatur: quanto hoc furiosius atque
Majus peccatum est? paullum deliquit amicus,
Quod nisi concedas, habeare insuavis, acerbus;
Odisti, et fugis, ut Drusonem debitor æris:
Qui nisi cum tristes misero venere Kalendæ,
Mercedem aut nummos unde unde extricat; amaras
Porrecto jugulo historias, captivus ut, audit.

---

164 gaol] goal *1750*

Who drags up all his visiters by force,
And, without mercy, reads them his discourse.
¹⁰ If sick at heart, and heavy at the head,   175
My drunken friend should reel betimes to bed;
And in the morn, with affluent discharge,
Should sign and seal his residence at large;
Or should he, in some passionate debate,
By way of instance, break an earthen plate;   180
Wou'd I forsake him for a piece of delph?
No—not for China's wide domain itself.
If toys like these were cause of real grief,
What shou'd I do, or whether seek relief,
Suppose him perjur'd, faithless, pimp, or thief?   185
Away—a foolish knavish tribe you are,
Who falsely put all vices on a par.
From this fair reason her assent withdraws,
E'en sordid Interest gives up the cause,
That mother of our customs and our laws.   190
When first yon golden sun array'd the east,
Small was the difference 'twixt man and beast;
With hands, with nails, with teeth, with clubs they fought,
'Till malice was improv'd, and deadlier weapons wrought.
Language, at length, and words experience found,   195
And sense obtain'd a vehicle in sound.

¹⁰ Comminxit lectum potus, mensave catillum
Evandri manibus tritum dejecit: ob hanc rem,
Aut positum ante mea quia pullum in parte catini
Sustulit esuriens, minus hoc jucundus amicus
Sit mihi? quid faciam, si furtum fecerit, aut si
Prodiderit commissa fide, sponsumve negarit?
Queis paria esse fere placuit peccata, laborant,
Cum ventum ad verum est; sensus, moresque repugnant.
Atque ipsa utilitas justi prope mater, et æqui.
Cum prorepserunt primis animalia terris,
Mutum et turpe pecus, glandem atque cubilia propter,
Unguibus, et pugnis, dein fustibus atque ita porro
Pugnabant armis, quæ post fabricaverat usus:
Donec verba, quibus voces, sensusque notarent,
Nominaque invenere; dehinc absistere bello,
Oppida cœperunt munire, et ponere leges;
Ne quis fur esset neu latro, neu quis adulter.

184 whether] whither *1791*

Then wholesome laws were fram'd, and towns were built,
And justice seiz'd the lawless vagrants guilt;
And theft, adultery, and fornication
Were punish'd much, forsooth, tho' much in fashion:
[11] For long before fair Helen's fatal charms   200
Had many a   .   .   .   .

.   .   .   .
.   .   .   .   . *Hiatus magnus lacrymabilis*

.   .   .   .
.   .   .   .   .   . set the world in arms.
But kindly kept by no historian's care,
They all, goodlack, have perish'd to an hair.
But be that as it may, yet in all climes,   205
There's diff'rent punishment for diff'rent crimes.
Hold, blockhead, hold—this sure is not the way,⎫
For all alike I'd slash, and all I'd slay,   ⎬
Cries W————N, if I had sovereign sway.   ⎭
Have sov'reign sway, and in imperial robe,   210
With fury † sultanate o'er half the globe.
Mean while, if I from each indulgent friend,
Obtain remission, when I chance t' offend,
Why, in return, I'll make the balance even,
And, for forgiving, they shall be forgiven.   215
[12] With zeal I'll love, be courteous e'en to strife,
More blest than Emperors in private life.

FINIS.

† *A word coin'd in the manner of Mr* W————N.

----

[11] Nam fuit ante Helenam cunnus teterrima belli
Causa: sed ignotis perierunt mortibus illi,
Quos Venerem incertam rapientes more ferarum
Viribus editior cædebat, ut in grege taurus.

.   .   .   .
.   .   . dum tu quadrante lavatum
Rex ibis, neque te quisquam stipator, ineptum
Præter Crispinum, sectabitur: et mihi dulces
Ignoscent, si quid peccavero stultus amici:
[12] Inque vicem illorum patiar delicta libenter,
Privatusque magis vivam te rege beatus.

----

208 slash] lash *1791*   209 I had] I'd *1791*

To Miss A—n

Long, with undistinguish'd flame,
I lov'd each fair, each witty dame,
My heart the belle-assembly gain'd,
And all an equal sway maintain'd.

But when you came, you stood confess'd   5
Sole sultana of my breast;
For you eclips'd, supremely fair,
All the whole seraglio there.

In this her mien, in that her grace,
In a third I lov'd a face;   10
But you in ev'ry feature shine
Universally divine.

What can those tumid paps excel,
Do they sink, or do they swell?
While those lovely wanton eyes   15
Sparkling meet them, as they rise.

Thus is silver Cynthia seen,
Glistening o'er the glassy green,
While attracted swell the waves,
Emerging from their inmost caves.   20

When to sweet sounds your steps you suit,
And weave the minuet to the lute,
Heav'ns! how you glide!—her neck—her chest—
Does she move, or does she rest?

As those roguish eyes advance,   25
Let me catch their side-long glance,

TO MISS A—N. MSS: *PC*; Bodl. Tenbury MS 1283 (*T*). First published in *LB* [Mar.
1747], i. 18–21. Text: *1752*. Collated: *PC*; *T*; *LB*; *MW* (Apr. 1751), ii. 36–8; *1791*.
Title. To Miss A—n *MW*] Sonnet *PC*   A Cantata *T*   Cantata *LB*   On Miss***
1752, *1791*
13 tumid paps] snow-white breasts *LB*   tumid paps *corrected to* snow-white breasts
T   17–20 *omitted*, *LB*   17 is] in *MW*

Soon—or they'll elude my sight,
Quick as light'ning, and as bright.

Thus the bashful Pleiad cheats
The gazer's eye, and still retreats,   30
Then peeps agen—then skulks unseen,
Veil'd behind the azure skreen.

Like the ever-toying dove,
Smile immensity of love;
Be Venus in each outward part,   35
And wear the vestal in your heart.

When I ask a kiss, or so—
Grant it with a begging no,
And let each rose that decks your face
Blush assent to my embrace.   40

Prologue to a Comedy call'd the Grateful Fair.

In ancient days (as jovial Horace sings)
When laurell'd bards were lawgivers and kings,
Bold was the comic muse, without restraint,
To name the vicious, and the vice to paint;
Th' enliven'd picture from the canvas flew,   5
And the strong likeness crowded on the view.
Our author practices more general rules,
He is no niggard of his knaves and fools.
Both small and great, both dull and pert he shews,
That every gentleman may pick and chuse.   10
The laws dramatic, tho', he scarcely knows ⎞
Of time and place, and all the piteous prose ⎟
Which pedant Frenchmen snuffle thro' their nose. ⎠

---

29 cheats] peeps *PC, T, LB, MW*   30 Charms her moment, and retreats, *PC, T,*
LB, MW   38 begging] willing *corrected to* begging *T*
PROLOGUE. First published in *GM* (Aug. 1747), p. 391. Text: *ST* (Feb. 1751), ii.
196–7. Collated: *GM*; *CJ* (19 Sept. 1747); *1791. Title from GM.* Prologue to a new
Comedy called the Grateful Fair *CJ*   Prologue to a Play intended for the Stage *ST*
No title in 1791
9 he shews] his Muse *1791*   10 That every gentleman] Displays, that every one
1791   11 laws] rules *GM, 1791*   13 Which] That *GM, 1791*   their] the
GM, CJ, 1791

Fools!—who prescribe what Homer shou'd have done,
Like tattling watches, they correct the sun.   15
Critics, like posts, undoubtedly may shew
The way to Pindus—but they cannot go:
For to delight and elevate the mind,
To heav'n-directed GENIUS is assign'd.
Whene'er immortal Shakespear's works we read,   20
He wins the heart, before he strikes the head;
Swift to the soul the piercing image flies,
More swift than Celia's wit, or Celia's eyes,
More swift than some romantic trav'ler's thought,
More swift than British fire, where Marlbro' fought.   25
Fancy precedes and conquers all the mind,
Deliberating judgment slowly lags behind,
Comes to the field with blunderbuss and gun,
Like heavy Falstaff when the work is done;
Fights when the battle's o'er, with wond'rous pain,   30
By Shrewsbury clock, and nobly slays the slain.—
—But critic censures are beneath his care,
Who strives to please the honest and the fair.
Their approbation is much more than fame,
He speaks—he writes—he breathes not—but for THEM.

[Soliloquy of the Princess Perriwinkle]

The Princess Perriwinkle sola, attended by fourteen Maids of great
honour.

Sure such a wretch as I was never born,
By all the world deserted and forlorn;
This bitter-sweet, this honey-gall to prove,
And all the sugar and vinegar of love.

15 they] they'd GM, CJ   16 posts GM, CJ, 1791] poets ST   18–19 omitted,
GM, 1791   18 For] Nor CJ   20 we] are GM, 1791   23, 24, 25 More
swift] Swifter 1791   23 Celia's] Harriot's GM, 1791   25 where Marlbro']
when William GM, CJ, 1791   27 lags] lays CJ   comes 1791   31
Shrewsbury] Shrewsbury's 1791   32 But] All GM   The 1791   his] our GM,
1791   33 Who strives] We strive GM, 1791   honest] generous 1791   34
To their decision we submit our claim; GM, 1791   35 We speak, we write, we
breath not ... GM   We write not, speak not, breathe not, ... 1791
SOLILOQUY. First published in MW (Oct. 1750), i. (iii). Text: MW. Collated: 1791.
4 sugar] oil 1791

Pride, Love and Reason will not let me rest, 5
But make a devilish bustle in my breast.
To wed with Fisgig, Pride, Pride, Pride denies, ⎫
Put on a Spanish padlock Reason cries; ⎬
But tender gentle Love with every wish complies. ⎭
Pride, Love and Reason fight till they are cloy'd, 10
And each by each in mutal wounds destroy'd.
Thus when a Barber and a Collier fight,
The Barber beats the luckless Collier—white;
The dusty Collier heaves his pond'rous sack,
And, big with vengeance, beats the Barber—black. 15
In comes the Brick-dust man, with grime o'erspread,
And beats the Collier and the Barber—red.
Black, red and white in various clouds are toss'd,
And in the dust they raise, the combatants are lost.

The Talkative Fair.

From morn to night, from day to day,
At all times and at every place,
You scold, repeat, and sing, and say,
Nor are there hopes, you'll ever cease.

Forbear, my Celia, oh! forbear, 5
If your own health, or ours you prize;
For all mankind that hear you, swear
Your tongue's more killing than your eyes.

Your tongue's a traytor to your face,
Your fame's by your own noise obscur'd, 10
All are distracted while they gaze;
But if they listen, they are cur'd.

7 Fisgig] Fizgig *1791*
THE TALKATIVE FAIR. First published in *MU* (12 Sept. 1747), iii. 493–4. Text: *1752*.
Collated: *MW* (Nov. 1750), i. 85; *MB*, i. 44–5; *1791*.
2 and at] and in *MU*   5 Celia] Fannia *MU*   12 they are] all are *MW*,
MB

Your silence wou'd acquire more praise,
Than all you say, or all I write;
One look ten thousand charms displays;   15
Then hush—and be an angel quite.

The Silent Fair.

From all her fair loquacious kind,
So different is my Rosalind,
That not one accent can I gain
To crown my hopes, or sooth my pain.

Ye lovers, who can construe sighs,   5
And are the interpreters of eyes,
To language all her looks translate,
And in her gestures read my fate.

And if in them you chance to find
Ought that is gentle, ought that's kind,   10
Adieu mean hopes of being great,
And all the littleness of state.

All thoughts of grandeur I'll despise,
Which from dependence take their rise;
To serve her shall be my employ,   15
And love's sweet agony my joy.

14 you say] I say *MU*
THE SILENT FAIR. MS: *PC*. First published in *MU* (12 Sept. 1747), iii. 493. Text:
1752. Collated: *PC*; *MW* (July 1751), ii. 168; *MB*, ii. 6; *1791*.
9 chance to] aught can *MU*   10 Ought that is] Aught that's *MU*
14 Which] That *PC*, *MU*, *MW*

THE
JUDGMENT
OF
MIDAS

A MASQUE.

Auriculas Asini Mida Rex habet.   Pers.

PERSONS REPRESENTED.

Apollo.
Pan.
Timolus, God of the Mountain.
Midas.
Calliope.
Melpomene.
Agno,
Melinoe,   } Two Wood-nymphs.
Satyrs, &c.

THE JUDGMENT OF MIDAS. First published in *1752*. Text: *1752*. Collated: *1791*.
Motto. Pers.] Juv. *1752, 1791*

THE JUDGMENT OF MIDAS.

TIMOLUS, MELINOE and AGNO, two Wood-nymphs.

TIMOLUS.

Agno, to-day we wear our acorn crown,
The parsley wreath be thine; it is most meet
We grace the presence of these rival gods
With all the honours of our woodland weeds.
Thine was the task, Melinoe, to prepare   5
The turf-built theatre, the boxen bow'r,
And all the sylvan scenery.

MELINOE.

                That task,
Sire of these shades, is done. On yester eve,
Assisted by a thousand friendly fays,
While fav'ring Dian held her glitt'ring lamp,   10
We ply'd our nightly toils, nor ply'd we long,
For Art was not the mistress of our revels,
'Twas gentle Nature, whom we jointly woo'd;
She heard, and yielded to the forms we taught her,
Yet still remain'd herself.—Simplicity,   15
Fair Nature's genuine daughter, was there too,
So soft, yet so magnificent of mien,
She shone all ornament without a gem.
The blithsome Flora, ever sweet and young,
Offer'd her various store: We cull'd a few   20
To robe, and recommend our darksome verdure,
But shun'd to be luxuriant.—

TIMOLUS.

                It was well.
Agno, thy looks are pensive: What dejects
Thy pleasure-painted aspect? Sweetest nymph,

---

1 acorn *1791*] acron *1752*   7 scenery *1791*] scen'ry *1752*   16 was there too]
too was there *1791*

That ever trod the turf, or sought the shade,   25
Speak, nor conceal a thought.

Agno.

                    King of the woods,
I tremble for the royal arbiter.
'Tis hard to judge, whene'er the great contend,
Sure to displease the vanquish'd: When such pow'rs
Contest the laurel with such ardent strife,   30
'Tis not the sentence of fair equity,
But 'tis their pleasure that is right or wrong.

Timolus.

'Tis well remark'd, and on experience founded.
I do remember that my sister Ida
(Whenas on her own shadowy mount we met,   35
To celebrate the birth-day of the Spring,
And th' orgies of the May) wou'd oft recount
The rage of the indignant goddesses,
When shepherd Paris to the Cyprian queen,
With hand obsequious gave the golden toy.   40
Heav'n's queen, the sister and the wife of Jove,
Rag'd like a feeble mortal; fall'n she seem'd,
Her deity in human passions lost:
Ev'n Wisdom's goddess, jealous of her form,
Deem'd her own attribute her second virtue.   45
Both vow'd and sought revenge.

Agno.

                    If such the fate
Of him who judg'd aright, what must be his
Who shall mistake the cause? for much I doubt
The skill of Midas, since his fatal wish:
Which Bacchus heard, and curs'd him with the gift.   50
Yet grant him wise, to err is human still,
And mortal is the consequence.

Melinoe.

                    Most true.
Besides, I fear him partial; for with Pan

He tends the sheep-walks all the live-long day,
And on the braky lawn to the shrill pipe   55
In aukward gambols he affects to dance,
Or tumbles to the tabor—'tis not likely
That such an umpire shou'd be equitable,
Unless he guess at justice.

TIMOLUS.

                    Soft—no more—
'Tis ours to wish for Pan, and fear from Phœbus,   60
Whose near approach I hear: Ye stately cedars
Forth from your summits bow your awful heads,
And reverence the gods. Let my whole mountain tremble,
Not with a fearful, but religious awe,
And holiness of horror. You, ye winds,   65
That make soft, solemn music 'mongst the leaves,
Be all to stillness hush'd; and thou their echo
Listen, and hold thy peace; for see they come.

SCENE *opens, and discovers* Apollo, *attended by* Clio *and* Melpo-
    mene, *on the right hand of* Midas, *and* Pan *on the left, whom*
    Timolus, *with* Agno *and* Melinoe, *join.*

MIDAS.

Begin, celestial candidates for praise,
Begin the tuneful contest: I, mean while,   70
With heedful notice and attention meet,
Will weigh your merits, and decide your cause.
APOLLO.

From Jove begin the rapturous song,
To him our earliest lays belong,
    We are his offspring all;   75
'Twas he, whose looks supremely bright,
Smil'd darksome chaos into light,
    And fram'd this glorious ball.
PAN.

Sylvanus, in his shadowy grove,
The seat of rural peace and love,   80
    Attends my Doric lays;

By th' altar on the myrtle mount,
Where plays the wood-nymph's favourite fount,
  I'll celebrate his praise.

CLIO.

Parnassus, where's thy boasted height,   85
Where, Pegasus, thy fire and flight,
Where all your thoughts so bold and free,
Ye daughters of Mnemosyne?
If Pan o'er Phœbus can prevail,
And the great god of verse shou'd fail?   90

AGNO.

From nature's works, and nature's laws,
We find delight, and seek applause;
The prattling streams and zephyrs bland,
And fragrant flow'rs by zephyrs fann'd,
The level lawns and buxom bow'rs,   95
Speak Nature and her works are ours.

MELPOMENE.

What were all your fragrant bow'rs,
Splendid days, and happy hours,
Spring's verdant robe, fair Flora's blush,
And all the poets of the bush?   100
What the paintings of the grove,
Rural music, mirth and love?
Life and ev'ry joy wou'd pall,
If Phœbus shone not on you all.

MELINOE.

We chant to Phœbus, king of day,   105
The morning and the evening lay.
But Pan, each satyr, nymph and fawn,
Adore as laureat of the lawn;
From peevish March to joyous June
He keeps our restless souls in tune,   110
Without his oaten reed and song,
Phœbus, thy days wou'd seem too long.

    104 you] them *1791*   107 satyr *1791*] satyre *1752*

Apollo.

Am I not he, who prescious from on high,
Sends a long look thro' all futurity?
Am I not he, to whom alone belong   115
The powers of Med'cine, Melody and Song?
Diffusely lib'ral, as divinely bright,
Eye of the universe and sire of light.

Pan.

O'er cots and vales, and every shepherd swain,
In peaceable pre-eminence I reign;   120
With pipe on plain, and nymph in secret grove,
The day is music, and the night is love.
I blest with these, nor envy nor desire
Thy gaudy chariot, or thy golden lyre.

Clio.

Soon as the dawn dispels the dark,   125
    Illustrious Phœbus 'gins t' appear,
Proclaimed by the herald lark,
    And ever-wakeful chanticleer,
The Persian pays his morning vow,
And all the turban'd easterns bow.   130

Agno.

Soon as the evening shades advance,
    And the gilt glow-worm glitters fair,
For rustic gambol, gibe and dance,
    Fawns, nymphs and dryads all prepare,
Pan shall his swains from toil relieve,   135
And rule the revels of the eve.

Melpomene.

In numbers as smooth as Callirhoe's stream,
Glide the silver-ton'd verse when Apollo's the theme;
While on his own mount Cyparissus is seen,
And Daphne preserves her immutable green.   140

113 prescious] prescient *1791*   114 Sends] Send *1791*

We'll hail Hyperion with transport so long,
Th' inventor, the patron, and subject of song.

MELINOE.

While on the calm ocean the Halcyon shall breed,
And Syrinx shall sigh with her musical reed,
While fairies, and satyrs, and fawns shall approve   145
The music, the mirth, and the life of the grove,
So long shall our Pan be than thee more divine,
For he shall be rising when thou shalt decline.

MIDAS.

No more—To Pan and to his beauteous nymphs
I do adjudge the prize, as is most due.   150

Enter two Satyrs, *and crown* MIDAS *with
a pair of ass's ears*

APOLLO.

Such rural honours all the gods decree,
To those who sing like Pan, and judge like thee.
                                        [*Exeunt Omnes.*

FINIS.

145 satyrs *1791*] satyres *1752*   147 thee] *1791*   *151* SD (Satyrs) *1791*]
Satyres *1752*

Christopherus Smart Samueli Saunders,

Col. Regal. S.P.D.

Phoebus et Liber Charitesque mecum
Nocte cœnabunt, (ita spondet Hermes)
Nostra sed prorsus, nisi te magistro,
    Poc'la recusant.

Attici dives venias leporis,   5
Non sine assueto venias chachinno, et
Blanda pinguedo explicita renidens
    Fronte jocetur.

Georgium expecto, salis architectum
Duplicis vafrum satis, æmulosque   10
Spero vos inter fore nunc, ut olim,
    Nobile bellum.

Dumque lucubrata per omne longi
Frigoris sæclum pueros tenellos
Alma nox pictas videt otiosos   15
    Volvere chartas,

Proh pudor! devota lucro juventus
(Ut puellarum numerus senumque)
Pallet insomnis repetita duri
    Jurgia ludi.   20

Sperne (nam multæ cerebrum Minervæ
Est tibi) nugas age quæstuosas,
Arduas, vanas, et amara curæ
    Elue mecum.

Jam riget tellus, hyemantque menses,   25
Vestra sed laurus vireat, tuisque
In genis dulcis rosa Sanitatis
    Sera moretur.

Aul. Pemb. CANTAB. *Cal. Jan.*

CHRISTOPHERUS SMART SAMUELI SAUNDERS. First published in *ST* (July 1750), i. 280. Text: *ST*. Collated: *1791*.
1 Liber] Liber, *ST, 1791*   16 chartas,] chartæ *ST*   chartas. *1791*

Translation

Christopher Smart to Samuel Saunders, *King's College*. Most hearty greetings.

Phoebus and Bacchus and the Graces will dine with me tonight—so Hermes promises—but they quite refuse our cups unless you are there as master of the feast.

May you come rich in Attic mirth; come with your accustomed laughter, and let your comfortable stoutness smilingly jest with unfurrowed brow.

I'm expecting George, shrewd enough architect of two-fold wit, and I hope that as rivals you will now, as in the past, join in noble battle.

And while kindly night, lamp-lit through a whole age of long cold, sees boys of tender years unroll their picture-books,

For shame!—our youth, devoted to gain (like many girls and old men), grows pale from sleeplessness in the repeated wranglings of hard gaming.

Come—for yours is a brain of great wisdom—disdain lucrative trifles, so arduous, so vain, and wash away, with me, the bitterness of care.

Now the earth is stiff and the months are wintry, yet may your laurel stay green, and may the rose of sweet healthiness long abide on your cheeks.

Pembroke Hall, Cambridge, *January*.

A Morning Piece,

or, An Hymn for the Hay-Makers.

Quinetiam Gallum noctem explaudentibus alis
Auroram clara consuetum voce vocare. LUCRET.

Brisk chaunticleer his mattins had begun,
    And broke the silence of the night,
  And thrice he call'd aloud the tardy sun,
    And thrice he hail'd the dawn's ambiguous light;
Back to their graves the fear-begotten phantoms run.   5

A MORNING PIECE. First published in *LM* (Dec. 1748), p. 564. Text: *1752*. Collated: *LM*; *ST* (July 1750), i. 274–5; *1791. No motto in LM.*

Strong Labour got up.—With his pipe to his mouth,
　　He stoutly strode over the dale,
He lent new perfumes to the breath of the south,
　　On his back hung his wallet and flail.
Behind him came Health from her cottage of thatch,　　10
Where never physician had lifted the latch.

First of the village Colin was awake,
And thus he sung, reclining on his rake.

　　Now the rural graces three
　　Dance beneath yon maple tree;　　　　　　15
　　First the vestal Virtue, known
　　By her adamantine zone;
　　Next to her in rosy pride,
　　Sweet Society, the bride;
　　Last Honesty, full seemly drest　　　　　20
　　In her cleanly home-spun vest.

The abby bells in wak'ning rounds
　　The warning peal have giv'n;
And pious Gratitude resounds
　　Her morning hymn to heav'n.　　　　　　25

All nature wakes—the birds unlock their throats,
And mock the shepherd's rustic notes.

　　All alive o'er the lawn,
　　Full glad of the dawn,
　　The little lambkins play,　　　　　　　　30
Syliva and Sol arise,—and all is day—

　　Come, my mates, let us work,
　　And all hands to the fork,
While the Sun shines, our Hay-cocks to make,
　　So fine is the Day,　　　　　　　　　　35

6–7 Strong Labour got up with his pipe in his mouth, / And stoutly *etc. All edd.*
8 He] And *LM*　　to the breath *1752 Errata*] to breath *1752*　　12 Colin was]
Strephon did *LM*　　13 reclining on] and leant upon *LM*　　20 seemly] neatly
LM　　22–3 The college bell, in solemn sounds, / The warning notes has giv'n;
LM　　31 Sylvia] Celia *LM*　　33–4 Let us handle the fork, / And in social
duties partake; *LM*　　35 So fine is] So glorious *LM*

And so fragrant the Hay,
That the Meadow's as blithe as the Wake.

Our voices let's raise
In Phœbus's praise,
Inspir'd by so glorious a theme,   40
Our musical words
Shall be join'd by the birds,
And we'll dance to the tune of the stream.

A Noon-Piece; or, The Mowers at Dinner.

Jam pastor umbras cum grege languido,
Rivumque fessus quaærit, et horridi
    Dumeta Silvani, caretque
        Ripa vagis taciturna ventis. HOR.

The Sun is now too radiant to behold,
    And vehement he sheds his liquid Rays of Gold;
No cloud appears thro' all the wide expanse;
    And short, but yet distinct and clear,
    To the wanton whistling air   5
The mimic shadows dance.

Fat Mirth, and Gallantry the gay,
And romping Extasy 'gin play.
Now Myriads of young Cupids rise,
And open all their joy-bright eyes,   10
Filling with infant prate the grove,
And lisp in sweetly-fault'ring love.
In the middle of the ring,
Mad with May, and wild of wing,
Fire-ey'd Wantonness shall sing.   15

36 fragrant] fragrant's *LM*   37 The meadows are fine as the wake. *LM*
39 In] To *LM*   40 glorious] noble *LM*
A NOON-PIECE. First published in *LM* (Dec. 1748), p. 564. Text: *1752*. Collated: *LM*;
ST (Aug. 1750), i. 305–7; *1791*. *No motto in LM*
2 liquid Rays of] rays of liquid *LM, ST*   3 expanse] expence *LM*
15 shall] does *LM*

By the rivulet on the rushes,
Beneath a canopy of bushes,
Where the ever-faithful Tray,
Guards the dumplings and the whey,
Colin Clout and Yorkshire Will   20
From the leathern bottle swill.

Their scythes upon the adverse bank
   Glitter 'mongst th' entangled trees,
Where the hazles form a rank,
   And court'sy to the courting breeze.   25

Ah! Harriot! sovereign mistress of my heart,
   Could I thee to these meads decoy,
New grace to each fair object thou'dst impart,
   And heighten ev'ry scene to perfect joy.

On a bank of fragrant thyme,   30
Beneath yon stately, shadowy pine,
We'll with the well-disguised hook
Cheat the tenants of the brook;
Or where coy Daphne's thickest shade
Drive amorous Phœbus from the glade,   35
There read Sydney's high-wrought stories
Of ladies charms and heroes glories;
Thence fir'd, the sweet narration act,
And kiss the fiction into fact.

Or satiate with nature's random scenes,   40
Let's to the gardens regulated greens,
   Where taste and elegance command
   Art to lend her dædal hand,
   Where Flora's flock, by nature wild,
   To discipline are reconcil'd,   45
   And laws and order cultivate,
   Quite civiliz'd into a state.

21 bottle] flasket *LM, ST*   23 'mongst] midst *LM*   26 Harriot! sovereign]
Delia, mighty *LM*   30 thyme] tanzy *LM*   31 Let us entertain our fancy,
LM   stately] shapely *ST*   32 We'll] And *LM*   35 amorous] ardent
LM   36 high-wrought] amorous *LM*   37 Of lady-charms and hero-glories;
LM

From the sun, and from the show'r,
Haste we to yon boxen bow'r,
Secluded from the teizing pry   50
Of Argus' curiosity:
There, while Phœbus' golden mean,
The gay meridian is seen,
Ere decays the lamp of light,
And length'ning shades stretch out to night—   55
Seize, seize the hint—each hour improve
(This is morality in love)
Lend, lend thine hand—O let me view
Thy parting breasts, sweet avenue!
Then—then thy lips, the coral cell   60
Where all th' ambrosial kisses dwell!
Thus we'll each sultry noon employ
In day-dreams of exstatic joy.

A Night-Piece; or, Modern Philosophy.

Dicetur merita nox quoque nœnia.   HOR.

'Twas when bright Cynthia with her silver car,
    Soft stealing from Endymion's bed,
Had call'd forth ev'ry glitt'ring star,
And up th' ascent of heav'n her brilliant host had led.

Night, with all her negro train,   5
Took possession of the plain;
In an hearse she rode reclin'd,
Drawn by screech-owls slow and blind:
Close to her, with printless feet,
Crept Stillness, in a winding sheet.   10

54 Ere] E'er *LM, ST*   55 to] the *LM*   58 thine] thy *LM*   59 breast's
sweet *LM*   62 Thus we'll each] Let's every *LM, ST*
A NIGHT-PIECE. First published in *LM* (Dec. 1748), pp. 564–5. Text: *1752*. Collated:
LM; ST (Sept. 1750), i. 353–4; *1791*. *Title*. Night Piece: Or, the philosopher *LM*   *No
motto in LM*
3 glitt'ring] glimmering *LM*   4 And girt the skies with horizontal red, *LM*
7 an] a *LM*   8 . screech] scritch *LM*   10 Crept] Walked *LM*

Next to her deaf Silence was seen,
Treading on tip-toes over the green;
Softly, lightly, gently she trips,
Still holding her fingers seal'd to her lips.

[Then came Sleep serene and bland,   15
Bearing a death-watch in his hand;
In fluid air around him swims
A tribe grotesque of mimic dreams.]

   You could not see a sight,
     You could not hear a sound,   20
   But what confess'd the night,
     And horror deepen'd round.

   Beneath a myrtle's melancholy shade,
   Sophron the wise was laid:
And to the answ'ring wood these sounds convey'd: 25

   While others toil within the town,
   And to Fortune smile or frown,
   Fond of trifles, fond of toys,
   And married to that woman, Noise;
   Sacred Wisdom be my care,   30
   And fairest Virtue, Wisdom's heir.

His speculations thus the sage begun,
   When, lo! the neighbouring bell
In solemn sound struck one:—
   He starts—and recollects—he was engag'd to Nell.   35

Then up he sprang nimble and light,
   And rapp'd at fair Ele'nor's door;
He laid aside virtue that night,
   And next morn por'd in Plato for more.

13 Softly, lightly,] Swiftly, softly *LM*   14 fingers] finger *ST*   seal'd to] close
in *LM*   15–18 *omitted, 1752, 1791*   16 Bearing *ST*] With *LM*
17–18 *transposed in LM*   21 what] all *LM, ST*   23 myrtle's] plantane's
LM   plantain's *ST*   25 wood] woods *LM*   34 sound] sounds *LM*
36 sprang] sprung *LM*

To the King.

STROPHE.

As some vast vista, whose extent
Scarce bounded by the firmament
   From whence its sweep begun;
Above, beneath, in every place,
Mark'd with some grand distinguish'd grace,   5
   Ends with the golden sun:
Thus, GEORGE, thy reign, to the impartial view
   In all its parts, in every light appears;
For ever happy, as for ever new,
   Rise the bright days, and roll the glorious years.   10
Yet—still—the voice, that bids the nations breathe
To hear fair justice, and the sword to sheathe,
   'Tis this, th' exertion of thy godlike soul,
'Tis this confirms, compleats, and nobly crowns the whole.

ANTISTROPHE.

Oh! born the nations to compose,   15
How doubly sweet thy olive blows
   O'er the triumphant palm!
After the blast, how bland the breeze!
How amiably superb the seas,
   When hush'd into a calm!   20
Say by what miracle, what pow'rful charm,
   Plan'd and accomplish'd was th' august design?
Was it thy WILLIAM's formidable arm
   Just and effectual, like the wrath Divine?
Was it thy fleet that smoak'd the depth along   25
Swift as the eagle, as the lion strong?—
   No—'twas that Wisdom bad the warfare cease,
Whose ways are pleasantness, and all whose paths are
               PEACE.

EPODON.

Of Camus oft the solitary strand
   Poetically pensive will I haunt: 30

TO THE KING. Text: *Gratulatio Academicæ Cantabrigiensis de reditu serenissimi Regis Georgii II. Post pacem et libertatem Europæ feliciter restitutam.* (Cambridge, 1748), sig. Gg–Gg^v.

And, as I view th' innumerable sand,
   Think on thy bounties; and with transport chaunt,
That now no more Bellona's brazen car
   Affrights Urania in her blissful seat;
Nor Stratagem, the subtlest snake of war,   35
   Plots to entangle every Pilgrim's feet:
That now no lures our vagrant steps mislead;
Except the harmless syrens of the mead,
   Deftly secrete in hawthorne ambuscade,
Charm the romantic rovers to the upland glade.   40

ON THE
ETERNITY
OF THE
SUPREME BEING.

Conamur tenues grandia——
Nec Dis, nec viribus æquis——

Hail, wond'rous Being, who in pow'r supreme
Exists from everlasting, whose great Name
Deep in the human heart, and every atom
The Air, the Earth or azure Main contains
In undecypher'd characters is wrote—   5
INCOMPREHENSIBLE!—O what can words
The weak interpreters of mortal thoughts,
Or what can thoughts (tho' wild of wing they rove
Thro' the vast concave of th' ætherial round)
If to the Heav'n of Heavens they'd win their way   10
Advent'rous, like the birds of night they're lost,
And delug'd in the flood of dazling day.—
    May then the youthful, uninspired Bard
Presume to hymn th' Eternal; may he soar
Where Seraph, and where Cherubin on high   15
Resound th' unceasing plaudits, and with them
In the grand Chorus mix his feeble voice?
    He may—if Thou, who from the witless babe
Ordainest honor, glory, strength and praise,
Uplift th' unpinion'd Muse, and deign t' assist,   20
GREAT POET OF THE UNIVERSE, his song.
    Before this earthly Planet wound her course
Round Light's perennial fountain, before Light
Herself 'gan shine, and at th' inspiring word
Shot to existence in a blaze of day,   25
Before "the Morning-Stars together sang"
And hail'd Thee Architect of countless worlds—
Thou art—all-glorious, all-beneficent,
All Wisdom and Omnipotence thou art.

ETERNITY. First published in 1750. Text: *E*. Collated: *E2*; *E3*; *1761*; *1791*. *No mottoes in*
E2, E3, 1761, 1791
20 deign *1791*] deign'st *E, E2, E3, 1761*

But is the æra of Creation fix'd   30
At when these Worlds began? Cou'd ought retard
Goodness, that knows no bounds, from blessing ever,
Or keep th' immense Artificer in sloth?
Avaunt the dust-directed crawling thought,
That Puissance immeasurably vast,   35
And Bounty inconceivable cou'd rest
Content, exhausted with one week of action—
No—in th' exertion of thy righteous pow'r,
Ten thousand times more active than the Sun,
Thou reign'd, and with a mighty hand compos'd   40
Systems innumerable, matchless all,
All stampt with thine uncounterfeited seal.
   But yet (if still to more stupendous heights
The Muse unblam'd her aching sense may strain)
Perhaps wrapt up in contemplation deep,   45
The best of Beings on the noblest theme
Might ruminate at leisure, Scope immense
Th' eternal Pow'r and Godhead to explore,
And with itself th' omniscient mind replete.
This were enough to fill the boundless All,   50
This were a Sabbath worthy the Supreme!
Perhaps enthron'd amidst a choicer few,
Of Spirits inferior, he might greatly plan
The two prime Pillars of the Universe,
Creation and Redemption—and a while   55
Pause—with the grand presentiments of glory.
    Perhaps—but all's conjecture here below,
All ignorance, and self-plum'd vanity—
O Thou, whose ways to wonder at's distrust,
Whom to describe's presumption (all we can,—   60
And all we may—) be glorified, be prais'd.
   A Day shall come, when all this Earth shall perish,
Nor leave behind ev'n Chaos; it shall come
When all the armies of the elements
Shall war against themselves, and mutual rage   65
To make Perdition triumph; it shall come,
When the capacious atmosphere above
Shall in sulphureous thunders groan, and die,
And vanish into void; the earth beneath

Shall sever to the center, and devour   70
Th' enormous blaze of the destructive flames.
Ye rocks, that mock the raving of the floods,
And proudly frown upon th' impatient deep,
Where is your grandeur now? Ye foaming waves,
That all along th' immense Atlantic roar,   75
In vain ye swell; will a few drops suffice
To quench the inextinguishable fire?
Ye mountains, on whose cloud-crown'd tops the cedars
Are lessen'd into shrubs, magnific piles,
That prop the painted chambers of the heav'ns   80
And fix the earth continual; Athos, where;
Where, Tenerif's thy stateliness to-day?
What, Ætna, are thy flames to these?—No more
Than the poor glow-worm to the golden Sun.

Nor shall the verdant vallies then remain   85
Safe in their meek submission; they the debt
Of nature and of justice too must pay.
Yet I must weep for you, ye rival fair,
Arno and Andalusia; but for thee
More largely and with filial tears must weep,   90
O Albion, O my Country; Thou must join,
In vain dissever'd from the rest, must join
The terrors of th' inevitable ruin.

Nor thou, illustrious monarch of the day;
Nor thou, fair queen of night; nor you, ye stars,   95
Tho' million leagues and million still remote,
Shall yet survive that day; Ye must submit
Sharers, not bright spectators of the scene.

But tho' the Earth shall to the center perish,
Nor leave behind ev'n Chaos; tho' the air   100
With all the elements must pass away,
Vain as an ideot's dream; tho' the huge rocks,
That brandish the tall cedars on their tops,
With humbler vales must to perdition yield;
Tho' the gilt Sun, and silver-tressed Moon   105
With all her bright retinue, must be lost;
Yet Thou, Great Father of the world, surviv'st
Eternal, as thou wert: Yet still survives
The soul of man immortal, perfect now,

And candidate for unexpiring joys.   110
   He comes! He comes! the awful trump I hear;
The flaming sword's intolerable blaze
I see; He comes! th' Archangel from above.
"Arise, ye tenants of the silent grave,
Awake incorruptible and arise: 115
From east to west, from the antarctic pole
To regions hyperborean, all ye sons,
Ye sons of Adam, and ye heirs of Heav'n—
Arise, ye tenants of the silent grave,
Awake incorruptible and arise."   120
   'Tis then, nor sooner, that the restless mind
Shall find itself at home; and like the ark
Fix'd on the mountain-top, shall look aloft
O'er the vague passage of precarious life;
And, winds and waves and rocks and tempests past,   125
Enjoy the everlasting calm of Heav'n:
'Tis then, nor sooner, that the deathless soul
Shall justly know its nature and its rise:
'Tis then the human tongue new-tun'd shall give
Praises more worthy the eternal ear.   130
Yet what we can, we ought;—and therefore, Thou,
Purge thou my heart, Omnipotent and Good!
Purge thou my heart with hyssop, lest like Cain
I offer fruitless sacrifice, and with gifts
Offend and not propitiate the Ador'd.   135
Tho' gratitude were bless'd with all the pow'rs
Her bursting heart cou'd long for, tho' the swift,
The firey-wing'd imagination soar'd
Beyond ambition's wish—yet all were vain
To speak Him as he is, who is INEFFABLE.   140
Yet still let reason thro' the eye of faith
View Him with fearful love; let truth pronounce,
And adoration on her bended knee
With Heav'n-directed hands confess His reign.
And let th' Angelic, Archangelic band   145
With all the Hosts of Heav'n, Cherubic forms,
And forms Seraphic, with their silver trumps

134 and *omitted, 1791*

And golden lyres attend:—"For Thou art holy,
For thou art One, th' Eternal, who alone
Exerts all goodness, and transcends all praise."   150

FINIS.

A Panegyrick on the Ladies.

Being Chaucer's Recantation for * *The blind eat many a fly.*
As it is sung at the Spring Gardens Vaux Hall, with great applause.

RECITATIVE.

Old Chaucer once to this re-echoing grove
Sung "of the sweet bewitching tricks of love;"
But soon he found, he'd sullied his renown,
And arm'd each charming hearer with a frown;
Then self-condemn'd anew his lyre he strung,   5
And in repentant strains this recantation sung.

AIR.

Long since unto her native sky
Fled heav'n-descended Constancy;
Nought now that's stable's to be had,
The world's grown mutable and mad: 10
Save WOMEN—they, we must confess,
Are miracles of stedfastness,
And every witty, pretty dame
Bears for her motto—*Still the same.*

The flow'rs that in the vale are seen,   15
The white, the yellow, blue and green,
In brief complexion idly gay
Still set with every setting day,
Dispers'd by wind, or chill'd by frost,
Their odours gone, their colour lost: 20
But what is true, tho' passing strange,
The WOMEN never—fade or change.

The wise man said that all was vain,
And folly's universal reign;

* *A song moderniz'd from the old English of* Chaucer.

A PANEGYRICK. First published in *ST* (June 1750), i. 230–2. Text: *ST*. Collated: *LM*
(Aug. 1750), p. 376; *VM* [Oct. 1750], ii. 38–42; *MB*, i. 8–9. *Title.* Chaucer's
Recantation *LM, VM.*
3 he'd] he *LM*   h' had *VM*   20 colour] colours *LM*

Wisdom its vot'ries oft enthralls,   25
Riches torment, and pleasure palls;
And 'tis, good lack, a general rule,
That each man soon or late's a fool:
In WOMEN 'tis th' exception lies,
For they are wond'rous, wond'rous wise.   30

This earthly ball with noise abounds,
And from its emptiness it sounds,
Fame's deafening din, the hum of men,
The lawyer's plea, and poet's pen:
But WOMEN here no one suspects,   35
Silence distinguishes that sex;
For, poor dumb things! so meek's their mould,
You scarce can hear them—when they scold.

CHORUS.

An hundred mouths, an hundred tongues,
An hundred pair of iron lungs,   40
Five heralds, and five thousand cryers,
With throats whose accent never tires,
Ten speaking trumpets of a size
Would deafness with their din surprize,
Your praise, sweet nymphs, shall sing and say,   45
And those that will believe it—may.

25 Its votries wisdom oft enthralls, *VM*   27 good lack] alas *VM*   34 and]
the *MB*   36 Silence distinguishes their sex *LM*   'Twere hard t' include that
silent sex *VM*   38 them] 'em *MB*   42 throats] voice *VM*   45 sweet]
dear *VM*

On the Fifth of December, being the Birth-day of a beautiful young Lady.

Hail, eldest of the monthly train,
    Sire of the winter drear,
December, in whose iron reign
    Expires the chequer'd Year.
Hush ail the blust'ring blasts that blow,   5
And proudly plum'd in silver snow,
    Smile gladly on this blest of Days.
The livery'd clouds shall on thee wait,
And Phoebus shine in all his state
    With more than summer rays.   10

Tho' jocund June may justly boast
    Long days and happy hours,
Tho' August be Pomona's host,
    And May be crown'd with flow'rs;
Tell June, his fire and crimson dyes,   15
By Harriot's blush and Harriot's eyes,
    Eclips'd and vanquish'd, fade away:
Tell August, thou canst let him see
A richer, riper fruit than he,
    A sweeter flow'r than May.   20

Sweet William.

By a prattling stream, on a Midsummer's eve,
Where the woodbine and jess'mine their boughs interweave,
Fair Flora, I cry'd, to my arbour repair,
For I must have a chaplet for sweet William's hair.

ON THE FIFTH OF DECEMBER. First published in *ST* (June 1750), i. 225. Text: *1752*.
Collated: *ST, 1791*. *Title*. Ode on the fifth of December, Being the birth-day of a very
beautiful Young Lady *ST*
15 dyes *ST*] dies *1752, 1791*
SWEET WILLIAM. First published in *ST* (July 1750), i. 273. Text: *1752*. Collated: *ST*;
MB, i. 9–10; *1791*. *Subtitled* A Ballad *ST*
3 arbour] harbour *1791*

She brought me the vi'let that grows on the hill,   5
The vale-dwelling lilly, and gilded jonquill:
But such languid odours how cou'd I approve,
Just warm from the lips of the lad that I love?

She brought me, his faith and his truth to display,
The undying myrtle, and ever-green bay: 10
But why these to me, who've his constancy known?
And Billy has laurels enough of his own.

The next was a gift that I could not contemn,
For she brought me two roses that grew on a stem:
Of the dear nuptial tie they stood emblems confest,   15
So I kiss'd 'em, and press'd 'em quite close to my breast.

She brought me a sun-flow'r—This, fair one's, your due;
For it once was a maiden, and love-sick like you:
Oh! give it me quick, to my shepherd I'll run,
As true to his flame, as this flow'r to the sun.   20

The Distressed Damsel.

Of all my experience how vast the amount,
Since fifteen long winters I fairly can count!
Was ever a damsel so sadly betray'd,
To live to these years and yet still be a maid?

Ye heroes triumphant, by land and by sea,   5
Sworn vot'ries to love, but unmindful of me;
You can storm a strong fort, or can form a blockade,
Yet ye stand by, like dastards, and see me a maid.

---

16 'em ... 'em] them ... them *ST, MB*   20 the] her *ST, MB*
THE DISTRESSED DAMSEL. First published in *ST* (Aug. 1750), i. 310. Text: *1752*.
Collated: *ST*; *MW* (Oct. 1750), i. 36; *VM* [Oct. 1750], ii. 36–7; *MB*, i. 10–11; *1791*.
Title. A Ballad *MW*   The Distress'd Maid *VM*
3 a] poor *ST, MW, VM, MB*   4 To live] For to live *ST, MW*   6 but]
yet *ST, MW, VM, MB*   7 Of prowess approv'd, of no danger afraid, *VM*
8 Yet] Will *VM*

Ye lawyers so just, who with slippery tongue,
Can do what you please, or with right, or with wrong,   10
Can it be, or by law or by equity said,
That a buxom young girl ought to die an old maid?

Ye learned physicians, whose excellent skill
Can save, or demolish, can cure, or can kill,
To a poor, forlorn damsel contribute your aid,   15
Who is sick—very sick—of remaining maid.

Ye fops, I invoke, not to list to my song,
Who answer no end—and to no sex belong;
Ye echoes of echoes, and shadows of shade—
For if I had you—I might still be a maid.   20

The Fair Recluse.

Ye ancient patriarchs of the wood,
    That veil around these awful glooms,
Who many a century have stood
    In verdant age, that ever blooms.

Ye Gothic tow'rs, by vapours dense,   5
    Obscur'd into severer state,
In pastoral magnificence
    At once so simple and so great.

Why all your jealous shades on me,
    Ye hoary elders do ye spread?   10
Fair Innocence shou'd still be free,
    Nought shou'd be chain'd, but what we dread.

9 Ye councellors sage, who with eloquent tongue, *VM*   10 or...or] both...and *VM*
11 be, or by] be by *VM*   12 buxom] comely *VM*   14 cure] heal *VM*
17 Ye fops,] You, Fops, *ST, MW, MB*
invoke], invoke *ST, MW, VM, MB*   19 of echoes] of echo *VM*
THE FAIR RECLUSE. First published in *ST* (May 1751), ii. 316–17. Text: *1752*.
Collated: *ST*; *1791*. Subtitled An Ode *ST*
3 Who] That *ST*   4 that] which *ST*

Say, must these tears for ever flow?
　Can I from patience learn content,
While solitude still nurses woe,   15
　And leaves me leisure to lament.

My guardian see!—who wards off peace,
　Whose cruelty is his employ,
Who bids the tongue of transport cease,
　And stops each avenue to joy?   20

Freedom of air alone is giv'n,
　To aggravate, not sooth my grief,
To view th' immensely-distant heav'n,
　My nearest prospect of relief.

On Good-Nature.

Hail cherub of the highest Heav'n,
Of look divine, and temper ev'n,
　Celestial sweetness, exquisite of mien,
　Of ev'ry virtue, ev'ry praise the queen!

Soft gracefulness, and blooming youth,   5
Where, grafted on the stem of truth,
　That friendship reigns, no interest can divide,
　And great humility looks down on pride.

Oh! curse on Slander's vip'rous tongue,
That daily dares thy merit wrong;   10
　Ideots usurp thy title, and thy frame,
　Without or virtue, talent, taste, or name.

Is apathy, is heart of steel,
Nor ear to hear, nor sense to feel,
　Life idly inoffensive such a grace,   15
　That it shou'd steal thy name and take thy place?

ON GOOD-NATURE. First published in *1752*. Text: *1752*. Collated: *1791*.

No—thou art active—spirit all—
Swifter than light'ning, at the call
   Of injur'd innocence, or griev'd desert,
   And large with liberality's thy heart.   20

Thy appetites in easy tides
(As reason's luminary guides)
   Soft flow—no wind can work them to a storm,
   Correctly quick, dispassionately warm.

Yet if a transport thou canst feel   25
'Tis only for thy neighbours weal:
   Great, generous acts thy ductile passions move,
   And smilingly thou weep'st with joy and love.

Mild is thy mind to cover shame,
Averse to envy, slow to blame,   30
   Bursting to praise, yet still sincere and free
   From flatt'ry's fawning tongue, and bending knee.

Extensive, as from west to east,
Thy love descends from man to beast,
   Nought is excluded little, or infirm,   35
   Thou canst with greatness stoop to save a worm.

Come, goddess, come with all thy charms
For Oh! I love thee, to my arms—
   All, all my actions guide, my fancy feed,
   So shall *existence* then be *life* indeed.   40

Against Ill-Nature.

I.

Offspring of folly and of pride,
To all that's odious, all that's base allied;

---

20 liberality's] liberality *1791*
AGAINST ILL-NATURE. First published in *1752*. Text: *1752*. Collated: *1791*. *Title*. On
Ill-Nature *1791*

Nurs'd up by vice, by pravity misled,
By pedant affectation taught and bred:
   Away, thou hideous hell-born spright, 5
Go, with thy looks of dark design,
   Sullen, sour, and saturnine;
Fly to some gloomy shade, nor blot the goodly light.
   Thy planet was remote, when I was born;
'Twas Mercury that rul'd my natal morn, 10
   What time the sun exerts his genial ray,
And ripens for enjoyment every growing day;
   When to exist is but to love and sing,
And sprightly Aries smiles upon the spring.

II.

There in yon lonesome heath, 15
Which Flora, or Sylvanus never knew,
   Where never vegetable drank the dew,
Or beast, or fowl attempts to breathe;
   Where Nature's pencil has no colours laid;
But all is blank, and universal shade; 20
   Contrast to figure, motion, life and light,
There may'st thou vent thy spight,
   For ever cursing, and for ever curs'd,
Of all th' infernal crew the worst;
   The worst in genius, measure and degree; 25
For envy, hatred, malice, are but parts of thee.

III.

Or woud'st thou change the scene, and quit thy den,
   Behold the heav'n-deserted fen,
Where spleen, by vapours dense begot and bred,
   Hardness of heart, and heaviness of head, 30
Have rais'd their darksome walls, and plac'd their
     thorny bed;
   There may'st thou all thy bitterness unload,
There may'st thou croak, in concert with the toad,
   With thee the hollow howling winds shall join,
Nor shall the bittern her base throat deny, 35

27 thy] the *1791*

The querulous frogs shall mix their dirge with thine,
Th' ear-piercing hern, and plover screaming high,
     While million humming gnats fit œstrum shall supply.

IV.

Away—away—behold an hideous band
     An herd of all thy minions are at hand,   40
Suspicion first with jealous caution stalks,
     And ever looks around her as she walks,
With bibulous ear imperfect sounds to catch,
     And prompt to listen at her neighbours latch.
          Next Scandal's meagre shade,   45
Foe to the virgins, and the poet's fame,
     A wither'd, time-deflow'red old maid,
That ne'er enjoy'd love's ever sacred flame.
     Hypocrisy succeeds with saint-like look,
And elevates her hands and plods upon her book.   50
Next comes illiberal scrambling Avarice,
     Then Vanity and Affectation nice—
See, she salutes her shadow with a bow
     As in short Gallic trips she minces by,
Starting antipathy is in her eye,   55
     And squeamishly she knits her scornful brow.
To thee, Ill-Nature, all the numerous group
     With lowly reverence stoop—
They wait thy call, and mourn thy long delay,
     Away—thou art infectious—haste away.   60

To the reverend and learned Dr. Webster.

Occasioned by his Dialogues on Anger and Forgiveness.

I.

'Twas when th' omniscient creative pow'r
     Display'd his wonders by a mortal's hand,

---

38 While million] Millions of *1791*   47 -deflow'red] -deflower'd *1791*
TO DR. WEBSTER. First published in *ST* (Dec. 1750), ii. 111–13. Text: *1752*. Collated:
ST, *1791*. *Title*. Ode to the Reverend, *etc. ST*

And, delegated at th' appointed hour,
   Great Moses led away his chosen band;
    When Israel's host, with all their stores,   5
    Past thro' the ruby-tinctur'd crystal shores,
The wilderness of waters and of land:
    Then persecution rag'd in heav'n's own cause,
And right on neighbouring kingdoms to infringe,
   Strict justice for the breach of nature's laws,   10
Strict justice, who's full-sister to revenge:
    The legislator held the scythe of fate,
      Where'er his legions chanc'd to stray,
      Death and destruction mark'd their bloody way;
Immoderate was their rage, for mortal was their hate.   15

II.

But when the king of righteousness arose,
   And on the illumin'd East serenely smil'd,
He shone with meekest mercy on his foes,
    Bright as the sun, but as the moon-beams mild;
      From anger, fell revenge, and discord free,   20
        He bad war's hellish clangor cease,
        In pastoral simplicity and peace,
And shew'd to men that face, which Moses could not see.

III.

Well hast thou, WEBSTER, pictur'd christian love,
   And copied our great master's fair design,   25
But livid Envy would the light remove,
   Or croud thy portrait in a nook malign—
The Muse shall hold it up to popular view—
Where the more candid and judicious few
   Shall think the bright original they see,   30
The likeness nobly lost in the identity.

IV.

Oh hadst thou liv'd in better days than these,
   Ere to excel by all was deem'd a shame!
Alas! thou hast no modern arts to please,
   And to deserve is all thy empty claim.   35

9, 11 *omitted, 1791*   23 men] man *1791*   33 Ere] E'er *ST, 1752*

Else thou'dst been plac'd, by learning, and by wit,
There, where thy dignify'd inferiors sit—
    Oh *they* are in their generation wise,
Each path of interest *they* have sagely trod,—
    To live—to thrive—to rise—and still to rise—   40
Better to bow to men, than kneel to God.

v.

Behold!—where poor unmansion'd Merit stands,
    All cold, and crampt with penury and pain;
Speechless thro' want, she rears th' imploring hands,
    And begs a little bread, but begs in vain;   45
While Bribery and Dulness, passing by,
Bid her, in sounds barbarian, starve and die.
        "Away (they cry) we never saw thy name
        Or in Preferment's List, or that of Fame;
    Away—nor here the fate thou earn'st bewail,   50
Who canst not buy a vote, nor hast a soul for sale."

vi.

Oh Indignation, wherefore wert thou given,
    If drowsy Patience deaden all thy rage?—
Yet we must *bear*—such is the will of heaven;
    And, WEBSTER, so prescribes thy candid page.   55
Then let us hear thee preach seraphic love,
Guide our disgusted thoughts to things above;
    So our free souls, fed with divine repast,
        (Unmindful of low mortals mean employ)
    Shall taste the present, recollect the past,   60
        And strongly hope for every future joy.

On the sudden Death of a Clergyman.

If, like th' Orphean lyre, my song could charm,
    And light to life the ashes in the urn,

38 generation] generations *1791*   50 thou earn'st] thou'st earn'd *ST*
ON THE SUDDEN DEATH. First published in *ST* (July 1751), ii. 393–4. Text: *1752.*
Collated: *ST, 1791.*

Fate of his iron dart I would disarm,
    Sudden as thy decease should'st thou return.
Recall'd with mandates of despotic sounds,   5
And arbitrary grief, that will not hear of bounds.
    But, ah! such wishes, artless muse, forbear;
        'Tis impotence of frantic love,
    Th' enthusiastic flight of wild despair,
        To hope the Thracian's magic power to prove.   10
Alas! thy slender vein,
    Nor mighty is to move, nor forgetive to feign,
    Impatient of a rein,
Thou canst not in due bounds the struggling measures keep,
—But thou, alas! canst weep—   15
Thou canst—and o'er the melancholy bier
Canst lend the sad solemnity a tear.
Hail! to that wretched corse, untenanted and cold,
And hail the peaceful shade loos'd from its irksome hold.
    Now let me say thou'rt free,   20
        For sure thou paid'st an heavy tax for life,
    While combating for thee,
    Nature and mortality
        Maintain'd a daily strife.
High, on a slender thread thy vital lamp was plac'd,   25
    Upon the mountain's bleakest brow,
To give a nobler light superior was it rais'd,
But more expos'd by eminence it blaz'd;
    For not a whistling wind that blew,
    Nor that drop-descending dew,   30
    Nor a bat that idly flew,
    But half extinguish'd its fair flame—but now
See—hear the storms tempestuous sweep—
Precipitate it falls—it falls—falls lifeless in the deep.
Cease, cease, ye weeping youth,   35
Sincerity's soft sighs, and all the tears of truth.
    And you, his kindred throng, forbear
    Marble memorials to prepare,
And sculptur'd in your breasts his busto wear.

'Twas thus when Israel's legislator dy'd,   40
No fragile mortal honours were supply'd,
    But even a grave denied.
Better than what the pencil's daub can give,
Better than all that Phidias ever wrought,
Is this—that what he taught shall live,   45
    And what he liv'd for ever shall be taught.

Inscriptions on an Æolian Harp.

On one end

Partem aliquam, O venti, divum referatis ad aures!

On one side

Salve, quæ fingis proprio modulamine carmen,
    Salve, Memnoniam vox imitata lyram!
Dulce O divinumque sonas sine pollicis ictu,
    Dives naturæ simplicis, artis inops!
Talia, quæ incultæ dant mellea labra puellæ,   5
    Talia sunt, faciles quæ modulantur aves.

On the other side

Hail heav'nly harp, where Memnon's skill is shewn,
That charm'st the ear with musick all thine own!
Which, tho' untouch'd, canst rapt'rous strains impart,
O rich of genuine nature, free from art!
Such the wild warblings of the sylvan throng,   5
So simply sweet the untaught virgin's song.

On the other end

CHRISTOPHERUS SMART HENRICO BELL Armigero.

---

21 an] a *ST*   31 *omitted, 1791*
INSCRIPTIONS. First published in *ST* (Aug. 1750), i. 311. Text: *ST*. Collated: *GM*
(Apr. 1754), p. 175; *1791*.
2 thine] thy *GM*   5 sylvan] chirping *GM*   CHRISTOPHERUS ... Armigero,
omitted, GM

Audivere, Lyce, Hor. Lib. 4. Ode 13.

At length mother Gunter the Gods hear my pray'r,
    They've heard me at length mother Gunter;
You're grown an old woman, yet romp, drink and swear,
    And ape all the tricks of a bunter.

You invoke with a voice that tremblingly squeaks   5
    Brisk Cupid, tho' sure of denial;
He shuns you, and basks in the blossomy cheeks
    Of Miss Gubbins, that plays on the viol.

He flies by the trunk that is sapless and bare
    To the pliant young branches he comes up;   10
Age has hail'd on thy face, and has snow'd on thy hair,
    And thy green teeth have eat all thy gums up.

Nor thy sack, nor thy necklace, thy watch, nor thy ring,
    Have restor'd thee to youth, or retarded
Those years which old Time, and his friend Vincent Wing, 15
    In the almanack long hath recorded.

Oh! where are those beauties, that bloom, and that grace,
    Those lips that could breath inspiration;
That stole me away from my self, and gave place
    To none other but Nan in the nation?   20

But poor Nan is dead, and has left you her years
    As a legacy, which the good heavens

AUDIVERE, LYCE. MS: *PC*. First known publication: *Magazine of Magazines* (Aug. 1750), i. 122–3. Text: *Magazine of Magazines*. Collated: *PC*; *LM* (Sept. 1750), pp. 421–2; *MB*, ii. 204–5; *Thraliana* (30 Oct. 1781). *Title*. Ode 13. B. 4. To Lyce *PC*
2 They've] They have *PC, Thraliana, MB*   3 You're] You are *MB*   romp, drink] romp & drink *PC*   4 And affect the tricks of a young bunter. *PC*   And affect the young tricks of a bunter. *Thraliana*   5 that] that now *Thraliana*   7 in] on *MB*   8 that] who *PC, MB*   9 by] from *PC, Thraliana*   11 on thy face] in thy face *PC* on your face *Thraliana, MB*   on thy hair] on your hair *Thraliana*   12 And your green teeth have eaten their gums up. *PC, Thraliana, MB*   13 thy watch, nor thy] the watch or the *Thraliana*   14 restor'd] recalled *Thraliana, MB*   16 hath] have *PC, Thraliana, MB*   17 are those beauties] is that beauty *PC, Thraliana, MB*   18 that could] that would *PC* which could *Thraliana*   19 That] Which *Thraliana, MB*   20 none other] no creature *PC, Thraliana, MB*   22 the good heavens] gracious heaven *PC, Thraliana, MB*

Have join'd to your own, and a century clears,
And is just, Mam, the age of your ravens.

Then remains a memento for each jolly soul,   25
Who of Venus's club's a staunch member;
That love, hot as fire, must be burnt to a coal,
As the broomstick concludes in an ember.

To Miss **** one of the Chichester Graces.

Written in Goodwood Gardens, September 1750.

"Ye hills that overlook the plains,
Where wealth and Gothic greatness reigns,
Where Nature's hand by Art is check'd,
And Taste herself is architect;
Ye fallows grey, ye forests brown,   5
And seas that the vast prospect crown,
Ye freight the soul with fancy's store,
Nor can she one idea more!"

I said—when dearest of her kind
(Her form the picture of her mind)   10
Chloris approach'd—The landskip flew!
All nature vanish'd from my view!
She seem'd all Nature to comprize,
Her lips! her beauteous breasts! her eyes!
That rous'd, and yet abash'd desire,   15
With liquid, languid, living fire!

But then—her voice!—how fram'd t' endear!
The music of the Gods to hear!

---

23 Have] Has *PC, Thraliana, MB*   and] which *PC*   that *Thraliana, MB*   24 your
ravens *LM*] you ravens *Mag. of Mags.* a raven *PC, Thraliana, MB*   25 for] to *PC,
Thraliana, MB*   26 Who] That *Thraliana*   27 must] may *Thraliana*
TO MISS ****. First published in *ST* (Now. 1750), ii. 65–6. Text: *1752*. Collated: *ST*;
1791.
7 freight] fright *1791*

Wit that so pierc'd, without offence,
So brac'd by the strong nerves of sense! 20
Pallas with Venus play'd her part,
To rob me of an honest heart;
Prudence and Passion jointly strove,
And Reason was th' ally of Love.

Ah me! thou sweet, delicious maid, 25
From whence shall I sollicit aid?
Hope and despair alike destroy,
One kills with grief, and one with joy.
Celestial Chloris! Nymph divine!
To save me, the dear task be thine. 30
Tho' conquest be the woman's care,
The angel's glory is to spare.

The Widow's Resolution.

A Cantata.

RECITATIVE.

Sylvia, the most contented of her kind,
Remain'd in joyless widowhood resign'd:
In vain to gain her ev'ry shepherd strove,
Each passion ebb'd, but grief, which drowned love.

AIR.

Away, she cry'd, ye swains, be mute, 5
Nor with your odious fruitless suit
   My loyal thoughts controul;
My grief on Resolution's rock
Is built, nor can Temptation shock
   The purpose of my soul. 10

THE WIDOW'S RESOLUTION. First published in *ST* (Suppl. Oct. 1750), i. 399–40.
Text: *ST*. Collated: *GM* (June 1754), p. 285; *1791*.
  1 most contented] gentlest, truest *GM*   3–4 In vain ten thousand lovers sought
relief / Her passions all were melted into grief. *GM*

Tho' blithe Content with jocund air
May ballance comfort against care,
   And make me life sustain;
Yet ev'ry joy has wing'd its flight,
Except that pensive dear delight,   15
   That takes its rise from pain.

RECITATIVE.

She said:—A youth approach'd of manly grace,
A son of Mars and of th' Hibernian race:—
In flow'ry rhetorick he no time employ'd,
He came,—he woo'd,—he wedded and enjoy'd.   20

AIR.

Dido thus of old protested,
   Ne'er to know a second flame;
But alas! she found she jested,
   When the stately Trojan came.

Nature a disguise may borrow,   25
   Yet this maxim true will prove;
Spite of pride, and spite of sorrow,
   She that has an heart must love.

What on earth is so enchanting,
   As beauty weeping on her weeds?   30
Thro' flowing eyes on bosom panting
   What a rapturous ray proceeds?

Since from death there's no returning,
   When th' old lover bids adieu,
All the pomp and farce of mourning   35
   Are but signals for a new.

11–12 Tho' calm content, to fate resign'd, / Has bless'd me with an equal mind,
GM   13 make] bids *GM*   16 That] Which *GM*   29–32 *omitted,*
GM   34 th' old lover bids] old lover's bid *GM*

The Author apologizes to a Lady, for his being a little man.

Natura nusquam magis, quam in minimis tota est. PLIN.
Ολιγον τε φιλον τε. HOM.

Yes, contumelious fair, you scorn
The amorous dwarf, that courts you to his arms,
But ere you leave him quite forlorn,
And to some youth gigantic yield your charms,
Hear him—oh hear him, if you will not try,   5
And let your judgment check th' ambition of your eye.

Say, is it carnage makes the man?
Is to be monstrous really to be great?
Say, is it wise or just to scan
Your lover's worth by quantity, or weight?   10
Ask your mamma and nurse, if it be so;
Nurse and mamma, I ween, shall jointly answer, no.

The less the body to the view,
The soul (like springs in closer durance pent)
Is all exertion, ever new,   15
Unceasing, unextinguish'd, and unspent;
Still pouring forth executive desire,
As bright, as brisk, and lasting, as the vestal fire.

Does thy young bosom pant for fame;
Woud'st thou be of posterity the toast?   20
The poets shall ensure thy name,
Who magnitude of *mind* not *body* boast.
Laurels on bulky bards as rarely grow,
As on the sturdy oak the virtuous misletoe.

Look in the glass, survey that cheek—   25
Where FLORA has with all her roses blush'd;
The shape so tender,—looks so meek,—
The breasts made to be press'd, not to be crush'd—

THE AUTHOR APOLOGIZES. First published in *ST* (Oct. 1750), ii. 26–8. Text: *1752*.
Collated: *ST*; *1791*. *Title.* Ode. The Author apologizes *etc.*, *Second motto omitted, ST*
18 and] as *ST*

Then turn to me,—turn with obliging eyes,
Nor longer Nature's works, in miniature, despise.   30

    Young AMMON did the world subdue,
  Yet had not more external man than I;
    Ah! charmer, should I conquer you,
  With him in fame, as well as size, I'll vie.
Then, scornful nymph, come forth to yonder grove,   35
Where I defy, and challenge, all thy utmost love.

The Decision.

  My Florio, wildest of his sex,
  (Who sure the veriest saint wou'd vex)
    From beauty roves to beauty;
  Yet, tho' abroad the wanton roam,
  Whene'er he deigns to stay at home,   5
    He always minds his duty.

  Something to every charming she,
  In thoughtless prodigality,
    He's granting still and granting,
  To Phyllis that, to Cloe this,   10
  And every madam, every miss;
    Yet I find nothing wanting.

  If haply I his will displease,
  Tempestuous as th' autumnal seas
    He foams and rages ever;   15
  But when he ceases from his ire,
  I cry, such spirit, and such fire,
    Is surely wond'rous clever.

  I ne'er want reason to complain;
  But sweet is pleasure after pain,   20

THE DECISION. First published in *ST* (Oct. 1750), ii. 28–9. Text: *1752*. Collated: *ST*; *LB* [Mar. 1754], iv. 65–6; *1791*.

2 Who] Which *ST*   3 From fair to fair is ranging *LB*   6 He's kinder for his changing. *LB*   7 Tho' something to each charming she *LB*

And every joy grows greater.
Then trust me, damsels, whilst I tell,
I should not like him half so well,
If I cou'd make him better.

The Trial of Chaucer's Ghost.

Sung at Vaux-Hall immediately after the *Recantation*; by Mr. Lowe,
Miss Norris, and Miss Stephenson.

Miss Norris.

Thou traitor, who with the fair-sex hast made war,
Come forward, and hold up your hand at the bar;
By a jury of damsels you now must be try'd,
For having your betters traduc'd and bely'd.

Miss Stephenson.

How could'st thou such base defamation devise,   5
And not have the fear of our sex in your eyes!
Is all decency gone—all good breeding forgot?
Speak, varlet, and plead—Art thou guilty or not?

Mr. Lowe.

Not guilty I plead—but submit to the laws,
And with pleasure I yield to these fair ones my cause;   10
But still, that my trial more just may appear,
Speak *louder* and *faster*, or how should I hear?

Miss Norris.

Hast thou not presum'd to alarm each bright toast,
By the conjuring up of an old English ghost;
And made fusty Chaucer, without a pretext,   15
Snarl posthumous nonsense against the fair-sex?

THE TRIAL. First published in *ST* (Nov. 1750), ii. 70–2. Text: *ST*. Collated: *MB*, i.
41–3.
2 forward] hither *MB*

Miss Stephenson.

Hast thou not presum'd to alarm each bright maid,
With that common-place trash, that each virgin must fade;
And, without fear or wit, most assuming and bold,
Hast dar'd to suggest that we paint and we scold?   20

Mr. Lowe.

For want of experience, when I was but young,
Perhaps, such *strange falshoods* might drop from my tongue;
But when I *recanted* for all my sins past,
I thought I had made you *amends* at the last.

Miss Norris.

I'll promise you, friend, you shall duly be paid   25
For the ample amends that you lately have made;
I find by your shuffling the whole charge is true,
So I bring you in guilty without more ado.

Miss Stephenson.

Ironical wits, like destroyers of game,
When they hide in a bush, 'tis to take surer aim—   30
By his shuffling I find too the whole charge is true,
So I bring him in guilty as willing as you.

Mr. Lowe.

Convicted I stand, and submit to my fate;
And fain would repent, but I find it too late;
If death then, alas! is to be my reward,   35
Why, then I must die—but, by Jove, I'll die hard.

Miss Stephenson.

Since to lengths so unbounded his malice he carried,
To hang him were kindness—

Miss Norris.

No, let, let him be married,
To some musty old maid, that's the dev'l of a shrew,
That will scold him—

38 let, let] let *MB*

Miss Stephenson.

And beat him,

Miss Norris.

And cuckold him too. 40

Both together.

To some musty old maid, that's the dev'l of a shrew,
That will scold him, and beat him, and cuckold him too.

The Bag-wig and the Tobacco-pipe.

A Fable.

A Bag-wig of a jauntee air,
Trick'd up with all a barber's care,
Loaded with powder and perfume,
Hung in a spendthrift's dressing-room;
Close by its side, by chance convey'd,   5
A black Tobacco-pipe was laid;
And with its vapours far and near,
Outstunk the essence of Monsieur;
At which its rage, the thing of hair,
Thus, bristling up, began declare.   10

"Bak'd dirt! that with intrusion rude
Breaks in upon my solitude,

THE BAG-WIG. MS: Bodl. Eng. misc. e. 241, fos. 19ᵛ–20 (*JP*). First published in *MW* (Dec. 1750), i. 120–2. Text: *1752*. Collated: *JP*; *MW*; *MO* (1763), pp. 54–5; *1791*. *Title.* The Tete and The Tobacco Pipe a fable *JP*

     1–6
                A modern tete of jaunty air,
                Wing'd off with all the friseur's care
                Five [feet?] of curls high at the least
                Flank'd round with cushions pins and paste,
                Beside the powder and perfume
                Stunk in Dorinda's dressing room. *JP*

2 up] out *MO*   *5 Close by*] And near *MO*   *7 And*] That *MO*   vapours]
vapour *JP*   *9 At this enraged the house of stuff *JP*   At which enrag'd, the
thing of hair *MO*   *10 declare*] to huff *JP*   *12 Breaks*] Breakst *JP, 1791*

And with thy fetid breath defiles
The air for forty thousand miles—
Avaunt—pollution's in thy touch—   15
O barb'rous English! horrid Dutch!
I cannot bear it—Here, Sue, Nan,
Go call the maid to call the man,
And bid him come without delay,
To take this odious pipe away.   20
Hideous! sure some one smoak'd thee, Friend,
Reversely, at his t'other end.
Oh! what mix'd odours! what a throng
Of salt and sour, of stale and strong!
A most unnatural combination,   25
Enough to mar all perspiration—
Monstrous! again—'twou'd vex a saint!
Susan, the drops—or else I faint!"
The pipe (for 'twas a pipe of soul)
Raising himself upon his bole,   30
In smoke, like oracle of old,
Did thus his sentiments unfold.

"Why, what's the matter, Goodman Swagger,
Thou flaunting French, fantastic bragger?
Whose whole fine speech is (with a pox)   35
Ridiculous and heterodox.
'Twas better for the English nation
Before such scoundrels came in fashion,
When none sought hair in realms unknown,
But every blockhead bore his own.   40
Know, puppy, I'm an English pipe,
Deem'd worthy of each Briton's gripe,
Who, with my cloud-compelling aid
Help our plantations and our trade,

13 with thy fetid] whose offensive *1791*   15 pollution's in] pollution is *JP*
16 Thou barbarous, horrid! english! dutch! *JP*   17 I cannot] Hideous! I cannot
MO   it] thee *JP*   20–9 printed 20, 27, 28, 21, 22, 25, 26, 29 (23–4 *omitted*)
in *MO*   21–8 *omitted, JP*   21 Sure some one hath smoak'd thee, Friend,
MO   22 Reversedly at the other end. *MO*   24 sour, of] sour, and
MW   27 Monstrous! again] Again! Egad *MO*   30 bole] bowl *JP*,
MW, MO   31 oracle] oracles *JP, MO*   35–40 *omitted, JP, which has instead:*
Thy merit's sure not worth one farthing / Thou dirty walking kitchen garden.
40 bore] wore *MO*   43–4 *omitted, MO*

And am, when sober and when mellow, 45
An upright, downright, honest fellow.
Tho' fools, like you, may think me rough,
And scorn me, 'cause I am in buff,
Yet your contempt I glad receive,
'Tis all the fame that you can give: 50
None finery or fopp'ry prize;
But they who've something to disguise;
For simple nature hates abuse,
And Plainness is the dress of Use."

Apollo and Daphne.

An Epigram.

When Phœbus was am'rous, and long'd to be rude,
Miss Daphne cry'd Pish! and ran swift to the wood,
And rather than do such a naughty affair,
She became a fine laurel to deck the God's hair.

The nymph was, no doubt, of a cold constitution; 5
For sure to turn tree was an odd resolution!
Yet in this she behav'd like a true modern spouse,
For she fled from his arms to distinguish his brows.

An Epigram on a Woman who was singing Ballads for Money to bury her Husband.

For her Husband deceas'd Sally chants the sweet lay,
  Why, faith, this is singular sorrow;
But (I doubt) since she *sings* for a dead man to day,
  She'll *cry* for a live one to-morrow.

45 and] or *JP*   49 your] their *MO*   50 fame] praise *MO*   51 None
artifice like yours can prize *JP*   None foppery or finery prize *MO*   52 they]
those *MO*

APOLLO AND DAPHNE. First published in *MW* (Dec. 1750), i. 137. Text: *1752*.
Collated: *MW*; *1791*.

5 was, no doubt,] was to be sure *1791*   6 To be turn'd to a tree was a strange
resolution! *1791*   7 Yet] But *1791*   behav'd like] resembled *1791*

AN EPIGRAM. First published in *MW* (Feb. 1751), i. 229. Text: *MW*. Collated: *1791*.

AN OCCASIONAL
PROLOGUE AND EPILOGUE TO *OTHELLO*.

As it was acted at the Theatre-Royal in Drury-Lane, on Thursday the 7th of March 1751, by persons of distinction for their diversion.

An Occasional Prologue to *Othello*.

While mercenary actors tread the stage,
And hireling scribblers lash or lull the age,
Ours be the task t' instruct, and entertain,
Without one thought of glory or of gain.
Virtue's her own—from no external cause—   5
She gives, and she demands the Self-applause:
Home to her breast she brings the heart-felt bays,
Heedless alike of profit, and of praise.
This now perhaps is wrong—yet this we know,
'Twas sense and truth a century ago: 10
When Britain with transcendent glory crown'd,
For high atchievements, as for wit renown'd;
Cull'd from each growing grace the purest part,
And cropt the flowers from every blooming art.
Our noblest youth, would then embrace the task   15
Of comic humour, or the mystic masque.
'Twas theirs t' incourage worth, and give to bards
What now is spent in *boxing* and in *cards*:
Good sense their pleasure—Virtue still their guide,
And English magnanimity—their pride.   20
Methinks I see with Fancy's magic eye,
The shade of Shakespear, in yon azure sky.
On yon high cloud behold the bard advance,
Piercing all Nature with a single glance:
In various attitudes around him stand   25
The passions, waiting for his dread command.
First kneeling Love before his feet appears,
And musically sighing melts in tears.

OCCASIONAL PROLOGUE AND EPILOGUE. First published separately on 6 Mar. 1751 (*OP*); 2nd and 3rd edns., 9 Mar. 1751 (*OP2*, *OP3*). Text: *OP*. Collated: *OP2*; *OP3*; *MW* (Mar. 1751), i. 271–3; *1752*; *1791*. *Prologue* 12 renown'd;] renown'd *MW*   24 Piercing *MW*, *1752*, *1791*] Grasping *OP*, *OP2*, *OP3*

Near him fell Jealousy with fury burns,
And into storms the amorous breathings turns;   30
Then Hope with heaven-ward look, and Joy draws near,
While palsied Terror trembles in the rear.
  Such Shakespear's train of horror and delight,
And such we hope to introduce to night.
But if, tho' just in thought, we fail in fact,   35
And good intention ripens not to act,
Weigh our design, your censure still defer,
When truth's in view 'tis glorious e'en to err.

Epilogue. Spoken by Desdemona.

True woman to the last—my *peroration*
I come to speak in spight of suffocation;
To shew the present and the age to come,
We may be choak'd, but never can be dumb.
Well now methinks I see you all run out,   5
And haste away to Lady Bragwell's rout;
Each modish sentiment to hear and weigh,
Of those who nothing think, and all things say.
Prudella first in parody begins,
(For Nonsense and Buffoonery are twins)   10
"Can beaux the court for theatres exchange?
I swear by Heaven 'tis strange, 'tis passing strange;
And very whimsical, and mighty dull,
And pitiful, and wond'rous pitiful:
I wish I had not heard it"—Blessed dame!   15
Whene'er she speaks her audience wish the same.
Next Neddy Nicely—"Fye, O fye, good lack,
A nasty man to make his face all black."
Then Lady Stiffneck shews her pious rage,
And wonders we shou'd act—upon a stage.   20
"Why Ma'me", says Coquetilla, "a disgrace?
Merit in any form may shew her face;
In this dull age the male things ought to play,
To teach them what to do, and what to say."
In short, they all with different cavils cram us,   25
And only are unanimous to *damn us.*

31 look *OP3, MW, 1752, 1791*] looks *OP, OP2*

But still there are a fair judicious few,
Who judge unbias'd, and with candour view;
Who value honesty, tho' clad in buff,
And wit, tho' dress'd in an old English ruff.   30
Behold them here—I beaming sense descry,
Shot from the living lustre of each eye.
Such meaning smiles each blooming face adorn,
As deck the pleasure-painted brow of morn;
And shew the person of each matchless fair,   35
Tho' rich to rapture, and above compare,
Is, even with all the skill of heaven design'd,
But an imperfect image of their mind;
While chastity unblemish'd and unbrib'd
Adds a majestick mien that scorns to be describ'd: 40
Such (we will vaunt) and only such as these,
'Tis our ambition, and our fame to please.

A Solemn Dirge,
Sacred to the Memory of His Royal Highness
Frederic Prince of Wales.

As it was Sung by Mr Lowe, Miss Burchell, and others, at Vaux-Hall.

CHORUS.

Hence clamour-loving joy be gone,—
Come sober, serious Muse, come on,
And mournfully majestic flow,
In the dread pomp of regal woe.

First, Mr. Lowe.

Her patron and her father banish'd,   5
   Every orphan muse shall mourn,
Honour's fled, and glory's vanish'd,
   To the death-devoted urn.

Epilogue 31 descry] decry 1791   38 their] her *MW*   41 Such (we will vaunt)] Such, we will vaunt, *OP3, MW, 1752, 1791.* A SOLEMN DIRGE. Text: *A Solemn Dirge,* 1751.

Second, Miss Burchell.

Sing some sad, some plaintive ditty,
    Steept in tears that endless flow;   10
Melancholy notes of pity,
    Notes that mean a world of woe.

Third, Mr. Lowe.

Charity no more shall charm us,
    But shall make a virgin's vow,
And thou, who fondly dreamt to warm us,   15
    Hope, ah! where's thy anchor now?

Fourth, Miss Burchell.

You, his offspring, cease to languish,
    Claim not sorrow for *your* due;
We demand our share of anguish,
    We were all his children too.   20

Fifth, Mr. Lowe.

Music's dumb, and Painting sighing,
    Drops her pencil from her hands,
Sculpture with her sisters dying
    See! herself a statue stands.

Sixth, Miss Burchell.

You, his consort, think on heaven,   25
    Blest, tho' immature he fled,
To him deathless joys are given,
    Weep not for the happy dead.

Seventh, Mr. Lowe.

Weep for us—we tears must borrow
    To express our misery,   30
Private grief to public sorrow,
    Is a riv'let to a sea.

Eighth, Miss Burchell.

Father! Master! Husband! Brother!
　Every blessed tender name!
Ye must dye—till such another,　　　　　　　35
　Call you back to life and fame.

Ninth, Mr. Lowe.

Such another?—we possess him,
　To revive his father's fame,
Honour, Glory, Wisdom, bless him,
　Not another, but the same.　　　　　　　40

Tenth, Miss Burchell.

Yes—He is the kingdom's glory,
　The advice his grandsire gave,
Shall secure his fame in story,
　＊ 'Twas, "Be honest and be brave."

CHORUS.

GEORGE is *Albion*'s consolation,　　　　　45
　The king's life's the common weal:
Every grief that wounds the nation,
　Long may he survive to heal!

Lovely Harriote,

A Crambo Song.

Great Phœbus in his vast career,
Who forms the self-succeeding year,
　Thron'd in his amber chariot,
Sees not an object half so bright,
Nor gives such joy, such life, such light,　　　5
　As dear delicious *Harriote.*

＊ *Be an honest man and be brave, but above all, be an honest man.*

LOVELY HARRIOTE. First datable publication: *MW* (Apr. 1751), ii. 31–3. Text: *MW*.
Collated: *SS* [n.d.] BL Mus. G.308 (36); *1791. Title.* Lovely Harriot, A Crambo Ballad
1791
6 et passim, Harriote] *Harriot 1791*

Pedants of dull phlegmatic turns,
Whose pulse not beats, whose blood not burns,
   Read Malbranche, Boyle, and Marriote,
I scorn their philosophic strife,   10
And study Nature from the life,
   (Where most she shines) in *Harriote*.

When she admits another wooer,
I rave like Shakespear's jealous Moor,
   And am, as ranting Barry hot;   15
True, virtuous, lovely was his dove,
But Virtue, Beauty, Truth, and Love,
   Are other names for *Harriote*.

Ye honest members, who oppose,
And fire both Houses with your prose,   20
   Tho' never can ye carry ought;
You might command the nations sense,
And without bribery convince,
   Had you the voice of *Harriote*.

You of the musick common weal,   25
Who borrow, beg, compose, or steal
   Cantata, air, or ariet;
You'd burn your cumbrous works in score,
And sing, compose, and play no more,
   If once you heard my *Harriote*.   30

Were there a wretch, who durst essay
Such wondrous sweetness to betray,
   I'd call him an Iscariot;
But her ev'n satyrs can't annoy,
So strictly chaste, tho' kindly coy,   35
   Is fair angelic *Harriote*.

While sultans, emperors, and kings
(Mean appetite of earthly things)
   In all the waste of war-riot;

15 ranting] raging *SS, 1791*   19 honest] factious *SS, 1791*   20 fire] tire
1791   24 you] ye *SS, 1791*   31 durst] dar'd *1791*   34 ev'n satyrs] e'en
satire *1791*   35 tho'] but *SS, 1791*

Love's softer duel be my aim,   40
Praise, honour, glory, conquest, fame,
  Are center'd all in *Harriote*.

I swear by Hymen, and the pow'rs
That haunt Love's ever-blushing bow'rs,
  So sweet a nymph to marry ought;   45
Then may I hug her silken yoke,
And give the last, the final stroke,
  T' accomplish lovely *Harriote*.

To Miss H——— ———— with some Musick;

   written by a poet outrageously in love.

Incomparable Harriot, loveliest fair,
That e'er breath'd sweetness on the vital air,
Whose matchless form to us below is giv'n,
As a bright pattern of the rest of heav'n,
Blest with a face, a temper, and a mind   5
To please, to sooth, and to instruct mankind!
Accept these notes—the warbling song begin,
And with your voice compleat the cherubin;
Swift with your iv'ry fingers wake the keys,
And make e'en ———'s desolation please.   10
O wou'd some God but listen to my pray'r,
And waft me to thee thro' the fields of air,
Thrown at thy feet a suppliant I'd reveal,
Each wish, each anguish, that my thoughts conceal,
In whisp'ring kisses I'd confess the whole,   15
And musically murmur out my soul.
May all the pow'rs that on fair virgins wait,
Heap on thee all that's happy, good, and great,
All that of earthly bliss you can conceive,
Your hopes can image, or your faith believe!   20

TO MISS H——— ————. Text: *GM* (June 1754), p. 285.

But vain are pray'rs, and all my wishes vain,
You are already all that I can feign.
With that sweet mind, to that fair body giv'n,
You must be blest—for all are blest in heav'n.
But you from *Time* th' improving form receive,   25
And he, alas! can take as well as give,
But that exalted soul which you enjoy,
Is what nor *Time* can give—nor can destroy.

Ode to Lady Harriot.

To Harriot all accomplish'd fair,
Begin, ye Nine, a grateful air;
Ye Graces join her worth to tell,
And blazon what you can't excell.

Let Flora rifle all her bow'rs,   5
For fragrant shrubs, and painted flow'rs,
And, in her vernal robes array'd,
Present them to the noble maid.

Her breath shall give them new perfume,
Her blushes shall their dyes outbloom;   10
The lilly now no more shall boast
Its whiteness, in her bosom lost.

See yon delicious woodbines rise
By oaks exalted to the skies,
So view in Harriot's matchless mind   15
Humility and greatness join'd.

To paint her dignity and ease,
Form'd to command, and form'd to please,
In wreaths expressive be there wove
The birds of Venus and of Jove.   20

There where th' immortal laurel grows,
And there, where blooms the crimson rose,
Be with this line the chaplet bound,
That beauty is with virtue crown'd.

ODE TO LADY HARRIOT. First published in *GM* (Feb. 1755), p. 86. Text: *1791*.
Collated: *GM*. *Title.* Lady Harriote *GM*

ON THE
IMMENSITY
OF THE
SUPREME BEING.

Once more I dare to rouse the sounding string
The Poet of my God—Awake my glory,
Awake my lute and harp—my self shall wake,
Soon as the stately night-exploding bird
In lively lay sings welcome to the dawn.   5
   List ye! how nature with ten thousand tongues
Begins the grand thanksgiving, Hail, all hail,
Ye tenants of the forest and the field!
My fellow subjects of th' eternal King,
I gladly join your Mattins, and with you   10
Confess his presence, and report his praise.
   O Thou, who or the Lambkin, or the Dove
When offer'd by the lowly, meek, and poor,
Prefer'st to Pride's whole hecatomb, accept
This mean Essay, nor from thy treasure-house   15
Of Glory' immense the Orphan's mite exclude.
   What tho' th' Almighty's regal throne be rais'd
High o'er yon azure Heav'n's exalted dome
By mortal eye unken'd—where East nor West
Nor South, nor blust'ring North has breath to blow; 20
Albeit He there with Angels, and with Saints
Hold conference, and to his radiant host
Ev'n face to face stand visibly confest:
Yet know that nor in Presence or in Pow'r
Shines He less perfect here; 'tis Man's dim eye   25
That makes th' obscurity. He is the same,
Alike in all his Universe the same.
   Whether the mind along the spangled Sky
Measures her pathless walk, studious to view
Thy works of vaster fabrick, where the Planets   30
Weave their harmonious rounds, their march directing

IMMENSITY. First published in 1751. Text: *IM*. Collated: *IM2*; *IM3*; *1761*; *1791*.
16 mite] might *1791*   29 Measures] Measure *1791*

Still faithful, still inconstant to the Sun;
Or where the Comet thro' space infinite
(Tho' whirling worlds oppose and globes of fire)
Darts, like a javelin, to his destin'd goal.   35
Or where in Heav'n above the Heav'n of Heav'ns
Burn brighter Suns, and goodlier Planets roll
With Satellits more glorious—Thou art there.
　　Or whether on the Ocean's boist'rous back
Thou ride triumphant, and with out-stretch'd arm   40
Curb the wild winds and discipline the billows,
The suppliant Sailor finds Thee there, his chief,
His only help—When Thou rebuk'st the storm—
It ceases—and the vessel gently glides
Along the glassy level of the calm.   45
　　Oh! cou'd I search the bosom of the sea,
Down the great depth descending; there thy works
Wou'd also speak thy residence; and there
Wou'd I thy servant, like the still profound,
Astonish'd into silence muse thy praise!   50
Behold! behold! th' unplanted garden round
Of vegetable coral, sea-flow'rs gay,
And shrubs of amber from the pearl-pav'd bottom
Rise richly varied, where the finny race
In blithe security their gambols play: 55
While high above their heads Leviathan
The terror and the glory of the main
His pastime takes with transport, proud to see
The ocean's vast dominion all his own.
　　Hence thro' the genial bowels of the earth   60
Easy may fancy pass; till at thy mines
Gani or Raolconda she arrive,
And from the adamant's imperial blaze
Form weak ideas of her maker's glory.
Next to Pegu or Ceylon let me rove,   65
Where the rich ruby (deem'd by Sages old
Of Sovereign virtue) sparkles ev'n like Sirius
And blushes into flames. Thence will I go
To undermine the treasure-fertile womb
Of the huge Pyrenean, to detect   70

53 shrubs of amber] shrubs, with amber, *1791*

The Agàt and the deep-intrenched gem
Of kindred Jasper—Nature in them both
Delights to play the Mimic on herself;
And in their veins she oft pourtrays the forms
Of leaning hills, of trees erect, and streams   75
Now stealing softly on, now thund'ring down
In desperate cascade with flow'rs and beasts
And all the living landskip of the vale:
In vain thy pencil Claudio, or Poussin,
Or thine, immortal Guido, wou'd essay   80
Such skill to imitate—it is the hand
Of God himself—for God himself is there.
    Hence with the ascending springs let me advance,
Thro' beds of magnets, minerals and spar,
Up to the mountain's summit, there t' indulge   85
Th' ambition of the comprehensive eye,
That dares to call th' Horizon all her own.
Behold the forest, and the expansive verdure
Of yonder level lawn, whose smooth-shorn sod
No object interrupts, unless the oak   90
His lordly head uprears, and branching arms
Extends—Behold in regal solitude,
And pastoral magnificence he stands
So simple! and so great! the under-wood
Of meaner rank an awful distance keep.   95
Yet Thou art there, yet God himself is there
Ev'n on the bush (tho' not as when to Moses
He shone in burning Majesty reveal'd)
Nathless conspicuous in the Linnet's throat
Is his unbounded goodness—Thee her Maker,   100
Thee her Preserver chants she in her song;
While all the emulative vocal tribe
The grateful lesson learn—no other voice
Is heard, no other sound—for in attention
Buried, ev'n babbling *Echo* holds her peace.   105
    Now from the plains, where th' unbounded prospect
Gives liberty her utmost scope to range,
Turn we to yon enclosures, where appears
Chequer'd variety in all her forms,

97 *Moses*] *Moses) 1791*   98 reveal'd)] reveal'd *1791*

187

Which the vague mind attract and still suspend   110
With sweet perplexity. What are yon tow'rs
The work of lab'ring man and clumsy art
Seen with the ring-dove's nest—on that tall beech
Her pensile house the feather'd Artist builds—
The rocking winds molest her not; for see,   115
With such due poize the wond'rous fabrick's hung,
That, like the compass in the bark, it keeps
True to itself and stedfast ev'n in storms.
Thou ideot that asserts, there is no God,
View and be dumb for ever—   120
Go bid Vitruvius or Palladio build
The bee his mansion, or the ant her cave—
Go call Correggio, or let Titian come
To paint the hawthorn's bloom, or teach the cherry
To blush with just vermilion—hence away—   125
Hence ye prophane! for God himself is here.
Vain were th' attempt, and impious to trace
Thro' all his works th' Artificer Divine—
And tho' nor shining sun, nor twinkling star
Bedeck'd the crimson curtains of the sky;   130
Tho' neither vegetable, beast, nor bird
Were extant on the surface of this ball,
Nor lurking gem beneath; tho' the great sea
Slept in profound stagnation, and the air
Had left no thunder to pronounce its maker;   135
Yet man at home, within himself, might find
The Deity immense, and in that frame
So fearfully, so wonderfully made,
See and adore his providence and pow'r—
I see, and I adore—O God most bounteous!   140
O infinite of Goodness and of Glory!
The knee, that thou hast shap'd, shall bend to Thee,
The tongue, which thou hast tun'd, shall chant thy praise,
And, thine own image, the immortal soul,
Shall consecrate herself to Thee for ever.

FINIS.

119 asserts] assertst *1791*   144 thine] thy *1791*

The Miser and the Mouse.

An Epigram from the Greek.

To a mouse says a Miser "my dear Mr. Mouse,
Pray what may you please for to want in my house?"
Says the Mouse "Mr. Miser, pray keep yourself quiet,
You are safe in your person, your purse, and your diet:
A lodging I want, which ev'n you may afford,   5
But none wou'd come here to beg, borrow, or board."

The Physician and the Monkey.

An Epigram.

A lady sent lately to one Doctor Drug,
To come in an instant, and clyster poor Pug—
As the fair one commanded he came at the word,
And did the grand office in tie-wig and sword.

The affair being ended, so sweet and so nice!   5
He held out his hand with—"You know, ma'am, my price."
"Your price," says the lady—"Why Sir, he's your brother,
And doctors must never take fees of each other."

The Force of Innocence.

To Miss C ***.

The blooming damsel, whose defence
Is adamantine innocence,

THE MISER. First published in *ST* (Apr. 1751), ii. 270. Text: *ST*. Collated: *MW* (Apr. 1751), ii. 38; *UV* (Apr. 1756), p. 192; *1791*.
THE PHYSICIAN. First published in *MW* (May 1751), ii. 69. Text: *1752*. Collated: *MW*; *1791*. Title. The Sick Monkey *1791*   7 your brother] a brother *MW*
THE FORCE OF INNOCENCE. First published in *MW* (June 1751), ii. 111–12. Text: *1752*. Collated: *MW*; *MB*, i. 183–4; *LTM* (Feb.–Mar. 1757), ii. 96; *1791*. Title. The Power of Innocence *MW*, *MB*, *LTM*   To Miss C*** *omitted*, *MW*, *MB*, *LTM*

Requires no guardian to attend
Her steps, for modesty's her friend:
Tho' her fair arms are weak to wield   5
The glitt'ring spear, and massy shield;
Yet safe from force and fraud combin'd,
She is an Amazon in mind.

With this artillery she goes,
Not only 'mongst the harmless beaux: 10
But even unhurt and undismay'd,
Views the long sword and fierce cockade.
Tho' all a syren as she talks,
And all a goddess as she walks,
Yet decency each action guides,   15
And wisdom o'er her tongue presides.

Place her in Russia's showery plains,
Where a perpetual winter reigns,
The elements may rave and range,
Yet her fix'd mind will never change.   20
Place her, Ambition, in thy tow'rs,
'Mongst the more dang'rous golden show'rs,
E'en there she'd spurn the venal tribe,
And fold her arms against the bribe.

Leave her defenceless and alone,   25
A pris'ner in the torrid zone,
The sunshine there might vainly vie
With the bright lustre of her eye;
But Phœbus' self, with all his fire,
Cou'd ne'er one unchaste thought inspire.   30
But virtue's path she'd still pursue,
And still, my fair, wou'd copy you.

15 action] motion *MW*   17 showery] frozen *LTM*   32 my] ye *MW, MB,*
LTM

On seeing the Picture of Miss R—— G——n,

Drawn by Mr. Verelst of Threadneedle-street.

Shall candid * Prior, in immortal lays,
Thy ancestor with generous ardour praise;
Who, with his pencil's animating pow'r,
In liveliest dies immortaliz'd a flow'r?
And shall no just, impartial bard be found,   5
Thy more exalted merits to resound;
Who giv'st to beauty a perpetual bloom,
And lively grace, which age shall not consume;
Who mak'st the speaking eyes with meaning roll,
And paint'st at once the body, and the soul?   10

* See Verses on a Flower painted by Verelst.

A Morning Hymn,

For all little good boys and girls: which is
also proper for people of riper years.

O Thou! who lately clos'd my eyes,
    And calm'd my soul to rest,
Now the dull blank of darkness flies,
    Be thank'd, be prais'd, and blest.

And as thou sav'st me in the night   5
    From anguish and dismay,
Lead through the labours of the light,
    And dangers of the day.

Tho' from thy laws I daily swerve,
    Yet still thy mercy grant;   10
Shield me from all that I deserve,
    And grant me all I want.

ON SEEING THE PICTURE. First published in *ST* (June 1751), ii. 354. Text: *ST*.
Collated: *1791*.
A MORNING HYMN. Text: *Lilliputian Mag.* (June 1751), pp. 102–3.

Howe'er she's tempted to descend,
   Keep reason on her throne;
From all men's passions me defend,   15
   But chiefly from my own.

Give me a heart t' assist the poor,
   Ev'n as thy hand bestows;
For thee and man a love most pure,
   And friendship for my foes.   20

This, thro' the merits, death and birth
   Of our bless'd Lord be giv'n;
So shall I compass peace on earth,
   And endless bliss in heav'n.

Epigram of Martial, Lib. VIII, Ep. 69.

Imitated.

No praise the grutching Rosalinda yields
To bards, till they are in th' Elysian fields.
She says that every modern is a dunce,
Forgetting Homer was a modern once.
Die—Die—she cries—and then I'll deign a smile,   5
Your servant, Ma'm,—but 'tis not worth my while.

The Lass with the Golden Locks.

No more of my Harriot, of Polly no more,
Nor all the bright beauties that charm'd me before;
My heart for a slave to gay Venus I've sold,
And barter'd my freedom for ringlets of gold:
I'll throw down my pipe, and neglect all my flocks,   5
And will sing to my lass with the golden locks.
Tho' o'er her white forehead the gilt tresses flow,
Like the rays of the sun on a hillock of snow;

EPIGRAM. Text: *MW* (June 1751), ii. 177.

THE LASS. First published in *VM* [Aug. 1751], iii. 12–13. Text: *1752*. Collated: *VM*; *1791*.

3 heart] self *VM*   5 I'll] I *VM*   6 to] of *VM*

Such painters of old drew the Queen of the Fair,
'Tis the taste of the antients, 'tis classical hair: 10
And tho' witlings may scoff, and tho' raillery mocks,
Yet I'll sing to my lass with the golden locks.

To live and to love, to converse and be free,
Is loving, my charmer, and living with thee:
Away go the hours in kisses and rhime, 15
Spite of all the grave lectures of old father Time;
A fig for his dials, his watches and clocks,
He's best spent with the lass of the golden locks.

Than the swan in the brook she's more dear to my sight,
Her mien is more stately, her breast is more white, 20
Her sweet lips are rubies, all rubies above,
Which are fit for the language of labour of love;
At the park in the mall, at the play in the box,
My lass bears the bell with her golden locks.

Her beautiful eyes, as they roll or they flow, 25
Shall be glad for my joy, or shall weep for my woe;
She shall ease my fond heart, and shall sooth my soft pain,
While thousands of rivals are sighing in vain;
Let them rail at the fruit they can't reach, like the fox,
While I have the lass with the golden locks. 30

The Long Nose'd Fair.

Once on a time I fair Dorinda kiss'd,
Whose *nose* was too distinguish'd to be miss'd:
My dear, says I, I fain wou'd kiss you closer,
But tho' your lips say *Aye*—your nose says *No, Sir*—
The maid was equally to fun inclin'd, 5
And plac'd her lovely lilly-hand BEHIND:
Here, swain, she cry'd, may'st thou securely kiss,
Where there's no nose to interrupt thy bliss.

12 to] of *VM*   13–18 *omitted*, *VM*   21 sweet lips are] lips are like *VM*
22 Which] They *1791*   language or labour] labour or language *VM*
THE LONG-NOSE'D FAIR. First published in *MW* (Sept. 1751), ii. 258–9. Text: *MW*.
Collated: *GM* (Aug. 1754), p. 382; *1791*.
5 maid] nymph *GM*   7 she cry'd, may'st thou] (says she) may you *GM*   kiss,
1791] kiss; *MW*   8 thy] your *GM*

Care and Generosity.

A Fable.

Old Care with Industry and Art,
At length so well had play'd his Part;
He heap'd up such an ample store,
That Av'rice cou'd not sigh for more:
Ten thousand flocks his shepherd told,   5
His coffers overflow'd with Gold;
The land all round him was his own,
With corn his crouded granaries groan.
In short so vast his charge and gain,
That to possess them was a pain;   10
With happiness oppress'd he lies,
And much too prudent to be wise.
Near him there liv'd a beauteous maid,
With all the charms of youth array'd;
Good, amiable, sincere and free,   15
Her name was Generosity.
'Twas hers the largess to bestow
On rich and poor, on friend and foe.
Her doors to all were open'd wide,
The pilgrim there might safe abide: 20
For th' hungry and the thirsty crew,
The bread she broke, the drink she drew;
There Sickness laid her aching head,
And there Distress cou'd find a bed.—
Each hour with an all-bounteous hand,   25
Diffus'd she blessings round the land:
Her gifts and glory lasted long,
And numerous was th' accepting throng.
At length pale Penury seiz'd the dame,
And Fortune fled, and Ruin came,   30
She found her riches at an end,
And that she had not made one friend.—

CARE AND GENEROSITY. First published in *MW* (Sept. 1751), ii. 277–8. Text: *1752*.
Collated: *GM* (Oct. 1751), p. 472; *LM* (Oct. 1751), p. 472; *UV* (June 1756), pp. 282–3;
1791. *Title*. A Fable] A Tale *UV*

All curs'd her for not giving more,
Nor thought on what she'd done before;
She wept, she rav'd, she tore her hair,   35
When lo! to comfort her came Care.—
And cry'd, my dear, if you will join
Your hand in nuptial bonds with mine;
All will be well—you shall have store,
And I be plagu'd with Wealth no more.—   40
Tho' I restrain your bounteous heart,
You still shall act the generous part.—
The Bridal came—great was the feast,
And good the pudding and the priest;
The bride in nine moons brought him forth   45
A little maid of matchless worth:
Her face was mix'd of Care and Glee,
They christen'd her Œconomy;
And styled her fair Discretion's Queen,
The mistress of the golden mean.   50
Now Generosity confin'd,
Is perfect easy in her mind;
She loves to give, yet knows to spare,
Nor wishes to be free from Care.

Fashion and Night.

A Fable

Quam multa prava atque injusta fiunt moribus? TERENT.

Fashion, a motley nymph, of yore
The Cyprian Queen to Proteus bore:
Various herself, in various climes,
She moulds the manners of the times;
And turns in every age and nation,   5
The chequer'd wheel of variegation;

33 All curs'd her] And blam'd her *GM*   40 Wealth] health *GM*   45 moons]
months *GM, LM*   52 Is perfect] Perfectly *1791*   53 She] Still *1791*
FASHION AND NIGHT. First published in *MW* (Jan. 1752), iii. 46–8. Text: *MW*.
Collated: *GM* (Oct. 1754), p. 479; *1791*.

True female, that ne'er knew her will,
Still changing, tho' immortal still.
One day as the inconstant maid
Was careless on her sofa laid,   10
Sick of the sun, and tir'd with light,
She thus invok'd the gloomy night:
"Come—these malignant rays destroy,
Thou skreen of shame, and rise of joy,
Come from thy western ambuscade,   15
Queen of the rout and masquerade;
Nymph, without thee no cards advance,
Without thee halts the loitering dance,
Till you approach, all, all's restraint,
Nor is it safe to game or paint;   20
The belles and beaux thy influence ask,
Put on the universal mask;
Let us invert, in thy disguise,
That odious nature, we despise."
She ceas'd—the sable mantled dame,   25
With slow approach and awful came,
And frowning with sarcastic sneer
Reproach'd the female rioteer:
"That nature you abuse, my fair,
Was I created to repair   30
And contrast with a friendly shade,
The pictures heav'n's rich pencil made,
And with my sleep-alluring dose,
To give laborious art repose;
To make both noise and action cease,   35
The queen of secrecy and peace.
But thou a rebel vile and vain,
Usurp'st my lawful old domain;
My sceptre thou affect'st to sway,
And all the various hours are day;   40
With clamours of unreal joy,
My sister Silence you destroy,
The blazing lamp's unnatural light
My eye balls weary and affright;

31 contrast *GM*, *1791*] contract *MW*

196

But if I am allow'd one shade,   45
Which no intrusive eyes invade,
There all th' atrocious imps of hell,
Theft, murder, and pollution dwell;
Think then how much, thou toy of chance,
Thy praise is like my worth t'inhance;   50
Blind thing, that run'st without a guide,
Thou whirlpool in a rushing tide,
No more my fame with praise pollute,
But damn me into some repute."

Ode on the 26th of January,

Being the Birth-day of a young Lady.

All hail, and welcome, joyous morn,
    Welcome to th' infant year;
Whether smooth calms thy face adorn,
    Or lowring clouds appear:
Tho' billows lash the sounding shore,   5
And tempests thro' the forests roar,
    Sweet Nancy's voice shall sooth the sound;
Tho' darkness shou'd invest the skies,
New day shall beam from Nancy's eyes
    And bless all nature round.   10

Let but those lips their sweets disclose,
    And rich perfumes exhale,
We shall not want the fragrant rose,
    Nor miss the southern gale.
Then loosely to the winds unfold   15
Those radiant locks of burnish'd gold;
    Or on thy bosom let them rove;
His treasure-house there Cupid keeps,
And hoards up, in two snowy heaps,
    His stores of choicest love.   20

46 no *GM, 1791*] do *MW*   50 like my] likely *1791*
ODE ON 26TH JAN. First published in *MV* (June 1753), iii. 129–30. Text: *MW*.
Collated: *1791*.

This day each warmest wish be paid
 To thee, the Muse's pride,
I long to see the blooming maid
 Chang'd to the blushing bride.
So shall thy pleasure and thy praise   25
Increase with the increasing days,
 And present joys exceed the past;
To give and to receive delight,
Shall be thy task both day and night,
 While day and night shall last.   30

Epithalamium.

I.

Descend, descend, ye sweet Aonian maids,
 Leave the Parnassian shades,
 The joyful Hymeneal sing,
  And to a lovelier Belle
Than fiction e'er devis'd, or eloquence can tell,   5
  Your vocal tributes bring.
And you, ye winged choristers, that fly
In all the pensile gardens of the sky,
 Chant thro' th' enamel'd grove,
Stretch from the trembling twigs your little throats, 10
With all the wide variety of artless notes,
  But let each note be love.
 Fragrant Flora, queen of May,
 All bedight with garlands gay,
 Where in the smooth-shaven green   15
The spangled cowslips variegate the scene,
  And the rivulet between,
  Whispers, murmurs, sings,
 As it stops, or falls, or springs;
There spread a sofa of thy softest flowers, 20

EPITHALAMIUM. MS: *PC*. First published in *1752*. Text: *1752*. Collated: *PC*; *1791*.
4 Belle] Fair *1791* 5 Than fiction can devise, or eloquence declare, *1791*
10 twigs] leaves *1791* 11 artless *omitted, PC*

There let the bridegroom stay,
There let him hate the light, and curse the day,
   And dun the tardy hours.

II.

But see the bride—she comes with silent pace,
    Full of majesty and love;   25
    Not with a nobler grace
    Look'd the imperial wife of Jove,
  When erst ineffably she shone
In Venus' irresistible, inchanting zone.
    Phœbus, great god of verse, the nymph observe   30
      Observe her well;
    Then touch each sweetly-trem'lous nerve
      Of thy resounding shell:
    Her like huntress-Dian paint,
    Modest, but without restraint;   35
    From Pallas take her decent pace,
    With Venus sweeten all her face,
    From the Zephyrs steal her sighs,
    From thyself her sun-bright eyes;
    Then baffled, thou shalt see,   40
    That as did Daphne thee,
  Her charms thy genius' force shall fly,
And by no soft persuasive sounds be brib'd
  To come within INVENTION's narrow eye;
But all indignant shun its grasp, and scorn to be describ'd. 45

III.

  Now see the bridegroom rise,
    Oh! how impatient are his joys!
  Bring me zephrys to depaint his voice,
    But light'ning for his eyes.
He leaps, he springs, he flies into her arms,   50
    With joy intense,
    Feeds ev'ry sense,
And sultanates o'er all her charms.

23 dun] blame *1791*   28 ineffably] ineffable *PC*   35 Modest, but] Modest
still *PC*   42 thy genius'] description's *1791*   48 me zephyrs] thunders
PC   zephyrs *1791*   49 But] And *PC*

Oh! had I Virgil's comprehensive strain,
Or sung like Pope, without a word in vain,   55
Then should I hope my numbers might contain,
Egregious nymph, thy boundless happiness,
    How arduous to express!
  Such may it last to all eternity:
    And may thy Lord with thee,   60
  Like two coeval pines in Ida's grove,
  That interweave their verdant arms in love,
  Each mutual office chearfully perform,
  And share alike the sunshine, and the storm;
  And ever, as you flourish hand in hand,   65
  Both shade the shepherd and adorn the land,
  Together with each growing year arise,
Indissolubly link'd, and climb at last the skies.

To my worthy Friend, Mr. T.B. one of the People called Quakers,

written in his Garden, July 1752.

Free from the proud, the pompous, and the vain,
How simply neat and elegantly plain,
Thy rural villa lifts it's modest head,
Where fair convenience reigns in fashion's stead;
Where sober plenty does it's bliss impart,   5
And glads thine hospitable, honest heart,
Mirth without vice, and rapture without noise,
And all the decent, all the manly joys!
Beneath a shadowy bow'r, the summer's pride,
Thy darling * Tullia sitting by my side;   10
Where light and shade in varied scenes display
A contrast sweet, like friendly *Yea* and *Nay*,
My hand, the secretary of my mind,
Left thee these lines upon the *poplar*'s rind.

  * Mr. B——'s daughter.

---

57 Egregious] Engaging *1791*   59 eternity] perennity *PC*
TO MY WORTHY FRIEND. First published in *MW* (June 1753), iii. 149–50. Text:
MW. Collated: *1791*.
4 stead; *1791*] stead? *MW*   10 my side] thy side *1791*   14 Left] Leaves *1791*

The Pig.

In every age, and each profession,
Men err the most by prepossession.
But when the thing is clearly shown,
And fairly stated, fully known,
We soon applaud, what we deride,   5
And penitence succeeds to pride.
  A certain baron, on a day,
Having a mind to show away,
Invited all the wits and wags,
Foot, Massey, Shuter, Yates, and Skeggs,   10
And built a large commodious stage
For the choice spirits of the age.
But, above all, among the rest
There came a genius, who profest
To have a curious trick in store,   15
Which never was perform'd before.
  Thro' all the town this soon got air,
And the whole house was like a fair.
But soon, his entry as he made
Without or prompter or parade,   20
'Twas all expectance, all suspence,
And silence 'gag'd the audience.
He hid his head behind his wig,
And so exact TOOK OFF a pig,
All swore 'twas serious, and no joke,   25
For that, or underneath his cloak
He had conceal'd some grunting elf,
Or was a real hog himself.
A search was made—no pig was found—
With thund'ring claps the seats resound,   30
And pit, and box, and galleries roar
With—O rare! Bravo! and Encore!

THE PIG. First published in *MW* (Aug. 1752), iii. 77–9. Text: *MW*. Collated: *CP6* [6th edn., *c*.1758], p. 128; *MO* (1763), pp. 31–3; *1791*. *Title*. The Pig *1791*   The Critics Mistaken. A Tale *CP6*   *Untitled*, *MW*, *MO*
3 clearly shown] fully known *MO*   4 Fully stated, clearly shewn *MO*
13 among] amongst *MO*   16 Which] That *MO*   20 or prompter] a prompter *1791*   22 'gag'd] gagg'd *1791*   24 And so exact] And with such truth *1791*   26 that, or] doubtless *1791*   31 galleries] gall'ry *MO*
32 Bravo!] Bravo, Bravo, *MO*

Old Roger Grouse, a country clown,
Who yet knew something of the town,
Beheld the mimic and his whim,   35
And on the morrow challeng'd him,
Declaring to each beau and bunter,
That he'd out-grunt th' egregious grunter.
    The morrow came—the crowd was greater—
But prejudice and rank ill-nature   40
Usurp'd the minds of men and wenches,
Who came to hiss, and break the benches.
    The mimic took his usual station,
And squeak'd with general approbation.
Again Encore! Encore! they cry—   45
'Twas quite THE THING—'twas VERY HIGH:
Old Grouse conceal'd, amidst this racket,
A real pig beneath his jacket.—
Then forth he came—and with his nail
He pinch'd the urchin by the tail.   50
The tortur'd pig from out his throat
Produc'd the genuine nat'ral note.
All bellow'd out 'twas very sad!
Sure never stuff was half so bad!
    That like a pig!—each cry'd in scoff,   55
Pshaw! Nonsense! Blockhead! Off! Off! Off!
The mimic was extoll'd, and Grouse
Was hiss'd and catcall'd from the house.—
"Soft ye, a word before I go,"
Quoth honest Hodge—and stooping low,   60
Produc'd the pig, and thus aloud
Bespoke the *stupid*, partial crowd—
BEHOLD AND LEARN FROM THIS POOR CREATURE,
HOW MUCH YOU CRITICS KNOW OF NATURE.

---

39 was] grew *MO*   46 'Twas ... 'twas] 'Tis ... 'tis *MO*   47 this] the
1791   56 Off! Off! Off!] Damn it! Off! *MO*   *Smart's revised version of the fable
appears under the title* The Buffoon and the Country Fellow *in his translation of Phaedrus
(vol. V in this edn.)*

To Miss Kitty Bennet and her Cat Crop.

Full many a heart, that now is free,
May shortly, fair one, beat for thee,
   And court thy pleasing chain;
Then prudent hear a friend's advice,
And learn to guard, by conduct nice,   5
   The conquests you shall gain.

When Tabby Tom your Crop pursues,
How many a bite and many a bruise
   The amorous Swain endures?
Ere yet one favouring glance he catch,   10
What frequent squalls, how many a scratch
   His tenderness procures?

Tho' this, 'tis own'd, be somewhat rude,
And Puss by nature be a prude,
   Yet hence you may improve,   15
By decent pride and dint of scoff
Keep caterwauling coxcombs off,
   And ward th' attacks of love.

Your Crop a mousing when you see
She teaches you œconomy   20
   That makes the pot to boil:
And when she plays with what she gains,
She shews you pleasure springs from pains,
   And mirth's the fruit of toil.

Where's the Poker?—A Tale.

The poker lost, poor Susan storm'd
And all the rites of rage perform'd;

TO MISS KITTY BENNET. First published in *MW* (Aug. 1752), iii. 81–2. Text: *MW*.
Collated: *1791*.
21 That] Which *1791*
WHERE'S THE POKER? First published in *MW* (Aug. 1752), iii. 103–5. Text: *MW*.
Collated: *CP6* [6th edn., *c*.1758], pp. 23–4; *1791*.

As scolding, crying, swearing, sweating,
Abusing, figitting and fretting.
"Nothing but villainy and thieving;   5
Good heavens! What a world we live in!
If I don't find it in the morning,
I'll surely give my master warning.
He'd better far shut up his doors
Than keep such good-for-nothing whores,   10
For wheresoe'er their trade they drive,
We *vartous* bodies cannot thrive."
Well may poor Susan grunt and groan;
Misfortunes never come alone,
But tread each other's heels in throngs,   15
For the next day she lost the tongs:
The salt-box, cullender and grate,
Soon shar'd the same untimely fate.
In vain the vails and wages spent
On new ones—for the new ones went.   20
They'd been (she swore) some dev'l or witch in
To rob and plunder all the kitchin.
One night she to her chamber crept
(Where for a month she had not slept,
Her master being to her seeming   25
A better playfellow than dreaming)
Curse on the author of these wrongs!
In her own bed she found the tongs.
(Hang Thomas for an idle joker!)
And there, good lack! she found the poker,   30
With salt-box, pepper-box and kettle,
And all the culinary mettle.—
Be warn'd, ye fair, by Susan's crosses,
Keep chaste, and guard yourself from losses;
For if young girls delight in kissing,   35
No wonder, that the poker's missing.

6 in! CP6] in? MW, 1791   12 vartous] vartuous 1791   17 grate] pot
1791   18 fate] lot 1791   21 They'd] There'd CP6, 1791   22 and] or
1791   25-6 omitted, CP6   30 In her own bed she found the poker;
1791   32 And] With 1791

ON THE
OMNISCIENCE
OF THE
SUPREME BEING.

Arise, divine Urania, with new strains
To hymn thy God, and thou, immortal Fame,
Arise, and blow thy everlasting trump.
All glory to th' Omniscient, and praise,
And pow'r, and domination in the height!   5
And thou, cherubic Gratitude, whose voice
To pious ears sounds silverly so sweet,
Come with thy precious incense, bring thy gifts,
And with thy choicest stores the altar crown.
Thou too, my Heart, whom he, and he alone   10
Who all things knows, can know, with love replete,
Regenerate, and pure, pour all thyself
A living sacrifice before his throne:
And may th'eternal, high mysterious tree,
That in the center of the arched Heav'ns   15
Bears the rich fruit of Knowledge, with some branch
Stoop to my humble reach, and bless my toil!
    When in my mother's womb conceal'd I lay
A senseless embryo, then my soul thou knewst,
Knewst all her future workings, every thought,   20
And every faint idea yet unform'd.
When up the imperceptible ascent
Of growing years, led by thy hand, I rose,
Perception's gradual light, that ever dawns
Insensibly to day, thou didst vouchsafe,   25
And taught me by that reason thou inspir'dst,
That what of knowledge in my mind was low,
Imperfect, incorrect—in Thee is wondrous,
Uncircumscrib'd, unsearchably profound,
And estimable solely by itself.   30
    What is that secret pow'r, that guides the brutes,

on the omniscience. First published in 1752. Text: O. Collated: O2; 1761; 1791.
1 Arise, divine Urania, O2] Arise divine Urania O
10 Heart O2] heart O   28, 32 Thee O2] thee O

Which Ignorance calls instinct? 'Tis from Thee,
It is the operation of thine hands
Immediate, instantaneous; 'tis thy wisdom,
That glorious shines transparent thro' thy works.   35
Who taught the Pye, or who forwarn'd the Jay
To shun the deadly nightshade? tho' the cherry
Boasts not a glossier hue, nor does the plumb
Lure with more seeming sweets the amorous eye,
Yet will not the sagacious birds, decoy'd   40
By fair appearance, touch the noxious fruit.
They know to taste is fatal, whence alarm'd
Swift on the winnowing winds they work their way.
Go to, proud reas'ner philosophic Man,
Hast thou such prudence, thou such knowledge?—No.   45
Full many a race has fell into the snare
Of meretricious looks, of pleasing surface,
And oft in desart isles the famish'd pilgrim
By forms of fruit, and luscious taste beguil'd,
Like his forefather Adam, eats and dies.   50
For why? his wisdom on the leaden feet
Of slow experience, dully tedious, creeps,
And comes, like vengeance, after long delay.
    The venerable Sage, that nightly trims
The learned lamp, t'investigate the pow'rs   55
Of plants medicinal, the earth, the air,
And the dark regions of the fossil world,
Grows old in following, what he ne'er shall find;
Studious in vain! till haply, at the last
He spies a mist, then shapes it into mountains,   60
And baseless fabrics from conjecture builds.
While the domestic animal, that guards
At midnight hours his threshold, if oppress'd
By sudden sickness, at his master's feet
Begs not that aid his services might claim,   65
But is his own physician, knows the case,
And from th'emetic herbage works his cure.
Hark from afar the * feather'd matron screams,

* The Hen Turkey.

49 beguil'd, *O2*] beguil'd; *O*   60 mountains, *O2*] mountains *O*

And all her brood alarms, the docile crew
Accept the signal one and all, expert　　　　　　70
In th' art of nature and unlearn'd deceit:
Along the sod, in counterfeited death,
Mute, motionless they lie; full well appriz'd
That the rapacious adversary's near.
But who inform'd her of th' approaching danger,　　75
Who taught the cautious mother, that the hawk
Was hatcht her foe, and liv'd by her destruction?
Her own prophetic soul is active in her,
And more than human providence her guard.

　　When Philomela, ere the cold domain　　　　80
Of cripled winter gins t'advance, prepares
Her annual flight, and in some poplar shade
Takes her melodious leave, who then's her pilot?
Who points her passage thro' the pathless void
To realms from us remote, to us unknown?　　　85
Her science is the science of her God.
Not the magnetic index to the North
E'er ascertains her course, nor buoy, nor beacon.
She heav'n-taught voyager, that sails in air,
Courts nor coy West nor East, but instant knows　90
What * Newton, or not sought, or sought in vain.

　　Illustrious name, irrefragable proof
Of man's vast genius, and the soaring soul!
Yet what wert thou to him, who knew his works,
Before creation form'd them, long before　　　95
He measur'd in the hollow of his hand
Th' exulting ocean, and the highest Heav'ns
He comprehended with a span, and weigh'd
The mighty mountains in his golden Scales:
Who shone supreme, who was himself the light,　100
Ere yet Refraction learn'd her skill to paint,
And bend athwart the clouds her beauteous bow.

　　When Knowledge at her father's dread command
Resign'd to Israel's king her golden key,
Oh to have join'd the frequent auditors　　　105

* The Longitude.

In wonder and delight, that whilom heard
Great Solomon descanting on the brutes.
Oh how sublimely glorious to apply
To God's own honour, and good will to man,
That wisdom he alone of men possess'd   110
In plenitude so rich, and scope so rare.
How did he rouse the pamper'd silken sons
Of bloated ease, by placing to their view
The sage industrous ant, the wisest insect,
And best œconomist of all the field!   115
Tho' she presumes not by the solar orb
To measure times and seasons, nor consults
Chaldean calculations, for a guide;
Yet conscious that December's on the march
Pointing with icie hand to want and woe,   120
She waits his dire approach, and undismay'd
Receives him as a welcome guest, prepar'd
Against the churlish winter's fiercest blow.
For when, as yet the favourable Sun
Gives to the genial earth th' enlivening ray,   125
Not the poor suffering slave, that hourly toils
To rive the groaning earth for ill-sought gold,
Endures such trouble, such fatigure, as she;
While all her subterraneous avenues,
And storm-proof cells with management most meet   130
And unexampled housewifry she forms:
Then to the field she hies, and on her back,
Burden immense! she bears the cumbrous corn.
Then many a weary step, and many a strain,
And many a grievous groan subdued, at length   135
Up the huge hill she hardly heaves it home:
Nor rests she here her providence, but nips
With subtle tooth the grain, lest from her garner
In mischievous fertility it steal,
And back to day-light vegetate its way.   140
Go to the Ant, thou sluggard, learn to live,
And by her wary ways reform thine own.
But, if thy deaden'd sense, and listless thought
More glaring evidence demand; behold,

132 back, *O2*] back *O*

208

Where yon pellucid populous hive presents   145
A yet uncopied model to the world!
There Machiavel in the reflecting glass
May read himself a fool. The Chemist there
May with astonishment invidious view
His toils outdone by each plebeian Bee,   150
Who, at the royal mandate, on the wing
From various herbs, and from discordant flow'rs
A perfect harmony of sweets compounds.
    Avaunt Conceit, Ambition take thy flight
Back to the Prince of vanity and air!   155
Oh 'tis a thought of energy most piercing;
Form'd to make pride grow humble; form'd to force
Its weight on the reluctant mind, and give her
A true but irksome image of herself.
Woful vicissitude! when Man, fall'n Man,   160
Who first from Heav'n from gracious God himself
Learn'd knowledge of the Brutes, must know by Brutes
Instructed and reproach'd, the scale of being;
By slow degrees from lowly steps ascend,
And trace Omniscience upwards to its spring!   165
Yet murmur not, but praise—for tho' we stand
Of many a Godlike privilege amerc'd
By Adam's dire transgression, tho' no more
Is Paradise our home, but o'er the portal
Hangs in terrific pomp the burning blade;   170
Still with ten thousand beauties blooms the Earth
With pleasures populous, and with riches crown'd.
Still is there scope for wonder and for love
Ev'n to their last exertion—show'rs of blessings
Far more than human virtue can deserve,   175
Or hope expect, or gratitude return.
Then O ye People, O ye Sons of men,
Whatever be the colour of your lives,
Whatever portion of itself his Wisdom
Shall deign t'allow, still patiently abide,   180
And praise him more and more; nor cease to chant
ALL GLORY TO TH' OMNISCIENT, AND PRAISE,

161 Heav'n ... himself] Heav'n, ... himself, *1791*   180 abide, *O2*] abide *O*
182 OMNISCIENT, *O2*] OMNISCIENT *O*

AND POW'R, AND DOMINATION IN THE HEIGHT!
And thou, cherubic Gratitude, whose voice
To pious ears sounds silverly so sweet,   *185*
Come with thy precious incense, bring thy gifts,
And with thy choicest stores the altar crown.

ΤΩ ΘΕΩ ΔΟΞΑ.

183 POW'R, *O2*] POW'R *O*   184 *thou, O2*] *thou O*

A New Ballad.

When Arthur fill'd the British throne-*a*,
Comedians were a name unknown-*a*;
Punch's train they did admire-*a*,
Pleas'd enough with wood and wire-*a*;
    Paw, Paw Paw, &c.
    Doodle, Doodle, Doo, &c.

But when Shakespear charm'd the age-*a*,   5
The sire and sov'reign of the stage-*a*;
Then the English had discernment,
And good writers met preferment.
    Paw, Paw, Paw, &c.

But now your Shakespears and your Johnsons
Must give way to noise and nonsense;   10
Sense and taste no more are friends-*a*;
The palm from man to beasts descends-*a*,
    Paw, Paw, Paw, &c.

'Stead of tragi-comic choice tricks,
'Tis "*Walk in and see the ostrich*;"
Modern wits must give the wall-*a*   15
To the tyger from Bengal-*a*.
    Paw, Paw, Paw, &c.

Now Harlequin full well contents-*a*
The motley race he represents-*a*;
Now all genius must withdraw, Sir,
And give place to wire and straw, Sir.   20
    Paw, Paw, Paw, &c.

Manly judgement, wit and reason,
To our critics ears are treason,
And Rich's lion fights with Garrick,
As Dun Cow with Guy at Warwick.
    Paw, Paw, Paw, &c.

A NEW BALLAD. First published in *GJ*, No. 14 (20 Jan. 1753). Text: *GJ*. Collated: *The True Briton* (25 Jan. 1753), v. 64–5 (*TB*).
19 But he himself must soon withdraw, Sir! *TB*

Thus life's a stage; your aged boys, Sir,
Cry once more for children's toys, Sir;
The present is, as was the past-*a*;
Babes at first, and babes at last-*a*.
    Paw, Paw, Paw, &c.

THE

HILLIAD:

AN

EPIC POEM.

By C. SMART, A. M.
Fellow of Pembroke-Hall, in the University of Cambridge.

To which are prefixed,

Copious PROLEGOMENA and NOTES VARIORUM.

Particularly,

Those of QUINBUS FLESTRIN Esq; and MARTINUS MACULAR-
IUS, M. D. Acad. Reg. Scient. Burdig. &c. Soc.

————*Pallas te hoc vulnere, Pallas*
Immolat, et pænam scelerato ex sanguine sumit.

VIRG.

LONDON:

Sold by J. NEWBERY, in St. Paul's Church-Yard; and M. COOPER,
in Pater-Noster-Row.
MDCCLIII.

A
LETTER

TO A

FRIEND at the University of CAMBRIDGE.

DEAR * * * * *

I am now to acknowledge several letters, which I lately
received from you, without any return on my part. As I have
been very much hurried of late with a multiplicity of affairs, I
must beg you will not only be kind enough, to overlook my past
omission, but to indulge me for a little time longer. As soon as I
am master of sufficient leisure, I will give you my sentiments
without reserve, concerning the affair, about which you have
thought proper to consult me; for the present I desire you will
consider this as a receipt for your many favours, or a promis-
sory note to discharge my debt of friendship as soon as possible.

The design and colouring of a poem, such as you have
planned, are not to be executed in a hurry, but with slow and
careful touches, which will give that finishing to your piece,
remarkable in every thing that comes from your hand, and
which I could wish the precipitancy of my temper would
permit me to aim at upon all occasions. I long to see you take a
new flight to the regions of fame, not upon unequal wings, that
sometimes rise to a degree of elevation, and then fall again, but
with an uniform tenour, like the bird in VIRGIL,

Radit iter liquidum, celeres neque commovet alas.

I have been now for about three weeks in this scene of smoke
and dust, and I think the republic of letters seems to be
lamentably upon the decline in this metropolis. Attorneys

clerks, and raw unexperienced boys, are the chief critics we have at present. With a supercilious look and peremptory voice, which they have caught from a few of their oracles, as dark and ignorant as themselves, these striplings take upon them to decide upon fable, character, language and sentiment.

Nescis, heu nescis dominæ fastidia Romæ;
Crede mihi nimium martia turba sapit.

With regard to writers, the town swarms with them, and the aim of them all is pretty much the same, viz. to elevate and surprize, as Mr. Bays says. At the head of these still continues the INSPECTOR. As we frequently laughed together concerning this writer, when you were last in town, I need not here give you a description of his parts and genius. I remember you express'd great amazement at the reception his essays seemed to meet with in all our coffee-houses; but you must consider, that, there are artifices to gain success, as well as merit to deserve it. The former of these his INSPECTORSHIP is eminently possessed of, and sooner than fail, he will not hesitate, in order to make himself talked of at any rate, to become most glaringly ridiculous. This answers the purpose of the booksellers, as well perhaps as Attic wit, and hence it results that they are willing to continue him in their pay.

In the packet, which I have sent to you by the stage coach, you will find a paper called the IMPERTINENT, written by himself. In this curious piece he has not stopped at abusing his own dear person, which is the only subject he has not handled with his usual malice, and the rest of it is made a vehicle for invective against Mr. Fielding and me. It was ushered into the world in a pompous manner, as if intended to be continued, but no second number was ever published, and to shew you a further instance of his fallacy, he thence took occasion to triumph over a pretender to essay-writing, which, he would fain insinuate, cannot be executed by any one but himself.

This unfair dealing, so unworthy a man, who aspires to be a member of the serene republic of letters, induced me to wave, for a time, the design you know I was engaged in, in order to bestow a few lines upon this scribler, who in my eyes is a disgrace to literature. In the first heat of my poetic fury, I formed the idea of another DUNCIAD, which I intended to call after the name of my hero, THE HILLIAD. The first book of it you will receive, among others things, by the coach, and I shall be glad to be favoured with your opinion of it.

If it conduces to your entertainment, I shall have gained my end; for though I have received such provocation from this man, I believe I shall never carry it any further. I really find some involuntary sensations of compassion for him, and I cannot help thinking, that, if he could keep within the bounds of decency and good manners, he would be a rare instance of what may be done by a fluency of periods, without genius, sense, or meaning. Though I am persuaded he is quite incorrigible, I am still reluctant to publish that piece, for I would rather be recommended to posterity by the elegant and amiable muses, than by the satyric sister, politely called by an eminent author, *the least engaging of the Nine.*—

On this account I shall proceed no further 'till you have favoured me with your opinion, by which I will absolutely determine myself. I hope therefore you will peruse it as soon as you can with convenience, and return it to me by the stage. You may shew it to Jack * * * * * *, and to Mr. * * * *.

I am, with great sincerity,

Dear * * * * *,

London, 15 December, 1752   Your most obedient

humble servant,

CHRISTOPHER SMART

DEAR SMART,

The perusal of your poem has given me so much pleasure, that I cannot postpone thanking you for it, by the first opportunity that has offered. I have read it to the persons you desired I should, and they approve the design in the highest manner. I cannot conceive what should make you hesitate a moment about the publication, and to be free with you, you must not by any means suppress it. When I say this, I must observe, that I should be glad to see you better employed, than in the dissection of an insect; but since the work should be done by some body, and since you have made such a progress, I must take the liberty to insist, that you will not drop this undertaking.

To speak in plain terms; I look upon it to be indispensably incumbent on you to bring the miscreant to poetic justice; it is what you owe to the cause of learning in general, to your Alma mater this university, and, let me add, it is what you owe to yourself. The world will absolve you from any imputation of ill-nature, when it is considered that the pen is drawn in defence of your own character. Give me leave upon this occasion, to quote a passage from the SPECTATOR, which I think pertinent to the present subject. "Every honest man ought to look upon himself as in a natural state of war with the libeller and lampooner, and to annoy them, where ever they fall in his way. This is but retaliating upon them, and treating them as they treat others."

Thus thought the polite Mr. Addison in a case where he was not immediately concerned; and can you doubt what to do, when personally attacked? As soon as the hissing of the snake is heard, some means should be devised to crush him. The advice of VIRGIL is, — "Cape saxa manu, cape robora pastor."

I can tell you that your friends here expect this of you, and we are all unanimous in thinking, that a man who has the honour of belonging to this learned university, and to whom the prize, for displaying with a masterly hand the attributes of his maker, has been adjudged for three years successively, should not on any account suffer himself to be trifled with, by so frigid and empty a writer. I would have you reflect that you launched into the world with many circumstances, that raised a general expectation of you, and the early approbation of such a genius as Mr. POPE, for your elegant version of his ode, made you considered as one, who might hereafter make a figure in the literary world; and let me recommend to you, not to let the laurel, yet green upon your brow, be torn off by the prophane hands of an unhallowed hireling. This, I think, as is observed already, you owe to yourself, and to that university which has distinguished you with honour.

Besides the motives of retaliation, which I have urged for the publication of your poem, I cannot help considering this matter in a moral light, and I must avow, that in my eyes it appears an action of very great merit. If to pull off the mask from an imposter, and detect him in his native colours to the view of a long-deluded public, may be looked upon as a service to mankind (as it certainly is) a better opportunity never can offer itself.

In my opinion the cause of literature is in imminent danger of a total degeneracy, should this writer's diurnal productions meet with further encouragement. Without straining hard for it, I can perceive a corruption of taste diffusing itself, throughout the cities of London and Westminster. For a clear vein of thinking, easy natural expression, and an intelligible stile, this pretender has substituted brisk question and answer, pert, unmeaning periods, ungrammatical construction, unnatural metaphors, with a profusion of epithets, inconsistent for the most part with the real or figurative meaning of his words, and, in short, all the masculine beauties of stile, are likely to be banished from among us by the continuation of his papers for almost two years together.

Now, sir, I submit it to you, whether this may not lead on a total depravity of sense and taste. Should the more sober at our coffee-houses be dazzled with false embellishments; should boys admire this unnatural flourishing, I do not in the least question, but the rising generation will be totally infected with this strange motley stile, and thus antithesis and point will be the prevailing turn of the nation.

It is to prevent a contagion of this sort, that HORACE took the pen in hand: for this Quintilian favoured the world with his excellent work. The ingenious authors of France have carefully attended to this point. Truth, they insisted, is the very foundation of fine writing, and that no thought can be beautiful, which is not just, was their constant lesson. To enforce this, and to preserve a manly way of thinking BOILEAU lashed the scriblers of his time, and in our own country the Spectators, Tatlers, and Guardians have laboured for this end. To this we owe the Bathos, in which we find exposed, with the most delicate traits of satire, all false figures in writing; and finally to this we owe the Dunciad of Mr. POPE.

These instances, dear Smart, are sufficient to justify your proceeding, and let me tell you, that the cultivation of taste is a point of more moment than perhaps may appear at first sight.

In the course of my reading, I have observed that a corruption in morals has always attended a decline of letters. Of this Mr. POPE seems to be sensible, and, hence we find in the conclusion of his Dunciad, the general progress of dulness over the land is the final coup de grace to every thing decent, every thing laudable, elegant and polite.

> Religion blushing veils her sacred fires,
> And unawares morality expires.
> Nor public fame, nor private dares to shine,
> Nor human spark is left, nor glympse divine.
> Lo! thy dread empire, CHAOS! is restored,
> Light dies before thy uncreating word.
> Thy hand great ANARCH lets the curtain fall,
> And universal darkness buries all.

I am aware that you may answer to what has been premised, that the man is not of consequence enough for all this, and you may observe to me, that at first setting out, I myself called him by the figurative and typical appellation of an insect. But if an insect gets into the sunshine, and there blazes, shines and buzzes to the annoyance of those, who may be basking in the beams, it is time for the muses wing to brush the thing away. In plain English, the rapidity, with which this writer went on in his progress, was so astonishing, that I really looked upon him to be reserved for the great instrument of dulness in the completion of her work, which certainly must be accomplished, unless a speedy stop be put to that inundation of nonsense and immorality with which he has overwhelmed the nation.

I have mentioned immorality, nor will I retract the word. Has he not attacked, maliciously attacked the reputations of many gentlemen, to whom the world has been greatly obliged?—He did not brandish his goose-quill for any length of time, before he discharged a torrent of abuse upon the reverend Mr. Francis, whose amiable character, and valuable translation of HORACE, have endeared him both to those, who are, and those who are not acquainted with him. Even beauty and innocence were no safe-guards against his calumny, and the soft-eyed virgin was by him cruelly obliged to shed the tender tear.

Upon the commencement of the Covent-Garden Journal, Mr. Fielding declared an humourous war against this writer, which was intended to be carried with an amicable pleasantry, in order to contribute to the entertainment of the town. It is recent in every bodies memory, how the INSPECTOR behaved upon that occasion. Conscious that there was not an atom of humour in his composition, he had recourse to his usual shifts, and instantly disclosed a private conversation; by which he reduced himself to the alternative mentioned by Mr. POPE; "and if he lies not, must at least betray". Through all Mr. Fielding's inimitable comic Romances, we perceive no such thing as personal malice, no private character dragged into light; but every stroke is copied from the volume which nature has unfolded to him; every scene of life is by him represented in its natural colours, and every species of folly or humour is ridiculed with the most exquisite touches. A genius like this is perhaps more useful to mankind, than any class of writers; he serves to dispel all gloom from our minds, to work off our ill-humours by the gay sensations excited by a well directed pleasantry, and in a vein of mirth he leads his readers into the knowledge of human nature; the most useful and pleasing science we can apply to. And yet so deserving an author has been most grossly treated by this wild Essayist, and, not to multiply instances, has he not attempted to raise tumults and divisions in our theatres, contrary to all decency and common sense, and contrary to the practice of all polite writers, whose chief aim has ever been to cherish harmony and good manners, and to diffuse through all ranks of people a just refinement of taste in all our public entertainments?

These considerations, dear Sir, prompt you to the blow, and will justify it when given. I believe, I may venture to add, never had poet so inviting a subject for satire; POPE himself had not so good an hero for his DUNCIAD. The first Worthy who sat in that throne, viz. Lewis Theobald of dull memory, employed himself in matters of some utility, and, upon his being dethroned, the person, who succeeded, was one, who formerly had some scattered rays of light; and in most of his comedies, though whimsical and extravagant, there are many strokes of drollery; not to mention that the Careless Husband is a finished piece.

But in the Hero of the Hilliad all the requisites seem to be united, without one single exception. You remember, no doubt, that in the dissertation prefixed to the Dunciad the efficient qualities of an hero for the little epic are mentioned to be vanity, impudence and debauchery. These accomplishments, I apprehend, are glaring in the person you have fixed upon. As a single and notable instance of the two first, has he not upon all occasions joined himself to some celebrated name, such as the Right Honourable the Earl of Orrery, or some other such exalted character? I have frequently diverted myself by comparing this proceeding to the cruelty of a tyrant, who used to tie a living person to a dead carcass; and as to your hero's debauchery, there are, I am told, many pleasant instances of it.

Add to these several subordinate qualifications; such as foppery, a surprizing alacrity to get into scrapes, with a notable facility of extricating himself, an amazing turn for politicks, a wonderful knowledge of herbs, minerals and plants, and to crown all, a comfortable share of gentle dulness. This gentle dulness is not that impenetrable stupidity, which is remarkable in some men, but it is known by that countenance, which Dr. Garth calls, "demurely meek, insipidly serene". It is known by a brisk volubility of speech, a lively manner of saying nothing through an entire paper, and upon all occasions by a conscious simper, short insertions of witty remarks, the frequent exclamation of wonder, the self-applauding chit-chat, and the pleasant repartee.

Upon the whole, dear Smart, I cannot conceive what doubt can remain in your mind about the publication; it is conferring on him that ridicule, which his life, character, and actions deserve. I shall be in town in less than a fortnight, when I shall bring your poem with me, and if you will give me leave, I will help you to some notes, which I think will illustrate many passages.

———Satyrarum ego, (ni pudet illas)
Adjutor, &c.   JUV.

I am, dear Smart,

Cambridge, 21st Dec. 1752.   Yours very sincerely,
                                          * * * * * * *

PROLEGOMENA

TO THE

HILLIAD.

EXTRACT

FROM A

PAPER called the IMPERTINENT.

Published Aug. 13, 1752.

Written by Dr. HILL.

There are men who write because they have wit; there are those who write because they are hungry: There are some of the modern authors who have a constant fund of both these causes; and there are who will write, although they are not instigated either by the one or by the other. The first are all spirit; the second are all earth; the third disclose more life, or more vapidity, as the one or the other cause prevails; and for the last, having neither the one nor the other principle for the cause, they shew neither the one nor the other character in the effect: But begin, continue, and end; as if they had neither begun, continued, nor ended at all.

Of the first one sees an instance in Fielding; Smart with equal right stands foremost among the second; of the third, the mingled wreath belongs to Hill; and for the fourth, none who has been curious enough to read the college oration in honour of physic, and in defamation of quacks and quackery, will dare to dispute the pre-eminence with Sir William Brown.

Those of the first rank are the most capricious, and the most lazy of all animals: the monkey genius would rarely exert itself, if even idleness innate did not give way to the superior love of mischief. The ass that characters the second is as laborious, and as dull, and as indefatigable as he is empty: Stranger to the caprice of genius, he knows none of its risings or its fall; but he wears a ridiculous comicalness of aspect, that makes people smile when they see him at a distance: His mouth opens, because he must be fed; and the world often joins with the philosopher in laughing at the insensibility and obstinacy that makes him prick his lips with thistles.

EXTRACT

FROM THE

GENTLEMAN's MAGAZINE,

For August 1752. Page 387

The Impertinent, printed [in the manner of the Rambler,] for J. Bouquet, price two-pence. To have been continued every Thursday. Of this piece, Dr. Hill, in his Inspector of the Tuesday following, says. "Of all the periodical pieces set up in vain during the last eighteen months, I shall mention only the most pert, the most pretending, and short lived of any. I have in vain sent to Mr. Bouquet for the second number of the Impertinent. There must have been indignation superior even to curiosity, in the sentence passed on this assuming piece, and the public deserves applause of the highest kind, for having crushed in the bud so threatening a mischief. It will be in vain to accuse the town either of patronizing dullness, or ill-nature, while this instance can be produced, in which a load of personal satyr could not procure purchasers enough to promote a second number. It will not be easy to say too much in favour of that candour, which has rejected, and despised a piece that cruelly and unjustly attack'd Mr. Smart, &c."—This character of the Impertinent, and an account of its reception, however quaint, and inaccurate the expressions, as they are indisputably just, might be thought a sufficient gratification of public curiosity; but there is yet an interesting anecdote behind with which "the world has a right to be acquainted."—The man who thus resents the cruel treatment of Mr. Smart in the Inspector, and he who thus cruelly treated him in the Impertinent, is known to be the same. The worthy and ingenious Dr. Hill, who every day obliges the world with a moral, or a philosophical essay; and on Saturday with a lecture on religion, is the scribler who published the load of personal abuse, that excited the indignation of the public, and produced the most pert, assuming, and short lived of all the periodical pieces which have lately appeared; and in this abuse and pertness, he would probably have persisted till the work had swelled to a volume; but that the contempt, and indignation with which his attempt was treated, discouraged him from risking the necessary expense of paper and printing, and induced him to join in the public censure, as a detected felon, when he is pursued, cries out stop thief, and hopes to escape in the croud that follows him.

AN

Accurate and Impartial STATE

OF THE

ACCOUNT

BETWEEN

Mr. SMART and Dr. HILL.

Mr. SMART Debtor to Dr. HILL,
for his PRAISES.

Saturday, March 9th, 1751. Inspector, Number VI. at the Close of the Essay.

Mr. J. D—— spoke an excellent * prologue, and this lady an epilogue, hardly at all inferior to it; the least we can say in regard to this part of the performance, is, that they both deserved all the applause they received on their delivering them.

Tuesday, April 14th, 1752. Inspector Number 350.

We find Mr. Smart, a person of real and of great genius, in a late poem on one of the attributes of the supreme being, in the midst of passages that would have done honour to many an ancient, talking of shrubs of amber, as if that mineral substance had been a plant growing at the bottom of the sea.

* This prologue and epilogue were written by Mr. Smart.

PER CONTRA Creditor,
For his ABUSE.

Thursday, August 13th, 1752. Impertinent, Number I and last.

Wednesday the 6th of December, 1752. Inspector Number 543.

"There is one Smart also, against whose severity I have still less to plead—'twas I that introduced him to the world—his *Bookseller took him into salary on my approbation of the specimens which he offered.—I betrayed him into the profession, and having starved upon it, he has a right to abuse me.—I am afraid I have since been guilty of saying that he had genius,—has he not reason to make me the hero of a Dunciad?"

Thursday, December 7th, 1752. Number 544. The whole Inspector.

* "Whereas the Inspector in his paper of the 7th instant, has confidently asserted, that he recommended Mr. Smart to me, and made us acquainted; I think it my duty to undeceive the publick, and contradict an assertion so absolutely false.

The truth is—Dr. Hill (the supposed author of the Inspector) called at my house one Sunday in the afternoon, about six months after Mr. Smart and I had been concerned together in business, and expressed a desire of being made known to him. As Mr. Smart was then above stairs, I brought them together, when the doctor complimented him on his writings, and gave both him and me an invitation to his house, which was never complied with. By the manner of their addressing each other they appeared to be absolute strangers, and after the doctor was gone, Mr. Smart told me he had never seen Dr. Hill before.

I farther declare, that to the best of my knowledge and belief, Mr. Smart never wrote any thing for hire, nor did he ever sell me any copy of his that I have published."

St. Paul's Church-Yard,
  December 9, 1752.   JOHN NEWBERY

Mr. SMART Debtor to Dr. HILL,
For his PRAISES.

The Monthly Review for August, 1752.

After bestowing some very high encomiums on the Penshurst of an unknown author, the Church-yard elegy of Mr. Gray, and the Elfrida of Mr. Mason, he adds; "Last in the point of time, but not last in any other consideration, stands Mr. Smart, the author of many entertaining pieces, and of the collection of miscellaneous poems, whose publication has given the immediate occasion to these observations."

Having said that the quantity of matter contained in his works, is not perhaps equal to the price at which it is set, he a few lines after asserts that, "A man of judgment and taste would scarcely grudge the price of the whole for the single ode to Ill-nature, if he could not have it on other conditions."

PER CONTRA, Creditor,
For his ABUSE.

The Monthly Review, August, 1752.

"The author of these poems is yet young enough to form himself: he seems to have been shamefully remiss on this head; and the alternative before him, at this time, is certainly that of care on his own part; or the utmost severity of censure on that of the world. Would one imagine, that the man we admire in one of these pieces, is the same we can scarce pardon in another? Could one suppose, that, in the compass of so few pages, the same writer shall make us applaud with the sincerest warmth, and condemn with no less reason? However, we hope this ingenious gentleman will understand this freedom as admonition rather than censure: it is intended so; for it were injustice to suppose that to be want of genius, which is indolence alone, or inattention."

On Mr. Smart's dedication, Dr. Hill has the following remark, "The man who could produce such lines as these, seems to hold the taste and spirit of his patron at but a low rate, when he supposes any consideration could be of superior power to recommend him to his protection. When we see what that superior consideration is, it is not easy to believe that the poet meant any thing but raillery.

"We are not so blinded by the beauties of the Ode, as not to see that the word œstrum, though of real and appropriated meaning, is chargeable with aukwardness and affectation, as introduced in this place: nevertheless the consideration of its expressing the sense of the author much more fully and emphatically than any word in our language could have done, is to be allowed a plea in great palliation, if not in absolute justification of the liberty of using it. Nor can the poetic ear allow the unmeasured harshness of the epithet, time deflower'd, as it stands printed; the line either wants a syllable, or what is worse, the epithet, from two syllables, deflower'd is to be stretched into four, deflowered; a poor expedient, savouring of those shifts which poets are often reduced to, who, for want

[continued overleaf

Mr. SMART Debtor to Dr. HILL,
For his PRAISES.

"Mr. Smart begun early to feel the fire of this enthusiastic passion. His twelfth ode, he tells us, was written when he was no more than thirteen, yet there is a vast deal of the true spirit of poetry, and, what is more wonderful at such an age, of elegance in it."

"We have mentioned the second ode as a very fine one; it would be injustice to the first not to acknowledge that it is very elegant."

---

of genius, or fondness for an already nearly-finished line, cannot, or will not, alter or improve it."

"The pieces in Latin verse, though accurate enough, and not wholly destitute of elegance and smoothness, bear no comparison in matter of form with the English. It is an *idle attempt, and savours more of industry than genius, to write in a language in which we can make no figure."

* An idle attempt, that savours of industry—What propriety of language have we here!

PER CONTRA, Creditor,
For his ABUSE.

"The eleventh Ode is an epithalamium. Pieces of this kind are generally indifferent performances, and this is not one of the best of them. It is an irregular and unmeasured ode, pretty much like one of those which it was an age ago, a fashion with writers who were acquainted with nothing but the irregularity of the length of lines in Pindar, (but not with the latent connexion and concert even in that) to call Pindaric. These things are like birth-day odes; they all seem to set out alike.

> Descend, descend, ye sweet Aonian maids,

Did any epithalamiast ever begin otherwise? was ever the repetition more spirited, or the epithet more sugared, or more appropriated?

> Leave the Parnassian shades,
> The joyful Hymeneal sing;
> And to a lovelier belle,
> Than fiction e'er devised, or eloquence can tell,
> Your vocal tributes bring.

Not to say any thing of the court-like dialect, in which the author talks of belle, to these people of the other world, what a use is made of the word tell, to form a jingle that is hardly rhime after all?

> And you, ye winged choristers that fly,
> In all the pensile gardens of the sky,
> Chant thro' th' enamel'd grove.

If one were in a humour to be impertinently inquisitive about these pensile gardens of the firmament, to ask how many there are of them, or in what part of each these enamel'd groves grow, what would the author have to say for himself; but it is not necessary. Does not the reader recollect Dean Swift's love-song, Fluttering spread thy purple pinions, &c.? If he does, there needs no further comment on this passage.

> Fragrant Flora, queen of May,
> All bedight with garlands gay,
> Where in the smooth-shaven green.

Mr. SMART Debtor to Dr. HILL,
For his PRAISES.

Speaking of the Latin poems, he says, "these are not indeed without beauties, and those very conspicuous ones in some parts, and in most the author is expressed justly, if not elegantly in all*".

* The very slight manner, in which the doctor passes over these Latin pieces, is a sufficient proof of his being (what some have censured Mr. Smart for calling him) an illiterate hireling.

PER CONTRA, Creditor,
For his ABUSE.

"How prettily these pilferings of the Miltonian epithets follow one another; and how happily are they connected with the rest of the pieces to which they are so very like! The infantine stile, the easy alertness of Philips, how happily are they here transplanted from the lips of a baby to the bed of a river?"

Two pages after, Dr. Hill says, "If our poet is chargeable with any fault in his better pieces, it is the being too free with the beauties of all other English writers. He is the boldest borrower we shall meet with among the men of real genius. He frequently uses, without scruple, the peculiar epithets of Pope, but much more those of Milton; and one sometimes sees more than their words, their very chain of thought taken in this free manner. Such thoughts and expressions will always please in the abstract; but when we recollect from whence they are taken, we shall not do any great honour to the borrower."

> And the rivulet between
> Whispers, murmurs, sings,
> As it stops, or falls or springs.
> There spread a sofa of the softest flowers.

On the last line the doctor has the following remark, "Every bellman could have said couch; but how elegantly does the court stile again disclose itself here?"

> There let the bridegroom stay,
> There let him hate the light and curse the day,
> And dun the tardy hours.

"We know not," says the doctor, "whether the metaphor of the last line is more polite or more expressive."

> Now see the bridegroom rise,
> Oh! how impatient are his joys!

The doctor's remark on these lines, is only the following exclamation, "Oh! how expressively are they painted!"

> At last he springs, he flies into her arms,
> With joy intense
> Feeds ev'ry sense,
> And sultanates o'er all her charms.

Mr. SMART Debtor to Dr. HILL,
For his PRAISES.

"As to the English poems, we have observed that the first ode is full of elegance; and the second is full of force. The last lines in most of the stanzas in the first ode, are remarkably beautiful and expressive: in the others the images are all well chosen and highly painted; and the conclusion is very fine and spirited."

PER CONTRA, Creditor,
For his ABUSE.

But what! some cold, untravelled, and unread reader will exclaim, what is that sultanates? a very pompous word, and never before introduced into our own, or any other language,

> With wrath far heard,
> She shuns the bard,
> And Billingsgates o'er all the field.

are lines it must be allowed, of the incomparable Sir Richard Blackmore. The resemblance, however, is not enough to take away the originality of Mr. Smart's sultanate: but perhaps it will not be so easy to excuse him from the charge of having borrowed the thought from Gorgias, celebrated many ages ago by Longinus, for having called Xerxes the Jupiter of the Persians.

To be serious, these things are not magnificent and great, as their authors intend them, but bloated and bombastic. Phrases thus embarrassed with unnatural ideas, disturb and spoil, instead of elevating the expression; and the forced manner in which they are introduced is sure to give us disgust.

The lines which succeed are too low for criticism,

> O had I Virgil's comprehensive strain,
> Or sung like Pope, without a word in vain,
> Then should I hope my numbers might contain,
> Egrarious nymph, thy boundless happiness!
> How arduous to express.

Astonishing! is it possible the man could be the author of these lines, who was capable of concluding the excellent Ode on Ill-nature with

> Next comes illiberal scrambling avarice, &c.

The Hop-garden is a Georgic, intended after the plan and manner of Virgil, but there is a very unfortunate error in the form: it is in blank verse, for we can hardly call it Miltonic, although the author does. It is that sort of verse which the laziness of the writer has robbed of the jingle of the last syllables, without adding to it that dignity of language, or

Mr. SMART, Debtor to Dr. HILL,
For his PRAISES.

"It would be contradicting our former assertion, and contra-
dicting truth, to say that Mr. Smart wants genius to have made
this poem* equal to any of the same kind."

"There are a great many truly poetical strokes in it, and
whole pages that abound with beauty."

"Mr. Smart has not injudiciously closed with it†, and we are
glad that he gives us an opportunity of concluding as we set
out, to his advantage. There is not much in the plan or design
of this piece: but what the author has proposed he has executed
in a masterly manner. There is great elegance, for nothing
more is intended, in most part of the versification: nor are there
any of those glaring inaccuracies in it, which disgrace some of
the other pieces.—The description of Midas's following Pan is
full of poetry as well as spirit.—The address of Timolus, to the
inanimate things about him, on the approach of the Gods, has
great dignity and propriety, as well as beauty in it.—The first
stanza of the song of Pan has great softness and an elegant ease
in it."

* The Hop-garden.
† The Judgment of Midas.

PER CONTRA, Creditor.
For his ABUSE.

variety of pauses, which make us rather rejoice in the absence of those fetters, than regret the want of the sound, in the author from whom the species is named: it would be difficult to assign any other cause for the omission of rhime in this piece, since there does not seem so much as an attempt to any of those graces, which not only support, but in a manner render it necessary."

"——But it would be as gross a contradiction to our understanding, not to perceive that application was greatly wanting.

It is not only that many of the verses are rough; but no small number of them want a foot in measure: unless we are to be obliged, for the making it up, to an extension of words by no means consonant with custom, much less with the dignity of a poem in this form."

"——But these are only a few fine flowers, appearing here and there in an uncultivated field, over-run with nettles and briars."

"The speech of Neptune, with which the author closes the poem gave him an opportunity of emulating the dignity of his divine original in the speeches of the angels: but mark how he closes it.

> ————France
> Shall bow the neck to Cantium's peerless offspring,
> And as the oak reigns lordly o'er the shrub,
> So shall the hop have homage from the vine.

That is, we suppose, claret shall confess itself a meaner liquor than two-penny, by as many degrees as there are between an oak and a gooseberry-bush*."

---

* This is one of the highest strokes of the Doctor's humour—and this piece of criticism may give a very adequate idea of that *learned, impartial, judicious, ingenious, useful* work—call'd the MONTHLY REVIEW.

"Enough will be seen in these, and the other specimens, selected from the more finished of these pieces to justify us in giving Mr. Smart a place among the first of the present race of English poets. If the censure, which it is the character of this work to bestow as freely as its praises, shall warn him to be more attentive to the finishing his works for the future, there is no doubt of his becoming equal to most who have done honour to the last, or the preceding age."

Due on the BALANCE to the INSPECTOR,

THE HILLIAD,

An Heroic POEM.

Bedford Coffee-House, Jan. 16, 1753.

Received then of* one Smart, the first book of the HIL-LIAD, in part of payment, for the many and great obligations he is under to me.

his

The + INSPECTOR

mark

Witness { QUINBUS FLESTRIN,
GABRIEL GRIFFIN.

* See Inspector, Number 543.

THE
HILLIAD.
BOOK THE FIRST.

Thou God of jest, who o'er th' ambrosial bowl,
Giv'st joy to Jove, while laughter shakes the pole;
And thou, fair Justice, of immortal line,
Hear, and assist the poet's grand design,

NOTES VARIORUM

Thou God of jest.] As the design of heroic poetry is to celebrate the virtues
and noble atchievements of truly great personages, and to conduct them
through a series of hardships to the completion of their wishes, so the little
epic delights in representing, with an ironical drollery, the mock qualities of
those, who for the benefit of the laughing part of mankind, are pleased to
become egregiously ridiculous, in an affected imitation of the truly renowned
worthies above-mentioned. Hence our poet calls upon Momus, at the first
opening of his poem, to convert his hero into a jest. So that, in the present case,
if cannot be said, *facit indignatio versum,* but, if I may be allowed the
expression, *facit titillatio versum*; which may serve to shew our author's temper
of mind is free from rancour, or ill-nature. Notwithstanding the great
incentives he has had to prompt him to this undertaking, he is not actuated
by the spirit of revenge; and to check the sallies of fancy and humorous
invention, he further invokes the goddess Themis, to administer strict, poetic
justice.

Shakes the pole.] Several cavils have been raised against this passage.
QUINBUS FLESTRIN, the unborn poet, is of opinion that it is brought in
merely to eke out a verse; but though in many points I am inclined to look
upon this critick as irrefragable, I must beg leave at present to appeal from
his verdict; and, though Horace lays it down as a rule not to admire any

THE HILLIAD. First published London, Feb. 1753; Dublin, May 1753,
substantially unchanged except for addition of an 'Imitation' (probably
supplied by Murphy), indicating sources which have been noted in the
Commentary. Textual variants in the prefatory material and Notes Var-
iorum, which are few and insignificant, have not been recorded but
corrections of spelling and punctuation have been silently incorporated.
Prefatory material was not included in *1791*. Text: *1753*. Collated: *1753D*,
1791.

Who aims at triumph by no common ways,   5
But on the stem of dulness grafts the bays.

    O thou, whatever name delight thine ear,
Pimp! Poet! Puffer! 'Pothecary! Play'r!

NOTES VARIORUM.

thing, I cannot help enjoying so pleasing an operation of the mind upon this
occasion. We are here presented with a grand idea, no less than Jupiter
shaking his sides and the heavens at the same time. The Pagan thunderer has
often been said to agitate the pole with a nod, which in my mind gives too
awful an image, whereas the one in question conveys an idea of him in good
humour, and confirms what Mr. Orator Henley says in his excellent tracts,
that "the deity is a joyous being."

MARTINUS MACULARIUS,
M. D. Reg. Soc. Bur. &c. Soc.

    Grafts the bays,] Much puzzle hath been occasioned among the naturalists
concerning the engraftment here mentioned. HILL's natural history of trees
and plants, vol. 52, page 336 saith, it hath been frequently attempted, but
that the tree of dulness will not admit any such inoculation. He adds in page
339, that he himself tried the experiment for two years successively, but that
the twig of laurel, like a feather in the state of electricity, drooped and died
the moment he touched it. Notwithstanding this authority, it is well known
that this operation has been performed by some choice spirits. ERASMUS in
his encomium on folly shews how it may be accomplished; in our own times
POPE and GARTH found means to do the same: and in the sequel of this
work, we make no doubt but the stem here-mentioned will bear some
luxuriant branches, like the tree in VIRGIL,

Nec longum tempus, et ingens
Exiit ad Cælum ramis felicibus arbos,
Miraturque novas frondes et non sua Poma.

    Pimp,] An old English word for a mean fellow; see CHAUCER and
SPENCER.

    Poet,] QUINBUS FLESTRIN faith, with his usual importance, that this is
the only piece of justice done to our hero in this work. To this assents the
widow at Cuper's, who it seems is not a little proud of the "words by Dr. Hill,
and the musick by Lewis Granon, Esq;" This opinion is further confirmed by
major England, who admires the pretty turns on Kitty, and Kate, and
Catherine and Katy, but from these venerable authorities, judicious Reader,
you may boldly dissent, *meo periculo.*

MART. MAC.

    Puffer,] Of this talent take a specimen. In a letter to himself he saith; "you
have discovered many of the beauties of the ancients; they are obliged to you;
we are obliged to you; were they alive they would thank you; we who are
alive do thank you." His constant custom of running on in this manner,
occasioned the following epigram,

240

Whose baseless fame by vanity is buoy'd,
Like the huge earth self-center'd in the void,   10
Accept one part'ner thy own worth t'explore,
And in thy praise be singular no more.

  Say, Muse, what Dæmon, foe to ease and truth,
First from the mortar dragg'd th' adventrous youth,
And made him, 'mongst the scribbling sons of men,   15
Change peace for war, the pestle for the pen?

NOTES VARIORUM.

  Hill puffs himself, forbear to chide;
    An insect vile and mean,
  Must first, he knows, be magnify'd
    Before it can be seen.

'*Pothecary, Play'r.*] For both these vide WOODWARD's letter, *passim.*
  Like the huge earth,] The allusion here seems to be taken from OVID, who
describes the earth fixed in the air, by its own stupidity, or *vis inertiæ:—*

    Pendebat in aere tellus,
  Ponderibus librata suis.—

But, reader, dilate your imagination to take in the much greater idea our poet
here presents to you: consider the immense inanity of space, and then the
comparative nothingness of the globe, and you may attain an adequate
conception of our hero's reputation, and the mighty basis it stands upon. It is
worth observing here, that our author, *quasi aliud agens*, displays at one touch
of his pen more knowledge of the planetary system, than is to be found in all
the volumes of the mathematicians.

This note is partly by Macularius, and partly by Mr. Jinkyns, Philomath.

  Say Muse] Observe, gentle reader, how tenderly our author treats his hero
throughout his whole poem; he does not here impute his ridiculous conduct,
and all that train of errors which have attended his consummate vanity, to his
own perverse inclination, but with great candour insinuates that some
Dæmon, foe to Hillario's repose, first misled his youthful imagination; which
is a kind of apology for his life and character. He is not the only one who has
been seduced to his ruin in this manner. We read it in POPE,

    Some Dæmon whisper'd Visto have a taste.

Hence then arise our hero's misfortunes; and that the Dæmon above-
mentioned was a foe to truth, will appear from Hillario's notable talent at
misrepresenting circumstances, for which vide all the INSPECTORS.

Twas on a day (O may that day appear
No more, but lose it's station in the year,
In the new style be not it's name enroll'd,
But share annihilation with the old!)   20
A tawny Sybil, whose alluring song,
Decoy'd the 'prentices and maiden throng,
First from the counter young HILLARIO charm'd,
And first his unambitious soul alarm'd—
An old strip'd curtain cross her arms was flung,   25
And tatter'd tap'stry o'er her shoulders hung;

NOTES VARIORUM.

May that day appear,] This seems to be wrote with an eye to a beautiful
passage in a very elegant poem;

> Ye Gods annihilate both space and time,
> And make two lovers happy.—

The request is extremely modest, and I really wonder it was never complied
with; but it must be said in favour of Mr. Smart, that he is still more
reasonable in his demand, and it appears by the alteration in the stile, that his
scheme may be reduced to practice though the other is mighty fine in theory.
The INSPECTOR is of this opinion, and so is Monsieur de Scaizau.

A tatter'd tap'stry] Our Author has been extreamly negligent upon this
occasion, and has indolently omitted an opportunity of displaying his talent
for poetick imagery. HOMER has describ'd the shield of Achilles with all the
art of his imagination; VIRGIL has followed him in this point, and indeed
both he and OVID, seem to be delighted when they have either a picture to
describe, or some representation in the labours of the loom. Hence arises a
double delight; we admire the work of the artificer, and the poet's account of
it; and this pleasure Mr. Smart might have impressed upon his readers in this
passage, as many things were wrought into the tapestry here-mentioned. In
one part our hero was administering to a patient, "and the fresh vomit runs
for ever green." The theatre at May-fair made a conspicuous figure in the
piece—the pit seemed to rise in an uproar,—the gallery opened its rude
throats—and apples, oranges and half-pence flew about our hero's ears.—
The mall in St. James's park was displayed in a beautiful Vista, and you
might perceive Hillario with his janty air wadling along.—In Mary le Bone
fields, he was dancing round a glow worm, and finally the rotunda at
Ranelagh filled the eye with its magnificence, and in a corner of it stood a
handsome young fellow holding a personage, dressed in blue silk, by the ear;
"the very worsted still look'd black and blue." There were many other
curious figures, but out of a shameful laziness has our poet omitted them.

POLYMETIS CANTABRIGIENSIS.

20 with] in *1791*

Her loins with patch-work cincture were begirt,
That more than spoke diversity of dirt;
With age her back was double and awry,
Twain were her teeth, and single was her eye,   30
Cold palsy shook her head—she seem'd at most
A living corps, or an untimely ghost,
With voice far-fetch'd from hollow throat profound,
And more than mortal was th' infernal sound.

   "Sweet boy, who seem 'st for glorious deeds design'd,   35
O come and leave that clyster-pipe behind;
Cross this prophetic hand with silver coin,
And all the wealth and fame, I have, is thine—
She said—he (for what stripling cou'd withstand?)
Straight with his ONLY six-pence grac'd her hand.   40

And now the prescious fury all her breast
At once invaded, and at once possess'd;
Her eye was fixt in an extatic stare,
And on her head uprose th' astonish'd hair:
No more her colour, or her looks the same,   45
But moonstruck madness quite convuls'd her frame,
While, big with fate, again she silence broke,
And in few words voluminously spoke.

   "In these three lines athwart thy palm I see,
Either a tripod, or a triple-tree,   50
For Oh! I ken by mysteries profound,
Too light to sink thou never can'st be drown'd—

NOTES VARIORUM.

Th' astonish'd hair:] This passage seems to be an imitation of the Sybil in
the sixth book of VIRGIL;

> *Subito non vultus, non color unus*
> *Nec comptæ mansere comæ.*——

and is admirably expressive of the witch's prophetic fury, and ushers in the
prediction of Hillario's fortune with proper solemnity.—
   This note is by one of the Æolists, mentioned with honour in the Tale of a
Tub.

Whate'er thy end, the fates are now at strife,
Yet strange variety shall check thy life—
Thou grand dictator of each publick show,   55
Wit, moralist, quack, harlequin, and beau,
Survey man's vice, self-prais'd, and self-prefer'd,
And be th' INSPECTOR of th' infected herd;
By any means aspire at any ends,
Baseness exalts, and cowardice defends,   60
The checquer'd world's before thee—go—farewell,
Beware of Irishmen—and learn to spell,
Here from her breast th' inspiring fury flew,
She ceas'd—and instant from his sight withdrew.
Fir'd with his fate, and conscious of his worth, 65
The beardless wight prepar'd to sally forth.
But first ('twas just, 'twas natural to grieve)
He sigh'd and took a soft pathetic leave.
"Farewel, a long farewel to all my drugs,
My labell'd vials, and my letter'd jugs;   70

NOTES VARIORUM.

Be th' INSPECTOR, *&c.*] When the Distemper first raged among the horned cattle, the king and council ordered a certain officer to super-intend the beasts, and to direct that such, as were found to be infected, should be knocked in the head. This officer was called the INSPECTOR, and from thence I would venture to lay a wager, our hero derived his title.

BENTLEY, Junior.

Beware of Irishmen, &c.] It is extreamly probable that our poet is intimately acquainted with the classics; he seems frequently to have them in his eye, and such an air of enthusiasm runs through this whole speech, that the learned reader may easily perceive he has taken fire at some of the prophecies in HOMER and VIRGIL.— The whole is delivered in breaks, and unconnected transitions, which denote vehement emotions in the mind; and the hint here concerning the Irish is perfectly in the manner of all great epic poets, who generally give the reader some idea of what is to ensue, without unfolding the whole. Thus we find in VIRGIL,

Bella, horrida bella,
Et Tybrim multo spumantem sanguine cerno.

and again,   *Alius latio tibi partus Achilles.*

And in the sequel of this work, I believe, it will be found, that as Æneas had another Achilles, so our hero has had as formidable an adversary.

Farewel, a long farewel,] The ingenous Mr. L—der says that the following passage is taken from a work, which he intends shortly to publish by

244

And you, ye bearers of no trivial charge
Where all my Latin stands inscrib'd at large;
Ye jars, ye gallipots, and draw'rs adieu,
Be to my memory lost, as lost to view,
And ye, whom I so oft have joy'd to wipe,   75
Th' ear-sifting syringe, and back-piercing pipe,
Farewel—my day of glory's on the dawn,
And now,—Hillario's occupation's gone."

  Quick with the word his way the hero made,
Conducted by a glorious cavalcade;   80
Pert Petulance, the first attracts his eye,
And drowsy Dulness slowly saunters by,
With Malice old, and Scandal ever new,
And neutral Nonsense, neither false nor true.
Infernal Falsehood next approach'd the band   85
With * * * and the koran in her hand.

subscription, and he has now in the press a pamphlet, called "Mr. Smart's
Use and Abuse of the Moderns." But, with his leave, this passage is partly
imitated from Cardinal Wolsey's speech, and from Othello.

M. MACULARIUS.

Neutral nonsense, &c.] The train, here described, is worthy of Hillario,
pertness, dulness, scandal and malice, &c. being the very constituents of an
hero for the mock heroic, and it is not without propriety that nonsense is
introduced with the epithet, neutral, nonsense, being like a Dutchman, not
only in an unmeaning stupidity, but in the art of preserving a strict
neutrality. This neutrality may be aptly explained by the following epigram,

> Word-valiant wight, thou great he shrew,
>   That wrangles to no end;
> Since nonsense is nor false nor true,
>   Thou'rt no man's foe or friend.

Falshood,] This lady is described with two books in her hand, but our
author chusing to preserve a neutrality, though not a nonsensical one, upon
this occasion, the tories are at liberty to fill up this blank with Rapin, Burnet,
or any names that will fit the niches; and the whigs may, if they please insert
Echard, Higgons, &c. But why, exclaimeth a certain critic, should falshood
be given to Hillario?—Because, replieth Macularius, he has given many
specimens of his talent that way. Our hero took it into his head some time
since to tell the world that he caned a gentleman, whom he called by the
name of Mario; what degree of faith the town gave him upon that occasion,

Her motley vesture with the leopard vies,
Stain'd with a foul variety of lies.
Next spiteful Enmity, gangren'd at heart,
Presents a dagger and conceals a dart.   90
On th' earth crawls Flatt'ry with her bosom bare,
And Vanity sails over him in air.

    Such was the groupe—they bow'd and they ador'd,
And hail'd Hillario for their sovereign lord.
Flush'd with success, and proud of his allies,   95
Th' exulting hero, thus triumphant cries.
"Friends, brethren, ever present, ever dear,
Home to my heart, nor quit your title there,
While you approve, assist, instruct, inspire,
Heat my young blood, and set my soul on fire;   100
No foreign aid my daring pen shall chuse,
But boldly versify without a Muse.

NOTES VARIORUM.

may be collected from the two following lines, by a certain wag who shall be
nameless.

> To beat one man great Hill was fated;
> What man?—a man that he created.

  The following epigram may be also properly inserted here.

> What H–ll one day says, he the next does deny,
> And candidly tells us—'tis all a damn'd lye:
> Dear Doctor—this candour from you is not wanted;
> For why shou'd you own it? 'tis taken for granted.

Crawls Flatt'ry, &c.] Our hero is as remarkable for his encomiums, where it
is his interest to commend, as for his abuse, where he has taken a dislike; but
from the latter he is easily to be bought off, as may be seen in the following
excellent epigram.

> An author's writings oft reveal,
> Where now and then he takes a meal.
> Invite him once a week to dinner,
> He'll saint you, tho' the veriest sinner.
> Have you a smiling, vacant face,
> He gives you soul, expression, grace.
> Swears what you will, unswears it too;
> What will not beef and pudding do?

Without a muse, &c.] No! the devil a bit!—I am the only person that can do

I'll teach Minerva, I'll inspire the Nine,
Great Phœbus shall in consultation join,
And round my nobler brow his forfeit laurel twine."   105
  He said—and Clamour of Commotion born,
Rear'd to the skies her ear-afflicting horn,
While J ARGON grav'd his titles on a block,
And styl'd him M. D. Acad. Burdig. Soc.

· But now the harbingers of fate and fame   110
Signs, omens, prodigies, and portents came.
Lo! (though mid-day) the grave Athenian fowl,
Eyed the bright sun, and hail'd him with an howl,

NOTES VARIORUM.

that!—My poems, written at fifteen, were done without the assistance of any Muse, and better than all Smart's poetry.—The Muses are strumpets—they frequently give an intellectual *Gonorrhæa*—Court debt not paid—I'll never be poet laureate.—Coup de grace unanswerable—Our foes shall knuckle, and buckle, and truckle, and all our friends shall checkle and chuckle—five pounds to any bishop that will equal this—*Gum guiacum Latin* for *lignum vitæ*.—Adam the first Dutchman—victorious stroke for Old England—Tweedle-dum and Tweedle-dee.

Oratory-Right-Reason-Chapel, Saturday
13th of January, and old-stile for-ever.

Jargon grav'd, &c.] J ARGON is here properly introduced graving our hero's titles, which are admirably brought into verse, but the gentleman who wrote the last note, Mr. Orator H—ley, takes umbrage at this passage, and exclaimeth to the following effect. "Jargon is meant for me." There is more music in a peal of marrowbones and cleavers than in these verses.—I am a logician upon fundamentals.—A rationalist,—lover of *mankande*, Glastonberry thorn,—huzza, boys.—Wit a vivacious command of all objects and ideas.—I am the only wit in Great Britain. See Oratory tracts, &c. 10036."

Patience, good Mr. Orator! We are not at leisure to answer thee at present, but must observe that *Jargon* has done more for our hero, than ever did the society at Bourdeaux, as will appear from the following extract of a letter sent to M ARTINUS M ACULARIUS, by a fellow of that society.

J'ai bien reçue la lettre, dont vous m'avés fait l'honneur le 12me passé. A l'Egard de ce Monsieur Hillario, qui se vante si prodigieusement chez vous, je ne trouve pas qu'il est enrollé dans notre societe, & son nom est perfaitement inconnu ici. J'espere de vos nouvelles, &c.

Moths, mites, &c.] The important objects of his future speculations!

O would the sons of men once think their eyes,
And reason given 'em but to study flies.

M. MACULARIUS

113 an] a *1791*

Moths, mites, and maggots, fleas, (a numerous crew!)
And gnats and grubworms crouded on his view,   115
Insects! without the microscopic aid,
Gigantic by the eye of Dulness made!
And stranger still—and never heard before!
A wooden lion roar'd, or seem'd to roar.
But (what the most his youthful bosom warm'd,   120
Heighten'd each hope and every fear disarm'd)
On an high dome a damsel took her stand,
With a well-freighted jordan in her hand,
Where curious mixtures strove on every side,
And solids sound with laxer fluids vied—   125
Lo! on his crown the lotion choice and large,
She soused—and gave at once a full discharge.
Not Archimedes, when with conscious pride,

NOTES VARIORUM.

Dulness made] This passage may be properly illustrated by a recollection of
two lines in Mr. POPE's essay on criticism.

> As things seem large which we thro' mists discry,
> Dulness is ever apt to magnify.

Wooden lion roar'd,] Not the black lion in Salisbury court, Fleet-street, where
the New Craftsman is published, nor yet the red lion at Brentford, but the
beast of the Bedford, who may be truly said to have been alive, when
animated by Addison and Steel, though now reduced to that state of
Blockheadism, which is so conspicuous in his master. *Ficulnus, in utile lignum!*

BENTLEY, Junior.

A full discharge,] Reader do not turn up your nose at this passage! it is much
more decent that POPE's—Recollect what SWIFT says, that a nice man has
filthy ideas, and let it be considered this discharge may have the same effect
upon our hero, as a similar accident had upon a personage of equal parts and
genius.

> Renew'd by ordure's sympathetic force,
> As oil'd by magic juices for the course,
> Vig'rous he rises from th' effluvia strong,
> Imbibes new life and scours and stinks along.

POPE's Dunciad.

Archimides, &c.] As soon as the Philosopher here mentioned discovered the
modern *Save-all* and the *New-invented patent black-ball*, he threw down his pipe,
and run all along Piccadilly, with his shirt out of his breeches, crying out like
a madman, ευρηκα! ευρηκα! which in modern English is, the job is done! the
job is done!

VETUS SCHOL.

I've found it out! I've found it out! he cry'd,
Not costive bardlings, when a rhime comes pat,   130
Not grave Grimalkin when she smells a rat:
Not the shrewd statesman, when he scents a plot,
Not coy Prudelia, when she knows what's what,
Not our own hero, when (O matchless luck!)
His keen discernment found another Duck,   135
With such ecstatic transports did abound,
As what he smelt and saw, and felt and found.
"Ye Gods I thank ye to profusion free,
Thus to adorn and thus distinguish me,
And thou, fair Cloacina, whom I serve,   140
(If a desire to please, is to deserve)
To you I'll consecrate my future lays,
And on the smoothest paper print my soft essays."

Notes Variorum.

Another Duck,] Hillario having a mind to celebrate and recommend a genius to the notice of the world, compares him to Stephen Duck, and at the close of a late Inspector, crys out, "I have found another Duck, but who shall find a Caroline?"

Print my soft essays,] Our hero for once has spoken truth of himself, for which we could produce the testimonies of several persons of distinction. Bath and Tunbridge-wells have upon many occasions testified their gratitude to him on this head, as his works have been always found of singular use with the waters of those places. To this effect also speaketh that excellent comedian, Mr Henry Woodward, in an ingenious parody *on busy, curious, thirsty fly*, &c.

I.

Busy, curious, hungry Hill,
Write of me and write your fill.
Freely welcome to abuse,
Could'st thou tire thy railing muse.
Make the most of this you can,
Strife is short and life's a span.

II.

Both alike your works and pay,
Hasten quick to their decay,
This a trifle, those no more,
Tho' repeated to threescore.
Threescore volumes when they're writ,
Will appear at last b——t.

No more he spake; but slightly slid along,
Escorted by the miscellaneous throng.   145

    And now, thou Goddess, whose fire-darting eyes,
Defy all distance and transpierce the skies,
To men the councils of the Gods relate,
And faithfully describe the grand debate.

    The cloud-compelling thund'rer, at whose call   150
The Gods assembled in th' etherial hall,
From his bright throne the deities addrest;
"What impious noise disturbs our awful rest,
With din prophane assaults immortal ears,
And jars harsh discord to the tuneful spheres?   155
Nature, my hand-maid, yet without a stain,
Has never once productive prov'd in vain,
Till now—luxuriant and regardless quite
Of her divine, eternal rule of right,
Or mere privation sh'as bestow'd a frame,   160
And dignify'd a nothing with a name,

<hr>

Notes Variorum.

And now, thou Goddess, &c.] This invocation is perfectly in the spirit of
ancient poetry. If I may use Milton's words, our author here presumes into
the heavens, an earthly guest, and draws empyreal air. Hence he calls upon
the Goddess to assist his strain, while he relates the councils of the Gods.
VIRGIL, when the plot thickens upon his hands, as Mr. Bayes has it, has
offered up his prayers a second time to the Muse, and he seems to labour
under the weight of his subject, when he cries out,

      Majus opus moveo, major rerum mihi nascitur ordo.

This is the case at present with the writer of the HILLIAD, and this piece of
machinery will evince the absurdity of that Lucretian doctrine, which asserts
that the Gods are wrapped up in a lazy indolence, and do not trouble
themselves about human affairs. The words of Lucretius are,

      Omnis enim per se divum natura necesse est
      Immortali ævo summa cum pace fruatur,
      Semota a rebus nostris, disjunctaque longe.

It is now recommended to the editors of the Anti-Lucretius to make use of
this instance to the contrary in the next publication of that work.—

              M. MACULARIUS.

    144 spake] spoke *1791*   160 sh'as] she's *1791*

A wretch devoid of use, of sense and grace,
Th' insolvent tenant of incumber'd space."

"Good is his cause, and just is his pretence,"
(Replies the God of theft and eloquence.)   165
"A hand mercurial, ready to convey,
E'en in the presence of the garish day,
The work an English classic late has writ,
And by adoption be the sire of wit—
Sure to be this is to be something—sure,   170
Next to perform, 'tis glorious to procure.

NOTES VARIORUM.

Incumber'd space.] Jupiter's speech is full of pomp and solemnity, and is finely closed by a description of our hero, who is here said to take up a place in the creation to no purpose. What a different notion of the end of his existence has Hillario, from what we find delivered by the excellent Longinus in his treatise on the sublime. The passage is admirable, translated by the author of the pleasures of imagination. "The Godlike geniuses of Greece, were well-assured that nature had not intended man for a low spirited or ignoble being; but bringing us into life and the midst of this wide universe, as before a multitude assembled at some heroic solemnity, that we might be spectators of all her magnificence, and candidates high in emulation for the prize of glory: she has therefore implanted in our souls an inextinguishable love of every thing great and exalted, of every thing which appears divine beyond our comprehension. Hence by the very propensity of nature we are led to admire, not little springs or shallow rivulets, however clear and delicious, but the Nile, the Rhine, the Danube, and much more than all the Ocean."—Instead of acting upon this plan, Hillario is employed in pursuit of insects in Kensington-gardens, and as this is all the gratitude he pays for the being conferred upon him, he is finely termed an Insolvent tenant.

By adoption be the sire, &c.] Our hero has taken an entire letter from Sir Thomas Fitz-Osborne, and with inimitable effrontery published it in his INSPECTOR, No. 239, as a production of his own. We are informed that, having been taxed with this affair, he declares with a great deal of art, that it was given him by another person, to which all we have to say is, that the receiver is as bad as the thief.

M. MACULARIUS.

Glorious to procure.] If our author could be thought capable of punning, I should imagine that the word *procure*, in this place, is made use of in reference to an appellation given to our hero in the commencement of this poem, viz. a *Pimp*, but the reader will please to recollect that the term *Pimp*, is not in that passage used in its modern acceptation.

Small was th' exertion of my God-like soul.
When privately Apollo's herd I stole,
Compar'd to him, who braves th' all-seeing sun,
And boldly bids th' astonish'd world look on."   175

    Her approbation Venus next exprest
And on Hillario's part the throne addrest,
If there be any praise the nails to pare,
And in soft ringlets wreath th' elastic hair,
In talk and tea to trifle time away;   180
The mien so easy and the dress so gay!
Can my Hillario's worth remain unknown,
With whom coy Sylvia trusts herself alone.
With whom, so pure, so innocent his life,
The jealous husband leaves his buxom wife.   185
What tho' he ne'er assume the post of Mars,
By me disbanded from all amorous wars;
His fancy (if not person) he employs,
And oft ideal countesses enjoys—

NOTES VARIORUM.

Small was th' exertion, &c.] Not so fast, good poet, cries out in this place, M. MACULARIUS. We do not find that HILLARIO, upon any occasion whatever, has been charged with stealing Apollo's quiver, and certain it is, that those arrows, which he has shot at all the world, never were taken from thence. But of Mercury it is recorded by HORACE, that he really did deceive the God of wit in this manner;

> *Te boves olim nisi reddidisses*
> *Per dolum amotas, puerum minaci,*
> *Voce dum terret viduus pharetra.*
>   *Risit Apollo.*

Venus next express'd,] Venus rises in this assembly quite in the manner attributed to her in the ancient poets; thus we see in VIRGIL that she is all mildness, and at every word breathes Ambrosia;

> ——*At non Venus aurea contra,*
> *Pauca refert.*—

She is to speak upon this occasion, as well as in the case produced from the Æneid, in favour of a much loved son, though indeed we cannot say that she has been quite so kind to Hillario, as formerly she was to Æneas, it being evident that she has not bestowed upon him that lustre of youthful bloom, and that liquid radiance of the eye, which she is said to have given the pious Trojan.

Tho' hard his heart, yet beauty shall controul,   190
And sweeten all the rancour of his soul,
While his black self, Florinda ever near,
Shews like a Diamond in an Ethiop's ear."

    When Pallas—thus—"Cease—ye immortals—cease
Nor rob serene stupidity of peace—   195
Should Jove himself in calculation mad
Still negatives to blank negations add,
How could the barren cyphers ever breed,
But nothing still from nothing would proceed?
Raise or depress—or magnify—or blame,   200
Inanity will ever be the same."

NOTES VARIORUM.

    ——*Lumenque juventæ,*
Purpureum, et lætos oculis afflavit honores.

On the contrary Venus here talks of his black self, which makes it suspected that she reconciled herself to this hue, out of a compliment to Vulcan, of whom she has frequent favours to sollicit; and perhaps it may appear hereafter, that she procured a sword for our hero from the cælestial blacksmith's forge. One thing is not a little surprizing, that, while Venus speaks on the side of Hillario, she should omit the real utility he has been of to the cause of love by his experience as an apothecary, of which he himself hath told us, several have profited; and it should be remembered at the same time, that he actually has employed his person in the service of Venus, and has now an offspring of the amorous congress. It is moreover notorious, that having, in his elegant language, tasted of the cool stream, he was ready to plunge in again, and therefore publickly set himself up for a wife, and thus, became a fortune-hunter with his pen, and if he has failed in his design, it is because the ladies do not approve the new scheme of propagation without the knowledge of a man, which Hillario pretended to explain so handsomely in the *Lucina sine concubitu.*—But the truth is, he never wrote a syllable of this book, though he transcribed part of it, and shew'd it to a bookseller, in order to procure a higher price for his productions.

QUINBUS FLESTRIN.

    Diamond in an Æthiops ear,] There is neither morality, nor integrity, nor unity, nor universality in this poem.—The author of it is a SMART; I hope to see a SMARTEAD published; I had my pocket picked the other day, as I was going through Paul's Church-yard, and I firmly believe it was this little author, as the man who can pun, will also pick a pocket.

JOHN DENNIS, Junior.

    Inanity will ever be, &c.] Our author does not here mean to list himself

253

"Not so" (says Phœbus) "my celestial friend,
E'en blank privation has its use and end—
How sweetly shadows recommend the light,
And darkness renders my own beams more bright!   205
How rise from filth the violet and rose!
From emptiness, how softest musick flows!
How absence to possession adds a grace,
And modest vacancy to all gives place?
Contrasted when fair nature's works we spy,   210
More they allure the mind and more they charm the eye.

NOTES VARIORUM.

among the disputants concerning pure space, but the doctrine he would
advance, is, that nothing can come from nothing. In so unbelieving an age as
this, it is possible this tenet may not be received, but if the reader has a mind
to see it handled at large, he may find in Rumgurtius, vol. 16. pagina 1001.
"De hac re multum et turpiter hallucinantur scriptores tam exteri quam
domestici. Spatium enim absolutum et realtivum debent distingui, prius-
quam distincta esse possunt; neque ulla alia regula ad normam rei metaphy-
sicæ quadrabit, quam triplex consideratio de substantia inanitatis. sive
entitate nihili, quæ quidem consideratio triplex ad unam reduci potest
necessitatem; nempe idem spatium de quo jam satis dictum est." This opinion
is further corroborated by the tracts of the society of Bordeaux. "Selon la
distinction entre les choses, qui n'ont pas de différence, il nous faut
absolument agreer, que lis idees, qui ont frappè l'imagination, peuvent bien
etre, effacer, pourvu qu'on ne s'avise pas d'oublier cet espace immense, qui
envîronne toute la nature, et le systeme des etoiles." Among our countrymen,
I do not know any body that has handled this subject so well as the accurate
Mr. Fielding, in his essay upon Nothing, which the reader may find in the
first volume of his miscellanies; but with all due deference to his authority, we
beg leave to dissent from one assertion in the said essay; the residence of
nothing might in his time have been in a critick's head, and we are apt to
believe that there is something like nothing in most criticks heads to this day,
and this false appearance misled the excellent metaphysician just quoted; for
nothing, in its *puris naturalibus*, as Gravesend describes it in his experimental
philosophy, does subsist no where so properly at present as in the pericranium
of our hero.

MART. MACULARIUS.

Musick flows,] Persons of most genius, says the INSPECTOR, Friday Jan.
26, Number 587, "have in general been the fondest of musick; Sir Isaac
Newton was remarkable for his affection for harmony; he was scarce ever
missed at the beginning of any performance, but he was seldom seen at the
end of it." And indeed of this opinion is M. MACULARIUS; and he further
adds, that if Sir Isaac was still living it is probable he would be at the

So from Hillario some effect may spring,
E'en him—that slight Penumbra of a thing."
Morpheus at length in the debate awoke,
And drowsily a few dull words he spoke—   215
Declar'd Hillario was the friend of ease,
And had a soporific pow'r to please.—
Once more Hillario he pronounc'd with pain,
But at the very sound was lull'd to sleep again.

Notes Variorum.

beginning of the Inspector's next song at Cuper's, but that he would not
be at the end of it, may be proved to a mathematical demonstration, though
Hillario takes so much pleasure in beating time to them himself, and though
he so frequently exclaims, very fine!—O fine!—vastly fine!—Since the
lucubration of Friday Jan. 26th has been mentioned, we think proper to
observe here, that his Inspectorship has the most notable talent at a
motto—Quinbus Flestrin saith, "he is a tartar for that," and of this
learned reader take a specimen along with you. How aptly upon the subject
of musick does he bid his readers pluck grapes from the loaded vine!

>   *Carpite de plenis pendentes vitibus uvas.*   Ovid.

The above-mentioned Quinbus Flestrin, peremptorily says, this line has
been cavilled at by some minor critics, because, "the grapes are sour;" and
indeed of that way of thinking is Macularius, who hath been greatly
astonished at the taste of Hillario, in so frequently culling from Valerius
Flaccus. But he is clearly of opinion, that the lines from Welsted and Dennis,
are selected with great judgment, and are hung out as proper signs of what
entertainment is to be furnished up to his customers.

Penumbra of a thing,] Whatever mean opinion Dr. Phœbus may entertain of
his terestrial brother physician and poet: on earth, Hillario is talked of in a
different manner, as will appear from the following parody on the lines
prefixed by Mr. Dryden, to Milton's Paradise Lost.

>   Three great wise men in the same Æra born,
>   Britannia's happy island did adorn:
>   Henley in care of souls display'd his skill,
>   Rock shone in physick, and in both John H—ll,
>   The force of nature could no farther go,
>   To make a third, she join'd the former two.
>
>   Quinbus Flestrin.

Lull'd to sleep again.] The hypnotick, or soporiferous quality of Hillario's
pen, is manifest from the following asseveration, which was published in the
New Craftsman, and is a letter from a tradesman in the city.

"SIR,
From a motive of gratitude, and for the sake of those of my fellow-
creatures, who may unhappily be afflicted as I have been for some time past,

Momus the last of all, in merry mood,   220
As moderator in the assembly stood.
"Ye laughter-loving pow'rs, ye Gods of mirth,
What not regard my deputy on earth?
Whose chymic skill turns brass to gold with ease,
And out of Cibber forges Socrates?·   225
Whose genius makes consistencies to fight,
And forms an union betwixt wrong and right?
Who (five whole days in senseless malice past)
Repents, and is religious at the last?

NOTES VARIORUM.

I beg leave, through the channel of your paper, to communicate the disorder
I have laboured under, and the extraordinary cure I have lately met with. I
have had for many months successively, a slow nervous fever, with a constant
flutter on my spirits, attended with pertinacious watchings, twitchings of the
nerves, and other grievous symptoms, which reduced me to a mere shadow.
At length, by the interposition of the divine providence, a friend who had
himself experienced it, advised me to have recourse to the reading of the
INSPECTORS. I accordingly took one of them, and the effect it had upon me
was such, that I fell into a profound sleep, which lasted near six and thirty
hours. By this I have attained a more composed habit of body, and I now
doze away almost all my time, but for fear of a lethargy, am ordered to take
them in smaller quantities. A paragraph at a time now answers my purpose,
and under heaven I owe my sleeping powers to the above-mentioned
INSPECTORS. I look upon them to be a grand soporificum mirabile, very
proper to be had in all families. He makes great allowance to those who buy
them to sell again, or to send abroad to the plantations; and the above fact I
am ready to attest whenever called upon. Given under my hand this 4th
January 1753.

Humphrey Roberts, weaver in Crispin-street, Spittle-fields, opposite the
white horse."

Forges Socrates,] Socrates was the father of the truest philosophy that ever
appeared in the world, and though he has not drawn God's image, which was
reserved for the light of the gospel, he has at least given the shadow, which
together with his exemplary life, induced Erasmus to cry out, *Sancte Socrates
ora pro nobis*; of Mr. Cibber we shall say nothing; as he has said abundantly
enough of himself, but to illustrate the poet's meaning in this passage, it may
be necessary to observe, that when the British worthy was indisposed some
time since, the INSPECTOR did not hesitate to prefer him to the God-like
ancient philosopher. *O te, Bollane, cerebri felicem.*

M. MACULARIUS.

Consistencies to fight,] Alluding to his egregious talent at distinctions without
a difference.

Religious at the last?] On every Saturday the florid Hillario becomes, in
Woodward's phrase, a Lay-preacher; but his flimzy, heavy, impotent

A paltry play'r, that in no parts succeeds,   230
A hackney writer, whom no mortal reads.

lucubrations have rather been of prejudice to the good old cause; and we hear that there is now preparing for the press, by a very eminent divine, a defence of christianity against the misrepresentations of a certain officious writer; and for the present we think proper to apply an epigram, occasioned by a dispute between two beaux concerning religion.

I.

On grace, free will, and myst'ries high,
    Two wits harangu'd the table;
J—n H–ll believes he knows not why,
    Tom swears 'tis all a fable.

II.

Peace, idiots, peace, and both agree,
    Tom kiss thy empty brother;
Religion laughs at foes like thee,
    But dreads a friend like t'other.

A paltry play'r, &c.] It appears that the first effort of this universal genius, who is lately become remarkable as the Bobadil of literature, was to excel in Pantomime. What was the event?—he was damned.—Mr. Cross, the prompter, took great pains to fit him for the part of Oroonoko—he was damned.—He attempted Captain Blandford—he was damned.—He acted Constant in the Provok'd Wife—he was damned.—He represented the Botanist in Romeo and Juliet, at the little theatre in the Haymarket, under the direction of Mr. The. Cibber—he was damned.—He appeared in the character of Lothario, at the celebrated theatre in May-Fair—he was damn'd there too. Mr. Cross, however, to alleviate his misfortune, charitably bestowed upon him a 15th part of his own benefit. See the Gentleman's Magazine for last December, and also Woodward's letter, passim.

No mortal reads,] Notwithstanding this assertion of Momus, our hero pro ea, qua est, verecundia, compareth himself to Addison and Steel, which occasioned the following epigram, by the right honourable the earl of * * * addressed to the right honourable G——e D————n.

Art thou not angry, learning's great protector,
To hear that flimsey author, the INSPECTOR,
Of cant, of puff, that daily vain inditer,
Call Addison, or Steel, his brother writer?
So, a pert H–ll (in Æsop's fabling days)
Swoln up with vanity, and self-given praise,
To his huge neighbour Mountain would have said,
"See; (brother,) how We Mountains lift the head!
How great We shew! how awful, and how high,
Amidst these paultry Mounts, that here around us lie!"

The trumpet of a base deserted cause,
Damn'd to the scandal of his own applause;
While thus he stands a general wit confest,
With all these titles, all these talents blest,   235
Be he by Jove's authority assign'd,
The UNIVERSAL BUTT of all mankind."

So spake and ceas'd the joy-exciting God,
And Jove immediate gave th' assenting nod,
When Fame her adamantine trump uprear'd,   240
And thus th' irrevocable doom declar'd.

"While in the vale perennial fountains flow,
And fragrant Zephyrs musically blow;
While the majestic sea from pole to pole,
In horrible magnificence shall roll,   245
While yonder glorious canopy on high,
Shall overhang the curtains of the sky,

NOTES VARIORUM.

And now, reader, please to observe, that, since so ingenious a nobleman hath
condescended to take notice of his INSPECTORSHIP, Mr. Smart doth not
need any apology for the notice he hath also taken of him.

M. MACULARIUS.

The trumpet, &c.] In a very pleasant account of the riots in Drury-lane
Play-house, by Henry Fielding, Esq; we find the following humourous
description of our hero in the character of a trumpeter. "They all ran away
except the trumpeter, who having an empyema in his side, as well as several
dreadful bruises on his breech, was taken. When he was brought before
Garrick to be examined, he said the ninnies, to whom he had the honour to be
trumpeter, had resented the use made of the monsters by Garrick. That it was
unfair, that it was cruel, that it was inhuman to employ a man's own subjects
against him. That Rich was lawful sovereign over all the monsters in the
universe, with much more of the same kind; all which Garrick seemed to
think unworthy of an answer; but when the trumpeter challenged him as his
acquaintance, the chief with great disdain turned his back, and ordered the
fellow to be dismissed with full power of trumpeting again on what side he
pleased."—Hillario hath since trumpeted in the cause of Pantomime, the
gaudy scenery of which with great judgment he dismisses from the Opera-
house, and saith, it is now fixed in its proper place in the threatre. On this
occasion, MACULARIUS cannot help exclaiming, "O Shakespear! O John-
son! rest, rest perturbed spirits."

While the gay seasons their due course shall run,
Ruled by the brilliant stars and golden sun,
While wit and fool antagonists shall be,   250
And sense and taste and nature shall agree,
While love shall live, and rapture shall rejoice,
Fed by the notes of Handel, Arne and Boyce,
While with joint force o'er humour's droll domain,
Cervantes, Fielding, Lucian, Swift shall reign,   255
While thinking figures from the canvass start,
And Hogarth is the Garrick of his art.
So long in flat stupidity's extreme,
Shall H–ll th' ARCH-DUNCE remain o'er every dunce supreme."

NOTES VARIORUM.

Handel, Arne, and Boyce,] The first of these gentlemen may be justly looked
upon as the Milton of musick, and the talents of the two latter may not
improperly be deliniated by calling them the Drydens of their profession, as
they not only touch the strings of love with exquisite art, but also, when they
please, reach the truly sublime.

Hogarth is the Garrick, &c.] The opinion which Mr. Hogarth entertains of
our hero's writings, may be guess'd at, by any one who will take the pleasure
of looking at a print called Beer-street, in which Hillario's critique upon the
Royal Society is put into a basket directed to the trunk-maker in St. Paul's
Church-yard. I shall only just observe that the compliment in this passage to
Mr. Hogarth is reciprocal, and reflects a lustre on Mr. Garrick, both of them
having similar talents, equally capable of the highest elevation, and of
representing the ordinary scenes of life, with the most exquisite humour.

Conclusion] And now, candid reader, MARTINUS MACULARIUS hath
attended thee throughout the first book of this most delectable poem. As it is
not improbable that those will be inquisitive after the particulars relating to
this thy commentator, he here gives thee notice that he is preparing for the
press, Memoirs of MARTINUS MACULARIUS, with his travels by sea and
land, together with his flights aerial, and descents subterraneous, &c. And in
the mean time he bids thee farewell, until the appearance of the second book
of the HILLIAD, of which we will say, *speciosa miracula promet*. And so as
Terence says, *Vos valete et plaudite*.

The END of BOOK the FIRST.

ERRATUM Magnum Lacrimabile.

It is with the utmost regret, that I am obliged to accuse OUR EPIC POET
of a most notorious blunder, and that in the very introduction to this work.—

250 antagonists] antagonist *1753D*   258 flat] gross *1791*

Turpissimum est in ipso limine cespitasse.—He has made himself debtor to Dr. Hill for his praises, and creditor for his abuse; whereas in truth and nature the reverse must be right, viz. The Doctor's abuse is an obligation, and his praise is downright Billingsgate. Swift says,—

> On me when blockheads are satyric,
> I take it for a panegyric.

And again,

> When scoundrels give me the dominion,
> They damn me in my own opinion.

M. MACULARIUS.

On St. David's Day 1753.

Humbly presented to His Royal Highness the Prince of Wales, by a
Cambro Briton—

Phœbe pater, qui mellifluas Heliconis ad undas,
Dulcia divinæ fundis præcepta Thaliæ,
Linque sacra sedes, et jam majora canenti
Aspira, radiisque diem melioribus orna.
Sed quid opem hinc quæram? nostris in vallibus amnes   5
Dulce sonant, nostris in montibus augur Apollo
Regnat, et indigenas jactat quoque *Cambria* musas.
   Salve sancte dies, quo solvimus annua cuncti
Gaudia, adorantes nostrum de more *Patronum.*
Et Tu, qui patrem vita, virtute redonas,   10
Quique ornas titulos, decus et superaddis honori
O salve ante omnes salve, celeberrime PRINCEPS!
O faveas, populumque bees, *Britonum*que tuorum
Accipias vota, et noster dignare vocari:
Summe puer, quem Fama vocat, quem gloria adoptat,   15
Quem vasti pater oceani colit omnibus undis:
   Tempus erit, cum tu (non unquam indignus avorum
Ast atavos qui mente refers, et moribus æquas)
Ad Famæ templum porta Virtutis adibis,
Atque infra positos regesque sophosque videbis;   20
Tempus erit, cum te (qua gens nec inanior ulla)
Gallia tota colet, mixtoque timebit amore.
In manibus tibi erit mundis dare jura futuris,
Et nondum inventis populis imponere leges.
Dum vestris læta auspiciis celeberrima floret   25
Cambria, jam prisci gens antiquissima mundi,
Inque velut montes nostrates vertice Cœlum
Sublimi feries, et cedet Laurea *Porro*—

ON ST. DAVID'S DAY. MS: Richard Morris, *Miscellaneous Collections,* n.d. (BL Add.
MS 14936), fo. 87b. First published in *Diddanwch Teuluaidd* (1763), pp. 27–8 (*DT*).
Text: *MS.* Collated: *DT.*
3 sedes, *DT*] sedes. *MS*   5 quæram?] quæram, *MS, DT*   14 vocari:] vocari
MS, DT   21 ulla] ulta *MS, DT*

Translation

Father Phœbus, who by the sweet-flowing waves of Helicon pourest out the sweet precepts of divine Thalia, leave your holy abode and now breathe on me as I sing of greater themes and adorn the day with better rays. Yet why should I seek aid from here? In our own valleys the rivers sound sweetly, in our mountains Apollo the prophet holds sway, and Cambria too boasts of her native muses.

All hail, holy day, on which we all break into yearly rejoicing, worshipping our patron in due form. You who restore [to us] your father by your life and goodness, and who give lustre to titles and add glory to honour, O hail before all others, hail most famous PRINCE! O may you favour and bless your people and receive the prayers of your Britons, youth most exalted, condescending to be called our own, whom Fame summons, whom glory adopts as her own, whom the father of the vast ocean worships with all his waves.

There will be a time when you (never unworthy of your forebears but reflecting your ancestors in your intellect, and their equal in your conduct) will approach the temple of Fame by the gate of Virtue, and will see kings and wise men placed beneath you. There will be a time when all France (than which no race is more frivolous) will worship you and hold you in fear mixed with love. It will be in your hands to mete out justice for worlds to be, and impose laws on peoples as yet undiscovered. While Cambria most famous flourishes joyfully under your auspices—Cambria, already the most ancient race of the primeval world—you, with head held aloft, will strike the sky as if it were our country's mountains, and the Laurel shall give way to the Leek—

Prologue

intended to have been spoken by Mr. Woodward at his benefit, in the character of the Old Mock Doctor, to introduce the New one.

Too long by dint of dress and force of face,
And all th' hypocrisy of grave grimace;
Have Pæon's sons attracted vulgar eyes,
And made themselves *conspicuous* by *disguise*.
But now with heart-felt worth, and conscious pride,   5
WE ARE OURSELVES, and throw the mask aside.

PROLOGUE. First published in *PA* (28 Mar. 1753). Text: *MW* (June 1753), iii. 145–6.
Collated: *PA. Title.* An Occasional Prologue *etc. PA*   2 And] With *PA*

The slow,—funereal—sober—solemn pace,
Turns to the WADDLE, and the sliding grace;
That look, which death denounces, or defies;
The gape-distended mouth, and half-shut eyes,   10
No longer please—but in their place are seen
The smiles *so soft! so simple! so serene!*
Life's a *disease* we all a while endure,
And which most doctors seldom fail to *cure.*
But wou'd you with *politeness* lose your breath,   15
And go *genteely* to the realms of death?
The BEAU PHYSICIAN stands the first in place,
And *hands you off* with elegance and grace.
Therefore no more this *mockery* I'll wear,
This compound strange of phiz, and cane, and hair.   20
Deceiving now's a trite, and trivial task,
He's the best cheat, who bravely scorns a mask.
   But let not *wits* mistake our true intent,
Nor think that *spleen,* where only *mirth* is meant.
We reverence virtue in the truly good,   25
And honour Science, where she's understood.
But if in this refin'd judicious age,
There are MOCK-DOCTORS acting *off* the stage,
We must be pleasant, and we must be free,
And pay derision as their lawful fee;   30
Whether they wait at Opulency's door,
Or do they *charitably* kill the poor,
To give them up to ridicule's our plan,
But shou'd suspicion mark some single man,
Let *that same doctor* in his turn be free,   35
And as a *brother-actor* laugh at me.

7 sober—solemn] solemn sober *PA*   12 *so serene*] *and serene PA*   15 But] Yet
PA   16 go] slide *PA*   20 compound strange of phiz] old compound of face
PA   21 Deceiving] Dissembling *PA*   22 a] the *PA*   23 But let not]
Let not the *PA*   24 Nor] Not *PA*   26 where she's] when 'tis *PA*
30 pay] give *PA*   33 give them up] point them out *PA*

An Epilogue,

Spoken by Mrs. Midnight's Daughter, riding upon
an Ass dressed in a great Tie-Wig.

As hissing and pelting are so much in vogue,
You'll permit me to ride with my new epilogue,
That in case of a thump from a *Buck*,—or a *Beau*,
I may clap to my spurs, and gallop—ge-hoe!
And, like a brave general, after being beat,   5
Exult and rejoice in a prudent retreat.
   Nor should you despise this old senat'ress here,
Accoutred and dress'd in a caxon so queer;
For she is a person of learning profound,
Of sense most sagacious, of wisdom most sound,   10
So genteel in carriage, so sober and quiet,
And so useful—she serves me for physic and diet;
In arts *Æsculapian* sh' has wonderful knowledge,
And wrought greater cures than most of the college!
   Oh, could all the sick, who have cause to repine,   15
But bridle their doctors, as I bridle mine;
Wou'd they saddle an ass, to the country repair,
And drink of her milk in an open free air,
The dabblers in physick would quickly decay,
And the bills of mortality dwindle away.   20
   Or could the poor clients, who oft are bestridden,
But ride on their lawyers, as by them they're ridden;
Cou'd saddle a sergeant, and jog out of town,
And strife and contention in full bumpers drown,
The world would grow wise and better each day,   25
And envy, and malice, and mischief decay!
The sons of sound sense to this scheme will agree,
And applaud my poor ass, and my mamma, and me.

AN EPILOGUE. First published in *CP6* (1756). Text: *CP6* [6th edn., *c.*1758], pp. 16–18.
Collated: *MO* (1763), pp. 59–60.
4 ge-hoe] He-hoe *MO*   11 carriage, so *MO*] carriage so *CP6*   13 sh' has]
she's *MO*   19 dabblers *MO*] babblers *CP6*

The Dust Cart

a favourite Cantata sung in the Old Woman's Oratory
at the New Theatre in the Hay-Market in manner of
the Moderns.

Recit.

As Tink'ring Tom the streets his trade did cry,
He saw his lovely Silvia passing by:
In dust cart high advanc'd, the nymph was plac'd
With the rich cinders round her lovely waist.
Tom with uplifted hands th' occasion blest,   5
And thus in soothing strains the maid addrest.

Aria.

Oh Silvia! while you drive your carts
To pick up dust you steal our hearts,
  You take our dust and steal our hearts.
That mine is gone alas! is true,   10
And dwells among the dust with you,
  And dwells among the dust with you.
Ah lovely Silvia ease my pain!
Give me the heart you stole again,
  Give me my heart, out of your cart;   15
  Give me the heart you stole again.

Recit.

Silvia, advanc'd above the rabble rout,
Exulting roll'd her sparkling eyes about,
She heav'd her swelling breast as black as sloe
And look'd disdain on little folks below;   20
To Tom she nodded as the carr drew on,
And then resolv'd to speak, she cry'd "stop John!"

THE DUST CART. First published in undated songsheets (?Apr. 1753) and *The Town Whim* [?1753], pp. 5–6. Text: Songsheet issued by James Oswald (*SS1*). Collated: Songsheet in Bodl., Harding Mus. E562 fo. 86 (*SS2*); *Town Whim*.
3 high *omitted, Town Whim*   13 Ah] Oh *SS2*   O *Town Whim*   14, 16 the *SS2*] my *SS1, Town Whim*   18 Exulting] Exulted *Town Whim*   19 breast] breasts *Town Whim*   21 carr] cart *Town Whim*

Air

Shall I who ride above the rest
Be by a paltry crowd opprest?
Ambition now my soul does fire,   25
The youths shall languish and admire,
And ev'ry girl with anxious heart
Shall long to ride in my dust cart,
    Shall long to ride in my dust cart.

The Bite.

Not Marry when I please—Can That be true?
Gad but I'll bite 'em tho'—for I'll turn Jew!

Ode to Lord Barnard,

on his Accession to that Title.

Sis licet felix ubicunque mavis,
Et memor nostri.   Hor.

Melpomene, who charm'st the skies,
    Queen of the lyre and lute,
Say, shall my noble patron rise,
    And thou, sweet Muse, be mute?
Shall Fame, to celebrate his praise,   5
Her loudest, loftiest accents raise,
    And all her silver trumps employ,
And thou restrain they tuneful hand,
And thou an idle list'ner stand
    Amidst the general joy?   10

Forbid it, all ye powers above,
    That human hearts can try,
Forbid it gratitude and love,
    And every tender tye:

28 long to ride *repeated three times, SS1, SS2*
THE BITE. MS: BL. Add MS 51441 (fo. 7).
ODE TO LORD BARNARD. First published in *GM* (Dec. 1754), p. 575. Text: *1791*.
Collated: *GM. Title.* To the Rt. Hon. the Lord ———, *etc. GM*

Was it not he, whose pious cares   15
Upheld me in my earliest years,
   And chear'd me from his ample store,
Who animated my designs,
In Roman and Athenian mines,
   To search for learning's ore?   20

The royal hand my Lord shall raise
   To nobler heights thy name,
Who praises thee, shall meet with praise
   Ennobled in thy fame.
A disposition form'd to please,   25
With dignity endear'd by ease,
   And grandeur in good nature lost,
Have more of genuine desert,
Have more of merit of the heart,
   Than arts and arms can boast.   30

Can I forget fair Raby's * towers,
   How awful and how great!
Can I forget such blissful bowers,
   Such splendour in retreat!
Where me, ev'n me, an infant bard,   35
Cleveland † and Hope ‡ indulgent heard.
   (Then fame I felt thy first alarms)
Ah, much lov'd pair!—tho' one is fled,
Still one compensates for the dead,
   In merit and in charms.   40

O more than compensation, sure!
   O blessings on thy life!
Long may the three-fold bliss endure,
   In daughters, sons, and wife!
Hope, copyist of her mother's mind,   45
Is loveliest, liveliest of her kind,
   Her soul with every virtue teems,

* His Lordship's seat in the county of Durham.
† Her late Grace of Cleveland.
‡ The Honourable Mrs. Hope.

By none in wit or worth outdone,
With eyes, that shining on the sun,
   Defy his brightest beams.   50

Hark! Charity's cherubic voice
   Calls to her numerous poor,
And bids their languid hearts rejoice,
   And points to Raby's door;
With open heart and open hands,   55
There HOSPITALITY—she stands,
   A nymph, whom men and gods admire,
Daughter of heavenly GOODNESS she,
Her sister's GENEROSITY,
   And HONOUR is her sire.   60

What tho' my Lord, betwixt us lie,
   Full many an envious league,
Such vast extent of sea and sky,
   As even the eye fatigue;
Tho' interposing ocean raves,   65
And heaves his heaven assaulting waves,
   While on the shores the billows beat,
Yet still my grateful muse is free,
To tune her warmest strains to thee,
   And lay them at thy feet.   70

GOODNESS is ever kindly prone
   To feign what fate denies,
And others want of worth t'attone,
   Finds in herself supplies:
Thus dignity itself restrains,   75
By condescension's silken reins,
   While you the lowly Muse upraise;
When such the theme, so mean the bard,
Not to reject is to reward,
   To pardon is to praise.

54 to] at *GM*   67 shores] shore *GM*

To the Rev. Mr. Powell, on the Non-performance of a Promise he made the Author of a Hare.

Friend, with regard to this same hare,
Am I to hope, or to despair?
By punctual post the letter came,
With P***LL's hand, and P***LL's name:
Yet there appear'd, for love or money,   5
Nor hare, nor leveret, nor coney.
Say, my dear Morgan, has my lord,
Like other great ones kept his word?
Or have you been deceiv'd by 'squire?
Or has your poacher lost his wire?   10
Or in some unpropitious hole,
Instead of puss, trepann'd a mole?
Thou valiant son of great Cadwallader,
Hast thou a hare, or hast thou swallow'd her?
    But now, me thinks, I hear you say,   15
(And shake your head) "Ah, well-a-day!
Painful pre-em'nence to be wise,
We wits have such short memories.
Oh, that the Act was not in force!
A horse!—my kindom for a horse!   20
To love—yet be deny'd the sport!
Oh! for a friend or two at court!
God knows, there's scarce a man of quality
In all our peerless principality—"
    But hold—for on his country joking,   25
To a warm Welchman's most provoking.
[So truce with your reflections national
And to the point in order rational.]
As for poor puss, upon my honour,
I never set my heart upon her.   30

TO THE REV. MR. POWELL. First published in *GJ*, No. 32 (26 May 1753). Text: *1791*. Collated: *GJ*; *MW* (June 1753), iii. 120–1. *Title.* An Epistle to the Reverend Mr. Evan Pritchard of —— in Glamorganshire, *etc. GJ*   To the Rev. Mr. ****, *etc. MW* 4 P***LL's ... P***LL's] Evan's ... Pritchard's *GJ*   7 Morgan] Evan *GJ*   8 ones] men *GJ*   13 Thou valiant] Tell me, thou *GJ*   14 Hast] Hadst *GJ*   19 Act *GJ*] act *1791*   23 a man] three men *GJ*   27–8 *GJ*: omitted, *MW*, *1791*

But any gift from friend to friend,
Is pleasing in its aim and end.
I, like the cock, wou'd spurn a jewel,
Sent by th' unkind, th' unjust, and cruel.
But honest P***LL!— Sure from him   35
A barley-corn wou'd be a gem.
Pleas'd therefore had I been, and proud,
And prais'd thy generous heart aloud,
If 'stead of hare (but do not blab it)
You'd sent me only a Welch rabbit.   40

The Tea-Pot and Scrubbing-Brush.

A Fable.

A tawdry Tea-pot, *A-la-mode*,
Where Art her utmost skill bestow'd,
Was much esteem'd for being old,
And on its sides with red and gold
Strange beasts were drawn in taste Chinese,   5
And frightful fish and hump-back trees.
  High in an elegant beaufet
This pompous utensil was set,
And near it, on a marble slab,
Forsaken by some careless drab,   10
A veteran Scrubbing-brush was plac'd,
And the rich furniture disgrac'd.
The Tea-pot soon began to flout,
And thus its venom *spouted* out.
"Who from the scullery or yard,   15
Brought in this low, this vile black-guard,
And laid in insolent position,
Amongst us people of condition?

34

34 and] or *MW*   35 P***LL] Pritchard *GJ*   36 wou'd be] had been *GJ*
40 sent me only] only sent me *GJ*
THE TEA-POT. First published in *MW* (June 1753), iii. 134–6. Text: *MW*. Collated:
UV (Apr. 1756), pp. 190–1; *MO* (1763), pp. 56–8; *1791*.
2 bestow'd] had shew'd *MO*   4 with] in *MO*   5 drawn] done *UV*   6 And]
With *MO*   hump-back] humpback'd *UV*   10 careless] dirty *MO*   13 soon]
first *UV*   flout] lout *MO*   17 laid] plac'd *MO*   18 Amongst] Among
MO, 1791

Back to the helper in the stable,
Scour the close-stool, or wash-house table,   20
Or cleanse some horsing-block, or plank,
Nor dare approach us folk of rank.
Turn—brother Coffee-pot, your spout,
Observe the nasty stinking lout,
Who seems to scorn my indignation,   25
Nor pays due homage to my fashion:
Take, sister Sugar-dish, a view
And cousin, Cream-pot, pray do you."
"Pox on you all," replies old Scrub—
"Of coxcombs ye confederate club.   30
Full of impertinence, and prate,
Ye hate all things that are sedate.
None but such ignorant infernals,
Judge, by appearance, and externals.
Train'd up in toil and useful knowledge,   35
I'm fellow of the kitchen college,
And with the mop, my old associate,
The family affairs negociate—
Am foe to filth, and things obscene,
Dirty by making others clean—   40
Not shining, yet I cause to shine,
My roughness makes my neighbours fine;
You're fair without, but foul within,
With shame impregnated, and sin;
To *you* each impious scandal's owing,   45
You set each gossip's clack a-going.—
How Parson Tythe in secret sins,
And how Miss Dainty brought forth twins:
How dear delicious Polly Bloom,
Owes all her sweetness to perfume;   50
Tho' grave at church, at cards can bet,
At once a prude and a coquette.
'Twas better for each British virgin,

20 Scour the close-stool] Clean a joint-stool *MO*   21 Or cleanse some] Or cleanse
an *UV*   Go scour a *MO*   22 folk] folks *1791*   27 sister] silver
1791   28 pray] so *MO*   30 ye] you *MO*   32 Ye] You *MO*   34 Can
boast experience and externals. *MO*   42 roughness] foulness *UV*   48 Dainty]
Squeamish *UV, MO*   53 each British virgin] our British virgins *MO*

When on roast beef, strong beer, and sturgeon,
Joyous to breakfast they sat round,   55
Nor was asham'd to eat a pound.
These were the manners, these the ways,
In good Queen Bess's golden days,
Each damsel ow'd her bloom and glee,
To wholesome elbow-grease, and me.   60
But now they center all their joys
In empty rattle traps and noise.
Thus where the Fates send *you*, they send
Flagitious times, which ne'er will mend,
Till some Philosopher can find   65
A Scrubbing-brush to scour the mind."

To the Memory of Master [Newbery],

who died of a lingering illness, aged eleven.

Henceforth be every tender tear supprest,
Or let us weep for joy, that he is blest;
From grief to bliss, from earth to heav'n remov'd,
His mem'ry honour'd, as his life belov'd.
That heart o'er which no evil e'er had pow'r!   5
That disposition, sickness cou'd not sour!
That sense, so oft to riper years deny'd!
That patience, heroes might have own'd with pride!
His painful race undauntedly he ran,
And in the eleventh winter died a MAN.

54 sturgeon] sturgeons *MO*   55 sat] set *1791*   56 was] were *1791*   63 Thus
where] Where'er *UV*   Thus when *MO*   65 can] shall *UV*
TO THE MEMORY. First published in *MW* (June 1753), iii. 146. Text: *MW*. Collated:
1791. *Title*. To the Memory of Master **** *etc. MW*   On the Death of Master
Newbery, after a lingering Illness *1791*   10 in *1791*] on *MW*

The Fair Monopolist.

A Ballad.

When young, and artless, as the lamb,
That plays about the fondling dam,
  Brisk, buxom, pert, and silly;
I slighted all the manly swains,
And put my virgin heart in chains,   5
  For simple, smock-fac'd *Billy.*

But when experience came with years,
And rais'd my hopes and quell'd my fears,
  My blood grew blithe and bonny;
I turn'd off every beardless youth,   10
And gave my love and fix'd my truth
  On honest, sturdy *Johnny.*

But when at Wake I saw the 'squire,
For lace I found a new desire,
  Fond to outshine my mammy;   15
I sigh'd for fringe, and frogs, and beaux,
And pigtail'd wigs, and powder'd cloaths,
  And silken Master *Sammy.*

For riches next, I felt a flame,
When to my cot old Gripus came,   20
  To hold an am'rous parley;
For musick then I 'gan to burn,
And to my arms took in his turn
  The warbling, quavering *Charly.*

At length alike the fools and wits,   25
Fops, fidlers foreigners, and cits,
  All had me by rotation;
Then warn'd by me, ye Patriot Fair,
Ne'er make one single man your care,
  But sigh for all the nation.   30

THE FAIR MONOPOLIST. First published in *MW* (June 1753), iii. 150–1. Text: *MW*. Collated: *LB* [Mar. 1754], iv. 67–8; *European Mag.* (Dec. 1791), p. 461 (*EM*). *Title.* The Patriot Fair *LB, EM*
2 That] Who *LB*   about] around *EM*   9 grew] was *LB*   14 found] felt *EM*   17 powder'd *LB, EM*] powder *MW*   22 then] now *EM*   'gan] chanc'd *LB, EM*   23 to my arms took] fondly listen'd *LB, EM*   24 The] To *LB, EM*   25 At length] Thus all *EM*   27 had] struck *LB*   charm'd *EM*   28 warn'd by] learn from *LB, EM*

ON THE
POWER
OF THE
SUPREME BEING.

"Tremble, thou earth! th' anointed poet said,
At God's bright presence, tremble, all ye mountains
And all ye hillocks on the surface bound."
Then once again, ye glorious thunders roll,
The Muse with transport hears ye, once again   5
Convulse the solid continent, and shake,
Grand musick of omnipotence, the isles.
'Tis thy terrific voice, thou God of power,
'Tis thy terrific voice; all Nature hears it
Awaken'd and alarm'd; she feels its force,   10
In every spring she feels it, every wheel,
And every movement of her vast machine.
Behold! quakes Apennine, behold! recoils
Athos, and all the hoary-headed Alps
Leap from their bases at the godlike sound.   15
But what is this, celestial tho' the note,
And proclamation of the reign supreme,
Compar'd with such as, for a mortal ear
Too great, amaze the incorporeal worlds?
Shou'd ocean to his congregated waves   20
Call in each river, cataract, and lake,
And with the watry world down an huge rock
Fall headlong in one horrible cascade,
'Twere but the echo of the parting breeze,
When Zephyr faints upon the lilly's breast,   25
'Twere but the ceasing of some instrument,
When the last ling'ring undulation
Dies on the doubting ear, if nam'd with sounds
So mighty! so stupendous! so divine!
But not alone in the aërial vault   30
Does he the dread theocracy maintain;

POWER. First published in 1754. Text: *P*. Collated *P2*; *1761*; *1791*.
22 an] a *1791*

For oft, enrag'd with his intestine thunders,
He harrows up the bowels of the earth,
And shocks the central magnet.—Cities then
Totter on their foundations, stately columns,   35
Magnific walls, and heav'n-assaulting spires.
What tho' in haughty eminence erect
Stands the strong citadel, and frowns defiance
On adverse hosts, tho' many a bastion jut
Forth from the rampart's elevated mound,   40
Vain the poor providence of human art,
And mortal strength how vain! while underneath
Triumphs his mining vengeance in th' uproar
Of shatter'd towers, riven rocks, and mountains,
With clamour inconceivable uptorn,   45
And hurl'd adown th' abyss. Sulphureous pyrites
Bursting abrupt from darkness into day,
With din outrageous and destructive ire
Augment the hideous tumult, while it wounds
Th' afflicted ear, and terrifies the eye,   50
And rends the heart in twain. Twice have we felt,
Within Augusta's walls twice have we felt
Thy threaten'd indignation, but ev'n Thou,
Incens'd Omnipotent, art gracious ever,
Thy goodness infinite but mildly warn'd us   55
With mercy-blended wrath; O spare us still,
Nor send more dire conviction: we confess
That thou art He, th' Almighty: we believe.
For at thy righteous power whole systems quake,
For at thy nod tremble ten thousand worlds.   60
  ' Hark! on the winged Whirlwind's rapid rage,
Which is and is not in a moment—hark!
On th' hurricane's tempestuous sweep he rides
Invincible, and oaks and pines and cedars
And forests are no more. For conflict dreadful!   65
The West encounters East, and Notus meets
In his career the Hyperborean blast.
The lordly lions shudd'ring seek their Dens,
And fly like tim'rous deer; the king of birds,
Who dar'd the solar ray, is weak of wing   70

        54 ever,] ever: *1791*

And faints and falls and dies;—while He supreme
Stands stedfast in the center of the storm.
   Wherefore, ye objects terrible and great,
Ye thunders, earthquakes, and ye fire-fraught wombs
Of fell Volcanos, whirlwinds, hurricanes,   75
And boiling billows hail! in chorus join
To celebrate and magnify your Maker,
Who yet in works of a minuter mould
Is not less manifest, is not less mighty.
   Survey the magnet's sympathetic love,   80
That wooes the yielding needle; contemplate
Th' attractive amber's pow'r, invisible
Ev'n to the mental eye; or when the blow
Sent from th' electric sphere assaults thy frame,
Shew me the hand, that dealt it!—baffled here   85
By his omnipotence Philosophy
Slowly her thoughts inadequate revolves,
And stands, with all his circling wonders round her,
Like heavy Saturn in th' etherial space
Begirt with an inexplicable ring.   90
   If such the operations of his power,
Which at all seasons and in ev'ry place
(Rul'd by establish'd laws and current nature)
Arrest th' attention! Who? O Who shall tell
His acts miraculous, when his own decrees   95
Repeals he, or suspends, when by the hand
Of Moses or of Joshua, or the mouths
Of his prophetic seers, such deeds he wrought,
Before th' astonish'd Sun's all seeing eye,
That Faith was scarce a virtue. Need I sing   100
The fate of Pharaoh and his numerous band
Lost in the reflux of the watry walls,
That melted to their fluid state again?
Need I recount how Sampson's warlike arm
With more than mortal nerves was strung t' o'erthrow 105
Idolatrous Philistia? shall I tell
How David triumph'd, and what Job sustain'd?

86 omnipotence] omnipotence, *1761*   94 attention! *P2*] attention; *P, 1761,*
1791   105 was *omitted, 1761*

—But, O supreme, unutterable mercy!
O love unequal'd, mystery immense,
Which angels long t' unfold! tis man's redemption   110
That crowns thy glory, and thy pow'r confirms,
Confirms the great, th' uncontroverted claim.
When from the Virgin's unpolluted womb
Shone forth the Sun of Righteousness reveal'd,
And on benighted reason pour'd the day;   115
Let there be peace (he said) and all was calm
Amongst the warring world—calm as the sea,
When O be still, ye boisterous Winds, he cry'd,
And not a breath was blown, nor murmur heard.
His was a life of miracles and might,   120
And charity and love, ere yet he taste
The bitter draught of death, ere yet he rise
Victorious o'er the universal foe,
And Death and Sin and Hell in triumph lead.
His by the right of conquest is mankind,   125
And in sweet servitude and golden bonds
Were ty'd to him for ever.—O how easy
Is his ungalling Yoke, and all his burdens
'Tis ecstacy to bear! Him blessed Shepherd
His flocks shall follow thro' the maze of life   130
And shades that tend to Day-spring from on high;
And as the radiant roses after fading
In fuller foliage and more fragrant breath
Revive in smiling spring, so shall it fare
With those that love him—for sweet is their savour,   135
And all eternity shall be their spring.
Then shall the gates and everlasting doors,
At which the *King of Glory* enters in,
Be to the Saints unbarr'd: and there, where pleasure
Boasts an undying bloom, where dubious hope   140
Is certainty, and grief-attended love
Is freed from passion—there we'll celebrate
With worthier numbers, him, who is, and was,
And in immortal prowess King of Kings
Shall be the Monarch of all worlds for ever.   145

FINIS.

111 glory, *P2*] glory *P*   118 O] Peace *1791*

277

On my Wife's Birth-Day.

'Tis Nancy's birth-day—raise your strains,
Ye nymphs of the Parnassian plains,
And sing with more than usual glee
To Nancy, who was born for me.

Tell the blithe Graces as they bound   5
Luxuriant in the buxom round;
They're not more elegantly free,
Than Nancy, who was born for me.

Tell royal Venus, tho' she rove,
The Queen of the immortal grove;   10
That she must share her golden fee
With Nancy, who was born for me.

Tell Pallas, tho' th' Athenian school,
And ev'ry trite pedantic fool,
On her to place the palm agree,   15
'Tis Nancy's, who was born for me.

Tell spotless Dian, tho' she range,
The regent of the up-land grange,
In chastity she yields to thee,
O, Nancy, who wast born for me.   20

Tell Cupid, Hymen, and tell Jove,
With all the pow'rs of life and love,
That I'd disdain to breathe or *be*,
If Nancy was not born for me.

ON MY WIFE'S BIRTHDAY. First published in *GM* (Feb. 1754), pp. 88–9. Text: *1791*.
Collated: *GM*. Subtitled A Song *GM*   20 wast] was *GM*

The Brocaded Gown and Linen Rag.

From a fine lady to her maid,
A Gown descended of brocade.
French!—Yes, from Paris—that's enough,
That wou'd give dignity to stuff.
By accident or by design,   5
Or from some cause, I can't divine;
A Linen Rag, (sad source of wrangling!)
On a contiguous peg was dangling,
Vilely besmear'd—for late his master,
It serv'd in quality of plaister.   10
The Gown, contemptuous beholder,
Gave a French shrug from either shoulder,
And rustling with emotions furious,
Bespoke the Rag in terms injurious.
"Unfit for tinder, lint or *fodder*,   15
Thou thing of filth, (and what is odder)
Discarded from thy owner's back,
Dar'st thou proceed, and gold attack?
Instant away—or in this place,
Begar me give you *coup de grace*."   20
    To this reply'd the honest Rag,
Who lik'd a jest, and was a wag;
    "Tho' thy glib tongue without a halt run,
Thou shabby second-hand subaltern,
At once so antient and so easy,   25
At once so gorgeous and so greasy;
I value not thy gasconading
Nor all thy alamode parading.
But to abstain from words imperious,
And to be sober, grave, and serious,   30
(Tho' says friend Horace, 'tis no treason,
At once to giggle and to reason):

THE BROCADED GOWN. First published in *GM* (Feb. 1754), pp. 89–90. Text: *1791*.
Collated: *GM*. Subtitled *A Fable, GM*
9 his] it's *GM*   13 emotions] emotion *GM*   16 (and what is odder)] and
(what is odder) *GM*   17 back] issue *GM*   18 Dare you approach brocade
and tissue? *GM*   23 a] an *GM*   27–8 thy ... thy] your ... your *GM*
28 parading. *GM*] parading; *1791*   30 serious, *GM*] serious. *1791*   31–2 (Tho'
... reason.) *GM*] Tho' ... reason, *1791*

When me you lesson, friend, you dream,
For know I am not what I seem;
Soon by the mill's refining motion, 35
The sweetest daughter of the ocean,
Fair Medway, shall with snowy hue,
My virgin purity renew,
And give me reinform'd existence,
A good retention and subsistence. 40
Then shall the sons of genius join,
To make my second life divine.
O MURRAY, let me then dispense,
Some portion of thy eloquence;
For Greek and Roman rhetoric shine, 45
United and improved in thine.
The spirit stirring * sage alarms,
And Ciceronian sweetness charms.
Th' Athenian AKENSIDE may deign
To stamp me deathless with his pen. 50
While flows approv'd by all the Nine
Th' immortal soul of every line.
COLLINS, perhaps, his aid may lend,
Melpomene's selected friend.
Perhaps our great Augustan GRAY 55
May grace me with a Doric lay;
With sweet, with manly words of woe,
That nervously pathetic flow.
What, MASON, may I owe to you?
Learning's first pride, and nature's too; 60
On thee she cast her sweetest smile,
And gave thee Art's correcting file;
That file, which with assiduous pain,
The viper Envy bites in vain.—
Such glories my mean lot betide, 65
Hear, tawdry fool, and check thy pride.—
Thou, after scouring, dying, turning,
(If haply thou escape a burning)

---

* Demosthenes.

---

33 lesson] lessen *GM*   39 me] my *GM*   53-4 *omitted, GM*   55 Perhaps
ev'n all-accomplish'd Gray, *GM*   68 thou] you *GM*

From gown to petticoat descending,
And in a beggar's mantle ending,   70
Shalt in a dunghill or a stye,
'Midst filth and vermin rot and die."

The Blockhead and Beehive.

The fragrance of the new-mown hay
Paid incense to the god of day;
Who issuing from his eastern gate,
Resplendent rode in all his state.
Rous'd by the light from soft repose,   5
Big with the Muse, a Bard arose,
And the fresh garden's still retreat
He measur'd with poetic feet.
The cooling, high, o'er-arching shade,
By the embracing branches made,   10
The smooth shorn sod, whose verdant gloss,
Was check'd with intermingled moss,
Cowslips, like topazes that shine,
Close by the silver serpentine,
Rude rustics which assert the bow'rs,   15
Amidst the educated flow'rs.
The lime tree and sweet-scented bay,
(The sole reward of many a lay)
And all the poets of the wing,
Who sweetly without salary sing,   20
Attract at once his observation,
Peopling thy wilds, Imagination!
"Sweet nature, who this turf bedews,
Sweet nature, who's the thrush's muse!
How she each anxious thought beguiles,   25
And meets me with ten thousand smiles!
O infinite benignity!
She smiles, but not alone on me;
Oh hill, on dale, on lake, on lawn,
Like Celia when her picture's drawn;   30

THE BLOCKHEAD. Text: *1791*.
4 state.] state, *1791*

Assuming countless charms and airs,
'Till HAYMAN's matchless art despairs,
Pausing like me he dreads to fall
From the divine original."
More had he said—but in there came   35
A lout—Squire Booby was his name.—
The bard, who at a distant view,
The busy prattling blockhead knew,
Retir'd into a secret nook,
And thence his observations took.   40
Vex'd he cou'd find no man to teize,
The squire 'gan chattering to the bees,
And pertly with officious mien,
He thus address'd their humming queen:
"Madam, be not in any terrors,   45
I only come t' amend your errors;
My friendship briefly to display,
And put you in a better way.
Cease, Madam, (if I may advise)
To carry honey on your thighs,   50
Employ ('tis better, I aver)
Old Grub the fairies coach-maker;
For he who has sufficient art
To make a coach, may make a cart.
To these you'll yoke some sixteen bees,   55
Who will dispatch your work with ease;
And come and go, and go and come,
To bring your honey harvest home.—
Ma'm, architcture you're not skill'd in,
I don't approve your way of building;   60
In this there's nothing like design,
Pray learn the use of Gunter's line.
I'll serve your Highness at a pinch,
I am a scholar every inch,
And know each author I lay fist on,   65
From Archimedes down to Whiston.—
Tho' honey making be your trade,
In chemistry you want some aid.—
Pleas'd with your work, altho' you sing,
You're not quite right—'tis not the thing.   70

Myself wou'd gladly be an actor,
To help the honey manufacture.—
I hear for war you are preparing,
Which I should like to have a share in;
Yet tho' the enemy be landing,   75
'Tis wrong to keep an army standing.—
If you'll ensure me from the laws
I'll write a pamphlet in your cause.—
I vow I am concern'd to see
Your want of state-œconomy.   80
Of nothing living I pronounce ill,
But I don't like your privy-council.
There is, I know, a certain bee,
(Wou'd he was from the ministry)
Which certain bee, if rightly known,   85
Wou'd prove no better than a drone;
There are (but I shall name no names,
I never love to kindle flames)
A pack of rogues with crimes grown callous,
Who greatly wou'd adorn the gallows,   90
That with the wasps, for paltry gold,
A secret correspondence hold,
Yet you'll be great—your subjects free,
If the whole thing be left to me.—"

    Thus, like the waters of the ocean,   95
His tongue had run in ceaseless motion,
Had not the Queen ta'en up in wrath,
This thing of folly and of froth.
    "Impertinent and witless medler,
Thou smattering, empty, noisy pedlar!   100
By vanity, thou bladder blown,
To be the football of the town.
O happy England, land of freedom,
Replete with statesmen, if she need 'em,
Where war is wag'd by Sue or Nell,   105
And Jobson is a Machiavel!—
Tell Hardwick that his judgment fails,
Show Justice how to hold her scales.—
To fire the soul at once, and please,
Teach Murray and Demosthenes;   110

Say Vane is not by goodness grac'd,
And wants humanity and taste.—
Tho' Pelham with Mæcenas vies,
Tell Fame she's false, and Truth she lies;
And then return, thou verbal Hector, 115
And give the bees another lecture."
  This said, the portal she unbarr'd,
Calling the Bees upon their guard,
And set at once about his ears
Ten thousand of her granadiers.— 120
Some on his lips and palate hung,
And the offending member stung.
"Just (says the bard from out the grot)
Just, tho' severe, is your sad lot,
Who think, and talk, and live in vain, 125
Of sweet society the bane.
Business misplac'd is a mere jest,
And active idleness at best."

The Citizen and the Red Lion of Brentford.

I love my friend—but love my ease,
And claim a right myself to please;
To company however prone,
At times all men wou'd be alone.
Free from each interruption rude, 5
Or what is meant by solitude.
My villa lies within the bills,
So—like a theatre it fills:
To me my kind acquaintance stray,
And Sunday proves no Sabbath day; 10
Yet many a friend and near relation,
Make up a glorious congregation;
They croud by dozens and by dozens,
And bring me all their country cousins.
Tho' cringing landlords on the road, 15

125 vain,] vain. *1791*

THE CITIZEN. Text: *1791*.

Who find for man and horse abode,
Tho' gilded grapes to sign-post chain'd,
Invite them to be entertain'd,
And straddling across his kilderkin,
Tho' jolly Bacchus calls them in;   20
Nay—tho' my landlady wou'd trust 'em,
Pilgarlick's sure of all the custom;
And his whole house is like a fair,
Unless he only treats with air.
What? shall each pert half witted wit,   25
That calls me Jack, or calls me Kit,
Prey on my time, or on my table?
No—but let's hasten to the Fable.
   The eve advanc'd, the sun declin'd,
BALL to the *booby-hutch* was join'd,   30
A wealthy cockney drove away,
To celebrate Saint Saturday;
Wife, daughter, pug, all crouded in,
To meet at country house their kin.
Thro' Brentford, to fair Twickenham's bow'rs,   35
The ungreased grumbling axle scow'rs,
To pass in rural sweets a day,
But there's a Lion in the way:
This Lion a most furious elf,
Hung up to represent himself,   40
Redden'd with rage, and shook his mane,
And roar'd, and roar'd, and roar'd again.
Wond'rous, tho' painted on a board,
He roar'd, and roar'd, and roar'd, and roar'd.
"Fool!" (says the majesty of beasts)   45
"At whose expence a legion feasts,
Foe to yourself, you those pursue,
Who're eating up your cakes and you;
Walk in, walk in (so prudence votes)
And give poor BALL a feed of oats,   50
Look to yourself, and as for ma'm,
Coax her to take a little dram;
Let Miss and Pug with cakes be fed,
Then honest man go back to bed;

16 abode,] abode; *1791*

You're better, and you're cheaper there,   55
Where no hangers on to fear,
Go buy friend Newbery's new Pantheon,
And con the tale of poor Acteon,
Horn'd by Diana, and o'erpower'd,
And by the dogs he fed devour'd.   60
What he receiv'd from charity,
Lewdness perhaps may give to thee;
And tho' your spouse my lecture scorns,
Beware his fate, beware his horns."
    "Sir" says the Cit (who made a stand,   65
And strok'd his forehead with his hand)
"By your grim gravity and grace,
You greatly wou'd become the mace.
This kind advice I gladly take,—
Draw'r, bring the dram, and bring a cake,   70
With good brown beer that's brisk and humming."
"*A coming, Sir! a coming, coming!*"
The Cit then took a hearty draught,
And shook his jolly sides and laugh'd.
Then to the king of beasts he bow'd,   75
And thus his gratitude avow'd.—
"Sir, for your sapient oration,
I owe the greatest obligation.
You stand expos'd to sun and show'r,
I know Jack Ellis of the Tow'r;   80
By him you soon may gain renown,
He'll show your Highness to the town;
Or, if you chuse your station here,
To call forth Britons to their beer,
As painter of distinguish'd note,   85
He'll send his man to clean your coat."
The Lion thank'd him for his proffer,
And if a vacancy shou'd offer,
Declar'd he had too just a notion,
To be averse to such promotion.   90
The Citizen drove off with joy
"For London—Ball—for London—hoy."
Content to bed, he went his way,
And is no Bankrupt to this day.

Ode to a Virginia Nightingale,

which was cured of a Fit in the Bosom of a young Lady, who
afterwards nursed the Author in a dangerous Illness.

Sweet bird! whose fate and mine agree,
As far as proud humanity,
   The parellel will own;
O let our voice and hearts combine,
O let us, fellow-warblers join,   5
   Our patroness to crown.

When heavy hung thy flagging wing,
When thou could'st neither move nor sing,
   Of spirits void and rest;
A lovely nymph her aid apply'd,   10
She gave the bliss to heav'n allied,
   And cur'd thee on her breast.

Me too the kind indulgent maid,
With gen'rous care and timely aid,
   Restor'd to mirth and health;   15
Then join'd to her, O may I prove
By friendship, gratitude, and love,
   The Poverty of Wealth.

Martial. Book I, Ep. 26.

When Brutus' fall wing'd fame to Porcia brought,
Those arms her friends conceal'd, her passion sought.
She soon perceiv'd their poor officious wiles,
Approves their zeal, but at their folly smiles.
What Cato taught heaven sure cannot deny,   5
Bereav'd of all, we still have pow'r to die.
Then down her throat the burning coal conveyed,
Go now, ye fools, and hide your swords, she said.

ODE. First published in *GM* (Mar. 1754), p. 137. Text: *1791*. Collated: *GM*. *Title.*
which] who *GM*
12 on] in *GM*   17 By friendship,] A life of *GM*   18 And harmony and
wealth. *GM*
MARTIAL. First published in *GM* (Mar. 1754), p. 138. Text: *1791*. Collated: *GM*.
5 heaven sure cannot] not heaven can *GM*   7 the] *omitted, GM*   8 ye] you
GM

On a Lady throwing Snow-Balls at her Lover.

From the Latin of Petronius Afranius.

When, wanton fair, the snowy orb you throw,
I feel a fire before unknown in snow.
E'en coldest snow I find has pow'r to warm
My breast, when flung by Julia's lovely arm.
T' elude love's powerful arts I strive in vain,   5
If ice and snow can latent fires contain.
These frolicks leave: the force of beauty prove,
With equal passion cool my ardent love.

Antipater's Greek Epigram,

on the invention of water-mills, translated.

Ye female artizans, who grind the corn,
Indulge your slumbers all the live-long morn;
And let the cock, with impotent essay,
Recite his usual prologue to the day;
For Ceres now herself assistance lends,   5
And to the mills the green-hair'd Naiads sends.
See! on the summit buxomly they bound,
And with their gambols work the axle round.
True to th' impulsive waters, winds the wheel,
While four huge mill-stones crush the mouldring meal,   10
All-bounteous Ceres, as in * days of yore,
Your toil remits, yet still affords her store.

* Alluding to the golden age, when the earth was supposed to yield corn spontaneously. In this epigram the naiads, or water-nymphs, are beautifully said to be substituted by Ceres in the room of the women, who formerly worked their mills with their hands and feet.

ON A LADY. First published in *GM* (Mar. 1754), p. 138. Text: *1791*. Collated: *GM*. Afranius] Ascanius *GM, 1791*

ANTIPATER. First published in *GM* (Apr. 1754), p. 176. Text: *GM*. Collated: *Poetical Calendar* (1763), ii. 71. *Title from Poetical Calendar: no title in GM. Footnote in GM omits* In this epigram ... hands and feet.

The Famous Epigram of Sannazarius on Venice.

Translated.

Built amidst waves, whilst Neptune pleas'd surveys,
Fair Venice sovereign of the Adrian seas.
No more, said he, let Jove or Mars presume
To boast the dome and tow'rs of rival Rome.
Tho' Tiber more than stormy Adria please,
View both these cities with impartial eyes;
With wonder struck, this difference you'll assign,
This built by mortal, that by hands divine.

An Epitaph found about 30 years since in the church of St Botolph, Bishopsgate, London.

Hic conjuncta suo recubat Francisca marito,
  Et cinis est unus, quis fuit una caro.
Huc cineres conferre suos soror Anna jubebat,
  Corpora sic uno pulvere trina jacent.
Ille opifex rerum omnipotens, qui trinus et unus,
  Pulvere ab hoc uno, corpora trina dabet.

Translated.

Here lie interr'd, an husband and a wife,
One dust in death, as once one flesh in life.
A sister's mingled ashes here repose,
Three bodies thus, one heap of dust enclose.
Thou pow'r almighty, three in one wilt raise,
Three several bodies from one common mass.

Another.

Below an husband and a wife are laid,
One flesh when living, and one dust now dead.
A sister's ashes mingle in the urn,
And thus three bodies to one dust return.
But thou, O three in one, almighty pow'r,
From this one dust, three bodies wilt restore.

THE FAMOUS EPIGRAM. Text: *GM* (Apr. 1754), p. 183.
AN EPITAPH. Text: *GM* (Apr. 1754), p. 183.

To Miss S—— P——e.

Fair partner of my Nancy's heart,
Who feel'st, like me, love's poignant dart;
Who at a frown can'st pant for pain,
And at a smile revive again;
Who doat'st to that severe degree,   5
You're jealous, e'en of constancy;
Born hopes and fears and doubts to prove,
And each vicissitude of love!
To this my humble suit attend,
And be my advocate and friend.   10
So may just heav'n your goodness bless,
Successful ev'n in my success!
Oft at the silent hour of night,
When bold intrusion wings her flight,
My fair, from care and bus'ness free,   15
Unbosoms all her soul to thee,
Each hope with which her bosom heaves,
Each tender wish her heart receives
To thee are intimately known,
And all her thoughts become thy own: 20
Then take the blessed blissful hour,
To try love's sweet infectious pow'r;
And let your sister souls conspire
In love's, as friendship's calmer fire.
So may thy transport equal mine,   25
Nay—every joy be doubly thine!
So may the youth, whom you prefer,
Be all I wish to be to her.

TO MISS S—— P——E. First published in *GM* (May 1754), p. 236. Text: *1791*.
Collated: *GM*.
20 thy] thine *GM*   24 love's] love *GM*

Jenny Grey.

A Ballad.

Bring, Phoebus, from Parnassian bowers
A chaplet of poetic flowers,
   That far out bloom the May;
Bring verse so smooth, bring thoughts so free,
And all the Muses heraldry   5
   To blazon JENNY GREY.

Observe yon almond's rich perfume
Preventing spring with early bloom
   In ruddy tints how gay!
Thus foremost of the blushing fair   10
With such a blithesome, buxom air
   Blooms lovely JENNY GREY.

The merry, chirping, plumy throng
The bushes and the twigs among
   That pipe the sylvan lay,   15
All hush'd at her delightful voice
In silent ecstasy rejoice,
   And study JENNY GREY.

Ye wanton, odour-breathing gales,
That sweep along the green robed vales,   20
   And in each rose-bush play—
I know ye all—you're errant cheats,
And steal your more than mortal sweets
   From lovely JENNY GREY.

Pomona and that goddess bright,   25
  The florist's and the maid's delight,
    In vain their charms display;

JENNY GREY. First published in *Westminster Journal* (11 May 1954) (*WJ*). Text: *WJ*. Collated: *GM* (May 1754), p. 238; George Berg's *Collection of New English Songs* (1759), vi. 12–13 (*GB*); *1791. Title.* To Jenny Gray *GB, 1791*
4 bring thoughts] and thoughts *GB, 1791*   6 *et passim* GREY] GRAY *GB,*
1791   8 Preventing] Presenting *1791*   19 wanton] balmy *GB, 1791*
20 sweep along] lightly sweep *GB, 1791*   22 ye] you *GB, 1791*   errant] arrant
1791   23 mortal] natural *1791*

The luscious nectarine, juicy peach
In richness, nor in sweetness reach
   The lips of JENNY GREY.   30

To the sweet knot of Graces three,
Th' immortal band of bards agree
   A tuneful tax to pay;
There yet remains of matchless worth,
There yet remains a lovelier fourth,   35
   And she is JENNY GREY.

An Invitation to Mrs. Tyler, a Clergyman's Lady, to dine upon a Couple of Ducks on the Anniversary of the Author's Wedding-Day.

Had I the pen of Sir John Suckling,
And could find out a rhyme for duckling,
Why dearest madam, in that case,
I would invite you to a brace.
Haste, gentle * shepherdess, away,   5
To morrow is the gaudy day,
That day, when to my longing arms,
Nancy resign'd her golden charms,
And set my am'rous inclination
Upon the bus'ness of the nation.   10
Industrious Moll, † with many a pluck,
Unwings the plumage of each duck;
And as she sits a brooding o'er,
You'd think she'd hatch a couple more.
Come, all ye Muses, come and sing—   15
Shall we then roast them on a string?

   * As every good parson is the shepherd of his flock, his wife is a shepherdess of course.
† The Maid.

---

34 of] a *GB, 1791*   36 she] that *GM*
AN INVITATION. First published in *GM* (July 1754), p. 335. Text: *1791*. Collated:
GM. Title. Mrs. Tyler] Mrs T—— *GM*
5/6 *transposed in GM*   12 Unwings] Unrigs *GM*   13 sits] sets *GM*

Or shall we make our dirty jilt run,
To beg a roast of Mrs. ‡ Bilton?
But to delight you more with these,
We shall provide a dish of pease:
On ducks alone we'll not regale you,   20
We'll wine, we'll punch you, and we'll ale you.
To-morrow is the gaudy day,
Haste, gentle shepherdess, away.

‡ The Landlady of the Public House.

An Inscription on a Column

erected in a piece of land that had been often bought and sold.
Imitated in English from the Greek of Lucian.

I, whom thou see'st begirt with tow'ring oaks,
Was once the property of John o' Nokes;
On him prosperity no longer smiles,
And now I feed the flocks of John o' Stiles.
My former master call'd me by his name,   5
My present owner fondly does the same:
While I alike unworthy of their cares,
Quick pass to captors, purchasers, or heirs.
Let no one henceforth take me for his own,
For, Fortune! Fortune! I am thine alone.   10

The Duellists.

A Fable.

What's honour, did your Lordship say?
My Lord, I humbly crave a day.—

17 dirty jilt run] jilt dirty run *GM*
AN INSCRIPTION. First published in *GM* (July 1754), p. 335. Text: *GM*. Collated:
Poetical Calendar (1763), ii. 72. *Title.* Lucian's Greek Epigram, inscribed on a column,
etc., *Poetical Calendar*.
THE DUELLISTS. First published in *GM* (Aug. 1754), p. 381. Text: *1791*. Collated:
GM; Daily Magazine and London Advertiser (11 Oct. 1773), (*DM*). *Title.* The Duellists *GM*,
DM] The Duellist *1791*   1–8 *omitted, GM, DM*

'Tis difficult, and in my mind,
Like substance, cannot be defin'd.
It deals in numerous externals, 5
And is a legion of infernals;
Sometimes in riot and in play,
'Tis breaking of the Sabbath day:
When 'tis consider'd as a passion,
I deem it lust and fornication. 10
We pay our debts in honour's cause,
Lost in the breaking of the laws:
'Tis for some selfish impious end,
To murder the sincerest friend;
But wou'd you alter all the clan, 15
Turn out an honourable man.
Why take a pistol from the shelf,
And fight a duel with yourself.—
    'Twas on a time, the Lord knows when,
In Ely, or in Lincoln fen, 20
A Frog and Mouse had long disputes,
Held in the language of the brutes,
Who of a certain pool and pasture,
Shou'd be the sovereign and master.
Sir, says the Frog, and d—n'd his blood, 25
I hold that my pretension's good;
Nor can a *Brute* of *reason* doubt it,
For all that you can squeak about it.
The Mouse averse to be o'erpower'd,
Gave him the lie, and call'd him coward; 30
Too hard for any frog's digestion,
To have his *froghood* call'd in question!
A bargain instantly was made,
No mouse of honour could evade.
On the next morn, as soon as light, 35
With desperate bullrushes to fight;
The morning came—and man to man,
The grand *monomachy* began;

21 had long] had strong *GM*   held fierce *DM*   22 Held in the] In the
low *DM*   23 Who] Which *DM*   24 sovereign] sov'reign lord *DM*
25 d—n'd] d——d *DM*   31-2, 37-42 *omitted, DM*

Need I recount how each bravado,
Shone in *montant* and in *passado*;   40
To what a height their ire they carry'd,
How oft they thrusted and they parry'd;
But as these champions kept dispensing
Finesses in the art of fencing,
A furious vulture took upon her,   45
Quick to decide this point of honour,
And, lawyer like, to make an end on't,
Devour'd both plaintiff and defendant.
Thus, often in our British nation,
(I speak by way of application)   50
A lie direct to some hot youth,
The giving which perhaps was truth,
The treading on a scoundrel's toe,
Or dealing impudence a blow,
Disputes in politics and law,   55
About a feather and a straw;
A thousand trifles not worth naming,
In whoring, jockeying, and gaming,
Shall cause a challenge's inditing,
And set two loggerheads a fighting;   60
Meanwhile the father of despair,
The prince of vanity and air,
His querry, like an hawk discovering,
O'er their devoted heads hangs hovering,
Secure to get in his tuition,   65
These volunteers for black perdition.

---

40 *montant* and in] montalto and *GM*   43 They met—but while they kept
dispensing *DM*   44 art] act *DM*   46 this] the *DM*   49 Thus in this
fighting age and nation, *DM*   54 a] her *GM*   55–8 *omitted, DM*   63 an
hawk] a hawk, *DM*   65 Secure] Sure *DM*   66 for] of *DM*

The Snake, the Goose, and Nightingale.

Humbly addressed to the Hissers and Catcallers attending both
Houses.

When rul'd by truth and nature's ways,
When just to blame, yet fix'd to praise,
As votary of the Delphic God,
I reverence the critic's rod;
But when inflam'd with spite alone,   5
I hold all critics but as one;
For tho' they class themselves with art,
And each man takes a different part;
Yet whatsoe'er they praise and blame;
They in their motives are the same.   10
    Forth as she waddled in the brake,
A grey Goose stumbled on a Snake,
And took th' occasion to abuse her,
And of rank plagiarism accuse her.
"'Twas I," quoth she, "in every vale,   15
First hiss'd the noisy Nightingale;
And boldly cavill'd at each note,
That twitter'd in the Woodlark's throat:
I, who sublime and more than mortal,
Must stoop to enter at the portal,   20
Have ever been the first to show
My hate to every thing that's low;
While thou, mean mimic of my manner,
(Without inlisting to my banner)
Dar'st in thy grov'ling situation,   25
To counterfeit my sibilation."
    The Snake enrag'd, reply'd, "Know, Madam,
I date my charter down from Adam;

THE SNAKE. First published in *GM* (Dec. 1754), p. 574. Text: *1791*. Collated: *GM*.
Title. The Goose, the Snake, and the Nightingale. A Fable, *GM*, *omitting* Humbly, *etc.*
2 fix'd] fond *GM*   5 with] by *GM*   8 takes] take *GM*   9 praise and]
find to *GM*   10 They in their motives] Their motives always *GM*
16 noisy] yelping *GM*   18 twitter'd] twitters *GM*   19–22 *omitted*,
GM   23 While thou] Yet you *GM*   24 to] in *GM*   25 Presume,
where'er you take your station, *GM*   28 down] ev'n *GM*

Nor can I, since I bear the bell,
E'er imitate where I excell.   30
Had any other creature dar'd
Once to aver, what you've aver'd,
I might have been more fierce and fervent,
But you're a Goose,—and so your servant."
"Truce with your folly and your pride,"   35
The warbling Philomela cry'd;
"Since no more animals we find
In nature, of the hissing kind,
You should be friends with one another,
Nay, kind as brother is to brother.   40
For know, thou pattern of abuse,
Thou Snake art but a crawling goose;
And thou dull dabbler in each lake,
Art nothing but a feather'd Snake."

Epitaph on the Rev. Mr. Reynolds, at St. Peter's in the Isle
of Thanet.

Was Rhetoric on the lips of sorrow hung,
Or cou'd affliction lend the heart a tongue,
Then should my soul, in noble anguish free,
Do glorious justice to herself and thee.
But ah! when loaded with a weight of woe,   5
Ev'n nature, blessed nature is our foe.
When we should praise, we sympathetic groan,
For sad mortality is all our own.
Yet but a word: as lowly as he lies,
He spurns all empires and asserts the skies.   10
Blush, power! he had no interest here below;
Blush, malice! that he dy'd without a foe;

29 can] shall *GM*   30 where] what *GM*   39 with] to *GM*   40 Nay,]
And *GM*   43 each] the *GM*
EPITAPH. First known publication: Toldervy's *Select Epitaphs* (1755), ii. 219 (*TE*).
Text: *1791*. Collated: *TE. Title*. On a young Clergyman, at *etc. TE*
4 herself] her grief *TE*   7 should] wou'd *TE*

The universal friend, so form'd to engage,
Was far too precious for this world and age.
Years were deny'd, for (such his worth and truth)   15
Kind heaven has call'd him to eternal youth.

Mrs. Abigail and the Dumb Waiter.

With frowning brow and aspect low'ring,
As Abigail one day was scow'ring,
From chair to chair she past along,
Without soliloquy or song;
Content, in humdrum mood, t' adjust   5
Her matters to disperse the dust.—
Thus plodded on the sullen fair,
'Till a Dumb Waiter claim'd her care;
She then in rage, with shrill salute,
Bespoke the inoffensive mute:—   10
"Thou stupid tool of vapourish asses,
With thy brown shelves for pots and glasses;
Thou foreign whirligigg, for whom
US honest folks must quit the room;
And, like young misses at a christ'ning,   15
Are forc'd to be content with list'ning;
Tho' thou'rt a fav'rite of my *master's*,
I'll set thee gadding on thy castors."
This said—with many a rough attack,
She scrubb'd him 'till she made him crack;   20
Insulted stronger still and stronger,
The poor dumb thing could hold no longer.—
"Thou drab, born mops and brooms to dandle,
Thou haberdasher of *small* scandal,
Factor of family abuse,   25
Retailer of domestic news;
My lord, as soon as I appear,
Confines thee in thy proper sphere;
Or else, at ev'ry place of call,
The chandler's shop, or cobler's stall,   30

MRS. ABIGAIL. First published in *GM* (Feb. 1755), p. 84. Text: *1791*. Collated: *GM*.
Subtitled A Fable. *GM*   17 *master's GM*] *masters 1791*   30 or] and *GM*

Or ale-house, (where for petty tales,
Gin, beer, and ale are constant vails)
Each word at table that was spoke,
Wou'd soon become the public joke,
And chearful innocent converse,   35
To scandal warp'd—or something worse.—
Whene'er my master I attend,
Freely his mind he can unbend;—
But when such praters fill my place,
Then nothing should be said—but grace."   40

The English Bull Dog, Dutch Mastiff, and Quail.

Are we not all of race divine,
Alike of an immortal line?
Shall man to man afford derision,
But for some casual division?
To malice, and to mischief prone,   5
From climate, canton, or from zone,
Are all to idle discord bent,
These Kentish men—those men of Kent;
And parties and distinction make,
For parties and distinction's sake.   10
Souls sprung from an etherial flame,
However clad, are still the same;
Nor should we judge the heart or head,
By air we breathe, or earth we tread.
Dame Nature, who, all meritorious,   15
In a true Englishman is glorious;
Is lively, honest, brave and bonny,
In Monsieur, Taffy, Teague, and Sawney.
Give prejudices to the wind,
And let's be patriots of mankind.   20
Bigots, avaunt, sense can't endure ye,
But fabulists should try to cure ye.

31 (where for *GM*] where (for *1791*   32 beer, and ale] ale, and beer *GM*
THE ENGLISH BULL DOG. First published in *GM* (Dec. 1758), pp. 594–5. Text: *1791*.
Collated: *GM*. Subtitled *A Fable. GM*
10 distinction's] distinction *GM*   21 ye] you *GM*

A snub-nos'd Dog to fat inclin'd
Of the true hogan mogan kind,
The favourite of an English dame, 25
Mynheer Van Trumpo was his name:
One morning as he chanc'd to range,
Met honest Towzer on the 'Change;
And whom have we got here, I beg,
Quoth he,—and lifted up his leg; 30
An English dog can't take an airing,
But foreign scoundrels must be staring.
I'd have your French dogs and your Spanish,
And all your Dutch and all your Danish,
By which our species is confounded, 35
Be hang'd, be poison'd, or be drownded;
No mercy on the race suspected,
Greyhounds from Italy excepted:
By them my dames ne'er prove big bellied,
For they poor toads are Farrinellied. 40
Well of all dogs it stands confess'd,
Your English bull dogs are the best;
I say it, and will set my hand to't,
Cambden records it, and I'll stand to't.
'Tis true we have too much urbanity, 45
Somewhat o'ercharg'd with soft humanity;
The best things must find food for railing,
And every creature has its failing.
    And who are you? reply'd Van Trump,
(*Curling his tail upon his rump*) 50
Vaunting the regions of distraction,
The land of party and of faction.
In all fair Europe, who but we,
For national œconomy;
For wealth and peace, that have more charms, 55
Than learned arts, or noisy arms.
You envy us our dancing bogs,
With all the music of the frogs;

---

29 whom] who *GM*   33 French dogs and] French, and all *GM*   34 your . . .
your] the . . . the *GM*   36 drownded *GM*] drowned *1791*   37–40 *omitted*,
GM   41 stands] is *GM*   46 Somewhat o'ercharg'd] Are overcharg'd *GM*

Join'd to the Tretchscutz's bonny loon,
Who on the cymbal grinds the tune.   60
For poets, and the muses nine,
Beyond comparision we shine;
Oh! how we warble in our gizzards,
With X X's, H H's and with Z Z's.
For fighting—now you think I'm joking;   65
We love it better far than smoaking.
Ask but our troops, from man to boy,
Who all surviv'd at Fontenoy.
'Tis true, as friends, and as allies,
We're ever ready to devise   70
Our loves, or any kind assistance,
That may be granted at a distance;
But if you go to brag, good bye t' ye,
Nor dare to brave the High and Mighty.

    Wrong are you both, rejoins a Quail,   75
Confin'd within its wiry jail:
Frequent from realm to realm I've rang'd,
And with the seasons, climates chang'd.
Mankind is not so void of grace,
But good I've found in every place: 80
I've seen sincerity in France,
Amongst the Germans complaisance;
In foggy Holland wit may reign,
I've known humility in Spain;
Free'd was I by a turban'd Turk,   85
Whose life was one entire good work;
And in this land, fair freedom's boast,
Behold my liberty is lost.
Despis'd Hibernia have I seen,
Dejected like a widow'd queen;   90
Her robe with dignity long worn,
And cap of liberty were torn;
Her broken fife, and harp unstrung,
On the uncultur'd ground were flung;
Down lay her spear, defil'd with rust,   95
And book of learning in the dust;

Her loyalty still blameless found,
And hospitality renown'd:
No more the voice of fame engross'd,
In discontent and clamour lost.— 100
Ah! dire corruption, art thou spread,
Where never viper rear'd its head?
And didst thy baleful influence sow,
Where hemlock nor the nightshade grow?
Hapless, disconsolate, and brave, 105
Hibernia! who'll Hibernia save?
Who shall assist thee in thy woe,
Who ward from thee the fatal blow?
'Tis done, the glorious work is done,
All thanks to heav'n and HARTINGTON. 110

The Country Squire and the Mandrake.

The sun had rais'd above the mead,
His glorious horizontal head;
Sad Philomela left her thorn;
The lively linnets hymn'd the morn,
And nature, like a waking bride, 5
Her blushes spread on ev'ry side;
The cock as usual crow'd up Tray,
Who nightly with his master lay;
The faithful spaniel gave the word,
Trelooby at the signal stirr'd, 10
And with his gun, from wood to wood
The man of prey his course pursu'd;
The dew and herbage all around,
Like pearls and emeralds on the ground;
Th' uncultur'd flowers that rudely rise, 15
Where smiling freedom art defies;
The lark, in transport, tow'ring high,
The crimson curtains of the sky,
Affected not Trelooby's mind—

THE COUNTRY SQUIRE. First published in *GM* (Apr. 1755), pp. 178–9. Text: *1791*.
Collated: *GM*. *Subtitled* A Fable. *GM*   17 lark] larks *GM*

For what is beauty to the blind?   20
Th' amorous voice of *silvan* love,
Form'd charming concerts in the grove;
Sweet zephyr sigh'd on Flora's breast,
And drew the black-bird from his nest;
Whistling he leapt from leaf to leaf;   25
But what is music to the deaf?
 At length while poring on the ground,
With monumental look profound,
A curious vegetable caught
His—something similar to thought: 30
Wond'ring, he ponder'd, stooping low,
(Trelooby always lov'd a show)
And on the Mandrake's vernal station,
Star'd with prodigious observation.
Th' affronted Mandrake with a frown,   35
Address'd in rage the wealthy clown.
 "Proud member of the rambling race,
That vegetate from place to place,
Pursue the leveret at large,
Nor near thy blunderbuss discharge.   40
Disdainful tho' thou look'st on me,
What art thou, or what canst thou be?
Nature, that mark'd thee as a fool,
Gave no materials for the school.
In what consists thy work and fame?   45
The preservation of the Game.—
For what? thou avaricious elf,
But to destroy it all thyself;
To lead a life of drink and feast,
T' oppress the poor, and cheat the priest,   50
Or triumph in a virgin lost,
Is all the manhood thou canst boast.—
Pretty, in nature's various plan,
To see a weed that's like a man;
But 'tis a grievous thing indeed,   55
To see a man so like a weed."

19 Affected *GM*] Afflicted *1791* 21 Th' amorous] Harmonious *GM* 24 And fann'd the blackbird in her nest, *GM* 25 Whistling] Whisp'ing *GM* 40 near] here *GM* 45 Wherein consists thy worth and fame? *GM* 48 destroy] devour *GM*

Epitaph on Mrs. Rolt.

Tho' thou art gone from friendship and from me,
I'll give to justice what I can't to thee:
Mute hast thou left thy mourning partner's tongue,
And like his heart-strings is his lyre unstrung.
Oft he's had joys, when guiltless of disguise   5
It beam'd with tenfold transport from thy eyes.
Had he a grief, or was oppress'd with care,
Thou kept'st within thyself the greater share;
And, mild as air that fans the southern seas,
Thou calm'st his troubled mind till all was peace.   10
In chastity thou held'st thy husband's heart,
To all, but him, as cold as now thou art.
Yet thy breast breath'd benevolence divine,
As thou wert his, so all his friends were thine.
There's one at least who can affect no art,   15
Whose grief is nature, and who acts no part—
Who on thy bed of earth, and on thy bier,
Bled from the eye one unaviling tear,
The rest to him who has the pow'r to save,
And bid th' archangel sound thy triumph o'er the grave. 20

EPITAPH. Text: *GM* (June 1755), p. 278.

ON THE
GOODNESS
OF THE
SUPREME BEING

ORPHEUS, for * so the Gentiles call'd thy name,
Israel's sweet Psalmist, who alone couldst wake
Th' inanimate to motion; who alone
The joyfull hillocks, the applauding rocks,
And floods with musical persuasion drew;   5
Thou who to hail and snow gav'st voice and sound,
And mad'st the mute melodious!—greater yet
Was thy divinest skill and rul'd o'er more
Than art and nature; for thy tuneful touch
Drove trembling Satan from the heart of Saul,   10
And quell'd the evil Angel:—in this breast
Some portion of thy genuine spirit breathe,
And lift me from myself each thought impure
Banish; each low idea raise, refine,
Enlarge, and sanctify;—so shall the muse   15
Above the stars aspire, and aim to praise
Her God on earth, as he is prais'd in heaven.
    Immense Creator! whose all-pow'rful hand
Fram'd universal Being, and whose Eye
Saw like thyself, that all things form'd were good;   20
Where shall the tim'rous bard thy praise begin,
Where end the purest sacrifice of song,
And just thanksgiving?—The thought-kindling light,
Thy prime production, darts upon my mind
Its vivifying beams, my heart illumines,   25
And fills my soul with gratitude and Thee.
Hail to the chearful rays of ruddy morn,
That paint the streaky East, and blithsome rouse
The birds, the cattle, and mankind from rest!
Hail to the freshness of the early breeze,   30

* *See this conjecture strongly supported by Delany*, in his *Life of David.*

GOODNESS. First published in 1756. Text: *G.* Collated: *G2; 1761; 1791.*
9 and] or *1791*

And Iris dancing on the new-fall'n dew!
Without the aid of yonder golden globe
Lost were the garnet's lustre, lost the lilly,
The tulip and auricula's spotted pride;
Lost were the peacock's plumage, to the sight   35
So pleasing in its pomp and glossy glow.
O thrice-illustrious! were it not for thee
Those pansies, that reclining from the bank,
View thro' th' immaculate, pellucid stream
Their portraiture in the inverted heaven,   40
Might as well change their triple boast, the white,
The purple, and the gold, that far outvie
The Eastern monarch's garb, ev'n with the dock,
Ev'n with the baneful hemlock's irksome green.
Without thy aid, without thy gladsome beams   45
The tribes of woodland warblers wou'd remain
Mute on the bending branches, nor recite
The praise of him, who, ere he form'd their lord,
Their voices tun'd to transport, wing'd their flight,
And bade them call for nurture, and receive;   50
And lo! they call; the blackbird and the thrush,
The woodlark, and the redbreast jointly call;
He hears and feeds their feather'd families,
He feeds his sweet musicians,—nor neglects
Th' invoking ravens in the greenwood wide;   55
And tho' their throats coarse ruttling hurt the ear,
They mean it all for music, thanks and praise
They mean, and leave ingratitude to man;—
But not to all,—for hark! the organs blow
Their swelling notes round the cathedral's dome,   60
And grace th' harmonious choir, celestial feast
To pious ears, and med'cine of the mind;
The thrilling trebles and the manly base
Join in accordance meet, and with one voice
All to the sacred subject suit their song: 65
While in each breast sweet melancholy reigns
Angelically pensive, till the joy
Improves and purifies;—the solemn scene

48 ere] e'er *all edns.*   58 man; *G2*] man, *G*   59 hark! *G2*] hark *G*
63 and] of *1791*   65 song: *G2*] song. *G*

The Sun thro' storied panes surveys with awe,
And bashfully with-holds each bolder beam.   70
Here, as her home, from morn to eve frequents
The cherub Gratitude;—behold her Eyes!
With love and gladness weepingly they shed
Extatic smiles; the incense, that her hands
Uprear, is sweeter than the breath of May   75
Caught from the nectarine's blossom, and her voice
Is more than voice can tell; to him she sings,
To him who feeds, who clothes and who adorns,
Who made and who preserves, whatever dwells
In air, in stedfast earth, or fickle sea.   80
O He is good, he is immensely good!
Who all things form'd, and form'd them all for man;
Who mark'd the climates, varied every zone,
Dispensing all his blessings for the best
In order and in beauty:—rise, attend,   85
Attest, and praise, ye quarters of the world!
Bow down, ye elephants, submissive bow
To him, who made the mite; tho' Asia's pride,
Ye carry armies on your tow'r-crown'd backs,
And grace the turban'd tyrants, bow to him   90
Who is as great, as perfect and as good
In his less-striking wonders, till at length
The eye's at fault and seeks th' assisting glass.
Approach and bring from Araby the blest
The fragrant cassia, frankincense and myrh,   95
And meekly kneeling at the altar's foot
Lay all the tributary incense down.
Stoop, sable Africa, with rev'rence stoop,
And from thy brow take off the painted plume;
With golden ingots all thy camels load   100
T' adorn his temples, hasten with thy spear
Reverted and thy trusty bow unstrung,
While unpursu'd thy lions roam and roar,
And ruin'd tow'rs, rude rocks and caverns wide
Remurmur to the glorious, surly sound.   105
And thou, fair Indian, whose immense domain

80 earth, *G2*] earth *G*   82 things form'd, *G2*] things form'd *G*   85 rise] raise
1791

To counterpoise the Hemisphere extends,
Haste from the West, and with thy fruits and flow'rs,
Thy mines and med'cines, wealthy maid, attend.
More than the plenteousness so fam'd to flow   110
By fabling bards from Amalthea's horn
Is thine; thine therefore be a portion due
Of thanks and praise: come with thy brilliant crown
And vest of furr; and from thy fragrant lap
Pomegranates and the rich * ananas pour.   115
But chiefly thou, Europa, seat of grace
And Christian excellence, his goodness own,
Forth from ten thousand temples pour his praise;
Clad in the armour of the living God
Approach, unsheath the spirit's flaming sword;   120
Faith's shield, Salvation's glory,—compass'd helm
With fortitude assume, and o'er your heart
Fair truth's invulnerable breast-plate spread;
Then join the general chorus of all worlds,
And let the song of charity begin   125
In strains seraphic, and melodious pray'r.
"O all-sufficient, all-beneficent,
Thou God of Goodness and of glory, hear!
Thou, who to lowliest minds dost condescend,
Assuming passions to enforce thy laws,   130
Adopting jealousy to prove thy love:
Thou, who resign'd humility uphold,
Ev'n as the florist props the drooping rose,
But quell tyrannic pride with peerless pow'r,
Ev'n as the tempest rives the stubborn oak: 135
O all-sufficient, all-beneficent,
Thou God of goodness and of glory hear!
Bless all mankind, and bring them in the end
To heav'n, to immortality, and THEE!"

FINIS.

* Ananas the Indian name for Pine-Apples.

---

115 *footnote omitted, 1791*   137 goodness] Goodness, *1791*   glory] glory, *1791*

Epilogue.

Spoken by Mr. Shuter, at Covent Garden, after the Play of the CONSCIOUS
LOVERS, acted for the Benefit of the Middlesex Hospital for Lying-in
Women, 1755, in the Character of a Man-Midwife.

[Enters with a Child]

Whoe'er begot thee, has no cause to blush:
Thou'rt a brave chopping boy, [*child cries*] nay, hush!
    hush! hush!
A workman, faith! a man of rare discretion,
A friend to Britain, and to our profession;
With face so chubby, and with looks so glad,   5
O rare roast beef of England—here's a lad!

[Shews him to the Company
[Child makes a noise again]

Nay if you once begin to puke and cough,
Go to the nurse. Within!—here take him off.
Well, heav'n be prais'd, it is a peopling age,
Thanks to the bar, the pulpit, and the stage;   10
But not to th' army—that's not worth a farthing,
The captains go too much to Covent Garden,
Spoil many a girl,—but seldom make a mother,
They foil us one way—but we have them t'other.

[Shakes a box of pills

The nation prospers by such joyous souls,   15
Hence smokes my table, hence my chariot rolls.
Tho' some snug jobs, from surgery may spring,
Man-midwifry, man-midwifry's the thing!
Lean shou'd I be, e'en as my own anatomy,
By mere catharticks and by plain phlebotomy.   20
Well, besides gain, besides the pow'r to please,
Besides the music of such birds as these,

[Shakes a purse

It is a joy refin'd, unmix'd and pure,

115 *footnote omitted, 1791*   137 goodness] Goodness, *1791*   glory] glory, *1791*
EPILOGUE TO THE CONSCIOUS LOVERS. First published in the *PA* (19 Dec. 1755).
Text: *1791*. Collated: *PA*; *GM* (Dec. 1755), p. 567; *LM* (Dec. 1755), p. 592; *CP6* (6th
edn., *c.*1758), pp. 32–4.
10 pulpit] army *PA, GM, LM, CP6*   11–14 *omitted, PA, GM, LM, CP6*

To hear the praises of the grateful poor.
This day comes honest Taffy to my house, 25
"Cot pless her, her as sav'd her poy and spouse,
Her sav'd her Gwinnifrid, or death had swallow'd her,
Tho' creat crand, creat crand crand child of
     Cadwallader."
Cries Patrick Touzl'em, "I am bound to pray,
You've sav'd my Sue in your same physick way, 30
And further shall I thank you yesterday."
Then Sawney came, and thank'd me for my love,
(I very readily excus'd *his glove*)
He bless'd the mon, e'en by St. Andrew's cross,
"Who cur'd his bonny bearn and blithsome lass." 35
   But merriment and mimickry apart,
Thanks to each bounteous hand and gen'rous heart
Of those, who tenderly take pity's part;
Who in good-natur'd acts can sweetly grieve,
Swift to lament, but swifter to relieve. 40
Thanks to the lovely fair ones, types of heaven,
Who raise and beautify the bounty given;
But chief to *him in whom distress confides,
Who o'er this noble place so gloriously presides.

     * The Earl afterwards Duke of Northumberland.

---

26 her] hur *PA, GM, LM, CP6*   27 Her] Hur *PA, GM, LM, CP6*   her
Gwinnifrid] my Gwinnifrid *PA, GM, LM, CP6*   28 of] to *GM, CP6*
30 my] our *GM*

Epilogue to the Apprentice.
[Spoken by Mrs Clive]

[Enters reading a Play Bill]

A very pretty bill—as I'm alive!
The part of—nobody—by Mrs. Clive!
A paltry scribbling fool—to leave me out—
He'll say, perhaps—he thought I cou'd not *spout*.
Malice and envy to the last degree!   5
And why?—I wrote a farce as well as he,
And fairly ventur'd it—without the aid
Of prologue dress'd in black, and face in masquerade;
Oh! Pit—have pity—see how I'm dismay'd!
Poor soul! this canting stuff will never do,   10
Unless like Bayes he brings his hangman too,
But granting that from these same obsequies,
Some pickings to our bard in black arise;
Should your applause to joy convert his fear,
As Pallas turns to feast—*Lardella's bier*;   15
Yet 'twould have been a better scheme by half
T' have thrown his weeds aside, and learnt with me to
　　　laugh.
I cou'd have shewn him, had he been inclin'd,
A spouting junto of the female kind.
There dwells a milliner in yonder row,   20
Well-dress'd, full-voic'd, and nobly built for shew,
Who, when in rage she scolds at Sue and Sarah,
Damn'd, damn'd dissembler!—thinks she's more than Zara.
She has a daughter too that deals in lace,
And sings—*O ponder well*—and *Chevy Chase*,   25
And fain wou'd fill the fair Ophelia's place.
And in her cock'd up hat, and gown of camblet,
Presumes on something—*touching the Lord Hamlet*.
A cousin too she has with squinting eyes,
With wadling gait, and voice like *London Cries*;   30
Who for the stage too short by half a story,

EPILOGUE TO THE APPRENTICE. First published in Arthur Murphy's *The Apprentice* (1756), pp. 47–8 (*AM*). Text: *1791*. Collated: *AM*; *GM* (Jan. 1756), p. 36; *LM* (Jan. 1756), p. 40. *Title*. Epilogue written by a Friend, Spoken by Mrs. Clive *AM*

Acts Lady Townly—thus—in all her glory.
And while she's traversing her scanty room,
Cries—"Lord! my lord, what can I do at home!"
In short, we've girls enough for all the fellows, ⎫ 35
The ranting, whining, starting and the jealous, ⎬
The Hotspurs, Romeos, Hamlets, and Othellos. ⎭
Oh! little do these silly people know,
What dreadful trials—actors undergo.
Myself—who most in harmony delight, 40
Am scolding here from morning until night.
Then take advice from me, ye giddy things,
Ye royal milliners, ye apron'd kings;
Young men beware, and shun our slippery ways,
Study arithmetic, and burn your plays; 45
And you, ye girls, let not our tinsel train
Enchant your eyes, and turn your madd'ning brain;
Be timely wise, for oh! be sure of this;
A shop with virtue, is the height of bliss.

'Hail, Energeia! hail, my native tongue'

Hail, Energeia! hail, my native tongue,
Concisely full, and musically strong!
Thou, with the pencil, hold'st a glorious strife,
And paints the passions greater than the life:
In thunders now tremendously array'd, 5
Now soft as murmurs of the melting maid:
Now piercing loud, and as the clarion clear,
And now resounding rough to rouse the ear:
Now quick as light'ning in its rapid flow,
Now, in its stately march, magnificently slow. 10
    Hail, Energeia! hail, my native tongue,
    Concisely full, and musically strong!
    Thou, with the pencil, hold'st a glorious strife,
    And paints the passions greater than the life.

35 we've] there's *AM, GM, LM*   38 these] those *AM, LM*   45 burn your]
shun our *1791*   46 our] your *GM*
HAIL, ENERGEIA. Text: *UV* (Jan. 1756), p. 9.

To the Right Hon. the Earl of Darlington, on his being
appointed Paymaster of his Majesty's Forces.

What each prophetic muse foretold is true,
And royal justice gives to worth her due;
The Roman spirit now breathes forth again,
And virtue's temple leads to honour's fane:
But not alone to thee this grant extends,   5
Nor, in thy rise, great Brunswick's goodness ends.
Whoe'er has known thy hospitable dome,
Where each glad guest still finds himself at home;
Whoe'er has seen the num'rous poor that wait,
To bless thy bounty, at th' expanded gate;   10
Whoe'er has seen thee general joy impart,
And smile away chagrin from ev'ry heart:
All these are happy—pleasure reigns confest,
And thy prosperity makes thousands blest.

Stanzas, occasioned by the Generosity of the English, to the
distressed Portuguese.

Where arts and arms astonish all the globe;
   Where Science sweeps along with Roman mien;
Where more than empress in her royal robe,
   The majesty of Liberty is seen;
Where countless graces croud the circling shore,   5
Is there yet room for one perfection more?

Yes, CHARITY! Religion's darling child;
   See, the seraphic language of her look!
Without her, anchor'd Hope in vain had smil'd,
   And heav'n-ey'd Faith had almost clos'd her book: 10
Without her, Virtue barren wou'd remain,
And ENGLISHMEN, be ENGLISHMEN in vain.

TO THE EARL OF DARLINGTON. First published in *UV* (Jan. 1756), p. 42. Text: *UV*.
Collated: *1791*.
1 each] the *1791*   2 her] its *1791*
STANZAS. Text: *UV* (Jan. 1756), p. 42.

'The sword of liberty, with God-like view'

[Imitation of Callistratus]

The sword of liberty, with God-like view,
Armodius, and Aristogiton, drew:
The myrtled falchion has the tyrant slain,
And giv'n th' Athenians to themselves again.
   O brave Armodius! thou didst never die,   5
Thou only hast return'd unto the sky;
Thy glorious lot eternally is sped,
Where great Achilles reigns, and warlike Diomed.
   Bring me with speed, O bring the myrtle bough,
T' adorn my sword, and to fulfil my vow;   10
As when Hipparchus gloriously was slain,
And gave th' Athenians to themselves again.
   Armodius lives! Aristogiton lives!
Ev'n death a better life of glory gives:
Hipparchus, by those God-like youths, was slain,   15
They gave th' Athenians to themselves again.

To Health.

Buxom nymph! all nymphs excelling,
Say, where hast thou fixt thy dwelling?
Hast thou plac'd thy bed of rest
In *Arabia the blest*,
Where spicy Zephyrs, all the year,   5
Breathe upon the atmosphere;
Odours borrowing, and bestowing,
With eternal freshness glowing?
   Or, in Afric's auburn downs,
Where the sun the *Zenith* crowns,   10
Full of heat, and full of fire,
Do thy tumid veins perspire?
Dost thou, where the lion lies,
Ply the manly exercise,

THE SWORD OF LIBERTY. Text: *UV* (Feb. 1756), p. 74.
TO HEALTH. Text: *UV* (Mar. 1756), pp. 140–1.

Skill'd the winged spear to throw,   15
Or to bend the stubborn bow?
  Or rangest thou, where bleak and foul,
The ungenial north-winds howl?
Do Lapland's hamlets charm thy sight,
Candied o'er with glist'ning white?   20
On solid waters dost thou slide,
Or drawn by rapid rein-deer ride!
Or dost thou flourish strong and hale,
Ermin'd in Siberia's vale?
  Wafted o'er th' Atlantic waves,   25
To the land of gold and slaves;
To the land of fruit and flow'rs,
Constant winds, and punctual show'rs;
Where, far beyond th' Herculean bars,
Columbus found new lands, and stars;   30
All-coveted, all-courted fair,
Tell me, charmer! art thou there?
  Is thy course propitious bent,
To Europa's continent;
Forth to Gallia's southern shores,   35
Dost thou bear thy balmy stores?
Or the pride of haughty Spain,
In Andalusia dost thou reign?
Or where Brundusium stood of yore,
Or where Lisbon is—*no more?*   40
  Or, hither com'st, with all thy smiles,
To fair freedom's western isles?
—Thee, nor Araby can boast,
Thee, nor Afric's tawny coast;
Thou art not of local worth,   45
Not in west, or south, or north,
Not in climate, or in zone,
But in TEMPERANCE ALONE.

Faber Acicularius. *Anglice*, A Pin-Maker.

In tenui labor, at tenuis non gloria. VIRG.

Te cano, Amazoniæ, [domina] ingeniosa, sagittæ,
   Cui labor in tenui præmia larga parat:
Tu præbes nuribus decus et tutamen, amantque
   Vel tua pacificum Cypridos arma latus.
Phillis seu spissi spectacula grata theatri,   5
   Sive aulam junctis visere gestit equis,
Pendeat e zona curat bombycinus orbis,
   Qui capit exiguas mira pharetra neces.
Cum bellum capere arma monet metuenda virago,
   Quam multis stimulis horret echinus, adest.   10
In pace innocuæ rutilant, et quisque per artus
   Mobilis usque suum mutat, ut ipsa, locum:
Nunc latet in tergo; nunc, si volet usus, in ore est,
   Sustinet et queruli fata vicesque proci.
* Sæpe, ut sævit hiems, pugnas et prælia ludo   15
   Ante focum Phyllis cum Corydone ciet,
"Ambo animis, ambo insignes præstantibus armis."
   En! tripode in lævi tela minuta vibrant;
Nec mora, nec requies, ast alterno impete uterque
   Irruit, et pulsat mollia corda pavor.   20
Dum jaculum jaculo impediens, atque ariete facto,
   Tela hostis gaudens, *ille* vel *illa* rapit.
Quanquam Mæonides armavit Amazonias aere,
   Quanquam terrifica Gorgone Pallas ovet,
Audeo vel fictis componere Phyllida nymphis   25
   Quando hæc, queis sese protegat, ornet, habet.
Sed tale auxilium fugiat lasciva puella,
   Odit enim impurum serica sphæra latus.
Sic leo virginibus solis comes astat amicus,
   Fidaque sic gelidum diligit Arcton acus.   30

* Describitur hic lusus, vulgo dictus, *push-pin*.

FABER ACICULARIUS. Text: *UV* (Apr. 1756), p. 189.
1 Amazoniæ, [domina] ingeniosa,] Amazoniæ, ingeniosa, *UV*   3 amantque]
amantque, *UV*   19 alterno impete] alterna impeta *UV*   21 facto,] facto.
UV

Translation

Slight is the work, but not slight the glory.

Of you I sing, gifted [mistress] of the Amazonian arrow, whose toil over a small article yields generous rewards. You provide ornament and protection for young married women, and your weapons love even the peaceful side of male lovers. Phyllis, all agog to visit, with yoked horses, either the pleasing spectacles of the crowded theatre or the court, takes care to have a silken ball hanging from her girdle, a wonderful quiver which inflicts miniature deaths. When the formidable heroine threatens to take up arms for war, she presents herself bristling with as many spikes as a hedgehog. In time of peace they glitter harmlessly, and each, moving about her body, changes its place as she does herself. Now it lies hidden at the back, now, if need be, at the front, and withstands the changes and fortunes of a plaintive suitor. * Often, when winter rages, Phyllis stirs up battles and fights in sport before the hearth with her Corydon: "both conspicuous in spirit, both in splendid weaponry." Lo! they brandish their tiny spears on the small tripod. No delay, no respite, but attacking alternately each of them rushes in, and fear agitates their tender hearts; until, dart blocking dart, and making a kind of battering-ram, either *he* or *she* seizes with joy the enemy's weapons. Though Homer armed the Amazons in bronze, though Pallas exulted over the terrifying Gorgon, I venture to compare Phyllis even to these legendary nymphs since she has these means of protecting and adorning herself. But a wanton girl should shun such aid, for the silken ball loathes an impure side. As the lion stands by as a companion and friend to virgins alone, so the faithful needle loves the frozen North.

* Here is described the game commonly termed *push-pin*.

HYMN

TO THE

SUPREME BEING,

ON

Recovery from a dangerous Fit of Illness.

By CHRISTOPHER SMART, M.A.

LONDON.

Printed for J. NEWBERY, in St. Paul's Church-yard.

MDCCLVI.

HYMN. First published in June 1756. Text *1756.* Collated: *1791.*

HYMN
TO THE
SUPREME BEING.

When * Israel's ruler on the royal bed
  In anguish and in perturbation lay,
The down reliev'd not his anointed head,
  And rest gave place to horror and dismay.
Fast flow'd the tears, high heav'd each gasping sigh   5
When God's own prophet thunder'd— MONARCH,
    THOU MUST DIE.

And must I go, th' illustrious mourner cry'd,
  I who have serv'd thee still in faith and truth,
Whose snow-white conscience no foul crime has died
  From youth to manhood, infancy to youth,   10
Like David, who have still rever'd thy word
The sovereign of myself and servant of the Lord!

The judge Almighty heard his suppliant's moan,
  Repeal'd his sentence, and his health restor'd;
The beams of mercy on his temples shone,   15
  Shot from that heaven to which his sighs had soar'd;
The † sun retreated at his maker's nod
And miracles confirm the genuine work of God.

But, O immortals! What had I to plead
  When death stood o'er me with his threat'ning lance,   20
When reason left me in the time of need,
  And sense was lost in terror or in trance,
My sick'ning soul was with my blood inflam'd,
And the celestial image sunk, defac'd and maim'd.

I sent back memory, in heedful guise,
  To search the records of preceding years;
Home, like the * raven to the ark, she flies,

    * Hezekiah vide Isaiah xxxviii.
    † Isaiah, chap. xxxviii.
    * Gen. viii. 7.

---

    15 temples *1791*] temple *1756*   23 sick'ning] sinking *1791*

Croaking bad tidings to my trembling ears.
O Sun, again that thy retreat was made,
And threw my follies back into the friendly shade!   30

But who are they, that bid affliction cease!—
    Redemption and forgiveness, heavenly sounds!
Behold the dove that brings the branch of peace,
    Behold the balm that heals the gaping wounds—
Vengeance divine's by penitence supprest—   35
She † struggles with the angel, conquers, and is blest.

Yet hold, presumption, nor too fondly climb,
    And thou too hold, O horrible despair!
In man humility's alone sublime,
    Who diffidently hopes he's Christ's own care—   40
O all-sufficient Lamb! in death's dread hour
Thy merits who shall slight, or who can doubt thy power?

But soul-rejoicing health again returns,
    The blood meanders gently in each vein,
The lamp of life renew'd with vigour burns,   45
    And exil'd reason takes her seat again—
Brisk leaps the heart, the mind's at large once more,
To love, to praise, to bless, to wonder and adore.

The virtuous partner of my nuptial bands,
    Appear'd a widow to my frantic sight;   50
My little prattlers lifting up their hands,
    Beckon me back to them, to life, and light;
I come, ye spotless sweets! I come again,
Nor have your tears been shed, nor have ye knelt in vain.

All glory to th' ETERNAL, to th' IMMENSE,   55
    All glory to th' OMNISCIENT and GOOD,
Whose power's uncircumscrib'd, whose love's intense;
    But yet whose justice ne'er could be withstood,
Except thro' him—thro' him, who stands alone,
Of worth, of weight allow'd for all Mankind t' atone!   60
    † Gen. xxxii. 24, 25, 26, 27, 28.

_____

44 gently] gentle *1791*

He rais'd the lame, the lepers he made whole,
   He fix'd the palsied nerves of weak decay,
He drove out Satan from the tortur'd soul,
   And to the blind gave or restor'd the day,—
Nay more,—far more unequal'd pangs sustain'd,   65
Till his lost fallen flock his taintless blood regain'd.

My feeble feet refus'd my body's weight,
   Nor wou'd my eyes admit the glorious light,
My nerves convuls'd shook fearful of their fate,
   My mind lay open to the powers of night.   70
He pitying did a second birth bestow
A birth of joy—not like the first of tears and woe.

Ye strengthen'd feet, forth to his altar move;
   Quicken, ye new-strung nerves, th' enraptur'd lyre;
Ye heav'n-directed eyes, o'erflow with love;   75
   Glow, glow, my soul, with pure seraphic fire;
Deeds, thoughts, and words no more his mandates break,
But to his endless glory work, conceive, and speak.

O! penitence, to virtue near allied,
   Thou can'st new joys e'en to the blest impart;   80
The list'ning angels lay their harps aside
   To hear the music of thy contrite heart;
And heav'n itself wears a more radiant face,
When charity presents thee to the throne of grace.

* Chief of metallic forms is regal gold;   85
   Of elements, the limpid fount that flows;
Give me 'mongst gems the brilliant to behold;
   O'er Flora's flock imperial is the rose:
Above all birds the sov'reign eagle soars;
And monarch of the field the lordly lion roars.   90

What can with great Leviathan compare,
   Who takes his pastime in the mighty main?
What, like the *Sun*, shines thro' the realms of air,
   And gilds and glorifies th' ethereal plain—
              * Pind. Olymp. 1.

Yet what are these to man, who bears the sway?   95
For all was made for him—to serve and to obey.

Thus in high heaven charity is great,
  Faith, hope, devotion hold a lower place;
On her the cherubs and the seraphs wait,
  Her, every virtue courts, and every grace;   100
See! on the right, close by th' Almighty's throne,
In him she shines confest, who came to make her known.

Deep-rooted in my heart then let her grow,
  That for the past the future may atone;
That I may act what thou hast giv'n to know,   105
  That I may live for THEE and THEE alone,
And justify those sweetest words from heav'n,
"THAT HE SHALL LOVE THEE MOST
  * TO WHOM THOU'ST MOST FORGIVEN.

FINIS.

---

* Luke vii. 41, 42, 43.

A Story of a Cock and a Bull.

Yes—we excel in arts and arms,
In learning's lore, and beauty's charms;
The sea's wide empire we engross,
All nations hail the British cross;
The land of liberty we tread,   5
And wo to his devoted head,
Who dares the contrary advance,
One Englishman's worth ten of France.
These, these are truths what man won't write for,
Won't swear, won't bully, and won't fight for?   10
Yet (tho' perhaps I speak thro' vanity)
Wou'd we'd a little more humanity!
Too far, I fear, I've drove the jest,
So leave to Cock and Bull the rest.
   A Bull who'd listen'd to the vows   15
Of above fifteen hundred cows,
And serv'd his master fresh and fresh,
With hecatombs of special flesh,
Like to an hermit, or a dervise,
Grown old and feeble in the service,   20
Now left the meadow's green parade,
And sought a solitary shade.
The cows proclaim'd by mournful moowing
The Bull's deficiency in wooing,
And to their disappointed master   25
All told the terrible disaster.
   Is this the case (quoth Hodge) O rare!
But hold, to-morrow is the fair:
Thou to thy doom, old boy, art fated
To-morrow—and thou shalt be baited—   30
The deed was done—Curse on the wrong!
Bloody description, hold thy tongue—

A STORY. First published in *LTM* (May–June 1756), i. 102–3. Text: *LTM*. Collated: *CP6* (6th edn., *c.*1758), pp. 44–6; *1791*.
10 and] or *1791*   11 speak] spake *CP6*   19 an] a *CP6*   23 by mournful moowing] in mournful lowing *1791*

Victorious yet the Bull return'd,
And with stern silence inly mourn'd.
   A vet'ran, brave, majestic Cock,   35
Who serv'd for hour-glass, guard and clock,
Who crow'd the mansion's first relief,
Alike from goblin and from thief;
Whose youth escap'd the Christmas skillet,
Whose vigour brav'd the Shrovetide billet,   40
Had just return'd in wounds and pain,
Triumphant from the barbarous main.
By riv'lets brink, with trees o'ergrown,
He heard his fellow-suff'rer moan,
And greatly scorning wounds and smart,   45
Gave him three cheers with all his heart.
   "Rise, neighbour, from that pensive attitude,
Brave witness of vile man's ingratitude,
And let us both with spur and horn
The cruel reasoning monster scorn—   50
Methinks at ev'ry dawn of day,
When first I chant my blithsome lay,
Methinks I hear from out the sky
'All will be better by and by.'
When bloody, base, degenerate man,   55
Who deviates from his maker's plan,
Who Nature and her work abuses,
And thus his fellow-servants uses,
Shall greatly, and yet justly, want
The mercy he refused to grant.   60
And, when his heart, his conscience purges,
Shall wish to be the brute he scourges."

---

41 wounds] wound *CP6*   42 main] train *1791*   44 -suff'rer] 'suffrer's
1791   57 work] works *1791*   58 -servants] -servant *CP6*   61 And
(while his heart his conscience purges) *1791*

To the Author of some defamatory Verses against a worthy gentleman.

When the viper has vented its venom, 'tis said,
That the fat heals the wound which the poison has made.
Thus fares it with blockheads whenever they write,
Their dullness an antidote proves to their spight.
But had sense and keen satire attended the strain,   5
That sense and keen satire had still been in vain;
For ill-manag'd wit, like a suicide's sword,
Turns its virulent point on the heart of its lord.
And since Charles leads a life undeserving of blame,
Detraction is only a foil to his fame.

Ad Cicadam. Anacreontis Imitatio.

Audies felix, gracilis Cicada,
Rore quæ pascis, rosea sub herba,
Dulce stillanti, profugasque Cantu,
    Porrigis horas!—

Sive quas fruges alit aura campis,   5
Sive quas Sylvanus in Æsculetis,
His tibi dextra dedit haud avara
    Parca potiri.

Te manent almæ Cereris coloni
Nunciam; quando tenuis, laborum   10
Dulce lenimen, tua vox susurris
    Mulceat aures.

Diligunt te Pierides, Cicada;
Diligit Phœbus; tibi nam Camœnæ
Spiritum parvæ dedit, et stridentis   15
    Carminis artem.

TO THE AUTHOR. First published in *GM* (June 1756), p. 304. Text: *GM*. Collated: *MM* (July 1803), p. 539 (ll. 1–4 only). *Title*. On a malignant, dull Poet *MM*
1 When the viper its venom has spit, is is said *MM*   2 the ... the] its ... its *MM*   has] had *MM*   3 Thus it fares with the blockhead, who ventures to write, *MM*   4 Their ... their] His ... his *MM*
AD CICADAM. Text: *UV* (Aug. 1756), p. 382.

Pauperis Brumæ memor ore ducat
Sedulo formica cibos: senectus
Nulla te tristem minuit, nec aufert
    Cura futuri.   20

O *vagi* salve studiosa Cantus!
Tuque mi par esse Deo videris,
Lene quæ faustam sine carne vitam, et
    Sanguine degis.

'Beneath this fragrant myrtle shade'

'Επὶ μυρσίναις τερείναις, &c.   ANACREON.

Beneath this fragrant myrtle shade,
  While I my weary limbs recline,
O love, be thou my Ganymede,
  And hither bring the gen'rous wine!

How swift the wheel of time revolves!   5
  How soon life's little race is o'er!
And, oh! when death this frame dissolves,
  Mirth, joy, and frolick is no more!

Why then, ah! fool, profusely vain,
  With incense shall thy pavements shine?   10
Why dost thou pour, O wretch profane,
  On *senseless* earth, the nectar'd wine?

To me thy breathing odours bring,
  On me the mantling bowls bestow:
Go, Chloe, rob the roseate spring   15
  For wreaths to grace my honour'd brow.

Yes, ere the * airy dance I join
  Of flitting shadows, light and vain,
I'll wisely drown, in floods of wine,
  Each busy care, and idle pain.   20

* *Ghostly.*

BENEATH THIS. First datable publication: *UV* (Aug. 1756), p. 383. Text: *UV*.
Collated: *SS*, Bodl. Mus. 9 c. 5(60), n.d. *Title*. Ode, in Imitation of Anacreon *SS*
5 time] life *SS*   7 And] But *SS*   17 ere] e'er *UV*, *SS*

The Furniture of a Beau's Mind.

—O quantum est in rebus inane! PERS.

When infants are born, by experience we find,
    With ideas so few they're supply'd,
That Locke has most justly resembled their mind,
    To a cabinet empty and void.

A *Beau*, and a child, may in this be compar'd,   5
    For his mind would be quite a charte blanche,
If you strive (tho' I own that the labour is hard)
    What's trifling and vain to retrench.

First a set of shrew'd hints, innuendos, and slanders,
    And lyes that he tells with pert face: 10
A heap of stale phrases, and double entendres,
    Without sense to apply them in place:

Some new-fashion'd compliments ready at hand,
    Which he learns, like a parrot, by rote;
To bully and bluster, with oaths at command,   15
    "Blood, madam, I'll cut the rogue's throat!"

Four jokes and a half from *Joe Millar* purloin'd,
    Six lines out of *Hudibras* more;
Compose, if you nicely examine his mind,
    Of humour and wit his full store.   20

His learning just serves him to read a new song,
    Or chatter a sentence of French;
And what tho' 'em both he pronounces quite wrong?
    'Tis enough for his barber and wench.

Of Venus, and Cupid, and arrows, and darts,   25
    His tongue never ceasing runs on;
"Those eyes, my sweet angel, like swords pierce our hearts,
    Oh, close them—or else I'm undone!"

THE FURNITURE OF A BEAU'S MIND. Text: *UV* (Sept. 1756), pp. 429–30.

Add to these a few scraps of our modern romances,
    From *Grandison*, *Ramble*, or *Briggs*;   30
Three dozen at least of new country dances,
    With minuets, louvres, and gigs.

Oh yes! I give notice, if any one know
    More virtues than these we have reckon'd;
Let him send us the name, and abode of his *Beau*,   35
    To add in edition the second.

Thus accomplished a captain, a knight, or a 'squire,
    How great are his merit, and charms?
See ladies in troops his perfections admire,
    And with extasy spring to his arms!—

The Forty-Second Psalm.

E'en as the hart desires the streams
With ardour, when the sultry beams
    Embrown the withering sod;
My captive soul longs to be free,
And pants, and is athirst for thee,   5
    My Saviour, and my God.

She, with the sons of sin at strife,
Sighs for the fountain of her life,
    And seeks her native place:
Ah! when glad tidings shall she hear,   10
When shall she yet again appear
    Before the throne of grace?

Thro' dangerous days, and nights of fears,
My sustenance has been my tears,
    While infidels are nigh:—   15
"And what an abject thing art thou,
Who! who is thy defender now,
    And where's thy God?" they cry.

THE FORTY-SECOND PSALM. First published in *UV* (Oct. 1756), pp. 171–4. Text:
UV. Collated: *LTM* (Apr.–May 1757), ii. 205–6.
10 she] I *LTM*

Home at my heart, when this I hear,
I keep my thoughts in pensive pray'r,   20
   Nor trust them to my tongue:
For oh! far other times I've known,
When trumpets were in triumph blown,
   And festive songs were sung.

When, at the van, with joy I rode,   25
And to the temple of my God
   The multitude I brought:
There too I still have led the way,
And bade them praise, and bade them pray,
   By my example taught.   30

By sad solicitude opprest,
Why dost thou flag within my breast,
   And yield to grief the rein?
Why, oh, my soul, do woes increase,
Where once serenity and peace   35
   Held their divine domain?

Be constant to thyself and just,
Still in the Lord repose thy trust,
   Resolv'd and yet resign'd:
Let thanks, let gratitude endure;   40
All but in praises art thou poor,
   All else thy pow'r confin'd.

When melancholy thoughts return,
My heart with holy zeal shall burn,
   Thy mercies past to prize: 45
The land of Jordan, and thy hill,
O Hermon, I'll remember still,
   And check my rising sighs.

The depths in horrible despite,
Their dire alliances unite,   50

---

33 yield] yield'st *LTM*   the rein] and pain *LTM*   49–50 The depths hold
terrible converse, / And hoarsly their rough parts rehearse *LTM*

Prepar'd t' o'erwhelm my soul.
Thy waves and storms afflict the skies,
And o'er me rage, and round me rise,
   And all thy thunders roll.

Yet ever, both by night and day,   55
Thy loving-kindness wakes my lay,
   While I thy praise proclaim:
'Tis that which makes the east more bright,
'Tis that illuminates the light,
   And night is but a name.   60

It is the Lord that makes me strong,
And him, whene'er I frame my song,
   Alone, I will invoke,—
"Dost thou not hear thy servant's cry,
Dost thou forget me whilst I lie   65
   Beneath the hostile yoke?"

With many a fierce opprobrious sound,
My soul, as with a sword, they wound,
   And smite my bones in twain:
And those, by whom my heart is torn,   70
At once add cruelty to scorn,
   To insolence, disdain.

For day by day, t' augment my woe,
Their infidelity they show,
   And deeds of deepest die:—   75
"And what an abject thing art thou,
Who? who is thy defender now,
   And where's thy God?" they cry.

Ah! why does sad solicitude
Upon my bosom yet intrude
   And gird my heart with pain?—   80
Why, O my soul, do woes increase,
Where once serenity and peace
   Held their divine domain!

53 rage] wave *LTM*   71 Are adding cruelty to scorn, *LTM*   77 Who?
who] And who *LTM*

He bids thy countenance be bold,—   85
Confirm'd his saving health behold,
   Nor dread th' avenger's rod:
In him thy confidence repose,
Tho' still ten thousand are thy foes,
   Yet he is still thy God.   90

Disertissime Romuli Nepotum,

Imitated after Dining with Mr. Murray.

O Thou, of British Orators the chief
That *were*, or are in *being*, or belief;
All eminence and goodness as thou art,
Accept the gratitude of POET SMART,
The meanest of the tuneful train as far,
As thou transcend'st the brightest at the bar.

The 100th Psalm, for a Scotch Tune.

Rejoice in God, ye blithsome lands,
With all your voices all your hands,
   Bent knees and faces prone;
With mickle gladness and content
Your goodly songs and selves present   5
   Before his awful throne.

Nought in ourselves but life and limb,
We are the workmanship of him,
   He is our God be sure;
Our shepherd too, as well ye ken,   10
He feeds us congregated men,
   Like sheep upon the moor.

DISERTISSIME. First published in *1763B*. Text: *1763B*. Collated: *1791*.
THE 100TH PSALM. Text: *CM* (Suppl. Jan.–June 1761), ii. 349.

O gang your way and gang with glee,
Into his courts with melody,
   And do his goodness right.   15
His gates are not too straight nor strong
To keep out sicke a lively song,
   And sicke a menceful sight.

For gracious is the Lord our rest,
Sith by his merits we are blest,   20
   And rescued from our crimes.
And us his just decrees he learns,
For sires to teach their bonny barnes
   Through all succeeding times.

Epitaph on the late Mr. Sheels,

Written at the Request of his Father.

O young, yet apt and able in the word,
And at the morning-call to CHRIST preferr'd!
Our hope was longer time, and more commands,
So great the harvest, and so scarce the hands!—
See how the likeliest are not lent to last,   5
And love officious calculates too fast.
—If God had left thy lot for human praise,
A father's prayer had multiplied thy days.
But since to grieve is now the task injoin'd,
We've learnt full well to weep, and be resign'd;   10
Nay more, adore and bless the great decree,
And, in the spirit, still commune with Thee.
Let God's good will, at our expence be done,
As CHRIST demands a brother and a son.

EPITAPH. First published in *CM* (Jan. 1763), iv. 44. Text: *1763B*. Collated: *CM*; *CC* (5 Feb. 1763). *Title as in CM, CC.*

REASON AND IMAGINATION, A FABLE;

ADDRESS'D TO
Mr. KENRICK.

PRAVO FAVORE *labi* mortales *solent,*
Et pro judicio dum stant erroris *sui*
Ad pœnitendum REBUS MANIFESTIS *agi.*   PHÆD.

Amidst the ample field of things,
The doubtful Muse suspends her wings;
While Thoughts, Imagination's host,
Keep hov'ring over Reason's post
Maintain'd, O *Truth*, upon thy base,   5
Whose voice, and whose Angelic face,
Are what the prudent love and hear,
And by no other star they steer.

   In vain fair *Fancy* decks her bow'rs,
And tempts with fruits, and tempts with flow'rs;   10
Her wiles in ev'ry mode express'd,
Or leudly strip'd, or proudly dress'd;
Try all the little arts she can,
Firm stands the Attribute of Man;
And solid, weighty, deep, and sound,   15
Asserts its right, and keeps its ground.

   'Twas in that famous *Sabine* grove,
Where Wit so oft with Judgment strove,
Where Wisdom grac'd th' Horatian lyre,
Like weight of metal play'd by fire;   20
Where Elegance and Sense conferr'd,
Just at the coming of the WORD,
Who chose his reasons to convey
A plain and a familiar way,
Then, would you taste the moral tale,   25
First bless the banquet, and regale.

REASON AND IMAGINATION. 'irst published in *1763* (reprinted in *GM*, July 1763,
pp. 355–6, omitting ll. 1–16, 19–26, 139–60). Text: *1763*. Collated: *1791*. *Title*.
Address'd to Mr. Kenrick *omitted, 1791*   1–26 *omitted, 1791*

IMAGINATION, in the flight
Of young desire, and gay delight,
Began to think upon a mate,
As weary of the single state;   30
For sick of change, as left at will,
And cloy'd with entertainment still,
She thought it better to be grave,
To settle, to take up, and save.
She therefore to her chamber sped,   35
And thus at first attir'd her head.
Upon her hair, with brilliants graced,
Her tow'r of beamy gold she placed;
Her ears with pendant jewels glow'd
Of various water, curious mode,   40
As nature sports the wintry ice,
In many a whimsical device.
Her eye-brows arch'd, upon the stream
Of rays, beyond the piercing beam;
Her cheeks in matchless colour high,   45
She veil'd to fix the gazer's eye;
Her paps, as white as Fancy draws,
She cover'd with a crimson gauze;
And on her wings she threw perfume
From buds of everlasting bloom.   50
Her zone, ungirded from her vest,
She wore across her swelling breast;
On which, in gems, this verse was wrought,
"I make and shift the scenes of Thought."
In her right hand a Wand she held,   55
Which Magick's utmost pow'r excell'd;
And in her left retain'd a Chart,
With figures far surpassing art,
Of other natures, suns and moons,
Of other moves to higher tunes.   60
The Sylphs and Sylphids, fleet as light,
The Fairies of the gamesome night,
The Muses, Graces, all attend
Her service, to her journey's end:

30 the] a *1791*   34 save. *1791*] save, *1763*

And Fortune, sometimes at her hand,　65
Is now the fav'rite of her band,
Dispatch'd before the news to bear,
And all th' adventure to prepare.

　　Beneath an Holm-tree's friendly shade,
Was REASON's little cottage made;　70
Before, a river deep and still;
Behind, a rocky soaring hill.
Himself, adorn'd in seemly plight,
Was reading to the Eastern light;
And ever, as he meekly knelt,　75
Upon the Book of Wisdom dwelt.
The Spirit of the shifting wheel,
Thus first essay'd his pulse to feel.—
"The Nymph supreme o'er works of wit,
O'er labour'd plan, and lucky hit,　80
Is coming to your homely cot,
To call you to a nobler lot;
I, *Fortune*, promise wealth and pow'r,
By way of matrimonial dow'r:
Preferment crowns the golden day,　85
When fair Occasion leads the way."
Thus spake the frail, capricious dame,
When she that sent the message came.—

　　"From first Invention's highest sphere,
I, Queen of Imag'ry, appear;　90
And throw myself at REASON's feet,
Upon a weighty point to treat.
You dwell alone, and are too grave;
You make yourself too much a slave;
Your shrewd deductions run a length,　95
'Till all your Spirits waste their strength:
Your fav'rite logick is full close;
Your morals are too much a dose;
You ply your studies 'till you risk
Your senses—you should be more brisk—　100

98 too] to *1791*

336

The Doctors soon will find a flaw,
And lock you up in chains and straw.
But, if you are inclin'd to take
The gen'rous offer, which I make,
I'll lead you from this hole and ditch,   105
To gay Conception's top-most pitch;
To those bright plains, where crowd in swarms
The spirits of fantastic forms;
To planets populous with elves;
To natures still above themselves,   110
By soaring to the wond'rous height
Of notions, which they still create;
I'll bring you to the pearly cars,
By dragons drawn, above the stars;
To colours of Arabian glow;   115
And to the heart-dilating show
Of paintings, which surmount the life:
At once your tut'ress, and your wife."—
"—Soft, soft, (says REASON) lovely friend;
Tho' to a parley I attend,   120
I cannot take thee for a mate;
I'm lost, if e'er I change my state.
But whensoe'er your raptures rise,
I'll try to come with my supplies;
To muster up my sober aid,   125
What time your lively pow'rs invade;
To act conjointly in the war
On dullness, whom we both abhor;
And ev'ry sally that you make,
I must be there, for conduct's sake;   130
Thy correspondent, thine ally;
Or any thing, but bind and tye—
But, ere this treaty be agreed,
Give me thy wand and winged steed:
Take thou this compass and this rule,   135
That wit may cease to play the fool;
And that thy vot'ries who are born
For praise, may never sink to scorn."

133 ere] e'er *1763, 1791*   136 wit] Wit *1791*

O KENRICK, happy in the view
Of *Reason*, and of *Fancy* too; ₌   140
Whose friendship of a few days growth,
Is ripe, and greater than them both;
Who reconcil'st with Euclid's scheme,
The tow'ring flight, and golden dream,
With thoughts at once restrained and free,   145
I dedicate this tale to THEE.
But now, a vet'ran for the prize,
I claim a licence to advise.
Let not a fondness for the sage,
Decoy thee from a brighter page,   150
THE BOOK OF SEMPITERNAL BLISS,
The lore where nothing is amiss,
The truth to full perfection brought,
Beyond the sage's deepest thought;
Beyond the poet's highest flight;   155
Then let Invention reason right,
And free from prejudice and hate,
And false refinement's vain debate,
Since GOD's the WORD, that *Christians* read,
Be love their everlasting deed.   160

139–60 *omitted, 1791*

ODE
TO
Admiral Sir *GEORGE POCOCK.*

When CHRIST, the seaman, was aboard
  Swift as an arrow to the *White*,
While Ocean his rude rapture roar'd,
   * The vessel gain'd the Haven with delight:
We therefore first to him the song renew,   5
Then sing of POCOCK's praise, and make the point in view.

The Muse must humble e're she rise,
  And kneel to kiss her Master's feet,
Thence at one spring she mounts the skies
  And in *New Salem* vindicates her seat;   10
Seeks to the temple of th' Angelic choir,
And hoists the ENGLISH FLAG upon the topmost spire.

O Blessed of the Lord of Hosts,
  In either India most renown'd,
The Echo of the Eastern coasts,   15
  And all th' Atlantic shores thy name resound.—
The victor's clemency, the seaman's art,
The cool delib'rate head, and warm undaunted heart.

My pray'r was with Thee, when thou sail'd
  With prophecies of sure success;   20
My thanks to Heav'n, that thou prevail'd
  Shall last as long as I can breathe or bless;
And built upon thy deeds my song shall tow'r,
And swell, as it ascends, in spirit and in pow'r.

There is no thunder half so loud,   25
  As God's applauses in the height,
For those, that have his name avow'd,
  Ev'n *Christian* Patriots valorous and great;
Who for the general welfare stand or fall,
And have no sense of self, and know no dread at all.   30
  * John vi. 21.

ODE TO POCOCK. Text: *1763.*

Amongst the numbers lately fir'd
  To act upon th' heroic plan,
Grace has no worthier chief inspir'd,
  Than that sublime, insuperable man,
Who could th' out-numb'ring *French* so oft defeat,   35
And from th' HAVANNAH stor'd his brave victorious fleet.

And yet how silent his return
  With scarce a welcome to his place—
Stupidity and unconcern,
  Were settled in each voice and on each face.   40
As private as myself he walk'd along,
Unfavour'd by a friend, unfollow'd by the throng.

Thy triumph, therefore, is not here,
  Thy glories for a while postpon'd,
The hero shines not in his sphere,
  But where the Author of all worth is own'd.—   45
Where *Patience* still persists to praise and pray
For all the Lord bestows, and all he *takes away*.

Not HOWARD, FORBISHER, or DRAKE,
  Or VERNON's fam'd *Herculean* deed;   50
Not all the miracles of BLAKE,
  Can the great Chart of thine exploits exceed.—
Then rest upon thyself and dwell secure,
And cultivate the arts, and feed th' *increasing* poor.

O NAME accustom'd and inur'd   55
  To fame and hardship round the globe,
For which fair Honour has insur'd
  The warrior's truncheon, and the consul's robe;
Who still the more is *done* and *understood*,
Art easy of access, art affable and good.   60

O NAME acknowledged and rever'd
  Where ISIS plays her pleasant stream,
Whene'er thy tale is read or heard,
  The good shall bless thee, and the wise esteem;

And they, whose offspring * lately felt thy care,   65
Shall in TEN THOUSAND CHURCHES make their
    daily pray'r.—

"Connubial bliss and homefelt joy,
    And ev'ry social praise be thine;
Plant thou the oak, the poor employ;
    Or plans of vast benevolence design;   70
And speed, when CHRIST his servant shall release,
From triumph over death to everlasting peace."

ODE
TO
General *DRAPER.*

——*Utcunque ferant ea facta* minores
Vincat amor patriæ, laudumque immensa cupido.   VIRG.

Noble in Nature, great in arms,
    The Muses patron and thyself a bard,
Who sternly rushing from domestic charms
    And for thy country tow'ring upon guard,
As born against the foes of human kind,   5
Preced'st the march alone, and leav'st all rank behind.
A little leisure for a thankful heart,
    It's own peculiar workings to attend,
A little leisure to survey the Chart,
    Of all thy labours bearing to their end;   10
To hail Thee, at the head of all renown,
To plan thy private peace, and weave thy laurel crown.

The Fame of DRAPER is a pile
    Of God's erecting in th' embattled field;
An English fabrick in the Roman stile,   15
    To which all meaner elevations yield;
What ho! ye brave lieutenants of the van,
Within a thousand furlongs not a single man.

* Alluding to the Admiral's noble Benefaction to the Sons of the Clergy.

ODE TO DRAPER. Text: *1763.*

341

My Muse is somewhat stronger than she was,
    In spite of long calamity and time,   20
Arouse, Arouse ye! is there not a cause?
    Arouse ye lively spirits of my prime!
Breathe, breathe upon the lyre thy parting breath,
There is no thought of him but triumphs over death.

Ye boys of Eton take your theme,   25
    That heroes from heroic fathers come;
Ye sons of learned Granta draw the scheme
    Of Archimedes, on the warriour's drum:
No more let champions scorn the man of parts,
For DRAPER comes like MARLBRO' from the school of arts.
O early train'd and practis'd in desert,   31
    The son of emulation from the womb,
In antient arms and eloquence expert;
    And student of the themes of Greece and Rome,
Thou chose ACHILLES from th' *Homeric* throng,   35
Who sinks beneath thy deeds, tho' rais'd upon * thy song.

A CHRISTIAN HERO is a name
    To bards of Classic eminence unknown,
A heroe, that prefers a higher claim
    To God's applause, his country's and his own;   40
Than those, who, tho' the mirrour of their days,
Nor knew the Prince of Worth, nor principle of praise.
Advance, advance a little higher still—
    Th' Ideas of an Englishman advance!
Advance above his meaner strength or skill;   45
    Who solely grasps his pen or shakes his lance.
Thy talent ever flows to learning's hoard,
And bore to leisure fruit 'midst peril and the sword.

O ENGLISH aspect name and soul,
    All ENGLISH to our joyful ears and eyes!   50
Thy chariot cleanly risk'd upon the goal
    Has brought Thee winner for the Martial Prize;
And interval on interval succeeds,

* Alluding to a famous Copy of Latin Verses, written by DRAPER at *Eton.*

---

41 Than] That *1763*

Before thy second comes to signify his deeds.
A note above the Epic trumpet's reach   55
    Beyond the compass of the various lyre,
The song of all thy deeds, which sires shall teach
    Their children active prowess to inspire.—
Thou art a Master—whose exploits shall warm,
The valiant yet to come, and future heroes form.   60

It is an honest book, that writes
    Thy name as worthy honourable lot,
For fair and faithful * thy detail recites,
    The merits of thy brethren on the spot;
From gallant MONSON foremost of th' array,   65
To him that came the last, yet help'd to win the day.
What tho' no sense of gratitude be shown
    As heretofore, to chiefs of meaner rank;
No mason hew thy figure from a stone,
    Or painter daub thee staring on a plank;   70
No groupe of Aldermen proclaim thee free,
And in the Tayler's College give thee thy degree?

What tho' no bonfires be display'd,
    Nor windows light up the nocturnal scene;
What tho' the merry ringer is not paid,   75
    Nor rockets shoot upon the STILL SERENE;
Tho' no matross upon the rampart runs,
To send out thy report from loud redoubling guns?
What tho' thy precious health does not go round,
    Where'er the gormandizing sinner dines;   80
Thy name be kept in secrecy profound,
    O'er female converse and loquacious wines;
What tho' th' astonish'd rustic does not fawn,
On DRAPER made of wax, or on the bellows drawn?

No coin the medalists devise,   85
    With thankful captives crowding the *Reverse*;
Or *Plutus* leading *Merit* to the prize,

---

* See Gazette for the 16th of April, 1763.

69 hew] knew *1763*, *corrected to* hew *in Daily Advertiser* (19 July 1763)

Or ALBION wailing MORE's untimely hearse;
What tho' no bawling ballad singers rend
The skies with joy for thee, or dirges for thy friend?　　90
Not monumental marble or the life
　　Upon the rival canvass aptly feign'd,
Nor City-Speaker, licensed by his wife,
　　To skrew up panygyric, bridg'd and strain'd;
Not glass adorn'd with mottos and with boughs,　　95
Nor fires that light the mob to roar and to carouse.

Not the round peal or guns' salute,
　　Pronouncing still that DRAPER is the toast;
Not youth and blooming beauty, bearing fruit
　　To Justice, as they make A MAN their boast;　　100
Not Salmon's wax-work or the hackney muse,
Not all the prose and verse of all the Grub-street news.
Not anything they have denied to Thee,
　　Is half so great as that which your possess;
The patriot's hand, the honest parson's knee,　　105
　　And the GREAT BRITISH MONARCH's love express;
And if I may presume upon my mite,
This rough unbidden verse, that aims to do thee right.

Stupendous, surely, is thy chance,
　　If such a man as thou shou'd be despis'd;　　110
Advance—thy fav'rite word—advance, advance
　　To take thy rank with worthies in the skies;
The Captain of ten thousand in the sphere,
Where *Michael* draws the sword or throws the glitt'ring spear.
Thyself and seed for which there is no doom,　　115
　　Race rising upon race in goodly pride,
Shall ever flourish root, and branch, and bloom,
　　Shall flourish tow'ring high and spreading wide;
To carry God's applauses in their heart,
To shew an ENGLISH face, and act an ENGLISH part.　　120

AN
EPISTLE
TO
JOHN SHERRATT, Esq;

Hæc mihi semper erunt imis infixa medullis,
Perpetuusque ANIMI debitor HUJUS ero.

Ovid de Trist. Eleg. iv.

Of all the off'rings thanks can find,
None equally delights the mind;
Or charms so much, or holds so long,
As gratitude express'd in song.
We reckon all the BOOK of GRACE   5
By verses, as the source we trace,
And in the spirit all is great
By number, melody and weight.
By nature's light each heathen sage,
Has thus adorn'd th' immortal page;   10
Demosthenes and Plato's prose,
From skill in mystic measure flows;
And ROLT's sublime, historic stile,
Is better that the Muses smile.
Take then from heartiness profest,   15
What in the bard's conceit is best;
The golden sheaf desertion gleans
For want of better helps and means.

    Well nigh sev'n years had fill'd their tale,
From Winter's urn to Autumn's scale,   20
And found no friend to grief, and *Smart*,
Like Thee and Her, thy sweeter part;
Assisted by a friendly * pair
That chose the side of CHRIST and PRAY'R,
To build the great foundation laid,   25
By one † sublime, transcendent maid.

* Mr. and Mrs. ROLT.
† Miss A. F. S.———. of *Queen's-Square.*

EPISTLE TO SHERRATT. Text: *1763.*
3 long,] long. *1763*

'Tis well to signalize a deed,
And have no precedent to plead;
'Tis blessing as by God we're told,
To come and visit friends in hold;   30
Which skill is greater in degree,
If goodness set the pris'ner free.
'Tis you that have in my behalf,
Produc'd the robe and kill'd the calf;
Have hail'd the *restoration day*,   35
And bid the loudest music play.
If therefore there is yet a note
Upon the lyre, that I devote,
To gratitude's divinest strains,
One gift of love for thee remains;   40
One gift above the common cast,
Of making fair memorials last.

   Not He whose highly finish'd piece,
Outshone the chissel'd forms of Greece;
Who found with all his art and fame,   45
* A part'ner in the house I claim;
Not he that pencils CHARLOTTE's eyes,
And boldly bids for ROMNEY's prize;
Not both the seats, where arts commune
Can blazon like a word in tune;   50
But this our young scholasticks con,
As warrant from th' *Appulian* Swan.
Then let us frame our steps to climb,
Beyond the sphere of chance and time,
And raise our thoughts on HOLY WRIT,   55
O'er mortal works and human wit.
The lively acts of CHRISTIAN LOVE,
Are treasur'd in the rolls above;
Where Archangelic concerts ring,
And God's accepted poets sing.   60
So Virtue's plan to parry praise,
Cannot obtain in after days;
Atchievements in the Christian cause,
Ascend to sure and vast applause;

* Mr. *Roubilliac*'s first Wife was a *Smart*, descended from the same Ancestors as Mr. *Christopher Smart*.

346

Where Glory fixes to endure   65
All precious, permanent and pure.
Of such a class in such a sphere,
Shall thy distinguish'd deed appear;
Whose spirit open and avow'd
Array'd itself against the croud   70
With chearfulness so much thine own,
And all thy motive God alone;
To run thy keel across the boom,
And save my vessel from her doom,
And cut her from the pirate's port,   75
Beneath the cannon of the fort,
With colours fresh, and sails unfurl'd,
Was nobly dar'd to beat the world;
And stands for ever on record,
IF TRUTH AND LIFE BE GOD AND LORD. 80

Song.

Where shall Cælia fly for shelter,
    In what secret grove or cave?
Sighs and sonnets sent to melt her
    From the young, the gay, the brave.
Tho' with prudish airs she starch her,   5
    Still she longs, and still she burns;
Cupid shoots like Hayman's archer,
    Wheresoe'er the damsel turns.

Virtue, wit, good sense, and beauty,
    If discretion guide us not,   10
Sometimes are the ruffian's booty,
    Sometimes are the booby's lot:
Now they're purchas'd by the trader,
    Now commanded by the peer;
Now some subtle mean invader   15
    Wins the heart, or gains the ear.

SONG. First datable publication: Samuel Howard's *Collection of Songs sung by Miss Davies at Vaux Hall* [Aug. 1763], v. 4–6 (*SH*). Text: *1764*. Collated: *SH*.
9 wit] youth *SH*

O discretion, thou'rt a jewel,
  Or our grand-mammas mistake;
Stinting flame by bating fewel,
  Always careful and awake!   20
Wou'd you keep your pearls from tramplers,
  Weigh the licence, weigh the banns:
Mark my song upon your samplers,
  Wear it on your knots and fans.

On a Bed of Guernsey Lilies.

Written in September 1763.

Ye beauties! O how great the sum
  Of sweetness that ye bring;
On what a charity ye come
  To bless the latter spring!
How kind the visit that ye pay,   5
Like strangers on a rainy day,
  When heartiness despair'd of guests:
No neighbour's praise your pride alarms,
No rival flow'r surveys your charms,
  Or heightens, or contests!   10

Lo, thro' her works gay nature grieves
  How brief she is and frail,
As ever o'er the falling leaves
  Autumnal winds prevail.
Yet still the philosophic mind   15
Consolatory food can find,
  And hope her anchorage maintain:
We never are deserted quite;
'Tis by succession of delight
  That love supports his reign.   20

19 bating] baiting *1764*
ON A BED OF GUERNSEY LILIES. Text: *1764.*

MUNIFICENCE and MODESTY,
A POEM;

The Hint from a Painting of *GUIDO*.

Attende cur negare cupidis debeas,
Modestis etiam offerre, quod non petierint.

PHÆDRUS.

O VOICE of APPROBATION, bless
The spirits still demanding less,
The more their natures have to need,
The more their services can plead;
The more their mighty merits claim—   5
The voice of Approbation came.

FAIR MODESTY, divinely sweet,
With garb prepared, and lamp replete,
Lamented still from sun to sun
So much received, and nothing done.   10
Her abstinence was insincere,
Her studies not enough severe;
Her thoughts at fault, and still to seek,
Her words inadequate and weak;
Her actions wretched and restrain'd,   15
Her passions neither balk'd nor rein'd.
Her head she waved in meek distrust,
Her eyes were fix'd to read the dust;
Her cheeks were tinctured to receive
The blushes of the crimson eve,   20
Prophetic of a better day,
When thus she framed her hymn to pray.
"O Thou, whose bounties never fail,
Who smil'st upon the lowly vale,
And giv'st fertililty and peace   25
Their flow'ry lawn and golden fleece;
Who send'st the spirit of the breeze,
To bend the heads of stately trees,

MUNIFICENCE AND MODESTY. Text: *1763B*.
18 read *MS correction*] reach *1763B*

Till pines with all their state and rank,
Bow like the bullrush on the bank.   30
Who bid'st the little brook flow on,
And warbling sooth the silent swan,
And spreading form the shaded lake,
Untill th' emerging rays retake
The transcript of the scene to Thee,   35
O FATHER of SIMPLICITY.
As this thy glossy turf I press,
And prostrate on my forehead bless,
Consider for the poor infirm,
The harmless sheep, th' obnoxious worm,   40
The stooping yoke that turn the soil,
And all the children of thy toil.
In fine, of all the num'rous race,
Of all that crowd and ought to grace
Thy vast immeasurable board,   45
To me the lowest lot afford."

SHE bow'd, she sigh'd, and made her pause:
And instantly th' immense applause
Of thunder in the height was heard,
And all the host of Heav'n appear'd.   50
And thro' the great and glorious throng,
Of Seraphims, ten thousand strong
Came down that prince of high degree,
Th' archangel LIBERALITY.
A crown of Beryls graced his head,   55
His wings were closed, his hands were spread;
His stature nobler than the rest,
A sun and belt adorn'd his breast;
His voice was rapture to the ears,
His look like GRANBY in his geers;   60
When lighting on the dewy sod,
Thus spake the Almoner of God.
"Survey these scenes from east to west,
All earth in bloom and verdure drest;
Those olives planted by the line,   65
That forrest after God's design.
Those naked rocks that rise to bound,

The vine-invested elms around;
The golden meads that far extend,
And to the silver streams descend.   70
Those fields of corn in youthful green,
Where larks prepare the nest unseen.
Or turn your eyes, immortal Fair,
To yon gay walks of art and care,
Where the throng'd hive their sweets augment,   75
And murmur not, but thro' content.
That long canal so clear and deep,
Unmoved, but by the Crusion's leap;
That Grotto, which from Gani's mines,
And Ocean's ransack'd bosom shines.   80
I, whose commission's to dispense
The meed of God's munificence,
To thy undoubted worth resign,
These joys of thought and sense, as thine."

    I ASK NOT (MODESTY replied)   85
For wealthy regions far and wide;
I rest content, if you but spare,
What is the utmost of my pray'r;
A little cot my frame to house,
With room enough to pay my vows.   90
"Then take a view of yonder tow'rs,
Where Fortune deals her gifts in showr's;
Where that vast bulwark's proud disdain
Runs a long terras on the main;
Whose strong foundation Ocean laves,   95
And bustles with officious waves,
To bring with many a thousand sail,
Whate'er refinement can regale;
Rich fruits of oriental zest,
Perfumes of ARABY the blest,   100
With precious ornaments to wear,
Upon thine hands, thy neck, thy hair:
O Queen of the transcendent few,
All decoration is thy due."
Remote from cities and their noise   105
Serenity herself enjoys,

82 meed] mead 1763B

And free from grandeur and expence,
Had best be cloath'd with innocence.
"If such thine elevated mind,
Chuse pleasures for thy sex design'd;   110
A blooming youth I will provide,
To make thee a transported bride;
To give each day some new delight,
And bless the soft connubial night."
I may not act a double part,   115
And offer a divided heart;
Let other nymphs their swains endear,
For my affections are not here.
"Accomplish then that great desire,
To which the wise and good aspire;   120
A name that no detraction knows,
Whose fragrance is as SHARON's rose;
Which makes the highest flight of fame,
By vast and popular acclaim."
O rather may I still refrain,   125
Nor run the risk of being vain;
To peace and silence let me cleave,
And *give* the glory—not receive.
"Yet, yet accept a gift of love,
The royal Sceptre and the Dove;   130
All things on earth thou shalt command,
Whatever heart, whatever hand;
Why are those charming looks aground?
Arise, aspire, thou shalt be crown'd."
Talk not of crowns—I have no will,   135
No power, no thought.—"No more, be still.
"Who's there?" The vast Cherubic flight,
Of thousand thousands on the right.
"Who's there?" 'Tis ORIEL and his SONG,
Full eighty thousand legions strong.—   140
"Hand from the nether Zenith down
The chariot with the emerald crown
By Phœnix drawn.—Lo! this is SHE,
Which has atchieved the first degree;
And scorning MAMMON and his leav'n,
Has won Eternity and Heav'n."

146 won *MS correction*] one *1763B*

352

FEMALE DIGNITY,

INSCRIBED AND APPLIED TO
Lady *HUSSEY DELAVAL.*

Whate'er the sense, whate'er the face,
    Whate'er the beauties all combin'd;
'Tis DIGNITY, that gives the grace,
    And forms the Fair, as first design'd.
Thro' life we have a sterling rule   5
    To make the noblest points our aim;
And DIGNITY commands the school
    Of all that excellence, we claim.

O never yet the gift of chance,
    Or bought by wealth, or forced by pow'r;   10
For Thee, the Champion grasps his lance,
    For Thee, the flights of Fancy tow'r.
Thine is the great and perfect praise
    Of fathers kind, and lovers true;
Stern censure smiles thy worth to blaze,   15
    And owns the myrtle wreath thy due.

'Tis DIGNITY, supports the song
    By sense to choicest sounds allied;
The Muses do the Graces wrong,
    Unless her influence preside.   20
O Fountain of all Female worth,
    That play'st so sweet and so sublime;
To feed the flow of decent mirth,
    The PRIDE of PLACE, the LIFE of TIME.

Hail Condescension, heav'nly mild,   25
    By which no Majesty is lost;
Thee Faith and Truth their Queen have styl'd,
    And still with awful love accost.
On Thee, ten thousand blessings wait,
    In bright succession without pause;   30
If, CHARMER, thou hast found thy mate,
    His name is HONOUR and APPLAUSE.

FEMALE DIGNITY. Text: *1763B.*

EPITAPH,

On *HENRIETTA*, Late Dutchess of
CLEVELAND.

Born in those days, when Charity revived,
And from the Champion of the Church derived,
We claim a portion in the HOUSE of GRACE
For her, whose relicts shall adorn the place:
For her, who cherish'd with a mother's care,   5
And fill'd the Orphan's mouth with praise and pray'r.
Form'd for these deeds she bore her fruit *above*,
And left no issue to connubial love.
Yet was the noble matron well sustain'd,
And true politeness served, where prudence reign'd.   10
She check'd all thoughts in which the tempter lurks,
By keeping Fancy busied on her works.—
A taste for hist'ry with a gen'rous aim,
And strict attention to her country's fame.—
A skill in picture, genius in design,   15
'Twas nature copy'd nature line for line.
Such were her merits, when her faith was tried,
And to attain diviner things, she died.—
Amen.—The paths of life so justly trod,
Bespeak the welcome due, thro' CHRIST, from GOD.

Epitaph on Henry Fielding, Esq.

The Master of the GREEK and ROMAN page,
The lively scorner of a venal age,
Who made the publick laugh, at publick vice,
Or drew from sparkling eyes the pearl of price;
Student of nature, reader of mankind,   5
In whom the patron, and the bard were join'd;
As free to give the plaudit, as assert,

EPITAPH ON THE DUTCHESS OF CLEVELAND. Text: *1763B*.
EPITAPH ON HENRY FIELDING. First published in *St. James's Mag.* (July 1763), ii.
312 (*SJM*). Text: *1763B*. Collated: *SJM*; *LM* (Aug. 1763), p. 441.
6 In whom the poet and the patron join'd. *SJM, LM*   7 the plaudit] applauses
SJM, LM

And faithful in the practice of desert.
Hence pow'r consign'd the laws to his command,
And put the scales of Justice in his hand,   10
To stand protector of the Orphan race,
And find the female penitent a place.
From toils like these, too much for age to bear,
From pain, from sickness, and a world of care;
From children, and a widow in her bloom,   15
From shores remote, and from a foreign tomb,
Call'd by the WORD of LIFE, thou shalt appear,
To *please* and *profit* in a higher sphere,
Where endless hope, unperishable gain,
Are what the scriptures *teach* and *entertain*.   20

The Famous General Epitaph of Demosthenes,

translated from the original Greek.

These for their Country's cause were sheath'd in arms
    And all base imputations dared despise;
And *nobly* struck with GLORY's *dreadful charms,*
    Made death their aim, eternity their prize.
For never could their mighty spirits yield,   5
    To see themselves and country-men in chains;
And Earth's kind bosom hides them in the field
    Of battle, so the WILL SUPREME ordains;
To conquer chance and error's not reveal'd,
    For mortals sure mortality remains.   10

8 faithful] skilful *SJM, LM*   9 his] thy *SJM, LM*   10 his] thine *SJM,*
LM   13 age] eye *SJM, LM*
THE FAMOUS GENERAL EPITAPH. First published in *1763B*. Text: *1763B*. Collated:
1791. *Title*. of] from *1791*   2 dared] dare *1791*

Ode to the Right Honourable the Earl of Northumberland,

on his being appointed Lord Lieutenant of Ireland.
Presented on the Birth-Day of Lord Warkworth.

Quod verum atque decens curo— HOR.

ADVERTISEMENT

Though the following Piece was in a degree received at a certain place, and something handsome done (according to custom) yet such was the modesty of the excellent person to whom it was addressed, that the Printing of it was so far from being approved of, that very positive injunctions were given to the contrary.

The Author therefore was content to have the Manuscript handed about amongst his friends for their private entertainment, determining at all events to abide by his obedience.—But at length having the honour to communicate it to a great and worthy friend, who has been for some years in the country, he persuaded him to make it public, urging that the suppression would in a degree be a loss to letters; and as for any blame about the matter, he was ready to take that upon himself. This is an honourable Gentleman who has a most profound respect to my Lord Lieutenant, and whose commands were not likely to be resisted, as they were given with equal authority and benevolence, and in the true spirit of an Englishman, born to encounter opposition and triumph over difficulty.

> Whate'er distinguish'd patriots rise
> The times and manners to revise,
>   And drooping merit raise,
> The Song of Triumph still persues
> Their footsteps, and the moral Muse   5
>   Dwells sweetly on their praise.
>
> It is a task of true delight
> The ways of goodness to recite
>   And all her works refin'd;

ODE. First published in *1764*. Text: *1764*. Collated: *1791*. *Title*. Ode to the Earl of Northumberland, *etc. 1791*

Tho' modest greatness under-rate   10
Its lustre, 'tis as fix'd as fate,
  Says Truth, with music join'd.

All hail to this auspicious morn,
When we, for gallant WARKWORTH born,
  Our gratulations pay: 15
Tho' Virtue all the live-long year
Refuse her eulogy to hear,
  She must attend to-day.

All hail to that transcendent FAIR,
That crown'd thy wishes with an heir   20
  And bless'd her native land:
Still shoots thy undegen'rate line,
Like oak from oak, and pine from pine,
  As goodly and as grand.

Well therefore might thy grateful heart   25
Its just munificence impart
  For women in their throes;
And ope'd an hospitable door
To skreen the children of the poor
  From all their wonted woes.   30

O form'd the highest rank to grace,
And hold with dignity thy place,
  How great soe'er the trust:
No eminence can be so high,
But ease and native majesty   35
  Their conduct will adjust.

O free and open of access,
As well the grievance to redress,
  As honour to decree:
When tim'rous meekness wou'd be gone   40
Inviting goodness draws her on,
  And bids to make her plea.

25–78, 85–114 *omitted, 1791*

357

Thy love of seemliness was great
To beautify the judgment-seat,
   And licence to repel;   45
"In order and proportion due
Let ev'n the place be just and true,
   Where truth and justice dwell."

Hail, genuine patriotic zeal,
Which stedfast to the common-weal   50
   By loyalty adheres:
Thy vessel wins applause supreme,
As sailing safe from each extreme,
   In glorious pomp she steers.

From such an active spirit sprung   55
WARKWORTH the lov'd, the gay, the young,
   By hostile threats unaw'd,
Presented his victorious hand,
When valiant GRANBY made a stand
   For ages to applaud!   60

'Twas by this noble thirst of fame,
That in his absence he became
   Our universal choice,
Asserting with a gen'rous strife,
"Who for his country risks his life   65
   Deserves his country's voice!"

By such a spirit warm'd and sway'd,
Thou hast attain'd for Ireland's aid
   The zenith of thy sphere;
Thy deputation is profest   70
From GEORGE the EMP'ROR of the WEST,
   Whose title's now so clear.

And may the humble muse presume
To counter-work the mines of Rome,
   By what she shall conceive?—   75
'Tis thine to hear Religion's cries,
From foul and impious blasphemies
   Her honour to retrieve.

O how illustrious and divine
Were all the heroes of thy line   80
   'Gainst Rome's ambitious CHEAT!
Born all these base insidious arts,
Which work the most in weakest hearts,
   To dare and to defeat!

When arbitrary James, a name   85
Consign'd to everlasting shame,
   Against his charge rebell'd;
To rule the Lord's free sheep disdain'd,
And with a tyrant's grasp profan'd
   The sceptre that he held.   90

The delegate of Rome was sent
Contempt and sorrow to augment
   Throughout th' astonish'd realm,
And the great vessel of the state
Had well nigh sunk with all its freight,   95
   While folly kept the helm.

Great SOMERSET, thy house's pride,
With scorn majestic dar'd deride
   Th' attempt of rash despair;
And when the Babylonian Whore   100
Came thund'ring at the palace door
   Refus'd her entrance there.

The charge thou art about to take
Shall all those genuine sparks awake
   Residing in thy breast;   105
Each lurking priest thou shalt surprize,
And pluck the mask from black disguise,
   Whose sons the land infest.

Those enemies of human peace
The race that hate mankind's increase,   110
   And blood and rapine prize;
Who fill the soul with hellish fears,
Denying Scripture to our ears,
   And beauty to our eyes.

Live, then, and triumph o'er deceit,   115
That with new honours we may greet
   The house of ARMS and ARTS,
Till blest experience shall evince
How fairly you present that Prince,
   Who's sovereign of our hearts.   120

In pity to our sister isle,
With sighs we lend thee for a while;
   O be thou soon restor'd—
Tho' STANHOPE, HALIFAX were there,
We never had a man to spare   125
   Our love cou'd less afford.

115 and] in *1791*

TO THE
Honourable Mrs. DRAPER.

Noble, lovely, and judicious,
   Making worth thy aim and prize,
Hear the verse the muse officious
   Now presents thee to revise.

Thine is exquisite discernment,   5
   Zealous for thy country's cause
Thou hast heap'd the best preferment
   On the prince of all applause.

Thus I greet thee at a distance,
   Checking love by learning awe;   10
Grandeur gives the muse assistance,
   And the lighter thoughts withdraw.

All ideas are untainted
   When we think on heav'nly things;
Cherubs without sex are painted,   15
   Form'd alone of heads and wings.

When of Cherubs we conjecture,
   'Tis because we dwell on thee;
Looks and life thou art a lecture
   On th' angelical degree.   20

Take the laurel for thy frontlet,
   On thy breast the myrtles place,
For young DRAPER wears the gauntlet
   Of all chivalry and grace.

TO MRS. DRAPER. Text: *1764*.

On being asked by Colonel HALL to make Verses upon KINGSLEY at MINDEN.

I.

This task of me why dost thou crave?
Thyself ingenious, learn'd, and brave,
  And equal to th' immortal theme!
The scenes that you beheld display,
And draw the picture of the day   5
  With which thy great ideas teem.

But if like me you are at fault,
Nor can your utmost thought exalt,
  But needs must do the subject wrong;
Then let us both at once confess   10
Our meanness, and the man address
  Who soars above our song.

II.

"O heart-allow'd, by conscience prais'd,
As the vast envy thou hast rais'd,
  Such is the terror of thine arm: 15
The Muses and the Arts have join'd
The grudging silence of mankind,
  And our weak hands thy deeds disarm.

Say, Leader of the glorious few,
What can impoverish'd fancy do   20
  On paper, canvas, or on stone?
Thy work so great, thy name so bright,
That GOD himself with all his might
  Must give th' applause alone."

Epitaph on the late Duke of Argyle.

To Death's grim shades let meaner spirits fly,
Here rests JOHN CAMPBELL, who shall never die.

ON BEING ASKED. Text: *1764.*
EPITAPH. Text: *1764.*

[Epigram of Epictetus]

Imitated from the Greek.

By birth a servant, and in body maim'd;
By want a beggar;—worth, to beg asham'd:
Hardships like these to certain bliss commend;
For hence I boast immortal GOD my friend.

Epigramma Sannazarii,

Translated.

When in the Adriatic Neptune saw
Fair Venice stand, and give all ocean law;
Now Jove (he cried) the tow'rs of Mars compare,
And Rome's eternal bulwarks, if you dare:
If Tiber beats the main declare the odds,
Whose the mean craft of man, and which the plan of Gods.

The Sweets of Evening.

The sweets of Evening charm the mind,
    Sick of the sultry day;
The body then no more's confin'd,
But exercise with freedom join'd,
    When Phœbus sheathes his ray.   5

The softer scenes of nature sooth
    The organs of our sight;
The Zephyrs fan the meadows smooth,
And on the brook we build the booth
    In pastoral delight.   10

EPIGRAM. Text: *1764. Title.* ΕΠΙΚΤΗΤΟΣ *1764*
EPIGRAMMA SANNAZARII. Text: *1764.*
THE SWEETS OF EVENING. First published in *1764*. Text: *1764*. Collated: *1791.*
3 more's] more *1791*   6–10 *omitted, 1791*

While all-serene the summer moon
   Sends glances thro' the trees,
And Philomel begins her tune,
Asterie too shall help her soon
   With voice of skilful ease.   15

A nosegay every thing that grows,
   And music every sound
To lull the sun to his repose;
The skies are color'd like the rose
   With lively streaks around.   20

Of all the changes rung by Time
   None half so sweet appear,
As those when thoughts themselves sublime,
And with superior natures chime
   In fancy's highest sphere.   25

The Prize Carnation.

While for beauty, love and glory,
   She's so exquisitely form'd,
See, see alike the young and hoary,
   Crowding where the sweets have swarm'd.
Millions proud of human nature,   5
   As such excellence they see,
Give up folly, spleen and satire,
   Led to sense and praise by thee.

She was born for approbation
   Which she gives the last and least.   10
Blushing like the prize carnation,
   Shewn at Flora's summer feast.
May such sanctity of manners
   Soon another Juba gain;
And display the Cyprian banners,   15
   On the top of virtue's fane.

14 Asterie] Asteria *1791*
THE PRIZE CARNATION. Text: *SS*, Bodl. Johnson Mus. c.1 (7), *c.*1764.

[Epistle to Dr Nares]

Smart sends his compliments and pray'rs,
Health and long life to Dr Nares—
But the chief business of the card
Is "come to dinner with the bard,"
Who makes a mod'rate share of wit   5
Put on the pot, and turn the spit.
Tis said the Indians teach their sons
The use of bows instead of guns,
And, ere the striplings dare to dine,
They shoot their victuals off a pine.   10
The Public is as kind to me,
As to his child a Cherokee;
And if I chance to hit my aim,
I chuse to feast upon the game;
For panegyric or abuse   15
Shall make the quill procure the goose;
With apple-sauce and Durham mustard
And codling pye o'er-laid with custard.
Pray please to signify with this
My love to Madam, Bob, and Miss,   20
Likewise to nurse and little Poll,
Whose praise so justly you extoll.
P.S.
I have (don't think it a chimæra)
Some good sound port and right Madeira.

Song.

Tune, *Ye frolicksome sparks of the game.*

A MASON is great and respected,
    Tho' cavillers wrangle and mock;
His plan is in WISDOM projected,
    His edifice built on a rock.

EPISTLE TO DR. NARES. MS (Smart's holograph): *PC.* First published in *UMU* (Apr.
1764), i. 214. Text: *PC.* Collated: *UMU. Title.* A Card *UMU*
2 Nares] Nayres *UMU*   10 victuals] dinner *UMU*   12 As to the child of
Cherokee; *UMU*   16 procure] supply *UMU*   19–22 *omitted, UMU*
SONG. Text: *A Defence of Free-Masonry* (1765), p. 64.

Cho. The attempts of his foes miscarry,   5
  And ever in vain are found;
 Or so wide, that they need no parry,
  Or so weak, that they make no wound.

Good-nature's an Englishman's merit,
 A title all Britons desire;   10
But We claim the name and the spirit,
 From the corner-stone up to the spire.
Cho. The attempts of our foes miscarry, &c.

Tho' often decry'd and derided,
 No tyrant our freedom controuls,
With us mighty monarchs have sided,   15
 And emp'ror's are writ in our rolls.
Cho. The attempts of our foes miscarry, &c.

Then fill up the glass and be sunny,
 Attend to due method and form;
The bee that can make the most honey,
 Is fairly the flow'r of the swarm.   20
Cho. The attempts of our foes miscarry, &c.

Madam and the Magpie.

Ye thunders roll, ye oceans roar,
And wake the rough resounding shore;
Ye guns in smoke and flame engage,
And shake the ramparts with your rage;
Boreas distend your chops and blow;   5
Ring, ring, ye bonny bells of Bow;
Ye drums and rattles, rend the ears,
Like twenty thousand Southwark fairs;
Bellow ye bulls, and bawl ye brats,
Encore, encore, ye amorous cats;   10

MADAM AND THE MAGPIE. First published in *The Twelfth-Day Gift* (1767), pp. 74–6
(*TG*). Text: *1791*. Collated: *TG*. *Title*. Madam and the Magpye. A Fable. *TG*
9 brats *TG*] bats *1791*

In vain poor things ye squeak and squall,
Soft Sylvia shall out-tongue you all:
But here she comes—there's no relief,
She comes, and blessed are the deaf.
"A Magpie! why, you're mad, my dear,   15
To bring a chattering Magpie here.
A prating play thing, fit for boys—
You know I can't endure a noise.—
You brought this precious present sure,
My headach and my cough to cure.   20
Pray hand him in and let him stain
Each curtain, and each counterpane;
Yes, he shall roost upon my toilet,
Or on my pillow—he can't spoil it:
He'll only make me catch my death.—   25
O heavens! for a little breath!—
Thank God, I never knew resentment,
But am all patience and contentment,
Or else, you paltry knave, I shou'd
(As any other woman wou'd)   30
Wring off his neck, and down your gullet
Cram it, by way of chick or pullet.—
Well, I must lock up all my rings,
My jewels, and my curious things:
My Chinese toys must go to pot;   35
My deards, my pinchbecks:—and what not?
For all your Magpies are, like lawyers,
At once thieves, brawlers, and destroyers.—
You for a wife have search'd the globe,
You've got a very female Job,   40
Pattern of love, and peace and unity,
Or how cou'd you expect impunity?
O Lord! this nasty thing will bite,
And scratch and clapper-claw and fight.
O monstrous wretch, thus to devise,   45
To tear out your poor Sylvia's eyes.
You're a fine Popish plot pursuing,
By presents to effect my ruin;

31 his] its *TG*   36 deards, my pinchbecks *TG*] dear, my pinchbeck *1791*
38 thieves,] both *TG*   44 clapper-claw *TG*] clapper, claw *1791*   48 effect
TG] affect *1791*

367

And thus for good are ill retorting
To ME, who brought you such a fortune;　　　　　50
To ME, you low-liv'd clown, to ME,
Who came of such a family;
ME, who for age to age possess'd
A *lion rampant* on my crest;
ME, who have fill'd your empty coffers,　　　　　55
ME, who'd so many better offers;
And is my merit thus regarded,
Cuckold, my virtue thus rewarded?
O 'tis past sufferance—Mary—Mary,
I faint—the citron, or the clary."　　　　　60
　　The poor man, who had bought the creature,
Out of pure conjugal good-nature,
Stood at this violent attack,
Like statues made by Roubilliac,
Tho' form'd beyond all skill antique,　　　　　65
They can't their marble silence break;
They only breathe, and think, and start,
Astonish'd at their maker's art.
Quoth Mag, "fair Grizzle, I must grant,
Your spouse a magpye cannot want:　　　　　70
For troth (to give the dev'l his due)
He keeps a rookery in you.
Don't fear I'll tarry long, sweet lady,
Where there is din enough already,
We never shou'd agree together,　　　　　75
Although we're so much of a feather;
You're fond of peace, no man can doubt it,
Who make such wond'rous noise about it;
And your tongue of immortal mould
Proclaims in thunder you're no scold.　　　　　80
Yes, yes, you're sovereign of the tongue,
And, like the king, can do no wrong;
Justly your spouse restrains his voice,
Nor vainly answers words with noise;

---

53 who for] who've from *TG*　　　54 on] for *TG*　　　62 pure *TG*] poor
1791　　　64 statutes *TG*] statutes *1791*　　　80 thunder] thunders *TG*

This storm, which no soul can endure,   85
Requires a very different cure;
For such sour verjuice dispositions,
Your crabsticks are the best physicians."

Verses to the Author

[of *The Battle of Minden*]

If HOMER's SPIRIT ev'ry Soul enflames,
While charmed with a LIST* of WARRIORS' NAMES;
How shall the EAR of ANGELS take delight,
In many a GERMAN WARRIOR—BRITISH KNIGHT!—
Such as thine EPIC ELEGANCE recounts;   5
Where EACH, held up, e'en CHIVALRY surmounts.
A FERDINAND!—enchanting to the ear!—
And GRANBY! MUSIC, GODS THEMSELVES might hear!
   Sing, on, BRIGHT BARD, resound their lasting praise;
And as thou giv'st them—wear ETERNAL BAYS.   10

* List of Ships and Commanders.

---

85 soul] one *TG*
VERSES TO THE AUTHOR. Text: Sidney Swinney, *The Battle of Minden, a poem in three books* (1769), p. 127. *Title.* Verses to the Author on his Poem. *Swinney*

POEMS PUBLISHED
POSTHUMOUSLY

[Epigram on John Wilkes]

His eyes are surely of the am'rous kind,
For to *each other* they are *still inclin'd*.

The Wholesale Critic and the Hop-Merchant.

Hail to each ancient sacred shade
Of those, who gave the Muses aid,
Skill'd verse mysterious to unfold,
And set each brilliant thought in gold.
Hail Aristotle's honour'd shrine,   5
And great Longinus hail to thine;
Ye too, whose judgment ne'er cou'd fail,
Hail Horace, and Quintilian hail;
And, dread of every Goth and Hun,
Hail Pope, and peerless Addison.   10
   Alas! by different steps and ways
Our modern critics aim at praise,
And rashly in the learned arts,
They judge by prejudice and parts;
For crampt by a contracted soul,   15
How shou'd they comprehend the whole?
   I know of many a deep-learn'd brother,
Who weighs one science by another,
And makes 'mongst bards poetic schism,
Because he understands the prism;   20
Thinks in acuteness he surpasses,
From knowledge of the optic glasses.

EPIGRAM. First published in *London Chronicle* (17–19 Oct. 1771), p. 378. Text: *UMU* (Oct. 1771), p. 455.
THE WHOLESALE CRITIC. Text: *1791.*

There are some critics in the nation,
Profoundly vers'd in gravitation;
Who like the bulky and the great,   25
And judge by quantity and weight.
Some who're extremely skill'd in building,
Judge by proportion, form, and gilding,
And praise with a sagacious look
The architecture of a book.   30
    Soon as the hops arriv'd from Kent,
Forth to the quay the merchant went,
Went critically to explore
The merit of the hops on shore.
Close to a bag he took his standing,   35
And at a venture thrust his hand in;
Then with the face of a physician,
Their colour scann'd and their condition;
He trusts his touch, his smell, his eyes,
The goods at once approves and buys.   40
    Catchup so dextrous, droll, and dry,
It happen'd Catchup there was by,
Who like * Iago, arch on all,
Is nothing, if not critical.
He with a sneer and with a shrug,   45
With eye of hawk, and face of pug,
Cry'd; "fellow I admire thy fun,
Thou most judiciously hast done,
Who from one handful buyst ten ton.
Does it not enter in thy crown,   50
Some may be mouldy, some be brown;
The vacancies with leaves supplied,
And some half pick'd and some half dry'd?"
The merchant, who Tom Catchup knew,
(A merchant and a scholar too)   55
Said "what I've done is not absurd,
I know my chap and take his word.—
On thee, thou caviller at large,
I here retort thy random charge;

* O, gentle lady, do not put me to't,
  For I am nothing if not critical.

OTHELLO, Act 2, scene 5.

Who, in an hypercritic rage,   60
Judgest ten volumes by a page;
Whose wond'rous comprehensive view
Grasps more than Solomon e'er knew;
With every thing you claim alliance,
Art, trade, profession, calling, science;   65
You mete out all things by one rule,
And are an universal fool.
Tho' swoln with vanity and pride,
You're but one driv'ller multiplied,
A prig—that proves himself by starts,   70
As many dolts—as there are arts."

The Herald and Husband-man.

—Nobilitas sola est atque unica virtus.   JUVENAL.

I with friend Juvenal agree,
Virtue's the true nobility;
Has of herself sufficient charms,
Altho' without a coat of arms.
HONESTUS does not know the rules,   5
Concerning Or and Fez, and Gules,
Yet sets the wond'ring eye to gaze on,
Such deeds no herald e'er could blaze on.
Tawdry atchievements out of place,
Do but augment a fool's disgrace;   10
A coward is a double jest,
Who has a lion for his crest;
And things are come to such a pass,
Two horses may support an ass;
And on a Gamester or Buffoon,   15
A moral motto's a lampoon.
   An honest rustic having done
His master's work 'twixt sun and sun,
Retir'd to dress a little spot,
Adjoining to his homely cot,   20

THE HERALD. Text: *1791.*
6 Gules,] Gules. *1791*

Where pleas'd, in miniature, he found
His landlord's culinary ground,
Some herbs that feed, and some that heal,
The winter's medicine or meal:
The sage, which in his garden seen,   25
No man need ever die* I ween;
The marjoram comely to behold,
With thyme, and ruddiest marygold,
And mint and penny-royal sweet,
To deck the cottage windows meet;   30
And baum, that yields a finer juice
Than all that China can produce;
With carrots red, and turnips white,
And leeks, Cadwallader's delight;
And all the savory crop that vie   35
To please the palate and the eye.
Thus, as intent, he did survey
His plot, a Herald came that way,
A man of great escutcheon'd knowledge,
And member of the motley college.   40
Heedless the peasant pass'd he by,
Indulging this soliloquy;
"Ye gods! what an enormous space,
'Twixt man and man does nature place;
While some by deeds of honour rise,   45
To such a height, as far out-vies
The visible diurnal sphere;
While others, like this rustic here,
Grope in the groveling ground content,
Without or lineage or descent.   50
Hail, Heraldry! mysterious art,
Bright patroness of all desert,
Mankind would on a level lie,
And undistinguish'd live and die,
Depriv'd of thy illustrious aid,   55
Such! so momentous is our trade."

---

* Cur moriatur Homo, cui salvia crescit in horto?

24 meal:] meal. *1791*   54 die,] die; *1791*

"Sir," says the clown, "why sure you joke,"
(And kept on digging as he spoke)
"And prate not to extort conviction,
But merrily by way of fiction.   60
Say, do your manuscripts attest,
What was old father Adam's crest;
Did he a nobler *Coat* receive
In right of marrying Mrs. Eve;
Or had supporters when he kiss'd her,   65
On dexter side, and side sinister;
Or was his motto, prithee speak,
English, French, Latin, Welch, or Greek;
Or was he not, without a lye,
Just such a nobleman as I?   70
Virtue, which great defects can stifle,
May beam distinction on a trifle;
And honour, with her native charms,
May beautify a coat of arms;
Realities sometimes will thrive,   75
E'en by appearance kept alive;
But by themselves, Gules, Or, and Fez,
Are cyphers, neither more or less:
Keep both thy head and hands from crimes,
Be honest in the worst of times: 80
Health's on my countenance impress'd,
And sweet content's my daily guest,
My fame alone I build on this,
And garter King at Arms may kiss."—

Epistle to Mrs. Tyler.

It ever was allow'd, dear Madam,
Ev'n from the days of father Adam,
Of all perfection flesh is heir to,
Fair patience is the gentlest virtue;
This is a truth our grandames teach,   5
Our poets sing, our parsons preach;
Yet after all, dear Moll, the fact is

EPISTLE. Text: *1791*

374

We seldom put it into practice;
I'll warrant (if one knew the truth)
You've call'd me many an idle youth,   10
And styled me rude ungrateful bear,
Enough to make a parson swear.

   I shall not make a long oration
   In order for my vindication,
   For what the plague can I say more   15
   Than lazy dogs have done before;
   Such stuff is naught but mere tautology,
   And so take that for my apology.

First then for custards, my dear Mary,
The produce of your dainty dairy,   20
For stew'd, for bak'd, for boil'd, for roast,
And all the teas and all the toast;
With thankful tongue and bowing attitude,
I here present you with my gratitude:
Next for your apples, pears and plumbs   25
Acknowledgment in order comes;
For wine, for ale, for fowl, for fish—for
Ev'n all one's appetite can wish for:
But O ye pens and, O ye pencils,
And all ye scribbling utensils,   30
Say in what words and in what metre,
Shall unfeign'd admiration greet her,
For that rich banquet so refin'd
Her conversation gave the mind;
The solid meal of sense and worth,   35
Set off by the dessert of mirth;
Wit's fruit and pleasure's genial bowl,
And all the joyous flow of soul;
For these, and every kind ingredient
That form'd your love—your most obedient.   40

36 dessert] desert 1791

Lines with a pocket book.

Of all returns in man's device
'Tis gratitude that makes the price,
And what Sincerity designs
Is richer than Peruvian mines.
Hence estimate the heart's intent,   5
In what the thankful hands present.
This volume soon shall worth derive
From what your industry shall hive
Soon will it in each leaf produce
The tale of innocence and use.   10
O, what pleasure there appears
In a train of well spent years!
Think of this whene'er you look
On this small but useful book.
Here too let your appointments be,   15
And set down many a day for me.
Your Saviour shall himself record
The hours you lend unto the Lord;
Where angels sing and cherubs smile
And Truth's the everlasting style.   20
O may the year we now renew
Be stor'd with happiness for you!
With all the wealth your friends would chuse
And all the praise yourself refuse.
The guise of diffidence profest   25
And meekness bowing to be blest.

[To Mrs. Dacosta]

O fram'd at once to charm the ear and sight,
Thou emblem of all conjugal delight,
See Flora greets thee with her fragrant powers,
A groupe of Virtues claims a wreath of Flowers.

LINES. First published in *MM* (Mar. 1804), p. 126. Text: Letter from Mrs Le Noir to E. H. Barker (*c.*1825), Bodl. MS 1006, fo. 246. Collated: *MM. Title.* Lines for a Lady's Pocket Book *MM*
5 Hence] Thus *MM*   6 thankful] faithful *MM*   9 And then in every line produce *MM*   10 innocence] industry *MM*   11–14, 17–20 *omitted*, *MM*   24 yourself] which you *MM*   25–6 With love, sweet inmate of the breast, / And meekness, while in blessing, blest. *MM*
TO MRS. DACOSTA. Text: *GM* (Aug. 1818), p. 157.

On Gratitude.

To the Memory of Mr Seaton.

O Muse! O Music! Voice and Lyre,
   Which are together Psalm of Praise
From heav'n the kneeling bard inspire
   New thoughts, new grace of utt'rance raise,
That more acceptable with Thee   5
   We thy best service may begin
O thou that bent thine hallow'd knee,
   And bless'd to bleed for Adam's sin.
Then did the Spirit of a Man
   Above all height sublimely tow'r,   10
And then sweet Gratitude began
   To claim Supremacy from Pow'r.
But how shall we those steps ascend,
   By which the Host approach the Throne?—
Love thou thy brother and thy friend,   15
   Whom thou on earth hast seen and known.
For Gratitude may make the * plea
   Of Love by Sisterhood most dear—
How can we reach the first degree
   If we neglect a step so near?   20
So shall we take dear *Seaton*'s part
   When paths of topmost heav'n are trod,
And pay the talent of our heart
   Thrown up ten thousand fold to God.
He knew the art the World dispise   25
   Might to his Merit be applied
Who when for man he left the skies
   By all was hated, scorn'd, denied.
† "The man that gives me thanks and laud
   Does honour to my glorious name"   30
Thus God did David's works applaud,
   And seal'd for everlasting fame.
And this for SEATON shall redound
   To praise, as long as *Camus* runs;

* I John. iv. 20.
† Psalm I. 23.

ON GRATITUDE. Text: MS. Henry W. & Albert Berg Collection, New York Public Library.

Sure Gratitude by him was crown'd,   35
　Who bless'd her Maker and her Sons.
When *Spencer* virtuous *Sidney* prais'd
　When *Prior Dorsett* hail'd to heav'n;
They more by Gratitude were rais'd
　Than all the *Nine* and all the *Sev'n*.   40
Then, O ye emulative tribe
　Of Granta, strains divine persue;
The glory to the Lord ascribe,
　Yet honour *Seaton*'s memory too.
The *Throne* of *Excellence* accost   45
　And be the post of Pray'r maintain'd;
For Paradise had ne'er been lost
　Had heav'nly Gratitude remain'd.

APPENDIX A

I. POEMS FROM *THE MIDWIFE*
(See Mahony and Rizzo, Item 325)

An Occasional Prologue;

occasion'd by the two occasional prologues; to be spoken either by
Mr. Garrick or Mr. Barry, or both, assisted in the delivery thereof by
Mrs. Midnight, being the first time of her appearing on any stage.

Kind-hearted friends—behold these sobs and sighing!
I'd ask your pardon—but—I can't for crying.
'Twas vile in me your honours to offend,
And if you'll make me better—why—I'll mend.
'Twas wholly to my Brother-Bluster owing;   5
He was the man *did do* this sad *misdoing*;
He was the man whose proud indignant spirit,
Hating a rival, strove to hide my merit.
Ah Brother! Brother! think on Johnny Gay,
Think on the moral giv'n us in his play;   10
And let's like Peachum, and his brother Lockit,
Our own affronts—with others money, pocket.
                Enter Mrs. Midnight in haste.

Great is the noise, and clam'rous is the clash,
When two such *weighty wights* together dash!
Wit's mirth oft takes its rise from *folly*'s ire,   15
As *flint* strikes *steel*, and quarrels into *fire*.
I, even I, old woman as I am,
Have just pretence your poetry to damn;
To fix the standard between wrong and right,
And call you both a couple of—Good night.   20

*They bow to Mrs. Midnight, and then retire; after which, the old lady
sings the following simile.*

379

While Garrick smart, and blustring Barry jar,
Like rough and smooth, or oil and vinegar,
I, like an hard-boil'd egg come in between,
And mix their matters, as I intervene;
I form (*for rhyme's sake add, with* JUST INTENTION)   25
Betwixt the fighting fluids a convention;
Which being thus conjoin'd, please ev'ry palate,
And make a pretty figure in a sallad.

N.B. *If the reader has any objection to the above as a* PROLOGUE, *let him signify such his dislike in the Daily Advertiser, and it shall be called an* INTERLUDE.

MW (Oct. 1750), i. 39–40.

This was attributed to Smart in Gray's *Bibliography*, and printed by Callan. It is in the index of the *MW* under Mrs Midnight as "her Prologue for the Benefit of both Mr. Garrick and Mr. Barry". The two occasional prologues referred to are "The New Occasional Prologue, spoken at the Opening of Drury-Lane Theatre by Mr. Garrick" (*MW*, i. 37) and "The Occasional Prologue spoken at Covent Garden Theatre, by Mr. Barry" (*MW*, i. 38). These were missiles in the quarrel between the rival theatres. Barry and Mrs Cibber had seceded from Garrick's company at Drury-Lane in 1750, and set up in competition at Covent Garden under Rich.

9–12 Presumably refers to the conclusion of the quarrel between Peachum and Lockit in *The Beggar's Opera* II. x. *Peachum*: "Brother, brother, we are both in the wrong. We shall be both losers in the dispute, for you know we have it in our power to hang each other. . . . 'Tis our mutual interest, 'tis for the interest of the world we should agree." John Gay, *The Beggar's Opera*, ed. E. V. Roberts, 1969, p. 50.

Greek translation of Virgil's famous Epigram on Augustus.

Νυκτος ὑει πασης, ανεασι θεαματα ωρωι
    Αρκην μειρομενην ουν Δι Καισαρ εχει.

MW (Nov. 1750), i. 66.

This translation, "by Mrs. Midnight", follows "Some Reflections on the Neglect of the Greek Language" (attributed to Smart in Gray's *Bibliography*). The Latin original, *Nocte pluit tota redeunt spectacula mane | Division imperium cum Jove Cæsar habet*, ascribed to Virgil by Donatus

(*Vitae Vergilianae*, ed. J. Brummer, Leipzig, 1912, p. 31), was published in *GM* (May 1748), p. 228, with an English translation: "Rain all the night, with sports returns the day; / Great *Caesar* thus with *Jove* divides the sway."

An Epigram on the British Lion.

Our lion once did roar, and look so grim,
That his own shadow durst not follow him;
But now, he's so dejected and dismay'd,
He cannot face the shadow of his shade.

UV (Aug. 1756), p. 384. Also printed in *MW* (Nov. 1750), i. 90; *LTM* (July–Aug. 1756), i. 209; *CP6* [1757], p. 136.

Attributed to Smart by A. Sherbo, "Survival in Grub-street: Another Essay in Attribution", *BNYPL* 64 (1960), 153. It was published anonymously, but in *MW* it comes at the end of a dialogue between Mrs Midnight and "her Boy". It is an adaptation of a couplet from Pope's *Peri Bathous*:

He roar'd so loud, and look'd so wondrous grim,
His very Shadow durst not follow him.

(*Miscellanies, The Last Volume*, 1727, p. 51).

To the little Elevators in Poetry who love to Surprise.

As when in blustring, thund'ring, wintry days,
The bully Boreas on his bagpipe plays;
When old Aquarius ducks this earthly ball,
And empties on our heads his urinal;
When rumbling clouds on grumbling clouds *do* dash,   5
And 'midst the flashing lightnings lightnings flash;
Hogs, dogs, and men, perceive the troubled sky,
Hogs, dogs, and men, away for shelter fly;
While all around, the black, dark, gloomy scene
Looks grey, looks white, looks red, looks blue, looks green;   10
So green, so blue, so red, so grey, so white,
Look'd Don Grimalchio, when he saw the spright.

MW (May 1751), ii. 80–1.

Attributed to Smart in Gray's *Bibliography*. It comes in a letter from "M. Midnight" with the note, "The following sublime description of a storm was wrote, in manner of a certain *Great* Author, from which I hope you will receive a *great* deal of pleasure and benefit, as it is in all respects *greatly* worthy your imitation." The title is an allusion to *The Rehearsal* I. i, in which Bayes speaks of would-be wits as "fellows that scorn to imitate Nature: but are given altogether to elevate and surprise" (this passage is quoted in Smart's introductory letter to the *Hilliad*). In II. iii, Bayes gives it as a general rule that "you must ever make a *simile*, when you are surpris'd, 'tis the new way of writing."

Crambo Song, on Miss Scott,

A beautiful lady whom the author saw at Ruckholt-House, Essex, attended by a very ugly sea captain.

Come one of ye lasses,
Who dwell in Parnassus,
　To London on Pegasus trot;
And bring me some verse
That I may rehearse　　　　　　　　　　5
　The praises of pretty Miss *Scott*.

When I saw the fair maid
First in Ruckholt's gay shade,
　I wish'd—but I dare not say what;
If I had her alone,　　　　　　　　　　10
With a sigh and a groan
　I'd whisper it all to Miss *Scott*.

Full close by her side,
By way of a guide,
　A damn'd ugly fellow she'd got,　　　　15
The dog did appear,
Like the dev'l at Eve's ear,
　He's so foul, and so fair is Miss *Scott*.

He'd a traitorous face,
And a Jesuit's grace,   20
   Yet you'd swear he'd no hand in the plot;
He was fitter to go
With a drum at a show,
   Than to follow the charming Miss *Scott*.

Oh had I a part   25
In the heav'n of her heart,
   Contented I'd dwell in a cot;
What are titles but toys,
What is fame but a noise,
   When compar'd with the charms of Miss *Scott*.   30

The pain of dull pleasure,
The poorness of treasure,
   Are the rake's and the miser's sad lot;
But riches immense
And pleasure intense   35
   Can come from no fund but Miss *Scott*.

Whoe'er in this dearth
Of enjoyments on earth
   Thinks of bliss, is a fool and a sot:
But we that are wise   40
Know that happiness lies
   In heav'n, or pretty Miss *Scott*.

The scholar in books,
The glutton in cooks,
   The drunkard delights in his pot;   45
But what is dull thinking,
Or eating, or drinking,
   To the feasting on pretty Miss *Scott*?

Some greatly desire
Wisdom to acquire,   50
   Some after religion are hot;
But wisdom's a fool,
And zeal it is cool,
   If compar'd with my flame for Miss *Scott*.

Oh! she's all that is rare, 55
Engaging and fair,
  A good husband alone she has not.
And that, if I might,
I'd give her to-night,
  T'accomplish the charming Miss *Scott*. 60

MW (June 1751), ii. 108.

This was published anonymously but has been attributed to Smart by Brittain (Mahony and Rizzo, Item 65) and Sherbo (Mahony and Rizzo, Item 82) on internal evidence, supported by circumstantial evidence from Betty Rizzo, "Christopher Smart, Polemical Author of 'Crambo Song on Miss Scott'", *PBSA* 75 (1981), 65–75.

Epigram.
On a certain Scribbler.

Word-valiant wight, thou great he-shrew,
  That wrangles to no end;
Since nonsense is nor false nor true
  Thou'rt no man's foe or friend.

MW (June 1751), ii. 118. Also printed in the notes to the *Hilliad*.

Published anonymously, this was attributed to Smart by Brittain (Mahony and Rizzo, Item 65), because of its appearance in the *Hilliad*.

To Mæcenas.
[Horace, Book I, Ode i]

Thy noble birth, Mæcenas springs
From an illustrious race of kings,
  That in Etruria reign'd;
Thy kind protection is my boast,
My all without thee, had been lost, 5
  My patron and my friend.

Some in Olympick games delight,
Where clouds of dust obscure the sight,
 And darken all the skies;
Striving who first shall reach the goal,   10
Their kindling wheels around to roll,
 And gain the glorious prize.

The palm obtain'd, so great the odds,
It ranks the victors with the Gods,
 That rule the world below: 15
Others by low intrigues elate,
To shine a Minister of State,
 All less pursuits forego.

Some lur'd with hopes of ample gain,
Their garners fill with Lybian grain,   20
 Awaiting times of dearth:
Some wedded to paternal fields,
Admire the store that labour yields,
 Employ'd to till the earth.

Offer to these Peruvian mines,   25
Or all the glitt'ring wealth that shines,
 On India's distant shore;
They would not tempt the stormy main,
Where winds unequal war maintain,
 And waves incessant roar.   30

The merchant views, with fear aghast,
The fury of the Northern blast,
 When lofty billows foam;
Praises the country's calm retreats,
Yet soon his shatter'd bark refits,   35
 In trackless paths to roam.

Some cheer the hours with racy wine,
The product of the Massick vine,
 Reclin'd beneath a shade;
Or near a mossy sacred source,   40
Where streams begin their silent course,
 Their listless limbs are laid.

Others are pleas'd when monarchs jarr,
Admiring all the pomp of war,
   And ev'ry warlike air;   45
When trumpets fainting hearts inspire,
And clarions kindle martial fire,
   Detested by the fair.

The sportsman bent to chace the hind,
To all delights besides is blind,   50
   His spouse entreats in vain;
Despising wint'ry skies he bounds,
Attended by sagacious hounds,
   O'er hill, and dale, and plain.

Politer arts, Mæcenas, share,   55
Thy calmer hours and banish care,
   Th' employment of the wise;
An ivy wreath thy temples binds,
An honour due t'exalted minds,
   The kindred of the skies.   60

I love to sing the cooling grove,
Where nymphs and fawns in measures move;
   And if the Muses aid:
Euterpe shall the flute inspire,
And Polyhymnia touch the lyre,   65
   Deep in a sacred shade.

Thus rais'd above the vulgar throng,
To noble themes I'll suit my song,
   And if you rank my name;
Among the tuneful lyrick train,   70
My works shall envious Time disdain;
   Secure of deathless fame.

MW (July 1751), ii. 165–7.

This is presented by Mrs Midnight as by "my Niece Nelly". It is attributed to Smart in Gray's *Bibliography* and printed by Callan.

58 *thy temples*: "Nelly" argues that line 29 of the original, *Me doctarum hederæ præmia frontium* should read *Te doctarum*, etc., on the grounds

that Horace would not have been so vain as to claim the wreath for himself. In his prose translation of Horace, Smart notes the suggested emendation (attributed to Hare) but does not incorporate it.

On Jollity: An Ode, or Song, or both.

There was a jovial butcher,
He liv'd at Northern-fall-gate,
   He kept a stall
   At Leadenhall,
And got drunk at the Boy at Aldgate.

He ran down Houndsditch reeling,
At Bedlam he was frighted,
   He in Moorfields
   Be sh–t his heels
And at Hoxton he was wiped.

MW (July 1751), ii. 175–6.

Quoted in a letter from Mary Midnight "To the Criticks and Poets", attributed to Smart in Gray's *Bibliography*. It is said, but with mock seriousness, to be by "one of our poets of the last century" (p. 175), born at Hoxton (p. 180). The letter-writer argues that odes and songs are essentially different ("there is as much difference between an ode and a song, as between a high-heel'd and a low-heel'd shoe, or . . . between a *Whig* and a *Tory*"), but that the qualities proper to each are sometimes mixed to produce "a true and poetical hermaphrodite", of which *On Jollity* is "a most animated and extraordinary instance".

The Little Lighterman, or the dissembling Waterman,

(which was sung at the corner of Blow Bladder street on the 10th of June last, to the tune of the Rolling Hornpipe) Chirurgically dissected.

Pray did you never hear of a sad disaster—
'Twas but t'other day that he ran away from his master.
   Oh the little little lighterman, and the dissembling waterman;
   Molly's a girl that will dye, if she has not a kiss from the lighterman.

With his black shammy pumps and his rolling eye, Sir,
He did kiss ev'ry girl that he did come nigh, Sir.
   Oh the little, little, &c.

But when his master he found him he put him into Bridewell;
Molly she loved him so well that she gave him a pot of porter.
   Oh the little, &c.

MW (Aug. 1751), ii. 197–8.

This so-called "ballad" is described as "the reputed bantling of a gentleman of great eminence and distinction" in the facetious critical essay that follows (pp. 198–204), signed "M. Midnight". It is interpreted as Jacobite propaganda in allegorical disguise. The whole piece (text and explication) is attributed to Smart in Gray's *Bibliography*.

On the Merit of Brevity.

If you think that my works are too puft up with levity,
Yet at least approbation is due to my brevity,
The praises of which shou'd be now more egregious,
As our bards at this time are confoundedly tedious.

MW (Aug. 1751), ii. 234–5.

Published under the pseudonym "Mrs. Midnight", this is attributed to Smart in Gray's *Bibliography* and printed by Callan. It is a translation of the last three lines of Phaedrus' *Scurra et Rusticus* (Bk. V, fable 5) in old editions (in modern editions they form the conclusion of an epilogue to Bk. IV). Smart's translation of this fable under the title of *The Pig* was published in *MW* in Aug. 1752.

The Prologue to Mrs. Mary Midnight's Oratory.

To brand the murderer of common sense,
With all his accessary audience;
To give up infamy to ridicule,
And in impartial colours paint the fool;
To wean from wickedness, and bring to grace,   5
Th' undaunted owner of the copper-face;

To form more innocent, and make less dull,
The master of th' unmalleable skull;
To drag the grub-worm from it's inmost hole,
And bleach the blackness of a negroe soul;   10
This is our task—And if we shou'd succeed,
'Twill be a true Herculean feat indeed.
   But lest the manly miss, or female beau,
Shou'd think our satire nonsense, stuff and low;
Shou'd 'gainst poor salt-box arm their critic rage,   15
And hiss the harmless jew-strump off the stage,
We between whiles ('tis hop'd without offence)
Shall introduce that honest exile SENSE.
Whom, tho' he's English, beaus must needs prefer,
He'll seem to them—so like a foreigner.   20
   Well, says Don Pope,—*Whatever is, is right*:
So sav'd, or damn'd, all will be well to night.
Let others whom self-center'd interest sways,
Force the reluctant town and ravish praise,
While we more willing wou'd be led than lead;   25
More proud to please than joyous to succeed;
But if we shou'd offend in deed or word,
Let candid Justice draw th' impartial sword;
With wit retaliate, with sense revive,
That is, at once be MERRY and be WISE.   30

MW (Jan. 1752), iii. 57 (no signature).

The Oratory opened on 3 Dec. 1751. "An occasional Prologue, to be spoken by a gentleman" was advertised in the programme from 26 Dec. 1751.

The Song which was deliver'd by Old Time to Mrs. Midnight.

To be sung to the tune of the *Roast Beef of Old England.*

If virtue's in vogue, and if honesty thrives,
Then all our true Britons will get themselves wives;
So they'll die glorious deaths, as they liv'd sober lives.
   Oh the dear dames of Old England! and oh the Old English dear dames!

Our damsels created love's soft war to wage,　　　　5
With charms and accomplishments challenge the age;
And he's a rank coward that dares not engage.
　　Oh the dear dames, &c. &c.

A batchelor lives in fair Nature's despight,
He cumbers the earth without use or delight,　　　　10
And cheats Dame Posterity out of her right.
　　Oh the dear dames, &c. &c.

But those who are married, wise Nature obey,
And comfort each other by night and by day,
While round them their little ones prattle and play.　　15
　　Oh the dear dames, &c. &c.

Then come lads and lasses of ev'ry degree,
Observe and attend to Dame MIDNIGHT's decree;
All wed and make work for the parson and me.
　　Oh the dear dames, &c. &c.

MW (Jan. 1752), iii. 60 (no signature); frequently reprinted.

Attributed to Smart by Sherbo (see Mahony and Rizzo, Item 87, p. 38). It was performed at the first Oratory on 3 Dec. 1751.

Epilogue.

Spoken by Master * Hallet, in the character of Cupid.

From fair Venus, on the wing,
A joyous embassy I bring,
Her Majesty this mandate sends,
"That Virtue now and Love be friends;
That beaux and belles shou'd cease to roam,　　　5
And every heart shou'd find an home;
That their joint labours they bestow,
To make more business for my bow;

* A child not nine years old, who plays admirably upon the violencello, and in every other respect has a capacity greatly beyond his years. N.B. He is shortly to have a Benefit, at which, 'tis hoped, all Mrs. Midnight's friends will do him the honour of their presence.

That men may'nt fail by lewd transgression,
But grow immortal by succession."   10
Now while, to the etherial sky,
By Mammy's order, swift I fly,
Let MARY MIDNIGHT o'er the nation
Reign Queen of Love by deputation.

MW (Jan. 1752), iii. 61 (no signature).

The epilogue was advertised in the programme for the Oratory from
26 Dec. 1751.

Epithalamium on a late Happy Marriage.

When Hymen once the mutual bands has wove,
Exchanging heart for heart, and love for love,
The happy pair, with mutual bliss elate,
Own to be single's an imperfect state.
But when two hearts united thus agree   5
With equal sense, and equal constancy,
This, HAPPINESS, is thy extreamest goal,
'Tis marriage both of body, and of soul,
'Tis making heav'n below with matchless love,
And's a fair step to reach the heav'n above.   10

MW (Jan. 1752), iii. 64; frequently reprinted.

Published in *MW* under the pseudonym "Mrs. Midnight", this was
attributed to Smart in Gray's *Bibliography* and printed by Callan. If it
is Smart's, it may have been written for the marriage of Harriote
Pratt's brother Edward to the daughter of Sir Jacob Astley (who
subscribed to Smart's *Poems on Several Occasions*, 1752), which took
place on 30 Dec. 1751.

[Translation of A beautiful Passage in the *Anti-Lucretius* of the Cardinal De Polignac]

The witless hen, disturb'd by causeless fright,
With droll amusement oft diverts the sight,
For if the nurse, ev'n to herself unknown,
Mistakes the duck's production for her own,

Soon as the eggshell's broke and just alive,   5
Forth to the pond the little dablers drive,
And by their first efforts they plainly prove,
That swimming is the very thing they love;
Then mindful of their birthright high and low,
Thro' all their manor of the marsh they go.   10
Swift to their aid th' imagined parent flies,
With beak, and wing, and foot, and voice, and eyes, ⎫
Gives every hint, and each remonstrance tries.   ⎬
But when she sees her quaking brats proceed,   ⎭
High time she thinks to rave and scold indeed.   15
About she works 'midst rushes, reeds and sedge,
And blunders round, and round, and round the edge,
Flutters each feather while her eye-balls roll,
For all th' old woman centers in her soul:
For why? the sober matron errs thro' zeal,   20
Nor sees the safe impunity they feel;
Takes nature's instinct merely for a whim,
And thinks it very odd a duck shou'd swim.

MW (Aug. 1752), iii. 94–5. Also published in *A Collection of Pretty Poems for the amusement of children three foot high* [1756], pp. 91–2 (*CP3*), as "The Old Nurse Mistaken". 4 production] productions *CP3*   14 quaking] quacking *CP3*   23 odd] strange *CP3*

Published in *MW* under the pseudonym "Mary Midnight", this was attributed to Smart in Gray's *Bibliography* and printed by Callan. The Latin original (from Lib. vi. 821–32) in printed in *MW*. *Anti-Lucretius* was first published in Paris in 1747 (London, 1748). A specimen translation of Lib. I appeared in *GM* in 1748 (pp. 218–19). The purpose of the work was to counter modern atheism and scepticism, of which Epicureanism was seen as the progenitor; as such it would certainly have appealed to Smart (see *Materies gaudet vi inertiæ*, 19–20). The work is referred to in the notes to the *Hilliad*, 146. Voltaire described Cardinal de Polignac as one "who has taught *Philosophy* herself to speak the beautiful Language of *Poetry*, uniting the Harmony of *Virgil* with the reasoning of *Plato*; Heaven's Great Avenger, and Vanquisher of *Lucretius*", (*The Temple of Taste*, 1734, p. 2).

11–12 Cf. Pope's parody of Milton's simile (*PL* ii. 947–50): "As when a dab-chick waddles thro' the copse, / On feet and wings, and flies, and wades, and hops" (*Dunciad* (A), ii. 59–60).

The Epigrammatist advises a certain Gentleman to wear
a black Wig.

Since doubtless 'tis true, as by Scripture we're told,
   That Hell is the hypocrite's share,
Put on a *black wig* for the sake of thy soul,
   And look like a rogue, as you are.

MW (Aug. 1752), iii. 95.

Attributed to Smart by Betty Rizzo (Mahony and Rizzo, Item 93),
who takes it as a reference to the caning and dewigging of John Hill
in May 1752, an episode to which Smart alludes in the *Hilliad*.

[* Mons. Timbertoe]

Behold great Timbertoe—illustrious name,
Exalts the dance, and capers into fame!
Tho' his left leg a victim fell to fate,
His right officiates for its absent mate;
And with a wooden supplement engages   5
All tastes, all ranks, all sexes, and all ages.
Each fair is dubious, which should win her heart,
The limb of Nature, or the stump of Art;
And smiles to see this active artist do
More with one foot than others can with two.   10

* The celebrated one-leg'd dancer, who perform'd with universal ap-
plause at Mrs. Midnight's Oratory.

MW (Aug. 1752), iii. 108. Also published in the *General Advertiser* (22
May 1752) and *London Daily Advertiser* (23 May 1752), under the
pseudonym "Lewis Lun".

This was published anonymously in *MW*, but attributed to Smart by
Botting (see Mahony and Rizzo, Item 62, p. 27) on the strength of the
signature in the newspapers, and printed by Callan. Smart used the
pseudonym "Mr. Lun" for several poems in *ST*.

On Gentleness.

Come, *placid* Muse, come *Gentleness's child*,
So *soft*, so *smooth*, so *simple*, and so *mild*;
Oh! let me seek the *quiet* evening's *cool*,
Where no rough wind disturbs the *peaceful pool*.
There, where Melpomene her skill employs   5
With see-saw sing-song, and with jingling joys;
In soft insensibility embalm'd,
And by serene security be calm'd.
So pretty-pert! and finiking so fine!
To tickle, sooth, and lull the niggling Nine,   10
With suckling baby-rhimes the mind to please,
And give to *easiness* the means of EASE.

MW (June 1753), iii. 119. Also published as 'An Epigram in the Sing-Song Taste' in *LTM* (Sept.–Oct. 1756), i. 317. 2 *simple*] ample *LTM*   8 be calm'd] becalm'd *LTM*   12 *easiness*] emptiness *LTM* Attributed to Smart by Rizzo (see Mahony and Rizzo, Item 93, p. 40). In *MW* it comes in a letter from "Ralph Ragandjaw" to "Mrs. Midnight", and is said to have been recited by "Mr. Walter Wishy-Washy, the CORRECT poet". Rizzo suggests that it may have been written in retaliation to Hill who had derided the "infantine style" of Smart's *Epithalamium* in his review of Smart's poems (see Prolegomena to the *Hilliad*), but notes that it could be by Murphy, who writes of "gentle dulness" as a leading attribute of Hill in his introductory letter to the *Hilliad*, and refers to Hill's "pretty turns" in a note to line 8 of the poem.

II. POEMS FROM THE *LILLIPUTIAN MAGAZINE*

(See Mahony and Rizzo, Item 368)

The Happy Nightingale.

A Song.

By Polly Newbery.

The Nightingale, in dead of night,
On some green hawthorn, hid from sight,
    Her wond'rous art displays;
While all the feather'd choir's at rest,
Nor fowler's snares her joys molest,   5
    She sings melodious lays.

The groves her warbling notes repeat,
The silence makes her music sweet,
   And heightens every note.
Benighted travellers admire   10
To hear her thus exert her fire,
   And swell her little throat.

No fear of phantoms, frightful noise,
Nor hideous form her bliss destroys;
   Darkness no terror brings;   15
But each returning shade of night
Affords the songster new delight;
   Unaw'd she sits and sings.

So children who are good and wise,
Hobgoblin stories will despise,   20
   And all such idle tales;
Virtue can fortitude instil,
And ward off all impending ill,
   Which over vice prevails.

Lilliputian Mag. (Mar. 1751), pp. 44–5.

Attributed tentatively to Smart by Iona and Peter Opie, *The Oxford Book of Children's Verse* (Oxford, 1973), p. 390, and by Rizzo (Mahony and Rizzo, Item 93, p. 40). Polly Newbery, daughter of John Newbery, publisher of the *Lilliputian*, was nine at this date.

Riddle. By Master Hunter.

Like W———TON, in different dress,
   I either sex can ape,
And like her, all mankind confess,
   Have comeliness and shape:
Had she the innocence of me,
   And I her air and parts,
She would a perfect goddess be,
   And I should gain more hearts.

Lilliputian Mag. (Mar. 1751), p. 47, as no. iv of "New Riddles".

Attributed to Smart by Rizzo (see Mahony and Rizzo, Item 93, p.

40). Christopher Hunter (Smart's nephew), listed as a subscriber to the *Lilliputian*, was born in 1746.

1 W———TON: the actress, Peg Woffington, noted for her male impersonations.

An Epigram on a drowsy dull boy, who was often whipped for not learning his lesson.

By Miss Peggy Smart.

> HOMER, 'tis said, wou'd sometimes nod,
> *Humphry* no certain *Vigil* keeps;
> But like his top defies the rod;
> The more he's whipp'd the more he sleeps.

Lilliputian Mag. (Mar. 1751), p. 49, under "New Epigrams".
Attributed to Smart by Rizzo (see Mahony and Rizzo, Item 93, p. 40). Peggy (Margaret) was Smart's sister.
3–4 Cf. Pope, *Ess. on Criticism*, 600–1.

A Pastoral Hymn.

By a Gentleman.

> How chearful along the gay mead,
>   The daisies and cowslips appear,
> The flocks as they carelessly feed,
>   Rejoice in the spring of the year.
> The myrtles, that shade the gay bow'rs,   5
>   The herbage that springs from the sod,
> Trees, plants, cooling fruits, and sweet flow'rs,
>   All rise to the praise of my God.
>
> Shall man the great master of all,
>   The only insensible prove?   10
> Forbid it fair gratitude's call,
>   Forbid it devotion and love.

The Lord who such wonders could raise,
  And still can destroy with a nod,
My lips shall incessantly praise,   15
  My soul shall be wrapt in my God.

Lilliputian Mag. (Mar. 1751), p. 50. Reprinted in *LTM* (May–June 1756), i. 102, as "by Mr. Arne".

Attributed to Smart rather than Arne by Betty Rizzo on stylistic grounds: see "Arne's 'Hymn of Eve': by Christopher Smart?", *N&Q* (Aug. 1975), pp. 359–60. As "The Hymn of Eve" this first appeared in Arne's oratorio *The Death of Abel*, performed in Dublin in Feb. 1744, but was not printed under that title until the libretto was published in 1755. Rizzo notes the similarity of ll. 11–12 to *Ode to Lord Barnard*, 11–14.

III. POEMS FROM THE *LONDON MAGAZINE* 1746–7

The group of poems signed "C.S." which appeared in *LM* at intervals from June 1746 to April 1747 was first noted by Charles Ryskamp, "Problems in the Text of Smart", *The Library*, 5th ser. 14 (1959), 293–8. The evidence for attributing them to Smart, which remains inconclusive, is reviewed in detail by Betty Rizzo, "Christopher Smart, the 'C.S.' Poems, and Molly Leapor's Epitaph", *The Library*, 6th ser. 5 (1983), 22–31.

On a young Lady from whom I took a Ring.

  Ah! Chloe, why didst thou bewail
    The ring, alas, I took!
  At guilty me why do you rail?
    Why kill me with your look?

  Your eyes, revengeful of the theft,
    Quick shot the fatal dart:
  Chloe, I gave you back your ring;
    Pray give me back my heart.

(June 1746, p. 312)

To Miss H—hm—e of Lincoln's-Inn-Fields, on her going into the Country.

Tir'd of old conquests, and the noisy town,
Belinda, to the country hastens down:
When Kentish swains, with happy joy, shall know
The charms that wit and beauty can bestow:
Single, ah single! thousands will they gain,
But when united, oh, how great's the pain:
That pain, dear miss, I feel tho' cannot tell,
The Kentish smarts, no doubt, will know it well.

(Aug. 1746, pp. 420–1)

Identified by Rizzo as Susan Highmore, daughter of Joseph Highmore the portrait painter, who can be tenuously linked with Smart through their mutual friend, the novelist Samuel Richardson.

Ryskamp pointed out the possible punning reference to Smart in the last line.

On Delia.

When first bright Venus saw Adonis' charms,
She long'd to revel in his youthful arms;
But all her beauty could not move the swain,
And her black eyes with tears were stain'd in vain;
What shall I do! the Cyprian goddess cry'd;   5
What shall I do! th' Idalian groves reply'd;
Sudden as thought, fair Delia's form she took,
Then on the youth she cast a smiling look;
Now, silly swain, despise me if you can,
But that I'm sure's impossible to man.   10
Adonis said, now, by the gods, I love,
For Delia charms, when Venus fails to move.

(Sept. 1746, p. 475)

To the unknown Author of *War, an Epic Satire.*

When Pope, sweet bard! forsook the seats of men,
And join'd, in happy vales, th' Elysian train,

With kindred shades, thro' flow'ry paths to rove,
And animate with song the *vocal grove*;
"Our *Sun* (we cry'd) withdraws his wonted ray,   5
And robs this golded *atmosphere* of day;
No more these eyes shall view Pierian light;
Whelm'd in the gloom of *dulness* and of *night!*"
How vain our fears! for, lo! with equal flame,
Attends our *Sun*; another and the same!   10
His rival beams enlighten, as they roll,
Warm the dull clay and vivify the soul!
The source of Europe's dire disasters show,
And bid, as Britons ought, his Britons glow.
Blest sons of Phœbus, and the tuneful *nine*!   15
In whom the various charms of song combine;
Thee Spencer's fancy, Cowley's wit, inspire,
And Pope's sharp satire, join'd with Milton's fire:
While Shakespear's grace, and Dryden's happy vein,
Gild thy smooth numbers, and adorn thy strain.   20
Thy vast invention, which no limits bound,
Tow'rs o'er the skies, or shoots the deep profound:
Yet sober reason still its flights controuls,
In night's dark regions, or the starry poles.
How just thy portrait of the gloomy vale,   25
Where rage, where woes, despair and anguish dwell!
There *vice* is *virtue*, there fell *hate* is *love*,
Th' exact reverse of happier states above!
Not others so:- for, but remove the pain,
Their *hell*'s another *earth*, their *fiends are men*.   30
Proceed, sweet *Muse*'s son! and born to charm!
Sing how *Rebellion* sunk by WILLIAM's arm!
Not less from hell that horrid pest arose,
Dark as her native shades, and big with woes!
Too far, in quest of subject, hast thou gone;   35
Thy Albion boasts a *heroe* of her own;
A youth, in all the prowess of the plain,
And martial skill, not second to Lorrain!

(Apr. 1747, p. 189)

The author was in fact Stephen Barrett (1718–1801). His satire was published in Mar. 1747.

IV. POEMS FROM *MRS. MIDNIGHT'S ORATIONS*

Mrs. Midnight's Orations; and other select pieces; as they were spoken at the Oratory in the Hay-Market, London. Printed for the Editor, 1763.

This work, probably compiled and published for Smart's benefit (with or without his connivance) by John Newbery and Richard Rolt, includes several compositions known to be Smart's and it is likely that others in the collection, but not all, were also written by him: see Mahony and Rizzo, Item 679. The case for Smart's editorship is made by Arthur Sherbo in "Survival in Grub-Street: Another Essay in Attribution", *BNYPL* 64 (1960), 147–58. In *Christopher Smart: Scholar of the University* (East Lansing, 1967) Sherbo treats the entire work as Smart's (see pp. 167, 271–2). In the absence of reliable criteria for distinguishing Smart's contributions from the rest, the unidentified poems (listed below) have not been included in the present collection.

Prologue ("When Mary Midnight first her Rostrum rear'd"), pp. 13–15.

Epilogue to *Britannia's Triumph: A Masque* ("Our Author says, his Allegoric Meaning"), pp. 26–8.

Prologue on Mrs. Midnight's Oratory ("In ev'ry Sphere, in ev'ry Age we find"), pp. 28–30.

Occasional Prologues. Mrs. Midnight enters with a Whistle, or Cat-Call ("'Tis strange this little, trifling Bauble here"), pp. 34–6.

Prologue [to *Britannia's Triumph*] ("Now, Songs of Triumph gladden ev'ry Ear"), pp. 36–7.

Prologue ("As the Œconomist, when Shoes grow bare"), pp. 38–40.

"Deep in a Shade one sultry Day" [poem from an Oration], pp. 52–3.

A Prologue Spoken by Mrs. Midnight ("Well, Ladies, What d'ye think of me To-night?"), pp. 58–9.

The Gristle, pp. 60–1. Also published in *CP6*, 1756, as "The Difference between Youth and Age demonstrated" (see Mahony and Rizzo, Item 579): attributed to Smart by Sherbo, art. cit.

The Gifts: A Dramatic Interlude, pp. 67–75 (probably by Rolt, see Mahony and Rizzo, Item 679).

V. POEMS FROM OTHER SOURCES

Epigram extempore on a Cold Poet.

Frigidio's muse, from ardour free,
    Whene'er he tunes his lyre,
Gives him a leaden policy
    T' insure his works from fire.

"By Ebenezer Pentweazle, of Truro in the County of Cornwall, Esq.", *ST* (Sept. 1750), i. 357.

This was attributed to Smart in Gray's *Bibliography* and printed by Callan. But it is the one poem with this signature *not* included by Hunter, and the target appears to be Smart's friend, Richard Rolt, who is called "Frigidio" in William Kenrick's *Old Woman's Dunciad* (1751), and "dull Rolt" in the same author's *Pasquinade* (1753). In *The Magazines Blown Up* (1750) Kenrick notes that there are two Ebenezer Pentweazles, one from Oxford, the other from Cambridge (see Mahony and Rizzo, p. 144).

To Miss Harriot's Favourite Squirrel.

Ah! little dancer, us'd to stray,
O'er Harriot's charms in active play
    And wanton with the fair;
Now press her bosom, now her hand;
How little dost thou understand,   5
    The joys that revel there?

Pity, that breast more white than snow,
Where Nature's choicest beauties glow,
    Should by such feet be press'd:
Ha! must thou share her kisses too,   10
Sweeter than aromatick dew,
    From Araby the bless'd.

Unwounded by her sparkling eyes,
Thou, senseless creature, can'st not prize
    The gifts she throws away;   15
But Strephon could, with better grace,
Supply that happy, envied place,
    And love with love repay.

Then, trifler, yield to Strephon's arms,
That inexhausted store of charms,   20
   Thou has not sense to taste:
He'll not impoverish, but improve;
And life shall be with Harriot's love
   A never cloying feast.

Kapélion (Nov. 1750), 151–2. Also printed in *LTM* (May 1758), iii. 230.

Published anonymously, this was attributed to Smart by Arthur Sherbo, "Two Pieces newly ascribed to Christopher Smart", *MLR* 62 (1967), 219–20, on the strength of its similarities in metre and style to Smart's known love poems, the name Harriot, and the fact that Smart's friend Arthur Murphy was editor of the *LTM*. But arguments from internal evidence would equally support the hypothesis that the poem was a parody, especially since William Kenrick, editor of *Kapélion*, was engaged in a paper quarrel with Smart in 1750–1: see Williamson (1973), 120.

The Fruitless Endeavour.

When gentle Harriot first I saw,
Struck with a reverential awe,
   I felt my bosom mov'd;
Her easy shape, her charming face,
She smil'd, and talk'd with so much grace,   5
   I gaz'd, admir'd and lov'd.

Up to the busy town I flew,
And wander'd all its pleasure thro'
   In hopes to ease my care;
The busy town but mocks my pain,   10
Its gayest pleasures all are vain;
   For Harriot haunts me there.

The labours of the learned sage,
The comic humour of the stage,
   By turns my time employ;   15
I relish not the sage's lore,
The stage's humour please no more
   For Harriot's all my joy.

Sometimes I try the jovial throng,
Sometimes the female train among,   20
   To chase her form away;
The jovial throng is noisy, rude,
Nor other female dares intrude,
   Where Harriot bears a sway.

Since then nor art nor learning can,   25
Nor company of maid or man,
   For want of thee atone;
O come, with all thy conquering charms,
O come! and take me to thy arms,
   For thou art all in one.

Thomas Arne's *Monthly Melody* (1760), Sect. 2, p. 29. Previously published without first stanza in *GM* (Dec. 1757), p. 563, under the title "Love Triumphant. To Harriot". 8 pleasure] pleasures *GM*   17 please] glads *GM*   18 When Harriot's form is by. *GM*   21 her form] my woes *GM*   25 art] wit *GM*

Though published anonymously, this has been attributed to Smart because of the correspondences to Smart's own situation at the time he was pursuing Harriot Pratt, and similarities to his other songs: see Williamson (1974), pp. 415–17. If it were Smart's, it would have to belong to the period 1745–51, perhaps modelled on a song published in *ST* (July 1750, i. 268), signed M.S. but later printed in Andrew Hervey Mills's *Bagatelles* (1767). Beginning "Sick of the town at once I flew / To Contemplation's rural seat", it too relates the torments of a lover vacillating between social life and a learned retreat.

Epitaph on Molly Leapor.

Rest, gentle shade: Thy virtue, wit and worth,
Survive the tomb, and dignify thy birth.
Living, thy virtue eas'd a parent's care;
Dying, thy works suspend his dropping tear.
Wit, pure as flow'd from infant Nature's tongue;
Just—not severe; tho' inoffensive—strong.
Such worth as points to man, what heav'n design'd,
True human greatness, dignity of mind.

APPENDIX A

Poems Upon Several Occasions. By the late Mrs. Leapor, of Brackley in Northamptonshire. The Second and Last Volume, 1751, p. xxxii (no signature).

Noted by Betty Rizzo as a possible attribution in "Christopher Smart, the 'C.S.' Poems, and Molly Leapor's Epitaph", *The Library*, 6th ser. 5 (1983), 22–31. She quotes an unpublished letter from Samuel Richardson (printer of the second volume of Mary Leapor's poems), dated 10 Dec. 1750, saying that he had introduced Smart to Mary Leapor's work and had asked him to write an epitaph on her, but had not yet received it. Smart published an excerpt from the first volume of the *Poems Upon Several Occasions* in *MW* (Nov. 1750), i. 81–4.

APPENDIX B

POEMS ON SMART

Smart and Derrick.
An Epigram, Written by Mr. G————

Contradiction we find both in Derrick and Smart,
Which manifests neither can write from the heart;
The latter, which readers may think somewhat odd,
Tho' devoted to wine, sings the glories of God:
The former lives sober, altho' no divine;
Yet merrily carols the praises of wine;
Here let us a moment lay by our surprize;
And calmly survey where the preference lies:
Derrick foolishly revels in fancy'd delights;
But Smart, for the sake of a legacy, writes.

Published in *A Collection of Original Poems* by Samuel Derrick (1755),
p. 154. The author is identified by an eighteenth-century hand in the
BL copy as Francis Gentleman. The legacy referred to in the last line
was the bequest establishing the Seatonian Prize for religious poems.

A performance of Aaron Hill's *Merope* for the benefit of Smart was
organized by Garrick and advertised in Jan. 1759. The performance
took place at Drury Lane Theatre on 3 Feb. 1759: see Sherbo, pp.
118–19. The following poems were written by Smart's friends on the
occasion.

A Thought, on reading a bill for the acting of Merope at the Theatre
Royal in Drury-Lane, on Saturday the 3rd of February, for the benefit
of a Gentleman well known in the literary World.

Amazing change in that capacious mind,
Where piercing wit, with wisdom's charm was join'd!
Wrapt in a vision, he presum'd to sing
The attributes of Heav'n's eternal King:

405

But O! approaching tow'rds the Throne of light,
Its flashing splendors overpow'r'd his sight.
Hence blind on Earth, behold him sadly stray;
'Tis we must chear the horrors of his way.

John Lockman, *Owen's Weekly Chronicle* (27 Jan.–3 Feb. 1759): first
published in *Lloyd's Evening Post and British Chronicle* (26–9 Jan. 1759).

On hearing that the Tragedy of Merope was to be acted for the Benefit of Mr. Smart.

Unhappy Bard! whose elevated soul
From earth took flight and reach'd the starry pole;
Whose harp cœlestial lies in broken state;
Affecting emblem of its master's fate!
Ah me! no more, I fear, its tuneful strings,
Touch'd by his hand, will praise the *King of Kings*.
Oh SMART! to me, to all, for ever dear,
Thy friend here drops a sympathetic tear;
Nor doubts but Britons on that night will mourn
Thy genius blasted, and thy laurels torn.

"J. Copywell" [William Woty], *The Shrubs of Parnassus* (1760), p. 55:
first published in *Lloyd's Evening Post and British Chronicle* (29–31 Jan.
1759).

On Mr. Garrick's appearing in a new Entertainment for the Benefit of Mr. Smart.

When Genius, clad in Melancholy's guise,
No longer sought its own ætherial skies,
But listless lay upon the verge of Fate,
Apollo saw, and mourn'd the poet's state;
Then to his agent, Garrick, sent this card:
"Do thou, my son, protect my fav'rite bard,
Who from our sacred fountain science drew,
Celestial science, granted but to few,
Of which he quaff'd his fill, and all was well;
But seeking more, like Phaeton, he fell.

Tho' for a time he's lost, we love his name,
And have enroll'd it on the list of fame:
The rest to you, my son, we must consign.
Your's, with the compliments of all the *Nine*."

Parnassus, Jan. 31.   APOLLO.

Author unidentified, *The Polite Companion; or, Wit A-la-Mode* (1760),
pp. 108–9: first published in *Lloyd's Evening Post and British Chronicle*
(29–31 Jan. 1759).

*Occasioned by the Benefit advertised to be performed at Drury-Lane
this Evening for Mr. Smart.*

Mourn not, my Smart, that now no more the Muse
Brings to thy hallow'd lip Castalian dews;
That with thy Horace thou no more can'st sing,
Or with bold hand awake the sounding string.
What tho' thy pow'rs have felt th' envious blast?
Still to late time thy deathless fame shall last.
Cæcilia's praise Pope, taught by thee, shall tell
In numbers worthy of the Latian shell.
Tho' mute thy tongue, thy lines melodious flow,
And in the Hop Land thy own laurels grow.
Still mounting hence, on the rapt Seraph's ray,
To the All Good thy Muse attunes her lay.
To hear thee, angels from their golden beds,
Willing bend down their star-encircled heads
A soul congenial the whole host admire,
Thy hallelujahs kindling heav'nly fire.
This praise, my friend, nor this thy praise alone,
A higher claim, and nobler wreaths you own.
Thy wide benevolence, thy soul sincere,
Thy gen'rous friendship, and thy social tear.
Thy public spirit that disdain'd a slave;
Thy honest pride that still despis'd a knave.
Thy manly warmth each rival to commend;
Thy rapture for the merit of a friend.
Thy steady morals that ne'er lost their sway,
Nor, like thy vernal genius, felt decay.

All this was thine; this it's reversion brings,
When wit and poetry are idle things.

"A.M." [Arthur Murphy], *The Public Advertiser* (3 Feb. 1759): first published in *Lloyd's Evening Post and British Chronicle* (31 Jan.–2 Feb. 1759).

On the Tragedy of Merope being performed for the Benefit of the late ingenious Mr. Christopher Smart.

Oh, Smart! with thee I often us'd to rove,
In Fancy's wilds, and Wisdom's sacred grove!
Heart-piercing thought! no more those joys are mine;
Thy elevated genius soar'd divine:
And human nature dignified in thee,
Had almost shewn us the Divinity:
But wisdom there was lost, and we deplore
Thy loss, which ages never may restore.
Britons be mov'd, feel your best bard's distress,
'Twas his to please, and now 'tis yours to bless.

Richard Rolt, *Select Pieces, by the late R. Rolt* (1772), p. 203.

On reading a Paragraph, hinting at the kind Concern of a Manager of Drury-lane Playhouse for Mr. Smart; for whose benefit MEROPE, &c. is to be acted there To-morrow Evening.

Shakespear to Mr. Garrick.

Garrick! my fav'rite son! it glads my shade,
To hear thy talents a lov'd poet aid,
Whose heavenly Muse which charms our griefs to rest,
Can't draw the arrow from his tortur'd breast.
All praise thy judgment, genius, spirit, art:
This friendly deed proclaims a gen'rous heart.

J. L. [John Lockman?], *Lloyd's Evening Post and British Chronicle* (31 Jan.–2 Feb. 1759).

APPENDIX C

A NOTE ON CLASSIFICATION

Both Smart himself and Hunter after him made classification by kind
the principle of arrangement in their collected editions. Most of these
classifications are indicated in the titles or subtitles of the individual
poems, but for the sake of convenience the numbered series of
classified poems as printed in *1791* are given here.

Odes

    I. Idleness
   II. To Ethelinda
  III. On an Eagle confined in a College-Court
  IV. On the sudden Death of a Clergyman
   V. On Good-Nature
  VI. On Ill-Nature [Against Ill-Nature]
 VII. To the reverend and learned Dr. Webster
VIII. Epithalamium
  IX. The Author apologizes to a Lady
   X. An Ode on the 26th of January
  XI. On taking a Bachelor's Degree
 XII. A Morning Piece
XIII. A Noon-Piece
XIV. A Night-Piece
 XV. On Miss **** [To Miss A—n]
XVI. On the Fifth of December

Fables

    I. The Wholesale Critic and the Hop-Merchant
   II. The English Bull Dog, Dutch Mastiff, and Quail
  III. Fashion and Night
  IV. Where's the Poker?
   V. The Tea-Pot and Scrubbing-Brush
  VI. The Duellist[s]
 VII. The Country Squire and the Mandrake
VIII. The Brocaded Gown and Linen Rag
  IX. Madam and the Magpie
   X. The Blockhead and Beehive
  XI. The Citizen and the Red Lion of Brentford
 XII. The Herald and Husband-Man

XIII. A Story of a Cock and a Bull
XIV. The Snake, the Goose, and Nightingale
XV. Mrs. Abigail and the Dumb Waiter
XVI. The Bag-Wig and the Tobacco Pipe
XVII. Care and Generosity
XVIII. The Pig

Ballads

I. Sweet William
II. The Lass with the Golden Locks
III. On my Wife's Birth-Day
IV. The Decision
V. The Talkative Fair
VI. The Silent Fair
VII. The Force of Innocence
VIII. The Distressed Damsel
IX. The Fair Recluse
X. To Miss **** one of the Chichester Graces
XI. Lovely Harriot
XII. To Jenny Gray [Jenny Grey]
XIII. To Miss Kitty Bennet and her Cat Crop
XIV. The Pretty Bar-Keeper of the Mitre
XV. The Widow's Resolution

Epigrams

I. The Sick Monkey [The Physician and the Monkey]
II. Apollo and Daphne
III. The Miser and the Mouse
IV. On a Woman who was singing Ballads for Money to bury her Husband

COMMENTARY

'Madam if you please'

Written at the age of four, according to the letter from Smart's daughter, Elizabeth Le Noir: 'His eldest sister Margaret . . . has often repeated to me his first essay at numbers when about . . . 4 years old. . . . The young rhymester was very fond of a lady of about three times his own age who used to notice and caress him. A gentleman old enough to be her father to teaze the child would pretend to be in love with his favorite and threatened to take her for his wife—"You are too old," said little Smart; the rival answered, if that was an objection he would send his son; he answered in verse as follows, addressing the lady' (Elizabeth Le Noir, letter to E. H. Barker, c.1825, *Bodl.* Ms 1006, fo. 245).

To Ethelinda

According to Elizabeth Le Noir, 'Ethelinda' was Anne Vane, daughter of Henry Vane of Raby Castle, where the Smart children used to spend their school holidays (see note on *Ode to Lord Barnard*). Anne was then aged nine. Such was the effect of the poem that 'these young lovers had actually set off on a runaway match together', but were 'timely prevented' (quoted by Brittain, pp. 9–10).

Arion

Described in *UV* as 'by a boy of fourteen' and signed 'S'. Smart's authorship is confirmed by Hunter (I, p. xlii n.). A translation by 'D', dated 'Eton. Mar. 10, 1756' was published in the March issue of *UV*. The story of Arion comes from Herodotus, i. 23.

Fanny, Blooming Fair

Signed 'C.S. Aetat. 16' in *GM*. Smart modelled his Latin version on Vincent Bourne's popular collection of Latin poems and translations published in 1734. The original, a popular song often attributed to Lord Chesterfield, was probably written by the dramatist, Thomas Philips: see Williamson (1973), pp. 116–17.

27 *illam* in *1791* may be an editorial correction; *GM*'s *illum* (referring to the *cestus*, rather than Fanny) is an acceptable reading, especially since the girdle is still the focus of attention in l. 29, but it could be a corruption by association with *satellitium* and *amorum*.

Part of the first Canto of Hudibras

The heading in the Pembroke MS, 'Part of the first Canto of Hudibras translated into Latin Doggrel by a Freshman of Pembroke.—"Christopher Smart"', dates it 1739–40. *PC* is a somewhat careless copy, containing errors (presumably of transcription) which would not have been made by a classical student of Smart's ability, but representing Smart's first version of the translation. *ST* (1750) is not only more correct but also shows considerable revision. Zachary Grey's text (1752), which is ascribed to 'a Gentleman formerly (I think) of Pembroke Hall', is more accurate than *PC* but does not incorporate the revisions of *ST*. Grey was evidently using an early MS corresponding to the source of *PC*, apparently unaware of the version printed in *ST*. That there was some association between Smart and Grey in the 1740s is suggested by the fact that Smart subscribed to the first edition of Grey's *Hudibras* (1744) and that Grey, who was vicar of St Giles and St Peter's, Cambridge, in Smart's time, reciprocated by subscribing to Smart's poems in 1752.

3–4   Added in *ST* to render Butler's 'men fell out they knew not why' (*Hudibras* I. i. 2).

25–6   'Nor put up blow, but that which laid / Right Worshipfull on shoulder-blade' (*Hudibras* I. i. 19–20). The allusion to the ceremony of dubbing is made explicit by *ense* (*PC*, *Z*), 'sword', but *ente*, 'being', which is needed for the rhyme, makes sense as a mock-heroic use of the philosophic term (medieval L *ens*) meaning, here, 'personage'.

29–30   The lines in *PC* are barely relevant.

42–7   The expanded version in *ST* clarifies the point of the story (see *Hudibras*, ed. J. Wilders (1967), I. i. 38 n.).

89   *solutione*: *cum ratione* (*PC*, *Z*) is closer to Butler's 'with ratiocination' (I. i. 78), but Smart evidently preferred to sacrifice accuracy for the sake of the pun. *ST* otherwise provides closer renderings than *Z*.

112   *fu*: an exclamation (cf. Eng. 'phew!') found in Plautus' *Mostellaria*, 37. Grey's *fere* (*Z*), presumably an attempt to make sense of an unfamiliar word, is hypermetrical.

Datur Mundorum Pluralitas

The first set of Tripos Verses written by Smart as an undergraduate at Cambridge. 'The Verses so called are compositions published every year, when the Bachelors of Arts have compleated their degrees. Young men of poetical talents are appointed to this employment; and on one side of their paper, the names are printed of those students, who at the public examination, on the occasion just mentioned, have succeeded the best' (Hunter, I, p. ix n.). No copies of Tripos lists with Smart's verses have been discovered. The date at the end of *Datur Mundorum Pluralitas* indicates that it was written for the First Tripos, the results of which were published in Lent. All three sets were published in *1752* with the translations printed here by Francis Fawkes (1720–77), Smart's friend and contemporary at Cambridge.

Title: 'The Plurality of Worlds granted'.

5   *Fontinelle*: Bernard de Fontenelle, whose *Entretiens sur la Pluralité des Mondes* (1686) were frequently translated into English and reprinted, and were principally responsible for popularizing the idea of a plurality of inhabited worlds in the 18th c. See A. O. Lovejoy, *The Great Chain of Being* (Cambridge, Mass., 1936), ch. iv.

The Pretty Bar-Keeper of the Mitre

The MS version comes from a commonplace-book inscribed 'John Phillips. med: Temp: Lond: 1776' and is described as 'by Mr Lunn'. This is the pseudonym used by Smart in *ST*, but Phillips's text differs substantially from both the *ST* and *1791* versions. Phillips, the only son of Joseph Phillips 'of Mambury, Devon, gent.', was born in 1752, admitted to the Middle Temple in 1775, matriculated at Exeter College, Oxford, in 1779 and was a fellow from 1782 to 1791 (*Middle Temple Admissions Register* i. 379, *Exeter College Register*). How he came by an independent version of Smart's poem is unknown; the likeliest explanation is that he was copying from a periodical or collection which has not been traced.

The Mitre tavern 'stood at the south end of the site now occupied by the screen of King's College' (C. Whibley, *In Cap and Gown: three centuries of Cambridge wit*, 1889, p. 4).

38–40   Whether on account of their alleged 'squalid figures and low habits' or of their reputation as gourmands, men of St John's College were known as 'hogs': see Whibley, pp. xxv–xxvi.

42   *stake-stuck*: citing this occurrence only, *OED* suggests 'that stands like a stake', presumably referring to the pride of Clare Hall men.

43–4   *KAY's*: i.e. Caius College, 'always ... known as a place of good eating', Whibley, p. xxvii. Cf. 'culinary Caius, the headquarters of good living', G. O. Trevelyan, *The Cambridge Dionysia* (1858), quoted by Whibley, p. 269.

48   Cf. Milton's description of Death, *PL* ii. 846.

Materies gaudet Vi Inertiæ

Tripos Verses for 1742 (see commentary on *Datur Mundorum Plurali-tas*), but affinities with *Dunciad* iv suggest that the poem may have been revised after 1742 (when the *New Dunciad* was published) under the influence of Pope's attack on contemporary science. For Smart's attitude to science, see Williamson (1979).

Title: 'Matter rejoices in the force of inertia'.

1 Ireland was traditionally the realm of dunces in Augustan satire; see Pope's note on *Dunciad* (A), i. 23.

7 ff. A parody of the vision of the temple in Pope's *Temple of Fame*, 21 ff.

22–5 In *Dunciad* (A), i. 23–4, conversely, the reign of Dulness shifts from Bœotia (Ireland) to the 'sister realm' of England.

29–32 Cf. the four faces of Pope's *Temple of Fame*, 65 ff. with its 'Doric pillars' on the west and 'Gothic structure' on the north.

44 An adaptation of Smart's own 'extemporary spondiac' on three fat University beadles: 'Pinguia tergeminorum abdomina Bedellorum' (Hunter, I, p. xxix). See Sherbo, p. 28.

45–7 Cf. Pope's 'Mad Mathesis' in *Dunciad* (B), iv. 31–4.

57–64 Cf. the procession of virtuosi in *Dunciad* (B), iv. 397–458.

65–73 *Polypon*: a term applied to small organisms of various kinds. Smart's description seems to be drawing on a report published in *GM*, Nov. 1742 (strengthening the supposition that the poem was revised for *1752*), of the discovery of small insects named *Polypes*, which had 'this singular property, that being cut into several pieces, each piece in the space of 24 hours reproduces what is sufficient to make it a perfect animal; so that this insect being cut crosswise in three pieces, the head produces a tail, the tail produces a head, and the middle produces both head and tail' (p. 607). See 'Several Papers relating to the Fresh-water Polypus', *Philosophical Transactions* No. 467, published Jan. 1743, parodied by Fielding in 'Some Papers Proper to be Read before the R——l Society', *Miscellanies* Vol. i (1743), ed. H. K. Miller (Wesleyan Edn.: Oxford, 1972), pp. 191–204.

84–6 Cf. *Dunciad* (A), iii. 15–18.

Mutua Oscitationum Propagatio

Tripos Verses for 1743 (see note on *Datur Mundorum Pluralitas*).

Title: 'The mutual propagation of yawning'.

70–1 See note on *Inscriptions on an Aeolian Harp*.

Carmen Cl. Alexandri Pope

Published as a pamphlet in Cambridge in 1743 at Smart's expense by J. Bentham, the University printer. Hunter relates with scepticism a story that the translation was written on the occasion when Smart won the Craven Scholarship (June 1742), adding, 'His extraordinary success in this poem, induced him to turn his mind to other Translations from that favourite Bard' (I, p. x). On 6 Nov. 1743 a copy was sent to Pope, who replied courteously, commenting on the accuracy of the translation (Sherbo, pp. 32–3).

Motto. Pindar, *Ol.* iii. 45 ('What lies beyond that is inaccessible to the learned and unlearned alike. I will not go in quest of it; I should be disappointed if I did.')

  1   *Descende cælo*: Horace, *Odes* III. iv. 1.

  97 *Fata obstant*: Virgil, *Aen*, iv. 440.

Secular Ode. On the Jubilee at Pembroke-College

The Jubilee was probably celebrated at the Founder's Feast on New Year's Day, 1743/4: see L. Whibley, 'The Jubilee at Pembroke Hall in 1743', *Blackwood's Mag.* ccxxi (1927), 104–15. Whibley's attribution of the *Secular Ode* to Smart has been generally accepted, but the chain of evidence is by no means complete. Smart's status as a poet of Pembroke, indicated by his selection as composer of the Tripos Verses for three successive years, and his co-editorship of *UV* in which the ode was first published, are arguments in favour of his authorship; but the absence of his usual signature 'S', the omission of the ode from *1791*, and the fact that Hunter—who gives so full an account of Smart's career at Cambridge and records with such obvious pride his uncle's success at the university—makes no mention of it, are all puzzling features. There were in fact other occasional poets at Pembroke, including the Master Roger Long himself, who had also been chosen for the Tripos performance (in 1714) and contributed to university collections of elegies on the Prince of Wales (1751) and on George II (1760). Satirical verses referring to him as 'a reverend Bard of old' (J. Nichols, *Two Music Speeches at Cambridge*, 1819, pp. liv–lviii) attest to his reputation as a poet of sorts. James Brown, a Fellow of Pembroke in 1743, who helped Smart when he was in debt in 1747 (Gray, *Corresp.* i. 291), was another contributor to the elegies on the Prince of Wales. The coincidence in phraseology noted below, however, provides a little corroborative evidence for Smart's authorship, and on balance he remains the likeliest claimant.

    Reviewing the *UV* in 1756, Samuel Derrick described the *Secular Ode* as 'a work of genius, but executed in a loose and rambling manner'. Strophe II he called 'a pretty imitation of Spenser' (*Critical Rev.*, Feb. 1756, p. 88). Secular Odes, of which Horace's *Carmen Seculare* was the prototype, celebrate recurrent events. The legend of the Countess of Pembroke's ill-fated wedding which supposedly led to the foundation of the college is alluded to by Gray in his *Ode for Music* (1769).

18   *muse-resounding glades*: cf. 'muse-resounding groves', *Hop-Garden* i. 263.

39   *Libitina*: Death (used by Horace in *Odes* III. xxx, the model for Smart's *On taking a Batchelor's Degree*).

On taking a Batchelor's Degree

Smart received his BA degree in Jan. 1743/4.

The Hop-Garden

Advertised in proposals for *A Collection of Original Poems* in Jan. 1748, but 'half' written by 1743, since Smart describes his friend Theophilus Wheeler (who died in Dec. 1743) as taking 'imaginary walks' in Smart's 'hopland groves' (ii. 26–9).

For discussion of the *Hop-Garden* in the context of 18th-c. English georgics, see J. Chalker, *The English Georgic* (1969), pp. 46–51. In spite of Smart's claim to 'teach in verse Miltonian', the conspicuous feature of his poem is its variety of subject-matter and style. Polysyllabic words of Greek or Latin origin, often used with mock-heroic effect (*salutiferous, chalybiate, hyemate, saltation, uncauponated, callidity*), Latinate word-order and Miltonic use of participial adjectives jostle with archaisms (*maugre, bedight, wights, yclep'd*), new coinages (*dulsome, scancile*), poeticisms (*jocund, delightsome*) and deliberately 'low' diction (i. 255). Smart's command of register does not always appear certain or felicitous, but Chalker's contention that in the context of georgic tradition the mixture of styles enables Smart to express a variety of viewpoints is valid. For a contemporary opinion, see Hill's comments quoted in the Prolegomena to the *Hilliad*.

Motto. Jacques Vanière, *Prædium Rusticum* (1707), i. 1–5: 'Love of praise whirls me too over the hazardous peaks of Mount Parnassus: I pursue the poet's incurable passion, not daring to quail before either the task or the name of bard—name once revered but now almost pointed out by the finger of scorn.'

i. 7   Cf. J. Philips: 'in *Miltonian* Verse / Adventrous I presume to sing', *Cyder* (1708), i. 3–4.

i. 11–27   See Introduction, p. xxiv.

i. 18 n.　Homer, *Il.* v. 749.

i. 33 n.　Virgil, *Georg.* ii. 485–6.

i. 36　*Egregious*: a pun from L *egregius*, lit. 'out of the flock'.

i. 38–9　*in fair Madum's vale . . . dwell*: for Smart's idealization of his native countryside see also i. 170–2, below, and *JA*, B168.

i. 42　*chalybiate*: impregnated or flavoured with iron.

i. 47　*paternal acres*: an Horatian tag (*Epode* ii. 3), cf. Pope, *Ode on Solitude*, 3.

i. 51　*obnoxious*: in orig. sense of L *obnoxius*, exposed to harm.

i. 72　*grutch*: archaic form of *grudge*, always preferred by Smart.

i. 74　*hyemate*: v. intr., to winter.

i. 147　*Indesinently*: incessantly.

i. 156 n.　Virgil, *Georg.* ii. 173–6.

i. 163　*Ascræan*: of Ascra, birthplace of Hesiod.

i. 181　*uncauponated*: unadulterated.

i. 184　*floscles*: i.e. floscules, flowerets, a botanical term.

i. 188　*dulsome*: Smart's coinage, on the analogy of *delightsome* (i. 186).

i. 191 n.　William Lambarde, *Perambulation of Kent* (1576), ch. i.

i. 201　*Briareus*: a huge giant of Homeric legend.

i. 206　*callidity*: craftiness.

i. 209　*Preposterous*: contrary to nature.

i. 233　*propin'd*: offered.

i. 254　*scancile*: Smart's coinage, presumably from L *scansile*, climbable. *scantile* in *1791* is probably the editor's emendation: failing to recognize the coinage, he may have assumed that a derivative of *scant*, i.e. thin, was intended.

i. 270　A footnote in *1791* supplies a quotation from Horace: 'At ipse / Subtilis veterum judex et callidus audis' (*Sat.* ii. vii. 100–1).

i. 281　i.e. 21 Mar.–20 Apr.

i. 287　*Quincunx*: a group of five, arranged as on a playing-card, a standard pattern in tree-planting.

i. 293　*Jocus*: Jest, cf. *A Latin Version of Milton's L'Allegro*, 27. *Momus* in *1791* is probably an editorial sophistication. Momus, a mythical figure personifying criticism and fault-finding (as in *Mutua Oscitationum Propagatio*, 1), is out of place in this festive context, but the editor may have disapproved of the promiscuous coupling of

English and Latin substantives and thought a mythological character would dignify the line.

i. 313   *Vernon ... Warren*: naval heroes of the War of Austrian Succession (1739–45). Captain Edward Vernon (1684–1757) captured Porto Bello in 1739. Sir Peter Warren (1703–52) commanded the squadron which helped to take Louisburg in 1745.

i. 329 n.   Virgil, *Georg.* ii. 82.

i. 355–421   This story is discussed in the *ST* (Supp. i. 367): it is reported sceptically by Rapin-Thoyras, *Histoire d'Angleterre* (The Hague, 1724), ii. 11, cited in *ST*.

i. 389   *the Thracian*: Orpheus.

i. 393–5   Echoing Psalms 114: 4, 148: 9, and Isa. 55: 12.

i. 401   *inopine*: unexpected.

ii. *Motto.*   Virgil, *Georg.* i. 167–8: 'You will keep all these things stored in your memory long in advance, if the glory of a divine country is to be yours.'

ii. 25   Theophilus Wheeler, a native of Kent, was son of the rector of Otterden. He matriculated at Christ's College, Cambridge, in Jan. 1742, but died in 1743, aged eighteen.

ii. 106 n.   Virgil, *Georg.* i. 373–91. ii. 115 A footnote in *1791* identifies *Thaumantia* as *Iris*.

ii. 127–9   *Niobe*: perhaps a marble statuette. Smart may be referring to the tendency of stone and metal to 'sweat' in humid conditions. Cf. Pope's 'pitying saints, whose statues learn to weep', *Eloisa to Abelard*, 22. John Pointer notes under 'Signs of Rain' that 'Stones (especially *Marble*) when they sweat (or rather seem to sweat) ... are signs of *Wet* Weather', *A Rational Account of the Weather*. (2nd edn., 1738), pp. 41–2.

ii. 129   *prescious*: archaic form of *prescient* always used by Smart (his *Phædrus* III. ix is the last source of this usage noted in *OED*).

ii. 149–50   *Chanticleer ... wings*: borrowed from Lucretius iv. 710, part of the quotation used as motto to *A Morning Piece*.

ii. 167–74   Smart describes both of these customs in *ST* (ii. 202). The first is recorded in Hazlitt's *Dictionary of Faiths and Folklore* (1905), but Smart himself is cited as source and I have not traced it elsewhere.

ii. 203–9   Stephen Hales (1677–1761), a native of Kent, was renowned both for his inventions and for his goodness of heart: see Spence's *Anecdotes*, ed. James M. Osborn (Oxford, 1966), no. 268 and

n. An account of the usefulness of his ventilating fans for granaries appeared in *GM* in June 1746 (pp. 315–18), following the publication of his *Description of Ventilators* (1742).

ii. 209 n.   Virgil, *Georg.* i. 166.

ii. 254–6   *Prior's* patron was Charles *Sackville* (1638–1706), 6th Earl of Dorset.

ii. 257–9   An unsubtle bid for patronage. The volume in which the *Hop-Garden* was first published was dedicated to the grandson of Prior's patron, Charles Sackville (1711–69), then Earl of Middlesex: *orphan merit* is applicable to Smart himself, who was left fatherless at the age of eleven.

ii. 260   *Shipbourne*: Smart's birthplace, a few miles SE of Knole.

ii. 274–8   *Mereworth*: seat of the earls of *Westmoreland*, about five miles E. of Shipbourne. John Fane (1682?–1762). 7th Earl of Westmoreland, distinguished himself as a soldier under Marlborough. After his accession to the title he rebuilt Mereworth Castle to Palladian designs.

ii. 282–3   Cf. Pope, *Mor. Ess.* iv. 187–8.

ii. 293–304   Cf. the conclusion to Philips's *Cyder* (1708), ii. 665–9:

> ... where-e'er the *British* spread
> Triumphant Banners, or their Fame has reach'd
> Diffusive, to the utmost Bounds of this
> Wide Universe, *Silurian* Cyder borne
> Shall please all Tasts, and triumph o'er the Vine.

De Arte Critica

Advertised as 'Preparing for the Press' in *Carmen Cl. Alexandri Pope* (2nd edn., 1746), but begun by 6 Nov. 1743, when Smart sent a sample of 'between forty and fifty lines' (beginning from l. 339) to Pope, together with a proposal prompted by William Murray (later Lord Mansfield) for a Latin version of the *Essay on Man*: see John Holliday, *The Life of William late Earl of Mansfield* (1797), pp. 25–6. Pope replied by advising against the latter, but encouraging Smart to continue with the *Essay on Criticism* (see Sherbo, p. 32). According to Hunter (I, p. xi), the translation was received 'with much praise from the learned, but without either profit or popularity'.

Motto. Lucr. i. 136–9: 'Nor am I unaware that it is difficult to make things clear in Latin verses (especially since new words often have to be used) on account of the poverty of the language and novelty of the subject-matter'.

158   *enim*: a false quantity. Smart was misled by the old school pronunciation of Latin, in which accented syllables were pronounced long: *ĕnim* thus became *ēnim*.

220   *animabus*: a non-existent form, but *animis* would be unmetrical.

385-94   Halliday (loc. cit.) quotes these as the concluding lines of the specimen sent to Pope.

On an Eagle

Dated May 1751 in *ST* but evidently composed earlier: the eagle was kept in Trinity College in 1744-6 (Sherbo, p. 278 n. 13). Allusions to the poem in William Kenrick's *Old Woman's Dunciad*, published Jan. 1751, indicate that it was circulating before publication: see Botting, pp. 11 n., 19. In *ST* it is prefaced by two mottos: *Quis tam crudeles optavit sumere pœnas, / Cui tantum de te licuit?* ('Who chose to wreak so cruel a penalty? Who had so much power over you?'), Virgil, *Aen.* vi. 501-2; and *Atque affigit humi divinæ particulam auræ* ('And fixes to the earth that portion of divine spirit'), Horace, *Sat.* II. ii. 79.

39   *mathematic gloom*: perhaps alluding to the fact that Newton was Trinity College's most celebrated alumnus.

A Description of the Vacation

Published anonymously, but provenance and subject matter put Sherbo's attribution (p. 38) beyond reasonable doubt. Sherbo suggests that the poem was addressed to Charles Burney, but Burney was engaged in London in the summer of 1745 (R. Lonsdale, *Dr. Charles Burney*, 1965, p. 11). Resemblances between the *Description* and William Dodd's *A Day in the Vacation at College. A Burlesque Poem*, dated August 15, 1750 but published in July 1751, are interesting in view of the association between Smart and Dodd (see Sherbo, p. 166). Dodd entered Cambridge in 1745; if the *Description* was in circulation before publication it might have given him the idea for his own poem.

4   *gyps*: college servants, 'an idle useful Set of Hangers on the College, to procure Ale, Pence, &c. by running Errands, and doing little Services for their Masters', Dodd, op. cit., l. 79 n.

11-12   The standard treatment for syphilis was a course of mercury, which induced salivation.

20   *St. Mary's*: the University church.

23   *Johnian hogs*: see *The Pretty Bar-Keeper of the Mitre*, 38-40 n.

30   A British force under the Duke of Cumberland was engaged in Flanders during the War of Austrian Succession (1740-8).

40   *Piece*: i.e. Parker's Piece, a stretch of open ground.

Ode for Musick on St. Cecilia's Day

The last two strophes appeared in Dodsley's *Museum* (13 Sept. 1746), i. 496, under the title 'Warlike Music, and Church Music'.

Motto. Tibullus, III. viii. 21–4 ('Sing of her, you Pierian nymphs, on the festal Calends, and you, proud Phœbus, with your tortoiseshell lyre. Let this solemn rite be celebrated for many years; no maiden is worthier of your choir').

Preface. l. 11   *a Gentleman very eminent in the science of Musick*: perhaps William Boyce, composer to the Chapel Royal, who set Smart's *Idleness* to music in 1744. Smart had already met Charles Burney by this date, but the twenty-year-old Burney, who was still apprenticed to Arne, could not have been described in 1746 as 'very eminent'.

l. 44 n.   Homer, *Od*. i. 351–2 ('For men praise most the song that comes newest to their ears'); Pindar, *Ol*. ix. 48–9 ('and if old wine be best, yet among songs prefer the newer flowers').

l. 50   Thomas Comber was admitted to Jesus in 1741, and took his degree in 1744/5.

ll. 59–64   Du Fresnoy, *De Arte Graphica*, 365–70 ('’Tis labour in vain to paint a high noon, or mid-day light in your picture: because we have no colours which can sufficiently express it; but ’tis better counsel, to choose a weaker light; such as is that of evening with which the fields are gilded by the sun; or a morning light, whose whiteness is allay'd; or that which appears after a shower of rain, which the sun gives us through the breaking of a cloud; or during thunder, when the clouds hide him from our view, and make the light of a fiery colour.' Dryden's translation).

Ode. 45 Penshurst was the home of Lady Dorothy Sidney, Waller's 'Sacharissa'.

55   Cf. Waller: 'While in the park I sing, the listening deer / Attend my passion, and forget to fear'.
At Penshurst (II), *Poems*, ed. G. Thorn Drury (1893), p. 64.

74   *Orthian*: Orthia, a Dorian goddess, was identified with Artemis (Cynthia): see l. 76.

101 n.   From Gyraldus's *Historiæ Deorum Gentilium* v (*Opera Omnia*, 1696, i. 167).

A Latin Version of Milton's L'Allegro

Advertised as 'Preparing for the Press' in 1746 in *Carmen Cl. Alexandri*

Pope (2nd edn.). A translation of *Il Penseroso* was also promised, but never materialized.

Motto. Homer, *Il*. vi. 236 ('Golden armour for bronze, the price of five score oxen for nine'); referring to a transaction in which Glaucus accepts from Diomedes a gift very much inferior to his own.

Title. 'Gaiety', 'good spirits': used by Plutarch of Agesilaus.

72   *undiquaque*: 'every where; on every side' (Ainsworth).

The Precaution

Published anonymously, but Smart's authorship is attested by his friend, John Lockman. The song is based on one of the spurious Chaucerian poems, *A balade warnyng men to beware of deceitfull women*, attributed to Chaucer by Stowe and reprinted in Urry's edition (1721). See Betty W. Rizzo, 'Christopher Smart's "Chaucerian" Poems', *The Library*, 5th ser. xxviii (1973), 124–30.

On seeing Miss H——— P—t

Published anonymously, but provenance and subject strongly suggest Smart's authorship. It appears to be the first of his poems about Harriote Pratt: see Introduction.

28   *Harvey*: the celebrated physician, William Harvey (1578–1657), discoverer of the circulation of the blood.

36   *Hippomanes*: an aphrodisiac substance supposed to be found in the forehead of new-born foals (Pliny, *HN* 8. 66. 165).

Hudibras, Canto I

Introduced by the note, 'It is an assertion of Mr. Voltaire's, that *Hudibras* cannot possibly be translated into any other language, without losing all the drollery and spirit of the original; which perhaps you will not subscribe to without some hesitation, when you peruse the following lines, which were actually render'd extempore by a gentleman of Cambridge.' The reference is to Voltaire's *Lettres philosophiques*, translated as *Letters concerning the English Nation* (1734), Letter xxii.

A Song

Published anonymously, but the evidence for Smart's authorship is strong. In *LH* it is said to be 'Written by a Gentleman of Cambridge, On a Young Lady, who was so closely watch'd by an Aunt, her Guardian, that he cou'd never get an Opportunity to address her.'

The same situation provides the basis of Smart's comedy, *The Grateful Fair* (see note on *Prologue to a Comedy call'd the Grateful Fair*), and *The Fair Recluse*, except that in these the guardian is male.

10–11   Cf. *The Fair Monopolist*, 1–2.

The Pretty Chambermaid

An imitation of Horace, *Odes* II. iv, but Smart reverses the roles of poet and lover: in the original it is the poet who is the middle-aged friend advising the ardent young lover.

12   A footnote in *GM* refers to the source in Homer, *Il.* i. 39, ἐμὸν λέχος ἀντιόωσαν, which is translated by Pope 'to deck the bed she once enjoy'd', with a note explaining the pun: 'The Greek . . . signifies either *making* the bed or *partaking* it.' Agamemnon's captive was Chryseis.

The Horatian Canons of Friendship

This is probably the work to which Smart referred in a letter to Dodsley dated 30 Jan. 1746/7 (Puttick and Simpson Sale Catalogue, 4 June 1878, lot 267) when he mentioned having 'imitated a Satyr of Horace in the manner of Mr. Pope' (see Sherbo, p. 51). The dedication to Warburton, however, must have been written later, and may indeed have been an attempt to cash in on the publicity attached to Warburton's quarrels with his critics; but Smart was no doubt also glad of an opportunity to support his friends, at least three of whom (William Webster, Zachary Grey and Mark Akenside) had been embroiled in disputes with Warburton (see I. D'Israeli, *The Calamities and Quarrels of Authors*, new edn., 1859, pp. 105 and 233–77).

Motto. Pope, *Epilogue to the Satires*, Dia. i. 7.

Dedication. l. 5. *Edwards*: Thomas Edwards published a scathing exposure of the faults in Warburton's edition of Shakespeare as a 'Supplement' to the edition (1747), retitled *The Canons of Criticism* in 1748.

l. 6   *as Hudibras . . . Sidrophel*: see *Hudibras* II. iii. 999–1000.

ll. 11–13   *The other Gentleman . . . likeness* refers to a pamphlet attributed to Philip Carteret Webb, published as *A Letter to the Rev. Mr. William Warburton, A.M. occasioned by some passages in . . . The Divine Legation of Moses demonstrated. By a Gentleman of Lincoln's-Inn* (1742).

ll. 14–15   *Your Shakespeare . . . Dunciad*: Warburton's edition of Shakespeare was published in 1747, and his *Dunciad* in 1749.

ll. 29–31   *making a dead man . . . admired*: Warburton used his edition of the *Dunciad* as an opportunity to strike at his own enemies, including Edwards and Webster (see Pope's *Poems*, v. 398 n and 458).

l. 32   *Menander*: Fragment 257K (Loeb edn., p. 366).

l. 47   *balderdashing the English language*: this was a stock criticism of Warburton by his enemies, but *impuissance*, at least, had been in use in English since the 17th c.

ll. 50–4   *I might accuse ... dog*: Warburton proposed *ming* as an emendation for *wing* in *All's Well* I. i. 191 ('virtue of a good wing'), and glossed *hym* as a kind of dog in *K. Lear* III. vi. 68 ('Hound or spaniel, brach or hym'), ignoring Hanmer's emendation to *lym*, now generally adopted.

ll. 57–8   *a gentleman much my superior*: perhaps Zachary Grey, whose *Free and Familiar Letter to that great refiner of Pope and Shakespeare, the Rev. William Warburton* was published in Apr. 1750, followed by a second attack, *Remarks upon a late edition of Shakespear*, in 1755.

To the Trunk-maker: i.e. Henry Nickless, who died in Nov. 1750, 'worth near £20,000' according to *GM* (1750, p. 526).

l. 2   *the Castle*: a tavern in Paternoster Row, near St Paul's Churchyard.

Horatian Canons.   1–6   Quoted in the introduction to *MB*, i, p. vii as 'Directions to enable Ladies and Gentlemen to sing in a pleasing and graceful manner.'

14 n.   *Pyramus and Thisbe*: a mock-opera by J. F. Lampe, first performed in 1745.

15   'The morning lark to mine accords his note' was a soprano aria in Act i of the version of Handel's *Semele* performed in 1744; its top note is G.

16   *Beard, or Lowe*: John Beard and Thomas Lowe, celebrated singers on the London stage and in the pleasure gardens. Beard was Pyramus in the first performance of *Pyramus and Thisbe*.

49–50   Probably referring to Marlborough's notorious avarice (see 114–15 below) and Chesterfield's alleged pride (see *Boswell's Life*, i. 265).

91   Smart used this conceit of himself in *ST* (i. 249): 'My eyes, which are extremely small and hollow, may truly be styl'd of the *amorous* kind, for they are always looking at one another.' Cf. *Epigram on John Wilkes*. It is tempting to guess that *Jacky* refers to Wilkes, but there is no other evidence that Smart knew him at this early period.

95   *brachet*: little brat.

106 *Ned*: if Smart had a specific person in view, the obvious candidate would be Edward Young whose exploitation by the Duke of Wharton was notorious; but the following line is not applicable to him.

107 *In commendam*: in trust.

110–13 *Chamont*: the nickname of Charles Montagu, 1st Earl of Halifax (see Prior, *To Mr. Charles Montagu, on his Marriage*), who was satirized, probably unfairly, by Pope and Swift for his niggardly patronage. Smart's point, though obscurely expressed, seems to be the same as theirs: that Halifax was more generous with his hospitality than with offers of real help or preferment (see Pope, *Epistle to Arbuthnot* 231–48, and Swift, *A Libel on Doctor Delany and a Certain Great Lord* 1–20).

114 *a great gen'ral*: presumably Marlborough, but I have not traced the particular story to which Smart alludes.

129 *Lælius*: probably William Murray, brother-in-law of Smart's patron, the Duchess of Cleveland, who had already interested himself in Smart's poetic career (see note on *De Arte Critica*). Clearly a lawyer is addressed (132): Murray was appointed Solicitor-General in 1742.

132 *Coke and Littleton*: the standard legal textbook.

166 An 'infamous attorney' with a name rhyming with 'oaf' ought to be identifiable but has eluded me so far.

181 *delph*: a kind of glazed earthenware made at Delft in Holland.

208–9 For Warburton's numerous and acrimonious disputes, see A. W. Evans, *Warburton and the Warburtonians* (1932).

211 *sultanate*: Smart was pleased enough with this coinage to repeat it in *Epithalamium* 53 (see commentary).

To Miss A—n

The relationship between the sources collated in the textual notes cannot be precisely determined. The Tenbury MS (in an unknown 18th-c. hand) contains alterations in the hand of the composer, William Boyce, which were incorporated into the text of the song as published in *LB* (1747). It appears to represent the earliest version of Smart's poem, since it alone has 'willing' in line 38. The Pembroke MS differs in title from the *MW* text, but is otherwise substantially the same. A third MS in Gerald Coke's library, Bentley, Hants, dated 4 Oct. 1751 and containing words and music, was copied, apparently from *LB*, by Edmund Thomas Warren; it shows no significant variants from *LB*. In chronological terms, the order of the collated sources is *T*, *LB*, *MW*, *1752*, *1791*. *PC* cannot be accurately located: it is presumably later than *T* (because it incorporates the correction in line 38) and earlier than *1752* (because it gives the unrevised version of lines 29–30). For further discussion of the text, see R. Mahony, 'Revision and Correction in the Poems of Christopher Smart', *PBSA* 77 (1983), 200–2.

13   *snow-white breasts* was probably Boyce's substitution: see Williamson (1974), 413.

17–20   The omission of this stanza from *LB* may have been merely inadvertent, or a late decision not registered in *T*; but see Mahony, loc. cit., for a different conjecture.

Prologue to a Comedy call'd the Grateful Fair

Smart's comedy, *The Grateful Fair, or A Trip to Cambridge*, was performed in Pembroke College in April, 1747, by Smart himself and a cast of undergraduates, 'with universal applause' according to *CJ* (19 Sept. 1747). Thomas Gray, writing to Wharton in Mar. 1747, looked upon it as a typical piece of Smart's tomfoolery: 'he is amuseing himself with a Comedy of his own Writeing, wch he makes all the Boys of his Acquaintance act, & intends to borrow the Zodiack Room, & have it performed publickly. our Friend Lawman, the mad Attorney, is his Copyist; & truly the Author himself is full as mad as he. his Piece (he says) is inimitable, true Sterling Wit, & Humour by God; & he can't hear the Prologue himself without being ready to die with Laughter. he acts five Parts himself, & is only sorry, he can't do all the rest.' (*Corresp.*, i. 274–5).

A list of the cast and synopsis of the plot was supplied to Hunter (I, pp. xiii–xvi) by John Gordon, who took a leading part himself, and reprinted in *Biographica Dramatica* (1812), ii. 270–1: 'The business of the Drama was laid in bringing up an old country Baronet to admit his nephew a Fellow Commoner at one of the Colleges; in which expedition a daughter or niece attended. In their approach to the seat of the Muses, the waters from a heavy rain happened to be out at Fenstanton, which gave a young student of Emmanuel an opportunity of showing his gallantry as he was riding out, by jumping from his horse and plunging into the flood to rescue the distressed damsel, who was near perishing in the stream, into which she had fallen from her poney, as the party travelled on horseback. The swain being lucky enough to effect his purpose, of course gained an interest in the lady's heart, and an acquaintance with the rest of the family, which he did not fail to cultivate on their arrival at Cambridge, with success as far as the fair one was concerned. To bring about the consent of the father (or guardian, for my memory is not accurate) it was contrived to have a play acted, of which entertainment he was highly fond; and the Norwich company luckily came to Cambridge just at the time; only one of the actors had been detained on the road; and they could not perform the play that night, unless the Baronet would consent to take a part; which, rather than be disappointed of his favourite amusement, he was prevailed upon to do, especially as he was assured that it would amount to nothing more than sitting at a great table, and signing an instrument, as a Justice of Peace might sign a warrant; and, having been some years of the Quorum, he felt himself quite equal to the undertaking. The under play to be acted by the Norwich company on this occasion was the *Bloody War of the King of Diamonds with the King of Spades*; and the actors in it came on with their respective emblems on their shoulders, taken from the suits of the cards they represented. The Baronet was the king of one of the parties, and in signing a declaration of war, signed his consent to the marriage of his niece or daughter, and a surrender of all her fortune.' The part of the Baronet, 'Sir Taleful Tedious', was played by Smart himself.

1–4   *Horace sings*: see *Ars Poet.* 391–407, and *Sat.* i. iv. 1–5.

16   *posts* is explained in a footnote in *GM*: 'In a like sense (with this Author) some merry travellers call the finger posts on the road *Parsons*.'

23   *Celia's*: *Harriot's* in other versions suggest that the whole play may have been a personal joke involving Harriote Pratt, as the jealously guarded heroine, and her father and brother (see Introduction).

25   *Marlbro'*: *William* in other versions presumably refers to William Augustus, Duke of Cumberland, whose victorious battle at Culloden in 1745 lasted less than half an hour.

29–31   See *1 Henry IV*, v. 111–52.

Soliloquy of the Princess Perriwinkle

From Smart's comedy, *The Grateful Fair* (see commentary on *Prologue*, above). Fanny Burney quoted l. 7 in a letter to her sister Charlotte, with the comment, 'I have never forgotten our early favourite *Soliloquy* of the Princess Perewinkle' (27 Nov. 1791: *Journals and Letters*, ed. J. Hemlow, 1972, i. 80).

8   *Spanish padlock*: 'A kind of girdle contrived by jealous husbands of that nation, to secure the chastity of their wives' (Grose's *Dictionary of the Vulgar Tongue*, 2nd edn., 1788).

The Judgment of Midas

Written by Jan. 1748 when it was advertised in proposals for *A Collection of Original Poems* in London newspapers: see Mahony and Rizzo, Item 1.

Motto. Persius, *Sat*. i. 121 (Casaubon's edn.): 'King Midas has ass's ears'. Modern editions read *auriculas asini quis non habet*.

113   *prescious*: see *Hop-Garden* ii. 129 n.

Christopherus Smart Samueli Saunders

Written not later than Jan. 1748. Samuel Saunders entered King's College, Cambridge from Eton in 1741, at the age of eighteen. He became a Fellow in 1745, took orders in 1746, and died in 1748.

S.P.D: usually *S.D.P.*, *salutem dicit plurimam*, a standard form of greeting.

9   *Georgium*: perhaps George Hartley, or Heartly, of Christ's College, Cambridge, Fellow of Magdalene from 1747, to whom Smart refers in *JA* (D24).

9–10   *salis . . . duplicis*: perhaps 'punning' or 'repartee'; *duplex* can also mean 'ambiguous', but if Smart intended the modern *double-entendre* he had no precedent in classical Latin.

A Morning Piece

First published anonymously together with *Noon-Piece* and *Night-Piece* under the title *The Rural Day*. Smart claimed that the *LM* text was 'a very imperfect copy', inserted 'without the knowledge or consent of the author' (*ST* 1. 274 n), but this may have been disingenuous: the variants in *ST* look more like revisions than corrections. The piece became very popular: it was set to music by several composers, and sung at Marylebone Gardens in 1763 and 1769 to a setting by Samuel Arnold, under the title *Ode to the Haymakers*. An elaborate setting, scored for soprano and bass soloists with orchestra, dating mainly from 1763, by Philip Hayes (Professor of Music at Oxford, 1777–97) survives in MS. (Bodl. Tenbury MS 1156).

Motto. Lucr. iv. 710–11: 'Even the cock, clapping away the night with his wings, who is accustomed to summon the dawn with his clear voice . . .' The trope, *noctem explaudentibus*, is borrowed in *The Hop-Garden* ii. 148 and *Immensity*, 4.

6–7   The grammatical error, first corrected in Chalmers's edn. (1810), was pointed out in 1792 by Dr Burney, who said that a correction had been advertised in 1752 (the advertisement has not however been traced). 'The poet did not mean to insinuate that Labour had slept with his pipe in his mouth' (*Monthly Rev.*, Jan. 1792, p. 43). Error or no, these lines were particularly relished by Goldsmith, who read them aloud on a visit to Smart's daughter, exclaiming 'There is not a man now living who could write such a line.' (E. Le Noir, *Miscellaneous Poems*, 1825, ii. 182).

A Noon-Piece

Set as a cantata by John Stafford Smith (1750–1836), a pupil of William Boyce (Bodl. Tenbury MS 1321).

Motto. Horace, *Odes* III. xxix. 21–4: 'now the weary shepherd, with his languid flock, seeks the shade, and the river, and the thickets of rough Sylvanus; and the silent bank is free from wavering winds' (Smart).

26 *Harriot*: see Introduction.

36–7 *Sydney's . . . glories*: cf. *Hop-Garden* i. 11–25.

A Night-Piece

Motto. Horace, *Odes* III. xxviii. 16: 'let the night also be celebrated in a suitable lay' (Smart).

1–22 William Kenrick ridiculed Smart's logic in an *Epigram. Occasion'd by the Night Piece, or Modern Philosophy of Mr. Christopher Smart*, published in his magazine *Kapélion* (Nov. 1750), p. 153:

> The *Moon shone bright!* yet *dark the Night!*
> Sure *Kitt* has miss'd the Mark!
> Oh—No—'tis right—he wanted Light
> To see—*that it was dark.*

To the King

From a collection of addresses to George II published after the signing of the Peace of Aix-la-Chapelle (18 Oct. 1748), which concluded the War of Austrian Succession. The King returned to England on 22 Nov. 1748.

23 William Augustus, Duke of Cumberland, the third son of George II, commanded the British forces in Holland, 1747–8.

35–6 A favourite metaphor: see *JA*, A66, B24.

On the Eternity of the Supreme Being

The first of Smart's Seatonian poems (see Introduction). The prize was awarded on 25 Mar. 1750.

Mottoes. Horace, *Odes* i. vi. 9: '... we attempt lofty themes'. Virgil, *Aen*, v. 809: 'neither the gods nor [my] strength suffice'.

2–5 For the occult notion of the inscription of divine characters on natural objects, see *JA*, B477 and n.

21 Representation of God as *Poet* (ποιητής, maker) was a common Renaissance trope: see Sidney, *A Defence of Poetry* (*Miscellaneous Prose*, ed. K. Duncan-Jones and J. van Dorsten, Oxford, 1973, p. 79); Cowley, *Davideis* (*Poems*, ed. A. R. Waller, Cambridge, 1905, p. 253); Oldham, 'Upon the works of Ben Jonson' (*Poems*, ed. B. Dobrée, 1960, p. 70). As Nathaniel Whiting laboriously explained, the Greek language

> calls all that which takes not essence by
> A matter pre-existent, poesy.
> So makes the world a poem: and by this
> The great creator a great poet is.

(*Minor Poets of the Caroline Period*, ed. G. Saintsbury, Oxford, 1905–21, iii. 546).

26–7 See Job 38: 4–7.

41 *Systems innumerable*: see *Datur Mundorum Pluralitas*, 5 n.

133–5 *Purge ... hyssop*: Ps. 51: 7. For Cain's fruitless sacrifice, see Gen. 4: 3–5.

A Panegyrick on the Ladies

A retort to *The Precaution*, which has as refrain 'The blind eat many a fly'. First printed under Smart's name in the *Choice Spirit's Chaplet* (Whitehaven, 1771), but not included in *1791*. It is based on *A Balade whiche Chaucer made in the praise, or rather dispreise, of Women for ther doublenes*, printed by Stowe and reprinted in Urry's Chaucer (1721), but now attributed to Lydgate (see Betty W. Rizzo, 'Christopher Smart's "Chaucerian" Poems,' *The Library*, 5th ser., xxviii, 1973, p. 128). The headnote in *VM* explains: 'Chaucer ... being hard set upon by the ladies of his time for writing a song call'd (From sweet bewitching tricks of love) which was a great satire on that sex; in order to make them ample amends, wrote the following Recantation.'

On the Fifth of December

'Written on Miss Harriot Pratt, of Downham in Norfolk, a lady for whom our Author had entertained a long and unsuccessful passion', according to Hunter (see Introduction). Fanny Burney thought it 'sweetly elegant and pretty' (*Early Diary*, ed. A. R. Ellis, 1907, i. 28).

The writer of *The Art of Poetry on A New Plan* (1762) commented that it was 'much to be admired for the beauty of the thoughts, and the elegance and delicacy of the compliment. It has great fire, and yet great sweetness, and is the happy issue of genius and judgment united' (ii. 67). It inspired several imitations: see Mahony and Rizzo, Items 1106, 1114, 1196.

15   *dies* in *1752* is probably merely a spelling variant of *dyes* (sb.), but with Smart's eccentric syntax, *dies* (v. intr.) cannot be wholly ruled out.

The Distressed Damsel

A version with a new musical setting and additional stanzas, probably not by Smart, was published anonymously in *LM* (July 1760) as 'A New Song': see Williamson (1974), pp. 412–13, and Mahony and Rizzo, Item 631. The extra stanzas, added at the beginning and end, read as follows:

> As Colin rang'd early one morning in spring,
> To hear the wood's choristers warble and sing,
> Young Phebe he saw supinely was laid,
> And thus in sweet melody sung the fair maid.
> .   .   .   .
>
> Poor Colin was melted to hear her complain,
> Then whisper'd relief, like a kind-hearted swain;
> And Phebe, well pleas'd, is no longer afraid
> Of being neglected, and dying a maid.

The Fair Recluse

Listed in proposals for *1752* published in Aug. 1750. Perhaps written for Smart's comedy, *The Grateful Fair*, the plot of which turned on the efforts of a guardian to keep his charge away from her suitor. Cf. *Song*, 'Gay Florimel of noble birth'. According to Hunter (I, p. xii), a few songs from the play were still extant in 1791. It might also be connected with Harriote Pratt, whom Smart visited at 'her ancient mansion' in July 1749 (see Introduction).

On Good-Nature

Listed in proposals for *1752* published in Aug. 1750. For the conception of *good-nature* as a quasi-divine attribute and the essence of virtue, cf. Fielding's poem 'Of Good-Nature', *Miscellanies*, Vol. i (1743), ed. H. K. Miller (Wesleyan Edn: Oxford, 1972), pp. 30–5.

13–14, 25–6 'Good-Nature is that benevolent and amicable Temper of Mind which disposes us to feel the Misfortunes, and enjoy the Happiness of others': Fielding, *An Essay on the Knowledge and Characters of Men*, op. cit., p. 158.

Against Ill-Nature

Listed in proposals for *1752* published in Aug. 1750. In spite of minor cavils, this ode was singled out for praise by Hill (see Prolegomena to the *Hilliad*).

   10   *my natal morn*: 11 Apr. 1722.

   38   *œstrum*: gad-fly, hence *fig.* passion, frenzy. Smart uses it to translate 'rapture' in *De Arte Critica*, 251. Hill comments: 'The word *œstrum*, tho' of real and appropriated meaning, is chargeable with aukwardness and affectation'.

   47   Hill objected on metrical grounds to *time-deflow'red*. Perhaps the monosyllable *-flow'r'd* was intended.

To the reverend and learned Dr. Webster

Listed in proposals for *1752* published in Aug. 1750. William Webster (1689–1758), vicar of Ware and a Cambridge doctor of divinity, was editor of the *Weekly Miscellany*, an anti-Methodist journal. He earned the enmity of William Warburton in 1739 by attacking his *Divine Legation of Moses*, in revenge for which Warburton secured Webster a niche in the *Dunciad* (B) ii. 258. Webster's *Casuistical Essay on Anger and Forgiveness . . . in three dialogues* was published in April 1750. Whether Smart's ode was written primarily from theological or personal motives is debatable (see Devlin, p. 106, and Dearnley, pp. 118–23), but his preference here (1–23) for NT mercy over OT justice is entirely consistent with the spirit of his religious poetry.

   32–7   Webster was appointed to a curacy in 1716 but failed to gain a benefice until 1732, and his attempt to obtain a prebend was repulsed (see Dearnley, p. 122).

   38   See Luke 16: 8, 'the children of this world are in their generation wiser than the children of light': cf. Smart's *Parables* 25. 30–4, and commentary (Vol. ii, p. 452).

   42–5   Probably inspired by the description of a poverty-stricken parson's house in Webster's essay: see Dearnley, p. 120.

On the Sudden Death of a Clergyman

Listed in proposals for *1752* published in Aug. 1750. The clergyman may have been Cornelius Harrison, who died in 1748: see *JA*, D88 and n. The *Student* supplies a motto from Virgil, *Aen.* ii. 329–30, *Nec te tua plurima, Pantheu, / Labentem pietas, nec Apollinis infula texit*: 'nor could all your goodness, Pantheus, nor Apollo's fillet, shield you in your fall'.

1 *th' Orphean lyre*: Milton, *PL* iii. 17.

12 *forgetive*: 'apt at forging, inventive, creative' (*OED*).

40–2 Moses ('Israel's legislator') was buried in the land of Moab, 'but no man knoweth of his sepulchre unto this day.' Deut. 34: 6.

Inscriptions on an Æolian Harp

Printed in *GM* in a letter about Æolian harps from 'Philo-Musicus', who writes that the inscriptions were seen 'at a gentleman's seat in Norfolk'. This identifies the owner as Henry Bell of Wallington, Norfolk, whose death was reported in *GM* in Jan. 1754 (p. 47). Henry Bell was a subscriber to Smart's *Poems on Several Occasions* (1752); Smart probably knew him through the Pratts, whose seat is only a few miles from Wallington (see Introduction). The Æolian harp was still a novelty at this date: Thomson found it necessary to explain his reference to one in 1748 (*The Castle of Indolence* I. xl. 9). See G. Grigson, *The Harp of Aeolus* (1948).

Motto. Virgil, *Ecl.* iii. 73: 'Waft some part, O winds, to the ears of the gods'. A second motto was supplied in *GM*: see Introduction, p. xxviii.

1–3 Cf. *Mutua Oscitationum*, 70–1. Memnon's 'harp' was in fact a marble statue of Memnon which gave out a musical sound at sunrise, but the notion that the statue showed Memnon holding a lyre or harp, which is without classical authority, was current in the 18th c. See Akenside, *The Pleasures of Imagination* (1744), i. 109–13 and n.; Ainsworth, s.v. Memnon.

Audivere, Lyce

Published anonymously but ascribed to Smart both in the Pembroke MS and by Mrs Thrale (*Thraliana*, ed. K. Balderston, 2nd edn. 1951, i. 516). Her copy probably came from Charles Burney, to whom Smart gave several of his poems in manuscript, including 'A burlesque or Parody or imitation of the Ode of Horace', according to Fanny Burney (R. Lonsdale, *Dr. Charles Burney* (Oxford, 1965), p. 27). There is a reference in *The Fool* (1748), i. 231 (originally published 17 Sept. 1746) to 'that humorous Ode to Mother *Gunter*' in the *Daily Gazetteer* (not found). If this was Smart's piece, it was clearly written in the same period as *Horatian Canons* and his other early imitations of Horace.

433

4 *bunter*: a woman who picks up rags in the street.

15 Vincent Wing's almanack was the standard one in use from 1658 onwards.

To Miss **** one of the Chichester Graces

The gardens at Goodwood House, near Chichester, were laid out in the 18th c. 'in the most romantic and picturesque manner', with a magnificent view from Cairney Seat 'embracing the whole tract of plain beneath, from Portsmouth Harbour to Littlehampton' (D. Jaques, *A Visit to Goodwood*, Chichester, 1822).

The Author apologizes to a Lady

Smart frequently alludes to his small stature: in *ST* he describes himself as 'very low' (i. 249) and in *MW* as 'but four feet high' (ii. 146 n). Cf. *JA*, B45.

Mottoes. Pliny, *HN*, 11. 1. 4: 'Nature is never more complete than in her smallest creature.' Homer, *Il*. i. 167: 'small and dear'.

The Trial of Chaucer's Ghost

Published in *ST* as 'by the Author of the Recantation', i.e. *A Panegyrick on the Ladies*, q.v.

The Bag-wig and the Tobacco-pipe

The MS version comes from John Phillips's commonplace-book, dated 1776 (see commentary on *The Pretty Bar-Keeper of the Mitre*). Even allowing for inaccuracies in Phillips's transcription, it is clear that he was copying a version substantially different from the known printed texts. No author is ascribed, the source being noted simply as 'In a morning paper', but the paper has not been traced. The fable is described in *The Art of Poetry on a New Plan* (1762) as 'very original, as well as droll and satyrical' (i. 250).

An Epigram on a Woman who was singing

A letter in *MW* from 'Mary Midnight' explained that the woman was 'singing a sprightly song to one of the most dismal tunes I ever heard in my life. ... As there were such evident marks of sorrow in her countenance, I sent for her, and ask'd the reason of her singing such a humourous song to so lamentable a tune. *Oh Madam*, says she, *serious things will not go down now, and I am obliged to sing such as will bring in money immediately, for my poor husband died yesterday, and I have not a farthing to bury him, nor any thing for my babe and me to subsist on*. ... When

I came home, I mention'd this to Mr. Pentweazle, who being a poet, and a flighty spark you may suppose, wrote me the following epigram on the subject' (i. 228–9).

An Occasional Prologue and Epilogue to Othello

Published as a pamphlet in Mar. 1751, dedicated to Francis and John Delaval. The performance of *Othello* was a highlight of the season. The audience was august, and included the Prince and Princess of Wales and other members of the royal family. The leading parts were played by Francis Delaval and his brother John (Cassio was played by yet another brother), with Francis's mistress Elizabeth La Roche and her sister Deodata as Emilia and Desdemona respectively. Smart was private tutor to John Blake Delaval during his brief and flamboyant residence at Pembroke College (see Gray's *Corresp.* i. 256, 260–1).

Full reports and criticism of the performance appear in *GM* (Mar. 1751), pp. 119–23. John Hill described the prologue as 'excellent' and the epilogue 'hardly at all inferior to it' (p. 121). But 'B.C.', a correspondent from Cambridge, regarded them as a blot on Smart's reputation: 'I wish the world had not known that this prologue and epilogue were written by a gentleman, who has hitherto been esteem'd a genius and a scholar; for nothing but the publication of them with his name, would have convinced the world that he was the author' (p. 122).

Epilogue. 12–15. *Othello* i. iii. 160–2.

A Solemn Dirge

Dedicated to Prince George, elder son of the Prince of Wales. Frederick Louis, Prince of Wales (b. 1707) died on 20 Mar. 1751. After quarrelling with his father, George II, in 1737, he set up his own establishment at Leicester House, which became a centre for Opposition politicians and wits. He was a friend of many of the leading poets of the day, including Pope, Gay, and Thomson, and an enthusiastic patron of the arts. He married Princess Augusta of Saxe Gotha in 1736; Prince George (afterwards George III) was born in 1738. The Prince of Wales and his family were present at the performance of *Othello* for which Smart provided a prologue and epilogue.

Two stanzas were quoted in *GM* (Apr. 1751), p. 190, with the comment, 'All the poetical pieces on this occasion lament the father at the beginning, and at the end rejoice in the son; the following stanzas therefore may serve not only as an epitome of this piece but most of all the rest.' John Worgan, who provided the musical setting, received his Mus.B. at Cambridge in 1748. He was at this time organist (later composer) at Vauxhall Gardens.

44   Dearnley (p. 264) suggests that this refers to 'Instructions for my son George' drawn up by Frederick in 1748 and based on advice given by his grandfather, George I, but this document was not published until 1937. Horace Walpole reports George II telling his grandsons, 'They must be brave boys, obedient to their mother, and deserve the fortune to which they were born' (*Memoires of George the Second*, 1822, i. 83). Both Smart and Walpole must have been drawing on some story current at the time, but I have failed to trace it. In *1740. A Poem* Pope alludes to Frederick with the words, 'Let him be honest, and he must be wise' (*Poems* iv. 337).

Lovely Harriote

Set to music by Charles Burney, who according to Hunter (I, p. xviii) set 'several songs' for Smart, but this is the only one that has been traced. (For Harriote, see Introduction). A crambo song is one in which the name of the person addressed is incorporated as a rhyme-word in each stanza.

9   Cf. Pope's *Artimesia* (*Poems* vi. 48), who 'Reads Malbranche, Boyle, and Locke'. *Malbranche*: Nicole Malebranche (1638–1715), Cartesian philosopher. *Boyle*: Robert Boyle (1627–91), chemist and physicist. *Marriote*: Edmé Mariotte (d. 1684), physicist.

15   *Barry*: Spranger Barry (1719–77), a leading actor in Garrick's company, scored a particularly notable success as Othello in 1746, in spite of his tendency to 'rant' (see Gray, *Corresp.* i. 250).

To Miss H——— ———, with some Musick

Signed 'S' and printed immediately after *The Widow's Resolution* in *GM*; another of the Harriote poems. Composition must date from before Aug. 1751, when Smart started to woo Nancy Carnan (see *The Lass with the Golden Locks*). In his letter to Charles Burney in July 1749, Smart writes of Harriote playing 'on her spinnet & organ' (Introduction, p. xxiii).

10   Either *Downham* or *Norfolk* would fill the gap metrically.

On the Immensity of the Supreme Being

The second of Smart's Seatonian poems (see Introduction). The prize was awarded on 20 Apr. 1751.

2–5   Cf. Ps. 57: 9 (Psalter): 'Awake up my glory; awake lute and harp: I myself will awake right early.' The borrowing was noted in the *Monthly Rev.*, which commented: 'Mr. Smart has kept that most divine poet the *Psalmist* in his eye, almost through the whole of this work, and finely imitated him in several passages' (1751, p. 508).

4   *night-exploding bird*: see *The Hop-Garden* ii. 148–9.

32   Probably refers to the dual motion of the planets, constantly revolving round the sun, but simultaneously revolving on their own axis, and thus turning away from it.

36–8   Cf. Prior, *Solomon*, i. 512–35, and Pope, *Ess. on Man*, i. 21–6.

39–45   See Ps. 107: 23–30.

53   John Hill, in the *Inspector* (14 Apr. 1752), pointed out the error of describing amber as a plant (see prolegomena to the *Hilliad*). The clumsy correction in *1791* looks like an editorial, rather than authorial, attempt at emendation.

62   *Gani, Raolconda*: diamond-mines in India, discovered in the 16–17th c.

65   *Pegu*: a kingdom of Burma, famed in the 18th c. for its rubies. 'There are but two places in the East where the *Ruby* is found: the kingdom of Pegu, and the isle of Ceylon' (Chambers, s.v. *Ruby*).

66–7   'The antients . . . have attributed many virtues to the *Ruby*; as, that it expels poisons, cures the plague, abates luxury and incontinence, banishes sorrow, &c.' (Chambers, s.v. *Ruby*).

71–8   See Chambers, s.v. *Jasper*: 'a precious stone, not much different from the agate . . . In some of these, Nature has amused herself, in representing rivers, trees, animals, landskips, &c. as if they were painted.'

79–81   *Claudio*: Claude Lorraine (1600–82). *Poussin*: probably Nicholas Poussin (1594–1665). *Guido*: Guido Reni (1575–1642). Claude and Poussin were enormously popular as landscape-painters in the 18th c. but Reni, whose religious and allegorical paintings were no less renowned, is scarcely appropriate in this context. The usual trio was Claude, Poussin and Salvator Rosa (see e.g. Thomson, *Castle of Indolence* I. xxxviii).

111–20   Quoted in *The Art of Poetry on a New Plan* (1762) as a particularly noteworthy example of the 'agreeable thoughts' with which the poem was said to abound (i. 27). The skill and artistry of birds in nest-building is cited in Derham's *Physico-Theology* (1713), Bk. IV, ch. xiii, as evidence of God's wisdom in the creation.

121–2   *Go bid . . . mansion*: a favourite theme of the physico-theologians. Cf. Blackmore (of the beehive): 'Can *Euclid* more, can more *Palladio* teach?' (*Creation*, 1712, vii. 174).

123–6 Cf. Thomson, *The Seasons* (1746), 'Spring', 468–70; 'But who can paint / Like Nature? Can imagination boast, / Amid its gay creation, hues like hers?' But Smart goes further: Thomson contrasts Art and Nature, Smart points beyond Nature to God (cf. lines 79–82).

136–9 Cf. Henry More, *An Antidote against Atheism* (1653) II. xii:

But we needed not to have rambled so farre out into the works of Nature, to seek out Arguments to prove a *God*, we being so plentifully furnish'd with that at home which we took the pains to seek for abroad. For there can be no more ample testimony of a *God* & a *Providence* then the *frame* and *structure* of our own *Bodyes*.

This is one of the main themes of Bk. vii of Blackmore's *Creation*.

The Miser and the Mouse

The original is attributed to Lucilius in the Greek Anthology (*Pal. Anth.* xi. 391).

The Physician and the Monkey

A doctor who prescribes for a pet monkey called *Pugg* features in a satirical pamphlet, possibly by Smart, titled *The Genuine Memoirs . . . of a Very Unfortunate Goose-Quill*, dated 29 Apr. 1751 (see Mahony and Rizzo, Item 128). The doctor in the pamphlet appears to be John Hill.

The Force of Innocence

Miss C*** was probably Nancy Carnan: see note on *The Lass with the Golden Locks*. Burney describes the poem as 'an elegant application of the *Integer Vitæ* of Horace to female virtue' (*Monthly Rev.* Jan. 1792, p. 42): see Horace, *Odes*, i. xxii.

On seeing the Picture of Miss R—— G——n

William Verelst (d. 1756), a portrait-painter active in London in the 1740s, was a great-nephew of Simon Varelst (or Verelst), the flower-painter celebrated by Prior. His sitters included Smollett, Stephen Hales, and James Oglethorpe (see J. Kerslake, *Early Georgian Portraits*, 1977), but I have not traced the portrait to which Smart refers.

A Morning Hymn

Published as 'by a young gentleman' in the *Lilliputian Mag.* but 'Mr.

Kitty Smart' was named as the author in an advertisement for the magazine in the *London Daily Advertiser* (29 June 1751): see Roland B. Botting, 'Christopher Smart and the Lilliputian Magazine', *ELH* 9 (1942), 286–7.

Epigram of Martial, Lib. VIII, Ep. 69

Published under the pseudonym 'Mrs. Midnight'. Page numbers in *MW* ii. 177–80 are duplicated; the epigram is on the second p. '177'.

The Lass with the Golden Locks

According to Burney, the Lass was 'the beautiful Nancy Carnan', John Newbery's step-daughter, whom Smart married in 1752: see R. Lonsdale, *Dr. Charles Burney* (Oxford, 1965), p. 28.

  1 *Harriot*: see Introduction.

  24 *bears the bell*: takes the prize, cf. Spenser *FQ* vi. x. 26.

The Long-Nose'd Fair

An imitation of Sir Thomas More's Latin epigram, 'De Tyndaro' (*Epigrammata*, 1638, p. 88); the original is printed in *MW*. The connection between this poem and *Epigram on Dorinda's Fore-Teeth. Occasion'd by her denying the Author a Kiss*, published in *Kapélion* (Dec. 1750), is problematic. The latter appears to be a parody of Smart's epigram, but was published several months before Smart's.

Care and Generosity

Described as 'sweetly elegant and pretty' by Fanny Burney (*Early Diary*, ed. A. R. Ellis, 1907, i. 28), and as 'one of the most beautiful allegories that has ever been imagined' by Charles Burney (*Monthly Rev.*, Jan. 1792, p. 39). The author of the *Art of Poetry on a New Plan* (1762) quotes it in full as a specimen of *allegory*, although 'written on a more familiar plan than the generality of pieces in that stile' (ii. 30–1).

Fashion and Night

  Motto. Terence, *Heauton Timorumenos* iv. 839: 'How many perverse and unjust acts does fashion make one commit.'

Ode on the 26th of January

'Nancy' is Anna-Maria Carnan (see *On my Wife's Birth-Day*); the poem must therefore have been written before Smart's marriage in 1752 (see 23–4).

16   Cf. *The Lass with Golden Locks.*

Epithalamium

Perhaps written to celebrate the wedding of Anne Vane and Charles Hope Weir in 1746 (Ainsworth and Noyes, p. 14).

20   *sofa . . . flowers*: cf. *Idleness*, 12.

29   *Venus . . . zone*: the magic girdle which made everyone fall in love with the wearer. It was borrowed by Juno to excite Jove's passion (Homer, *Il.* xiv. 214–351).

53   *sultanates*: Smart's coinage, see *Horatian Canons*, 211 n. It was condemned by Hill as 'a very pompous word, never before introduced into our own or any other language' (quoted in Prolegomena to the *Hilliad*).

To my worthy Friend, Mr. T.B.

Mr. T.B. has been identified through the records of the Society of Friends as Timothy Bevan (1704–86), co-founder with his brother Silvanus of the apothecary's business in Plough Court, Lombard Street, which later became Allen and Hanbury's. His only daughter Priscilla was born 11 Oct. 1737 (Society of Friends: *London and Middlesex Quarterly Meeting Register 1720–1837*). Bevan was at this time owner of a large house in Hackney, in the area now occupied by Mare Street and Loddidge Street, a description of which survives: it was 'one of those sound Georgian villas with plenty of well-kept flower beds and shrubberies, where solid and expensive comfort was joined with the Quaker dread of worldly show' (quoted by Desmond Chapman-Huston and Ernest C. Cripps, *Through a City Archway: the story of Allen and Hanburys 1715–1954*, 1954, pp. 23–5). According to the same source, however, Bevan was 'of a temper the very opposite to cheerfulness and affability' (p. 24), but perhaps this was at a later stage. In 1752 he had just married, presumably for a second time.

The Pig

A translation of Phaedrus's *Scurra et Rusticus* (Bk. V, fable 5). Note in *CP6*: 'This tale is a proper lesson for the critics, as it evidently shows the necessity of a man's bearing his judgment about him; and having his head fraught with the rule of enquiry, and the scale of satisfaction. If the errors of our modern critics for the last ten years were pointed out in this minute manner, fifty volumes in folio would not contain them, so pregnant have they been in the business of blundering. VOLTAIRE.' (Source untraced).

The Pig was recited at a Medley Concert at the Haymarket Theatre on 11 Aug. 1757 by 'Miss Dorothy Midnight' (*London Stage*, Part 4, p. 604).

10 Well-known actors and performers on the London stage in the 1750s.

37 *bunter*: see *Audivere, Lyce*, 4 n.

To Miss Kitty Bennet

Kitty Bennet was probably the daughter of James Bennet, Master of Hoddesdon Grammar School: see *JA*, D35 n.

On the Omniscience of the Supreme Being

Smart's third Seatonian poem (see Introduction), for which he was awarded the prize on 2 Nov. 1752. It was dedicated to Thomas Herring, Archbishop of Canterbury, whose nephew John Herring subscribed to Smart's *Poems on Several Occasions* (1752).

6 For gratitude as a cherub, see *A Song to David*, 8–9, *Hymns* (1771) 22.3, and commentary to *Hymns* 6. 76–80.

14–17 *th' eternal, high mysterious tree*: the tree of life in the heavenly Jerusalem (Rev. 22: 2) whose *fruit* is the *Knnowledge* of God (2 Cor. 4: 6), in implicit contrast to philosophic knowledge to which man vainly aspires (see lines 54–9).

26–30 Cf. Milton, *PL* i. 17–23.

31 ff. The contrast between the God-given instinctive wisdom of brutes and the limited laborious learning of man was a standard theme of the physico-theologians: see esp. W. Derham, *Physico-Theology* (1713), Bk. IV, chs. xi and xiii, and cf. Pope, *Ess. on Man* iii. 83–98.

36–41 Cf. Pope, *Ess. on Man* iii. 99–100.

61 *baseless fabrics*: cf. Shakespeare, *Tempest* IV. i. 151. Smart used the same phrase for speculative notions in the *Student* i. 223.

80–102 Quoted in *The Art of Poetry on a New Plan* (1762) as a passage 'singularly sublime and beautiful' (i. 24). The migration of birds is discussed by Derham (op. cit., p. 38 n) as a notable manifestation of the wisdom of the animal world, quoting at length from Louis de Beaufort's *Cosmopœa Divina* (1656) about the skill of birds in navigation, a passage which Smart may have remembered:

Quis eas certum iter in aeris mutabili regione docuit? quis præteritæ signa, et futuræ viæ indicia; ... modumque eius modi loca in peregrinationibus suis inveniendi? Hæc sane superant hominum captum et industriam, qui non nisi longis experientiis, multis itinerariis, chartis graphicis—et acus magneticæ benefico—eiusmodi marium et terrarum tractus conficere tentant et audent.

91 n *Longitude*: in 1714 a Committee was appointed by the government to investigate the problem of finding longitude at sea; much of its most important evidence came from a written statement by Newton enumerating various different methods (see Rupert T. Gould, 'John Harrison and his Timekeepers', *The Mariner's Mirror* xxi, 1935). The search for a solution to this problem is cited by Smart in *ST* i (1750), 250, as an example of man's pursuit of chimeras, but the subject nevertheless engrossed him: see *JA*, B169, B190, B349.

94–9 Cf. Isa. 40: 12, 'Who hath measured the waters in the hollow of his hand, and meted out heaven with a span ... and weighed the mountains in scales, and the hills in a balance?'

100–2 Cf. Thomson, *The Seasons* (1746), 'Summer' 175–8, 'Spring' 203–5.

103–53 Cf. Prior, *Solomon*, Bk 1.

114–15 See Prov. 6: 6–8.

116–18 See *JA*, B340 n.

163 *scale of being*: for this standard conception of nature as a graduated scale or chain, extending upwards from microscopic forms of life to man, and thence through infinite gradations of supernatural beings to God himself, see A. O. Lovejoy, *The Great Chain of Being* (Cambridge, Mass., 1936).

169–70 *o'er the portal ... blade*: Gen. 3: 24.

ΤΩ ΘΕΩ ΔΟΞΑ: 'Glory to God', a liturgical formula, but δόξα also means 'opinion', 'knowledge'.

A New Ballad

Introduced in *GJ* (edited by Arthur Murphy, who collaborated with Smart on *The Hilliad*) with the note: 'The following satyrical ballad on the reigning taste of the town has been handed about here this week. It is said to be a *jeu d'esprit* of Mr. Smart's, whose genius sometimes deigns to descend from flights worthy of its eagle-wing, to the inferior regions of pleasantry, where it gaily amuses itself in pursuit of elegant trifles.' (Reprinted in the *Ladies Mag.* with additional details: see Mahony and Rizzo, Item 470). It is a close imitation of a ballad published in the *Ladies Mag.* on 6 Jan. 1753, called 'The New Comedians', ridiculing the animal acts put on by Rich at Covent Garden theatre, thus contributing to the theatre war between Garrick and Rich: see Betty Rizzo, 'A New Prologue by

Christopher Smart and a Forgotten Skirmish of the Theatre War',
PBSA 68 (1974), 305–10.

The Hilliad

The Hilliad was Smart's major contribution to the paper war started
by Fielding in the first issue of the *Covent-Garden Journal* (4 Jan. 1752)
as a general attack on hack writers. Fielding satirized John Hill
personally in the third number (11 Jan. 1752) but eventually
withdrew from direct engagement, leaving the cudgels to a host of
minor writers, including Arthur Murphy and William Kenrick (see
introduction to the *Covent-Garden Journal*, ed. G. E. Jensen, 1915, i.
29–98). The immediate occasion of the *Hilliad* was an attack on
Smart and Fielding in the first and only issue of a paper called *The
Impertinent* (no original copies of which appear to be extant), pub-
lished anonymously but actually written by Hill, on 13 Aug. 1752.
This was followed up by Hill's disingenuous counter-attack in *The
Inspector* (a daily essay by Hill published in the *London Daily Advertiser*),
no. 464 (25 Aug. 1752). Hill's condescending review of Smart's *Poems
on Several Occasions* in the same month, most of which is quoted
piecemeal in the Prolegomena, did not appease his enemies. Arthur
Murphy joined battle on Smart's behalf in *GJ* in Nov. 1752, but Hill
returned to the attack in Dec. These skirmishes were publicized in the
Supplement to *GM* in Dec. 1752, together with the retorts of Smart
and of John Newbery who by then had also been drawn in (see
Prologomena). For further details of the Smart–Hill quarrel, see
Betty Rizzo, 'Notes on the War between Henry Fielding and John
Hill, 1752–53', *The Library*, 6th ser. vii (1985), 338–53. If Mahony
and Rizzo are right in their attribution to Smart of a satirical
pamphlet dated 29 Apr. 1751 (Item 128), it would seem that the
initial provocation came from Smart even before Fielding began his
campaign: the pamphlet praises Fielding and satirizes his rivals,
including Hill. But Hill had already aroused antagonism in the
literary world in Feb.–Mar. 1751: see G. S. Rousseau, 'Controversy
or Collusion? The Lady Vane Tracts', *N&Q*, ns 19 (1972), 375–8.

John Hill (1714–75) started his career as apprentice to an apoth-
ecary, eventually setting up his own shop in Westminster. He also
studied botany, published numerous scientific works, and tried his
luck, haplessly, on the London stage, on the strength of which he
wrote a treatise on the art of acting. He began his *Inspector* essays in
1750, and published them in a two-volume edition in 1753. On the
quarrel with Smart, Charles Burney's verdict was that 'Hill seems to
have been insensible to the learning and genius of Smart; and Smart
only saw Hill in the light of a quack and a coxcomb: but posterity not

only allows the originality, the invention, and the poetical talents of Smart, but also regards Hill as an able botanist' (*Monthly Rev.*, Jan. 1792, p. 37). The best modern account of Hill's career and writings is G. S. Rousseau's 'John Hill, Universal Genius Manqué', *The Renaissance Man in the Eighteenth Century*, ed. D. Greene (Los Angeles, 1978), pp. 45–129.

The poem is prefaced by a letter from Smart and a lengthy reply, probably by Murphy. The purpose of both is to justify Smart's satire by associating it with the efforts by Pope and Fielding to defend the republic of letters against the corruption of modern taste. The *Notes Variorum* were supplied by Murphy, 'Mr. Smart walking up and down the room, speaking the Verses, and Mr. Murphy writing the notes to them' (Jessé Foot, *Life of Arthur Murphy*, 1811, p. 106). The pseudonym 'Quinbus Flestrin', borrowed from Swift, stands for Samuel Derrick, an Irish author and friend of Hill. 'Martinus Macularius' (from *macula*, a blemish or stigma), adapted partly from 'Martinus Scriblerus' of the *Dunciad*, partly from Kenrick's 'Margelina Scribelinda Macularia' of the *Old Woman's Dunciad* (a satire on the *Midwife*), represents Hill himself.

Motto. Virgil, *Aen.* xii. 948–9: 'It is Pallas, Pallas, who slays you with this stroke, and takes vengeance in your guilty blood.' Smart casts himself with mock-heroic bravura in the role of Aeneas, killing Turnus (Hill) in revenge for the death of young Pallas (Fielding). Fielding was actually Smart's senior by fifteen years.

7–8 The Dublin edition notes the imitation of *Dunciad* (B) i. 19–20: 'O Thou! whatever title please thine ear, / Dean, Drapier, Bickerstaff, or Gulliver!' Cf. Churchill on the 'Proteus Hill': 'Who could so nobly grace the motley list, / Actor, Inspector, Doctor, Botanist?' *The Rosciad* (1761), lines 111–12.

8 n *Hill puffs himself*, etc.: author unidentified. Woodward's *letter*: a satirical pamphlet published in Dec. 1752 in retaliation to an attack on the actor by Hill, with the title *A Letter from Henry Woodward, Comedian, the meanest of all characters, to Dr. John Hill*. The author described Hill's career as an apothecary and ignominious failure as an actor (quoted *GM*, Dec. 1752, pp. 568–9).

17 n *Ye Gods*, etc.: author unidentified, quoted in *Peri Bathous* (Swift–Pope *Miscellanies, The Last Volume*, 1727, p. 52).

19 *new style*: referring to the change in the calendar, which became law in 1752.

25–8 The Dublin edition notes the imitation of Otway's *The Orphan* (ii. 246–56):

I spy'd a wrinkled hag, ...
And on her crooked shoulders had she wrapt
The tatter'd remnant of an old strip'd hanging, ...
Her lower weeds were all o'er coarsely patch'd
With diff'rent colour'd rags, black, red, white, yellow,
And seem'd to speak variety of wretchedness.

50   *tripod*: seat of the Delphic oracle, hence a metonym for oracular power. *triple tree*: slang term for the gallows.

62   Alludes to the notorious occasion on 6 May 1752 when Hill was publicly thrashed at Ranelagh by a young Irishman, Capt. Mountefort Brown, whom he had ridiculed in the *Inspector* of 30 Apr. 1752 (see *The Letters and Papers of Sir John Hill*, ed. G. S. Rousseau, New York, 1982, p. 49). According to Hill, Brown wrote him a letter 'so illiterate that not a Line ... was without some false Spelling.' Hill had also sneered at Fielding's 'misspellings' (Jensen, *op. cit.*, i. 43). In *Libitina Sine Conflictu* (1752), a satirical account of the Ranelagh episode, perhaps written by Murphy, or by Smart himself, the line 'Beware of Irishmen, and learn to knit' is put into Hill's mouth. The source is Gay's 'Beware of Papishes, and learn to knit' (*The What D'ye Call It*, 1715, II. v), as the Dublin edition notes.

69-78   See Shakespeare, *K. Hen. VIII*, III. ii. 351, and *Oth.* III. iii. 352-61. The Dublin edition notes the imitation of Othello's *ear-piercing fife* in line 76, adding, 'which Mr. W. corrects Fear-spersing': a jibe at Warburton's editorial habits (see commentary on *Horatian Canons*).

84 n   *Word-valiant wight*, etc.: see *Epigram. On a certain Scribbler* (Appendix A).

85 n   The authorship of both epigrams is unknown. The second is quoted in Kenrick's *Pasquinade* (line 248 n), a satire published in Jan. 1753, in which both Smart and Hill are targets.

91 n   *An author's writings*, etc.: author unidentified.

108-9   Hill had a diploma in medicine from St Andrews, and was elected a Foreign Member of the Bordeaux Academy of Sciences (see *The Letters and Papers of Sir John Hill*, p. 34 n), on the strength of which he styled himself 'M.D., Acad. Reg. Scient. Burd. &c. Soc.' on the title-page of his *Review of the Works of the Royal Society* (1751).

108 n.   The errors of spelling and accenting in the spoof letter from Bordeaux and the supposed quotations from the tracts below (201 n.) are corrected in *1791* but not in the Dublin edition, and may have been intended as part of the joke.

114-15   The *Letter from Henry Woodward* to Hill refers sarcastically

445

to the 'incredible, nay uncredited Discoveries you have ... made in *Moss, Mites, Cabbage-Leaves, Cherry-Stones, Stinking Oysters,* and *Cockle-Shells*' (p. 7).

119   Hill set up a carved lion's head, said to have been acquired from Steele, at the Bedford Coffee-house as a receptacle for letters to the *Inspector* (Jensen, op. cit., i. 38).

125   The Dublin edition notes an allusion to *Hudibras* II. ii. 627–30, but adds, 'What means the Author by solids sound? A country lady conjectures solids round, or solids brown. Let the reader take which he will.'

143 n.   The parody of *Busy, curious, thirsty fly* was recited by Woodward at Drury Lane theatre in Dec. 1752 (see *GM*, 1752, p. 583).

173   See Horace, *Odes* I. x. 9–12.

176 n.   *Lucina sine concubitu*: a satire by Hill, on the concept of parthenogenesis, published in 1750.

193   *Diamond ... ear*: cf. *Rom. and Jul.* I. v. 44, 'a rich jewel in an Ethiop's ear'. Smart puns on the name of Hill's mistress, identified as 'Miss Diamond, a celebrated Lady, formerly intimately acquainted with the INSPECTOR' in an anonymous pamphlet on the Ranelagh affair, *The Inspector's Rhapsody or Soliloquy, on the loss of his wigg, in a scuffle with some Irish Gentlemen at Ranelagh* (1752), p. 3 n.

193 n   *The Smartiad*, a retort to the *Hilliad* attributed to Samuel Derrick, was in fact published in Feb. 1753 (see Mahony and Rizzo, Item 1183).

213 n.   *Three great wise men*, etc.: probably by Murphy, who printed it in *Gray's-Inn Journal* jokingly attributed to Quinbus Flestrin (Derrick).

229 n.   *On grace, free will*, etc.: author unknown, see Williamson (1973), pp. 118–19.

231 n.   *the earl of* *** ... *G——e D————n*: Mahony and Rizzo suggest the Earl of Middlesex to George Bubb Dodington (Item 134), but the epigram has not been traced.

On St. David's Day 1753

The circumstances in which this ode was written are explained by Moira Dearnley: 'Christopher Smart: some young Cymro in Cambridge', *RES*, NS 19 (1968), 53–8. Smart and the Welsh poet, Goronwy Owen, supplied renderings in Latin and Welsh respectively of a prose address in English, drawn up by an unknown hand, which was to be presented to the young Prince of Wales on St David's Day by his preceptor, the Bishop of Peterborough. For Smart's Welsh ancestry, through his mother, see *JA*, B91.

2 *Thalia* is the muse of Comedy: Smart doubtless alludes to his share in the writing and performance of the Old Woman's Oratory at this period.

10 *qui . . . redonas*: the verb seems to require an indirect object (*nobis*), as on both occasions on which it is used by Horace. Prince George (the future George III) was created Prince of Wales after the death of his father, Prince Frederick, in 1751.

17 *non unquam indignus avorum*: Virgil, *Aen.* xii. 649.

Prologue [*to the Mock Doctor*]

Published anonymously, but identified as Smart's in Cross's diary-notes on the performance of Fielding's *The Mock Doctor* at Drury Lane, 20 Mar. 1753, at which it caused a near-riot. Its satirical target was John Hill, whose feud with Fielding had developed from a paper-war into a theatre-war: see Betty Rizzo, 'A New Prologue by Christopher Smart and a Forgotten Skirmish of the Theatre War', *PBSA* 68 (1974), 305–10. According to Cross, the Prologue ('by the Author of the *Hilliad*') was banned by the licenser but left in the newspaper advertisements by mistake: 'a great noise for it, Wood-ward said; as he had face to study, he had not time to do it—more Noise—I went on—& told 'em the *Prologue* was forbid—Noise still—Woodward went on & said it was forbid by Ld Chamberlain—it cool'd a little but when he came on dress'd like Dr Hill, it began again, & so the farce ended' (*London Stage*, pt. 4, p. 359).

3 *Pæon* was physician to the gods (Homer, *Il.* v. 899).

An Epilogue, spoken by Mrs. Midnight's Daughter

A regular item in the programme of the Old Woman's Oratory from 27 Mar. 1753 onwards. First attributed to Smart in an advertisement for the Oratory in the *Kentish Post* (8–11 Nov. 1758). For full details, see Betty Rizzo, 'Enter the Epilogue on an Ass—By Christopher Smart', *PBSA* 73 (1979), 340–4. The epilogue, Rizzo shows, was 'a Parthian shot' at John Hill, following Smart's attacks in the *Hilliad* and *Prologue to the Mock Doctor*.

3 Alluding to the attack on Hill at Ranelagh in 1752 (see *Hilliad* 62 n). '*Bucks* are fools, who think they have wit, and who have impudence enough to do any thing but what is right. GROTIUS. *Beau*, a name for any thing that is insipid and ridiculous. PUFFENDORF.' Notes in *CP6*.

8 *caxon*: a kind of wig. The ass, with her wig and her 'arts Æsculapian', represents Dr Hill.

14 'It is a melancholly consideration, saith *Celsus*, but true it is, that when diseases have baffled the art of the physicians, they are obliged to call in the aid of the *ass*, who very often, by her secret cunning and wonderful workings, doth despise those disorders that were deemed incurable, and snatch the patient both from death and the doctors. This observation from the great *Celsus*, calleth to my mind the verdict of a jury, who sat on a man that died in consequence of a fall from one of the horses that started for the plate at —— races. In this case the horse is usually forfeited to the Lord of the Manor; to prevent which, or rather because he was attended by six physicians, the Jury brought in their verdict *Dead of the Doctors*. Jewson's *Reports*.' Note in *CP6*.

22 '*Ridden*. Clients are said to be ridden; because they pay the lawyer money; but the lawyer payeth them no money; (*ergo*) therefore is the lawyer not ridden. Coke *upon* Littleton.' Note in *CP6*.

The Dust Cart

Discovered by Betty Rizzo: see 'Christopher Smart's Burlesque Cantata, "The Dust Cart" ', *N&Q* 31 (1984), 11–13. It was set to music by James Oswald and first performed in the Old Woman's Oratory in Apr. 1753. Smart is named as the author in an advertisement for the Oratory in the *Bath Advertiser* (12 Mar. 1757). The only text with any sort of authority is the songsheet published at Oswald's music shop in St Martin's Church-yard, London, but punctuation etc. has been revised in accordance with the printed version in *The Town Whim*. Oswald was a close associate of Charles Burney: see R. Lonsdale, *Dr. Charles Burney* (Oxford, 1965), pp. 28–34.

The Bite

This epigram, signed 'Kitty Smart', and possibly in his handwriting, was discovered among the papers of Henry Fox (later Lord Holland) by Betty Rizzo, who notes (*RES* n.s. xxxvii, 1986) that it refers to two controversial bills which passed through parliament in May–June 1753: the Jewish Naturalization Bill, and the Marriage Act, outlawing clandestine marriages. Fox supported the first (as expected of a member of Government), but attacked the second. He had himself eloped in 1744 with Lady Georgiana Lennox. The point of the epigram depends on the fact that Jews were excepted from the Marriage Act.

Ode to Lord Barnard

Henry Vane, 3rd Baron Barnard (1705-58) succeeded to the title on the death of his father in April 1753. He was a Whig MP, Paymaster-General (1742-4), lord of the Treasury (1749-55), and lord-lieut. of Co. Durham, where Raby Castle, the family seat, is situated. Smart's father was steward to the junior branch of the Vanes in Kent, but when Christopher went north to Durham School he was taken under the wing of Henry Vane's family, and 'was cordially received at Raby Castle, when absent, during the holidays, from School' (Hunter, I, p. vii).

Motto. Horace, *Odes* III. xxvii. 13-14: 'May you be happy wheresoever you chuse to reside, and live mindful of me' (Smart).

21-2   Vane was created Earl of Darlington in Apr. 1754.

36   *Cleveland*: the duchess of Cleveland (1705-42), Vane's sister-in-law, 'discerned and patronized [Smart's] talents. She allowed him forty pounds a year until her death' (Hunter, I, p. vii): see *Epitaph on the late Dutchess of Cleveland. Hope*: Vane's daughter Anne, Smart's 'Ethelinda' (see commentary, *To Ethelinda*), married Charles Hope Weir, or Vere, brother of the Earl of Hopetoun, in 1746.

To the Rev. Mr. Powell

Introduced in *GJ* with the note, 'The Author of an excellent poem upon a very bad subject, *viz.* the *Hilliad*, has been indisposed for some time past, but we had the pleasure of seeing him here a few days since, and the following pleasant piece of poetry shews that he has again held dalliance with his Muse.' (The editor, Arthur Murphy, was Smart's collaborator on the *Hilliad*). Evan Pritchard, the original subject, has not been identified. Morgan Powell, a Cambridge contemporary of Smart's, came from Carmarthenshire; he entered St Catharine's College in 1742, received his BA in 1746 and took orders in the same year. He was a subscriber to Smart's *Psalms*.

13-14   Quoted by Coleridge as an example of the 'lower species of wit' provided by trisyllabic rhymes (*Biographia Literaria*, ed. G. Watson, 1975, p. 207).

19   The killing of hares was permitted only to those with property qualifications laid down under the Game Laws.

33   See 'The Cock and Pearl' in Smart's *Phædrus*, Book III, fable xi.

The Tea-Pot and Scrubbing-Brush

7   *beaufet*: sideboard (buffet).

To the Memory of Master Newbery

John Newbery, elder son of the publisher and a boy 'of singular acuteness and sense', according to his brother Francis, 'had the misfortune so to injure his spine by a fall down some stone steps when a child, that he died after a lingering illness, aged eleven years' (C. Welsh, *A Bookseller of the Last Century*, 1885, p. 7). He died in the winter of 1751.

The Fair Monopolist

Published anonymously in Smart's lifetime, but ascribed to him in the *European Magazine* (1791, p. 461), one of whose proprietors was Isaac Reed, a friend of Francis Newbery, Smart's stepbrother-in-law. See Betty Rizzo, 'Christopher Smart's Song "The Patriot Fair" ', *PBSA* 69 (1975), 394–8.

On the Power of the Supreme Being

The fourth of Smart's Seatonian poems (see Introduction). The prize was awarded on 5 Dec. 1753.

1–3   See Ps. 114.

51–6   Severe earth tremors shook London in Feb. and Mar. 1750, causing negligible damage but great consternation. Many families left town for fear of a third earthquake, the Bishop of Oxford preached a sermon on the event, and the Bishop of London published a *Letter . . . to the Clergy and People of London* (1750), interpreting the earthquakes as a warning against the sins of the citizens and a summons to repentance. Dearnley (p. 108) suggests that Smart's lines are a conscious paraphrase of the bishop's rhetoric. For a cool contemporary account of reactions to the shocks, see Walpole, *Corresp.* vol. 20, pp. 133–7.

80–1   *sympathy* was the pre-Newtonian explanation of magnetic attraction: cf. *JA*, B165–6.

82   'The most remarkable property of *Amber*, is, that, when rubbed, it draws or attracts other bodies to it' (Chambers).

83–4   *when . . . frame*: refers to experiments with electricity, using glass globes, which excited public interest in the 1740s. See *GM* (1745), pp. 193–7.

85–7   'Electricity is a vast country, of which we know only some bordering provinces; it is yet unseasonable to give a map of it, and pretend to assign the laws by which it is governed.' *GM* (1745) p. 195.

113–45   A tissue of Biblical allusions: the principal texts only are cited below.

114–15   Mal. 4: 2, Luke 1: 78–9.

116–19   Mark 4: 37–9.

127–9   Matt. 11: 30.

129–30   Ps. 23, Isa. 40: 11.

132–5   Isa. 61: 11, 2 Cor. 2: 15.

137–9   Ps. 24: 7, Rev. 21: 25–6.

143–5   1 Tim. 6: 15–16, Rev. 19; 16.

On my Wife's Birth-Day

1   *Nancy's birth-day*: 26 Jan. (see *Ode on the 26th of January*).

The Brocaded Gown

27   *gasconading*: extravagant boasting.

28–32   The punctuation of *GM* is preferred here to *1791*, which mangles the sense.

31–2   Probably an allusion to Horace, *Sat.* 1. x, who argues that satire is often most effective when it combines humour with gravity ('modo tristi, sæpe iocoso').

43   William *Murray*, 1st Earl of Mansfield (1705–93), was called to the bar in 1730 and rose through Solicitor-General (1742) and Attorney-General (1754) to Lord Chief Justice (1756–88). He was renowned for his oratory, which was based on intensive study of classical models (cf. *Disertissime Romuli Nepotum*). For his early interest in Smart's poetic career, see commentary on *De Arte Critica*. Murray's wife, Elizabeth Finch, was the sister of Smart's patron, the Duchess of Cleveland.

49   *Athenian AKENSIDE*: Mark Akenside (1721–70) dedicated his philosophic poem, *The Pleasures of Imgaination* (1744) to the 'Genius of ancient Greece', pledging himself to 'tune to Attic themes the British lyre' (i. 567–604).

53–4   William *Collins* (1721–59) is presumably associated with Melpomene, the muse of Tragedy, because of his *Dirge in Cymbeline* and his skill as a writer of elegiac odes.

55–8   Thomas *Gray* (1716–71) earns the epithet *Augustan* by the classical qualities of his odes, but the famous *Elegy* (1751) appears to be the subject of 57–8.

59–62   William *Mason* (1725–97) was a Fellow of Pembroke College, Cambridge; he had staked his claim as a poet with the publication in 1747 of *Musæus: a monody to the memory of Mr. Pope*, in imitation of Milton's *Lycidas*.

The Blockhead and Beehive

Written not later than Mar. 1754, when Henry Pelham died (see line 113).

15   *assert*: lay claim to (*OED* II. 4).

32   Francis *Hayman* (1708–76), a popular and successful painter, was one of the original members of the Royal Academy. He was a friend of Smart's and provided illustrations for his *Poems on Several Occasions* (1752).

59–61   The beehive was a stock example of the superiority of Nature to Art in architecture: cf. *Immensity*, 121–2 and n.

62   *Gunter's line*: the rule of proportion introduced by the Elizabethan mathematician, Edmund Gunter.

66   William *Whiston* (1667–1752) succeeded Newton as Lucasian Professor of Mathematics at Cambridge, and published numerous works on mathematical subjects.

76   Maintenance of a standing army was a perennial subject of dispute in the 18th c. Smart's allusion may have been prompted by the debate in parliament on this issue in Nov. 1753.

106   *Jobson*: a country fellow, a lout (*OED*).

107   *Hardwick*: Philip Yorke, Earl of Hardwicke (1690–1764) was Lord Chancellor 1737–56.

110   *Murray*: see *The Brocaded Gown and Linen Rag*, 43 n.

111   *Vane*: Smart's patron, Henry Vane: see note on *Ode to Lord Barnard*.

113   Henry *Pelham* (1696–1754), Prime Minister 1746–54, was courted as a patron of learning and the arts by most of the leading writers of the time, including Pope, Thomson, Fielding, and Young.

The Citizen and the Red Lion of Brentford

The reference to the *new Pantheon* (l. 57) suggests 1753–4 as the probable date of composition. *The New Pantheon: or, Fabulous History of the Heathen Gods*, by Samuel Boyse, was published in Nov. 1753. It was reprinted in 1760 and 1764, but by then Smart was estranged from Newbery. Hunter (I, pp. xxxviii–xxxix) criticized the poem on the grounds that it 'transgressed the limits of mythological probability' by giving the power of speech and action to a painted lion. He argued that it was acceptable to give human functions to natural creatures, 'But when art assumes the person of nature; when the lion of the painter roars, and shakes his mane, and reasons like his archetype in the forest; when imitation exercises functions, which it is an indulgence to suppose even in the original, the mind rejects the fiction as improbable, and revolts against it as absurd.'

7   *the bills*: i.e. the bills of mortality for London, hence the district of London.

19–20   Cf. *Hop-Garden* ii. 52.

22   *Pilgarlick*: poor creature, usually used of oneself, 'poor me'.

30   *BALL*: a horse's name. *booby-hutch*: small clumsy cart.

80   *Jack Ellis*: John Ellis, or Ellys (1701–57) who held the sinecure of master-keeper of the lions in the Tower of London was principal painter to Frederick, Prince of Wales.

Martial. Book I, Ep. 26

Martial's 'Coniugis audisset fatum cum Porcia Bruti', Ep. i. 42 in modern editions.

On a Lady throwing Snow-Balls

Published in Renaissance editions of Petronius Arbiter's *Satiricon*, but now regarded as spurious. It is printed in Ernout's edition (Paris, 1958), p. 203. For the appellation 'Afranius', see Ernout, p. xii n.

Antipater's Greek Epigram

Published with the signature 'C.S.' in the *Poetical Calendar*, which was edited by Smart's friends, Francis Fawkes and William Woty. The original appears in the Greek Anthology (*Pal Anth*. ix. 418); the first two lines are quoted in *JA*, B82.

The Famous Epigram of Sannazarius on Venice

Signed 'Z.A.', initials used by Smart for two other translations of Latin epigrams, printed in the previous issue of *GM*. This translation is printed together with the original and another English version by J. Banks (see Mahony and Rizzo, Item 493). Jacopo Sannazaro (1458–1530) was best known for his pastoral romance, *Arcadia*; the epigram on Venice is included in his *Opera Latina* (Amsterdam, 1689), Ep. I. xxxvi.

An Epitaph ... in the church of St. Botolph

Signed 'Z.A.' (see note on previous poem). The church was in fact in Aldersgate. For another translation, attributed to Pope, see Pope's *Poems* vi. 449.

To Miss S—— P——e

Published in *GM* with a letter signed 'J.K.' explaining that 'it was addressed to a young lady who was an intimate friend of the author's mistress, and who, at the time it was written, was in love with a gentleman of his acquaintance.'

1   *Nancy*: Smart's wife.

An Invitation to Mrs. Tyler

Mrs Tyler was probably the wife of Robert Tyler (1700–66), vicar of St Lawrence, Isle of Thanet, the neighbouring parish to St Peter's where Smart's friend Thomas Reynolds kept a school (see *Epitaph on the Rev. Mr. Reynolds*). Tyler had earlier been vicar of Sittingbourne, Kent (1723–40), near Smart's childhood home at Shipbourne. The model for these colloquial invitation poems was Prior's *Extempore Invitation to the Earl of Oxford: The Literary Works of Matthew Prior*, ed. H. B. Wright and M. K. Spears (Oxford 1971), i. 399–400.

An Inscription on a Column

[*Lucian's Greek Epigram* in Mahony and Rizzo]. Published in *Poetical Calendar* with the signature 'C.S.'; signed 'S.' in *GM* and published on the same page as *An Invitation to Mrs Tyler*. The original (Ep. 13 in the Teubner Lucian) appears in the Greek Anthology (ix. 74). First published under Smart's name in *Select Epigrams* (1797), i. 34.

2–4   *John o' Nokes* and *John o' Stiles* are conventional names for parties in a lawsuit.

The Duellists

The short-lived *Daily Magazine*, in which the fable was published in 1773, was edited by William Kenrick (see Mahony and Rizzo, Item 803). In view of Smart's friendship with Kenrick in the 1760s (see *Munificence and Modesty* and notes), it is possible that the textual variants in *DM* are based on authorial copy of some kind.

38   *monomachy*: single combat.

40   *montant* and *passado* are terms for sword-strokes in fencing.

60   *loggerheads*: thickheads, fools.

Epitaph on the Rev. Mr. Reynolds

Thomas Reynolds matriculated at University College, Oxford, in 1740. In 1752 he opened a school at Ramsgate, Isle of Thanet, which was attended by Francis Newbery, son of John Newbery, from 1752 to 1754. Reynolds died in Oct. 1754 and was buried at St Peter-in-Thanet (see Dearnley, pp. 129–30).

The English Bull Dog, Dutch Mastiff, and Quail
'Written ... when his Grace the Duke of Devonshire (then Lord Hartington) was appointed Lord Lieutenant of Ireland' (introductory note in *GM*). The appointment was gazetted on 27 Mar. 1755; Hartington succeeded to the dukedom on the death of his father in Dec. 1755.

8   The traditional distinction between those born west and east, respectively, of the Medway.

11   This idea, current in pre-Socratic philosophy, was revived in Berkeley's *Siris* (1744), sect. 166.

24   *hogan mogan*: contemptuous term for Dutchmen.

40   *Farrinellied*: i.e. castrated, from the name of the celebrated male soprano, Carlo Farinelli (1705–82).

44   'And thus much is certain, that British Dogs have been thought preferable to all others in Europe', William Camden, *Britannia*, tr. E. Gibson (2nd edn., 1722), i. 139. The use of the English bulldog for patriotic self-glorification was already standard in the 18th c; see e.g. *The Craftsman* (13 Sept. 1729): 'that antient genuine Race of *true-bred English Bull-Dogs* ... excelling in Fight; victorious over their Enemies; undaunted in Death', etc.

59–60   *Tretchscutz*: from Du. *trekschuit*, 'track-boat', a horse-drawn vessel in common use on canals and rivers in Holland. *cymbal*: applied in 18th c. loosely to various kinds of musical instrument, but here the reference is clearly to the hurdy-gurdy.

67–8   At the battle of *Fontenoy* (1745), in which the allies were heavily defeated by the French, the British and Hanoverians fought bravely but the Dutch forces took shelter from the enemy fire and failed to support them.

89 ff.   Alluding to the dispute of 1751–3 over the money-bill, which led to the appointment of Lord Hartington. The Irish parliament claimed the right to dispose of surplus revenue, but this was denied by the English government, which insisted that it was a royal prerogative. The dispute developed into an impassioned constitutional debate, against the background of continuing Irish grievances over poverty and neglect of the province. It reached a climax in 1753 when a bill incorporating a clause asserting the royal prerogative was defeated in the Irish parliament, to the jubilation of the Dublin populace. The removal of the previous Crown representa-

tive, the Duke of Dorset, and the appointment of Lord Hartington in his place, was intended as a conciliatory move and clearly welcomed by Smart as such. For background and details, see J. C. Beckett, *The Making of Modern Ireland 1603–1923* (1966), pp. 193–4, and W. E. Lecky, *A History of England in the Eighteenth Century* (1879), ii. 431–4.

The Country Squire and the Mandrake

10   The name *Trelooby* comes from *Squire Trelooby*, a farce by Vanbrugh, Congreve and others.

19   *Affected: Afflicted* in *1791* was said by Burney to be 'an error of the press' (*Monthly Rev.* 1792, p. 43).

53–4   The resemblance of a mandrake root to the figure of a man was legendary: see Sir T. Browne, *Pseudodoxia Epidemica; Works*, ed. G. Keynes (1964), ii. 140–2.

Epitaph on Mrs. Rolt

Signed 'S' in *GM*. Anne Rolt died 22 Feb. 1755, aged 24; she was the wife of Richard Rolt, a close friend of Smart and co-editor of the *UV*, in which Rolt's own epitaph for his wife was published.

On the Goodness of the Supreme Being

The fifth of Smart's Seatonian poems (see Introduction). The prize was awarded on 28 Oct. 1755. According to Hunter (I, p. xvi). Smart's entry was composed in London and delayed so long 'that there was barely opportunity to write it upon paper, and to send it to Cambridge by the most expeditious conveyance, within the time limited for the Compositions.' It was dedicated to the Earl of Darlington, Smart's old patron, Henry Vane. James Grainger, reviewing for the *Monthly Rev.* (June 1756, pp. 554–7) found it inferior to Smart's other prize poems, charging it with incorrect grammar and lack of logical coherence.

1–2   'What if *Orpheus* in *Thrace* was no other than *David* in *Paran?*' Patrick Delany, *An Historical Account of the Life and Reign of David King of Israel* (1740), i. 195. Delany argued that the legend of Orpheus was derived from the actual history of David.

11–15   Cf. Milton, *PL* i. 17–23.

15–17   Cf. Milton, *PL* vii. 12–14.

59–70   Cf. Milton, *Il Penseroso*, 155–66.

72   *cherub Gratitude*: see *Omniscience*, 6 n.

94   *Araby the blest*: Milton, *PL* iv. 163.

119–23   See Eph. 6: 11–17, and *Hymns* (1771) 8. 9–16.

124–6   Cf. *Hymns* 1. 37–44.

Epilogue [to The Conscious Lovers]

The benefit performance of Steele's comedy, for which this epilogue was written, was part of a 'grand Entertainment' given for governors of the Middlesex Hospital and other guests on 5 Dec. 1755 by the Earl of Northumberland to celebrate the countess's birthday: see C. Ryskamp, 'Christopher Smart and the Earl of Northumberland', *The Augustan Milieu: essays presented to Louis A. Landa*, ed. H. K. Miller, E. Rothstein, and G. S. Rousseau (Oxford, 1970), pp. 323–7. But by casting Shuter as man-midwife, Smart contrived to combine a compliment to Northumberland with publicity for 'Mrs. Midnight' and the Old Woman's Oratory.

10–14   The alteration in line 10 and addition of lines 11–14 were made in an announcement in *LM* (Appendix, 1755, p. 626) and incorporated in *1791* but not in earlier publications.

Epilogue to the Apprentice

Arthur Murphy's comedy *The Apprentice*, was first performed on 2 Jan. 1756 at Drury-Lane. Kitty Clive (1711–85), Garrick's leading lady, was renowned for her gifts as a comic actress (see Boswell's *Life of Johnson*, iv. 243, and Churchill, *The Rosciad*, 686–94). The play concerns a group of apprentices who are members of a 'spouting club' (i.e. amateur theatrical company). The epilogue was said by the *Critical Rev.* to contain 'some humour and a good deal of pert vivacity' (1756, p. 82), but the *Monthly Rev.* commented that it 'affords nothing remarkable, except the last two lines, which are certainly the most unfortunate ones that ever were penned by a man of genius' (1756, p. 78).

6   Mrs Clive's *The Rehearsal, or Bayes in Petticoats* was published and performed in 1753.

8   The prologue to the *Apprentice*, written by Garrick and spoken by Woodward, began: 'Prolgues precede the piece in mournful verse, / As UNDERTAKERS walk before the hearse'.

11   In Buckingham's *The Rehearsal* Bayes describes his model prologue, in which 'I come out in a long black veil, and a great huge hang-man behind me'.

15   Alluding to Buckingham's *Rehearsal*, IV. i. In a performance on 15 Sept. 1755 the part of Pallas was played by 'Mrs. Midnight', possibly Smart himself (*London Stage*, Pt. 4, p. 491).

23   *Damn'd, damn'd dissembler*: spoken by Zara in Congreve's *The Mourning Bride*, III. ii (the part of Zara was played by Mrs Clive herself in 1753).

25   *O ponder well ... Chevy Chase*: popular broadside ballads, adapted by Gay in *The Beggar's Opera*.

32–4   See Vanbrugh and Cibber, *The Provok'd Husband*, I. i (performed at Covent Garden 1755–6).

'Hail, Energeia!'

From an essay titled 'Some Thoughts on the English Language', signed 'S.' and confirmed by Ann Gardner: see Introduction (ii). On the subject of English heroic verse, the essay concludes: 'The iambic, though used by the *Latin* tragedians, is too quick a measure for the purpose. But the *English* tongue, abounding more with monosyllables and consonants, adds a weight and dignity to the spirit of the measure, so that, upon the whole, it is extremely animated and majestic.'

1   Cf. Milton: 'Hail, native language, that by sinews weak / Didst move my first endeavoring tongue to speak' (*At a Vacation Exercise in the College*, 1–2).

5–10   Cf. Pope, *Essay on Criticism*, 366–71.

To the Earl of Darlington

Henry Vane, created Earl of Darlington in Apr. 1754, was appointed Paymaster to the Forces on 16 Dec. 1755.

1–2   Lines 21–4 of *Ode to Lord Barnard*, prophesying Vane's promotion, are printed as epigraph to this poem in *1791*.

4   Cf. *On St. David's Day 1753*, 19.

Stanzas, occasioned by the Generosity of the English

Signed 'S.' and printed on the same page as *To the Earl of Darlington*. The great Lisbon earthquake occurred in Nov. 1755; the English parliament immediately voted £100,000 for relief. The 'Monthly Memorialist' in *UV* commented: 'We have lived to see the most remarkable and tremendous accident that ever happened in the world, except the general deluge: *Portugal* has more immediately felt the blow; and, as she has the most intimate connexions with *Great-Britain*, she has received the strongest proofs of its favour and affection, in alleviating her distress by an uncommon generosity peculiar to the *British* nation' (p. 48).

'The sword of liberty, with God-like view'

Signed 'S.' and confirmed by Ann Gardner: see Introduction (ii). The original text (from Athenaeus, xv. 695) is printed in 'Further Remarks on Dr. Lowth's celebrated Prelections' with the comment: 'The preceding *Greek* ballad (for such it is) written by one *Callistratus*, and sung in all the streets of *Athens*, kept up a spirit of liberty amongst the people, which the morals of muzzy philosophers, and the declamations of orators, never could do' (*UV*, p. 74). Harmodius and Aristogiton were celebrated in Athens as champions of liberty after their attempt to kill the tyrant, Hippias, in 514 BC. They slew his younger brother, Hipparchus, but Harmodius was killed by a guard and Aristogiton was caught and executed.

To Health

Signed 'S.' and confirmed by Ann Gardner: see Introduction (ii).

1–2 Cf. Dryden's song from *King Arthur*, 'Fairest isle, all isles excelling, / . . . Venus here, will chuse her dwelling'.

4–8 See Milton, *PL* iv. 161–3, and *Goodness*, 94–5.

40 Another allusion to the Lisbon earthquake: see *Stanzas, occasioned by the Generosity of the English.*

Faber Acicularius

Signed 'S.' and confirmed by Ann Gardner: see Introduction (ii).

Motto: Virgil, *Georg.* iv. 6.

1 The line is metrically defective: I am grateful to Mr J. G. Griffith for suggesting *domina* to fill the gap.

6 *junctis . . . equis*: perhaps intended metonymically for a carriage.

7 *bombycinus orbis*: presumably a pin-cushion.

9 *metuenda virago*: the phrase is used by Ovid of Minerva (Pallas Athene, see line 24 *infra*) in combative mood, *Met.* ii. 765.

15 ff. The game of *push-pin* involved two players, each attempting by pushing their respective weapons to cross the pin of the other.

17 Virgil, *Aen.* xi. 291, referring to Hector and Aeneas.

18. *tripode*: perhaps a three-legged stool or stand used for the game.

24 Pallas Athene provided Perseus with the mirror which enabled him to kill the Gorgon Medusa.

29 *leo virginibus . . . amicus*: Thomas Warton notes, 'It is the doctrine of romance, that a lion will offer no injury to a true virgin.'

Observations on the Faery Queen of Spenser (2nd edn., London 1762), ii. 128–9. See *FQ* I. iii. 5 ff.

30 Smart's conceit depends on the double equation of the pin with the magnetic needle and the coldness of chastity with the frozen north.

Hymn to the Supreme Being

Published in June 1756. Title and content suggest that the Hymn was intended as a pendant to the Seatonian Prize poems on the attributes of the Supreme Being, to which specific allusion is made (55–6). The poem was dedicated to Dr James, inventor of the famous fever powder and author of a compendious *Medicinal Dictionary* (see *Johnson's England*, ed. A. S. Turberville, 1933, ii. 276). In his dedicatory letter, Smart attributes his recovery from the illness which occasioned the poem to Dr James, whose 'judgment and medicines rescued me from the grave . . . in a manner almost miraculous.' But it is clear from the poem itself that Smart had passed through a spiritual as well as a physical crisis, and had emerged with a new sense of Christian commitment (67–78). This did not however commend it to the *Critical Rev.* which found 'more gratitude than genius, and more piety than poetry' in the Hymn (June 1756, p. 482).

Title-page: ΤΩ ΘΕΩ ΔΟΞΑ: 'Glory to God' (cf. end of *Omniscience*).

55–6 *Eternity, Immensity, Omniscience* and *Goodness*, in that order, are four of the five attributes celebrated in Smart's Seatonian poems.

85–6 Pindar, *Ol.* i. 1–2.

91–2 Cf. *Immensity*, 56–9.

97–102 Charity is similarly elevated in *Hymns* (1771), 3: the source is 1 Cor. 13. Cf. also *Goodness*, 119–26.

A Story of a Cock and a Bull

8 Cf. Garrick, 'Upon Johnson's Dictionary', *GM* (Apr. 1755), p. 190, ll. 1–2: 'Talk of war with a Briton, he'll boldly advance, / That one English soldier is worth ten of France.' The supposed superiority (by various ratios) was proverbial: see Addison, *Spectator* No. 383, Chesterfield's *Letters*, 7 Feb. 1749, Goldsmith, *Citizen of the World*, Letter 119. The chain that 'One Englishman can beat *five* Frenchmen' is quoted in *MW* (i. 246) among 'Things to be laugh'd at: Or a Collection of honest Prejudices'.

19 *dervise*: dervish.

42 *main*: cock-fight.

To the Author of some defamatory Verses

Published anonymously in *GM* (see R. Lonsdale, 'Christopher Smart's first publication in English', *RES*, NS 12 (1961), 403). The first four lines were ascribed to Smart in George Dyer's 'Cantabrigiana' column in *MM* (July 1803), p. 539. Dyer was a close friend of Elizabeth Le Noir, who also contributed *Lines with a pocket book* to Dyer's column.

1–2 Cf. *JA*, B118. The simile also occurs in an epigram of unknown date, beginning 'When Chloe I confess my pain', ascribed to Kenrick in *A Collection of Select Epigrams*, ed. J. Hackett (1757), no. 255:

> Thus for the viper's sting we know,
>   No surer remedy is found,
> Than to apply the tort'ring foe,
>   And squeeze his venom on the wound.

9–10 No *Charles* among the many so-named among Smart's friends has been convincingly identified as the victim of vilification.

Ad Cicadam

Signed 'S.' and confirmed by Ann Gardner: see Introduction (ii). A free rendering of *Anacreontea*, Ode 34 (Loeb edn.).

10–11 *laborum / Dulce lenimen*: Horace, *Odes* i. xxxii. 14–15.

14–15 Perhaps an echo of Horace, *Odes* ii. xvi. 37–9.

22 An adaptation of Catullus, li. 1, 'Ille mi par esse deo videtur'.

'Beneath this fragrant myrtle shade'

Signed 'S.' and confirmed by Ann Gardner: see Introduction (ii). A free rendering of *Anacreontea*, Ode 32 (Loeb edn.).

The Furniture of a Beau's Mind

Signed 'S.' and confirmed by Ann Gardner: see Introduction (ii). Modelled on Swift's *The Furniture of a Woman's Mind*.

Motto. Persius, *Sat.* i. i. 1: 'What emptiness there is in human affairs!'

17 *Joe Millar*: i.e. *Joe Miller's Jests*, a popular compilation, first published in 1739.

30 Alluding to Richardson's *Sir Charles Grandison* (1753–4); Edward Kimber's *Life and Adventure's of James Ramble, Esq*; (1755); *The Adventures of the Rev. Mr. Judas Hawkes, the Rev. Mr. Nathan Briggs, Miss Lucretia Briggs, &c., late inhabitants of the island Querumania, after the manner of Joseph Andrews* (1751).

33–6   Cf. Swift, *The Furniture of a Woman's Mind*, 57–62:

> O Yes! If any Man can find
> More Virtues in a Woman's Mind,
> Let them be sent to Mrs. *Harding*;
> She'll pay the Charges to a Farthing:
> Take Notice, she has my Commission
> To add them in the next Edition.

The Forty-Second Psalm

Signed 'S': not confirmed by Ann Gardner, but accepted by Jones and there is no reason to doubt the attribution, even though Smart used a different version in his *Psalms*. The present text follows the 15-verse arrangement of the Psalter, not the 11-verse AV version, but draws on both for its phraseology.

28–30   Neither the Psalter nor the AV assigns such a crusading role to the speaker. Psalter: 'I went with the multitude, and brought them forth into the house of God; In the voice of praise and thanksgiving'. AV: 'I went with them to the house of God, with the voice of joy and praise'.

86   *saving health* Christianized the original: Psalter 'help of my countenance', AV 'health of my countenance'.

Disertissime Romuli Nepotum

An imitation of Catullus, *Carm.* xlix (the original is printed in *UV*). Written not later than 1756, when Murray was created Baron Mansfield. See *The Brocaded Gown and Linen Rag*, 43 n.

The 100th Psalm

Published under Smart's name in *CM*, a Newbery publication, edited by William Dodd.

18   *menceful*: a genuine dialect word, but scarcely appropriate here; it means well-behaved, sensible, generous (*Scot. Nat. Dict.*).

19–20   As in *The Forty-Second Psalm*, Smart Christianizes the original ('For the Lord is gracious, his mercy is everlasting: and his truth endureth from generation to generation', Psalter).

Epitaph on the late Mr. Sheels

Published in *1763B* with the inscription: 'Sacred to the memory of the Rev'd James Sheeles A.B. late of Trinity College, in the University of Cambridge; and by the honourable patronage of the Earl of Northumberland, minister of this parish [identified in footnote as

Long-Burton]; a young gentleman of great hopes, and singular benevolence: who having served in the church no longer than one year and three months, was remanded to his master on the 29th day of October, 1762, in the 24th year of his age. His affectionate father has indulged his grief with this tribute to his ashes.'

Sheeles was educated at Eton and Trinity; at the time of his death he was curate and vicar-designate of Long-Burton, Dorset, where both he and his father, John Sheeles (master of a well-known boarding school in Queen's Square, London) are buried (Hutchins's *History of Dorset*, 3rd edn., 1873, iv. 135). Smart's connection with the family probably came through Charles Burney, who was music-master at the Sheeles's school. James Sheeles contributed a Hebrew poem to the Cambridge University obsequies on George II (1760), and published an elegy for Lady Elizabeth Percy titled *Threnodia Northumbrica* (1761), and a *Sermon on the Fast* (1762).

2   *preferr'd*: presented (*OED* II. 4).

4   Cf. Christ's words at the appointment of the seventy disciples: 'The harvest truly is great, but the labourers are few' (Luke 10: 2), and Smart's *Parables*, 55.

5   *likeliest*: most promising (*OED* 4a).

Reason and Imagination

The text appears in full only in *1763*: the suppression of all or part of 1–26 and 139–60 in *GM* and *1791* was probably due to their obscurity (see Introduction).

William Kenrick (1725?–79), a journalist and miscellaneous writer, was witheringly characterized by Johnson as 'one of the many who have made themselves *publick*, without making themselves *known*' (*Boswell's Life*, i. 479). He was a literary rival and opponent of Smart in the 1750s but a reconciliation, it appears from the poem (141), had recently taken place. Among his more serious writings was *Epistles Philosophical and Moral* (1759), a set of verse discourses in octosyllabic couplets, designed to establish science and reason as the grounds of truth. *Reason and Imagination* seems to be intended as an answer to this contention. Kenrick's third epistle contains an illustrative fable of Reason and Genius, which may have prompted Smart to cast his answer in the form of a fable, although it is possible, as Callan suggested (i. 372), that the fable itself was of earlier composition, furnished with an introduction and epilogue for the occasion.

Smart concurs with Kenrick in valuing reason and distrusting fancy (139–40), but argues for an alliance between the two rather than a slavish subjection of one to the other (124–32). Where he disagrees most radically with Kenrick is in his belief in a supra-rational truth. The frame passages are in fact consonant with Smart's religious poetry of the same period, and need to be read in that context. In *JA* and the *Hymns* he constantly insists on the supremacy of revelation as the source of truth, and on the sufficiency of the Christian message for man's guidance. His belief centres, above all, on the saving power of the Word, incarnate in Christ and revealed in the scriptures. Kenrick's scheme, which is heavily indebted to Locke and to Pope's *Essay on Man*, acknowledges a divine plan in the universe, but subordinates revelation to reason and demonstrative science as the source of truth. His final epistle debates the question of the immortality of the soul but bypasses the Christian scheme of salvation altogether, grounding the hope of everlasting life on man's godlike powers of understanding. Science, he concludes, is the 'Jacob's ladder whereby man attains to heaven' (Ep. viii. 486–8). For Smart, on the contrary, it is the founding truth embodied in Christ and manifested in the gospels which shows the way to eternal happiness (151–60).

Motto (from title-page of *1763*). Phaedrus v. v. 1–3: 'Men are wont to err through prejudice, and when they stand up in defence of their error are liable to be forced to admit their mistake by the plain facts.'

17–22 Smart places his fable within both classical and Christian tradition (see Introduction). The *Sabine grove* is Horace's famous retreat (Kenrick too claimed Horace as his mentor); *Where Wisdom ... lyre* perhaps alludes to Horace's well-known dictum, *Scribendi recte sapere est et principium et fons* ('Wisdom is the source and fount of good writing', *Ars Poet.* 310). The story dates from the birth of Christ (the coming of the WORD) which signalized the conjunction of *Elegance* and *Sense* (21). *Elegance* is the special attribute of a consecrated language for Smart (see *Hymns* 2. 49–54 and commentary): cf. *Hymns* (1771) 13, in which *Elegance* is the umbrella term for the conduct of faithful Christians ('the great elect'). Smart apparently had in mind the putative derivation of *elegance* from L *eligere*, to choose: language may be 'chosen' in the sense that the faithful are God's 'chosen' people. *Conferr'd*, similarly, is used with its root meaning from L *conferre*, '(were) brought together', an archaic sense of *confer* still current in the 18th c. For the combination of *elegance* and *sense*, cf. *Female Dignity*, 18.

20 Cf. *Hymns* 9. 39–40.

23–6 Probably referring to the parables: cf. *Parables* 22. 11–14.

37–60 The portrayal of Imagination as a winged nymph may have been intended to remind readers of the figure of Fancy in Joseph

Warton's popular ode *To Fancy*, but for the purpose of contrast rather than analogy. The terms Fancy and Imagination were virtually synonymous in the 18th c. But whereas Warton's Fancy is a devotee of Nature, Smart's Imagination is a creature of artifice. Warton's nymph has 'loosely-flowing hair' and 'bosom bare', a waist 'with myrtle-girdle bound' and brows 'with Indian feathers crown'd' (*Odes on Various Subjects*, 1746, p. 6), where Smart's has an elborate coiffure ornamented with precious stones (37–42), a bosom covered with crimson gauze (47–8), and a bejewelled girdle (51–4). This stress is in contrast also to Smart's own portrait of Fancy in *The Hop-Garden* i. 257–64.

55–6 Cf. Warton's Fancy, 'Waving in thy snowy hand / An all-commanding magic wand' (loc. cit.).

121–2 Probably an allusion to the Book of Wisdom, of which Reason has already been shown to be a devotee (76). Wisdom is described as a 'pure influence' (7: 25) drawing to herself the total devotion of 'holy souls . . . For God loveth none but him that dwelleth with wisdom' (7: 27–8).

147 *the prize*: i.e. of salvation, as in Col. 2: 18, Phil. 3: 14. cf. *Hymns* (1771) 2. 16.

Ode to Admiral Sir George Pocock

George Pocock (1706–92) entered the navy in 1718. He commanded the West Indian squadron which routed a French convoy in 1747, and scored notable successes against the French fleet on the East India station in 1758–9, but his greatest exploit was the capture of Havana in 1762 (see *JA*, D112). He was knighted and made Admiral of the Blue in 1761. Pocock's return to Plymouth on 13 Jan. 1763, after a hazardous trip from Havana, was announced in the *Public Advertiser* on 18 Jan. Reports of his arrival in London ten days later stated that he had an audience with the king and was to be rewarded with a peerage.

The stanza form is the same as that used in *Hymns*, 17, in which naval heroes are again glorified.

1–4 Cf. *Hymns* 26. 9–10.

2 *the White*: i.e. the white band on the target used in archery, but also a naval term, Admiral of the White [squadron] being the most senior flag-officer beneath the Admiral of the Fleet.

4 n. 'Then they willingly received him into the ship: and immediately the ship was at the land whither they went.'

7–10 See Luke 14: 11, 'For whosoever exalteth himself shall be abased; and he that humbleth himself shall be exalted.'

12 See *Hymns* 11. 121–4.

14 *either India*: i.e. the East and West Indies (see headnote above).

God's applauses: see introduction, p. xxxv.

37–42 This is largely invention, but presumably based on the fact that Pocock felt himself unjustly treated when he failed to get the appointment as first commissioner of the Admiralty for which he was nominated in Dec. 1762; he resigned from the service as a result (Charnock's *Biographia Navalis*, 1796, iv. 405–6).

49–51 The naval heroes listed by Smart were all, like Pocock, celebrated for victories against Spain: Charles *Howard*, Sir Martin *Frobisher* (for the spelling *Forbisher* see *Hymns* 17. 28 n.) and Sir Francis *Drake* for the defeat of the Armada in 1588; Edward *Vernon* for the capture of Porto Bello in 1739; Robert *Blake* for the destruction of the Spanish fleet at Santa Cruz in 1657.

58 *consul's robe*: Pocock was MP for Plymouth 1760–8.

66 Cf. *Hymns* 27. 23.

67–72 Charnock reports of Pocock: 'Nor were his private virtues less the subject of regard and honour than those of greater and more public notoriety. As a parent he was, with the greatest truth, unexcelled: as a brother, most truly benevolent: and, as a relative, affectionate in the highest degree.' He was noted also for 'an extensive generosity, which raised him up as a blessing to all his neighbours, whose indigence called forth his ever attentive bounty' (op. cit., iv. 406–7).

Ode to General Draper

William Draper (1721–87) was educated at Eton and King's College, Cambridge. He joined the army in 1744, fought with distinction as Lieut.-Col. of the 79th regiment at Fort St George, Madras (1758–9), and as Brig.-Gen. commanded the expedition which captured Manila (1762). He was knighted in 1766. He was clearly a good friend to Smart, subscribing both to *Poems on Several Occasions* (1752) and to the *Psalms* (40 books), and twice mentioned in *JA* (B19, B606).

Motto. Adapted from Virgil, *Aen.* vi. 822–3: 'However lesser men may report those deeds, patriotism and passion for renown shall prevail.'

30 Draper was a Fellow of King's before enlisting. *MARLBRO'*: probably the 3rd Duke, Charles Spencer Churchill (1706–58) whom Draper served as aide-de-camp in 1756. He distinguished himself at the battle of Dettingen (1743) and was Commander-in-Chief of the

expedition against Cherbourg and St Malo (1758). He was made DCL at Oxford in 1746.

63 n.   Refers to the report of the capture of Manila.

65   *MONSON*: Col. George Monson was in command of a landing force in the assault on Manila.

69   *hew*: for the correction see R. Mahony, 'Revision and Correction in the Poems of Christopher Smart', *PBSA* 77 (1983), 198.

72   *Tayler's College*: i.e. Merchant Taylors Hall, seat of the livery company, referring to the practice of honouring prominent men by conferring freedom of the company on them.

77   *matross*: gunner's mate.

88   *MORE*: Major More, of the 79th regt., was killed in the attack on Manila.

101   *Salmon's wax-work*: Mrs Salmon's Wax-work in Fleet St. was one of the popular sights of London in the 18th c. (see R. D. Altick, *The Shows of London*, Cambridge, Mass., 1978, pp. 52–3).

An Epistle to John Sherratt

For full biographical details of John Sherratt (b. 1718), see Betty Rizzo, 'John Sherratt, Negociator', *Bulletin of Research in the Humanities* 86 (1983–5), 373–429. He was a London entrepreneur of wide-ranging (sometimes shady) activities. Smart may first have known him when he was manager of Marybone Gardens in the early 1750s, but it was in his role as reformer of private madhouses that Sherratt contrived Smart's release from confinement in 1763, apparently by tricking his keeper (Rizzo, 420).

Motto.   Ovid, *Tr.* I. v. 9–10: 'These things will always be fixed deep in my heart, and I shall be perpetually his debtor for my life'.

1–4   Cf. *Hymns* 3. 27–32.

7–8   Cf. Wisd. 11: 21, 'thou hast ordered all things in measure and number and weight.' This text, cited by Augustine as evidence of the mathematical ordering of the Creation (*Civ. Dei.* xi. 30), became the basis of Renaissance analogies between divine and artistic creation and a key test in numerological theory. Smart's substitution of *melody* for *measure* is in keeping with this tradition, which assimilated mathematical conceptions of creation to the idea of *harmonia mundi*. See C. Butler, *Number Symbolism* (1970), and M.-S. Røstvig, 'Structure as prophecy: the influence of Biblical exegesis upon theories of literary structure', *Silent Poetry*, ed. A. Fowler (1970), pp. 32–72.

12   *mystic measure*: cf. *Hymns* 3. 31

13-14   The syntax would be smoother if *that* were emended to *than*, but Smart's point appears to be that Rolt's historical poetry is better than his prose: *that* is causal ('Rolt's historical writing is the better for being graced by verse'). The allusion is probably to Rolt's *Cambria* (1749), an ambitious poem in blank verse furnished with elaborate historical notes, as contrasted with his prose *History of South America* (1756).

17-18   Cf. *JA*, B333: 'For being desert-ed is to have desert in the sight of God and intitles one to the Lord's merit.' Poetry is the spiritual reward ('golden sheaf') which the poor and outcast may still 'glean' when material advantages are lacking: the metaphor is from Ps. 126: 5-6.

19-20   i.e. from Jan.–Feb. (Aquarius) 1756 to Sept.–Oct. (Libra) 1762. Smart's confinement actually ended in Jan. 1763, but evidently he dates the end of his sufferings from the negotiations for his release. The seven years were doubtless of numerological significance to Smart.

23 n.   Rolt married Mary Perrins in 1756 after the death of his first wife for whom Smart's epitaph was written (see *Epitaph on Mrs. Rolt*).

26 n.   *Miss A. F. S———*: probably Anna, the sister of James Sheels (see commentary on *Epitaph on the late Mr. Sheels*).

29-30   See Matt. 25: 34-6.

33-6   Cf. *JA*, B15, and Luke 15: 11-12. The allusion is to the parable of the prodigal son.

43-6   Louis Francis *Roubiliac* (1705?-62) came to London about 1732 and made his name with a statue of Handel for Vauxhall Gardens in 1737. One of his most famous works was the statue of Newton erected in Trinity College, Cambridge, in 1755.

47   *he ... eyes*: probably Allan Ramsey (1713-84), whose splendid portrait of Queen Charlotte in the Royal Collection was painted *c.*1762 (see M. Levey, *A Royal Subject: portraits of Queen Charlotte*, 1977).

48   George *Romney* (1734-1802) established himself as a fashionable portrait painter in London in 1762.

52   *th' Appulian Swan*: Horace, whose tag *ut pictura poesis* was the rallying-cry in contemporary arguments about the relations between painting and poetry. Smart's point seems to be that the 'young scholasticks' are conducting a futile debate, since neither poetry nor painting ('both the seats where arts commune') can vie with the song of gratitude.

63-4   See Introduction, p. xxxv.

73-8   The nautical imagery suggests an allusion to the capture of the French prize ship by the *Antigallican* privateer in 1756, an affair in which Sherrat was involved (see Rizzo, *art. cit.* 395-409). The 'pirate' was Smart's father-in-law, John Newbery, who was responsible for Smart's committal to the madhouse (Rizzo, 420-1).

73   *boom*: a barrier stretched across a river or harbour mouth to obstruct nevigation. Smart may be recalling the celebrated exploits of the Dutch fleet who in 1667 sailed up the Medway, crossing the boom designed to defend it.

Song ('Where shall Celia fly for shelter')

7   *HAYMAN's archer*: Francis Hayman executed many of the paintings decorating the pavilions in Vauxhall Gardens, among which was one representing 'An archer and a landscape' (*A Description of Vaux-Hall Gardens*, 1762, p. 30). The apparent pun, 'Hymen's archer', which occurs in an undated song-sheet (Bodl. Harding Mus. E562, fo. 62), may be accidental: *Hymen* was an alternative spelling of the artist's name, found on an 18th-c. series of prints of the Vauxhall paintings (Bodl. Douce Prints a. 49, fos. 86-90). The names of both *Hayman* and *Celia* occur in *The Blockhead and Beehive* (*c.*1754), which suggests that the song may date from the same period.

19   *bating*: reducing (*OED* v² 4). *1764* 'baiting' was an older spelling of the same verb.

On a Bed of Guernsey Lilies

Dearnley (pp. 210-11) notes the affinity in subject and theme between this poem and an essay titled 'Some Account of the Guernsey Lilly, with Animadversions thereon', published in *CM* (1760) under the pseudonym 'Juvenis'. She cites particularly Juvenis's conclusion:

Be not disheartened at your lot, O Christian, when God seems to have withdrawn his holy assistance from you; contemplate on the various changes which this flower undergoes; submit and support yourself with Christian fortitude and resignation; and rely on this, that God will not utterly forsake you, but that the sun of righteousness shall rise on you again, shall enable you to conquer that three headed monster, sin, death, and hell; and shall raise you to the greatest splendor in heaven, there to dwell when time shall be no more.

18   Cf. *Epistle to John Sherratt*, 17-18, and *JA*, B333.

Munificence and Modesty

The principal poem in *1763B*, but excluded from *1791*. Every copy of

1763B I have examined contains the corrections in Smart's hand to lines 18 and 146. The first of these corrections was announced in the *Daily Advertiser* on 4 Nov. 1763 (see R. Mahony, 'Revision and Correction in the Poems of Christopher Smart', *PBSA* 77 (1983), 198).

For an interpretation of the allegory, see Introduction, p. xxxvi. The identity of the painting by Guido Reni from which the 'Hint' in the subtitle was taken has been debated. Devlin (p. 157) suggested the *Coronation of the Virgin*, now in the National Gallery in London. This depicts a peasant Madonna enthroned in the heavens with the crown held above her head by two cherubs, and hosts of angels singing and playing musical instruments, as in Smart's baroque tableau at the end of the poem. But this painting was not in England in Smart's time and it is doubtful whether he could have known it. Dearnley's suggestion (pp. 206–8) that Reni's *Liberality and Modesty* was the picture in question is surely right. This painting was well known in England. One version was in the possession of Henry Furnese, a lord of the Treasury when it was engraved (in reverse) in 1755. It was purchased at the sale of Furnese's effects in 1758 by John, later first Earl Spencer, and remained at Althorp until it was sold in 1981. Other copies were in private collections in England in the 18th c. The Althorp picture shows two semi-naked female figures on a terrace: Liberality holds out a bowl of jewels from which Modesty, with downcast eyes, is picking one small brooch; a putto (or cherub) flies overhead, and in the background is a view of the sea with a wooded headland and a spire just visible among the trees. From this Smart could have taken not only his title and temptation-scheme but also some pictorial details (see lines 91–102). There are discrepancies in the treatment of the theme between his poem and the painting, the most conspicuous being in the representation of Liberality, but there is little reason to doubt that this was the painting to which Smart was alluding. (See C. Garboli and E. Baccheschi, *L'opera completa di Guido Reni*, Milan 1971; C. Whitfield, *England and the Seicento*, Catalogue of an exhibition at Agnews, 1973, no. 49; K. Garlick, Catalogue of Pictures at Althorp, *The Walpole Society* xlv, 1976, no. 521). Both the *Coronation of the Virgin* and Strange's print of *Liberality and Modesty* are reproduced by Dearnley (plates III–IV, facing p. 18).

The main literary source appears to be Milton: Smart's temptation-scheme follows the pattern of *Paradise Regained*, and he may have taken hints for the portrayal of Modesty from *Comus* and *Il Penseroso*. Crashaw (an alumnus of Smart's own college) is another possible influence: both *On the Blessed Virgins bashfulnesse* and *On the Assumption*, from *Steps to the Temple* (1646) are germane.

Motto (from title-page of *1763B*). Phaedrus, II. i. prol. 'Mark the reason why you should refuse the greedy, but give to the modest what they will not ask for'.

1–5   The *voice of Approbation* (Christ) is asked to fulfil the promise implicit in the Sermon on the Mount: 'Blessed are the poor in spirit: for theirs is the kingdom of heaven.' (Matt. 5: 3).

6   Anticipating the climax of the story, when 'Oriel' (Christ?) comes to receive Modesty into heaven.

8   Alluding to the parable of the ten virgins (Matt. 25: 1–13): the wise virgins prepared themselves for the coming of the bridegroom with lamps filled with oil. This parable is traditionally interpreted in relation to the Second Coming.

17–20   The self-distrust, downcast eyes, and blushes are reminiscent of Spenser's Shamefastnesse (*FQ* II. ix. 40–3); but cf. Crashaw, *In the Glorious Epiphanie* (*Carmen Deo Nostro*, 1652), line 67, for the 'blushes' of the Virgin Mary, and *JA*, B664: 'For the blessing of God upon purity is in the Virgin's blushes.'

36   See note on 115–18.

40   *obnoxious*: liable to harm (*OED* 1c); cf. *Hop-Garden* i. 51.

47–54   Cf. the narrative of St John the Divine: 'And she [Mary] spread forth her hands unto heaven and prayed, saying: I worship and praise and glorify thy name ... O Lord, because thou hast regarded the lowliness of thine handmaiden ... And after the prayer she said unto the apostles: Cast on incense and pray. And when they had prayed there came thunder from heaven and a terrible sound as of chariots, and lo, a multitude of the host of angels and powers, and a voice as of the Son of man was heard, and the Seraphim came round about the house wherein the spotless mother of God, the virgin, lay' (*The Apocryphal New Testament*, trans. M. R. James (1924), p. 204).

55–62   In the apocryphal narratives, the assumption is announced by the archangel Gabriel, but Smart's iconography suggests a composite figure based on the three principal archangels. Michael, the warrior angel, is usually depicted in armour ('geers', 60), and as chief of the archangels would appropriately be of greater stature (57). Gabriel is often depicted at the Annunciation wearing a crown (55) and carrying a sceptre (130). Raphael is often depicted with a golden belt (58), and is associated with alms-giving (62) in Tobit 12: 8–9.

60   *GRANBY*: John Manners, Marquis of Granby (1721–70), was the hero of the day. Appointed commander of the British forces in

Germany after the battle of Minden (1759), he scored a brilliant cavalry success at Warburg (1760) and had the lion's share of the fighting and the glory in the final campaign of the Seven Years' War, returning to a hero's welcome in England in 1763. *geers*: armour (*OEC*, s.v. gear I. 2).

78   *Crusion*: goldfish (see commentary on *A Song to David*, 341).

79   *Gani's mines*: famous diamond-mines in India (cf. *Immensity*, 62).

90   Besides characterizing Modesty's nun-like piety, *vows* may allude to the vows of virginity made by Mary, according to apocryphal legends of her nativity and and childhood: see *Catholic Encyclopaedia* (New York, 1907), xv. 464.

100   *ARABY the blest*: Milton, *PL* iv. 163, cf. *Goodness*, 94, and *To Health*, 4.

103   Perhaps alluding to Song of Songs 6: 8–9: 'There are threescore queens, . . . and virgins without number. My dove, my undefiled is but one; she is the only one of her mother, she is the choice one of her that bare her.' Passages relating to the bride in the Song are applied to Mary in the Office of the Blessed Virgin. Crashaw addresses the virgin as 'holy Queen of humble hearts' in *On the Assumption*, 29.

115–18   Modesty's declaration, coupled with her prayer to God as 'Father of Simplicity' (36), suggests that Smart had 2 Cor. 11: 2–3 in mind: 'I have espoused you to one husband, that I may present you as a chaste virgin to Christ. But I fear, lest . . . your minds should be corrupted from the simplicity that is in Christ.'

122   The bride in Song of Songs 2: 1 is self-styled 'the rose of Sharon'.

128   Cf. Milton, *Paradise Regained*, iii. 105–7: 'Shall I seek glory then, as vain men seek, / Oft not deserved? I seek not mine, but his / Who sent me.'

130   Both *Sceptre* and *Dove* are associated with the Annunciation in Christian iconography, the sceptre (carried by Gabriel) representing divine sovereignty, the dove representing the Holy Spirit and Mary's purity. The sceptre is associated with the kingdom of heaven in Ps. 45: 6 and Heb. 1: 8; *dove* is used of both bride and bridegroom in the Song of Songs; cf. Crashaw, *On the Assumption*, 7, 14.

134   Cf. Crashaw, *On the Assumption*, 55–7.

137–46   Cf. the coming of Christ in the apocryphal narrative of St John: '. . . behold Christ cometh sitting upon the throne of the

Cherubim. And as we all prayed there appeared innumerable multitudes of angels, and the Lord riding upon the Cherubim in great power ... And the Lord abode by her [Mary], saying: Behold, henceforth shall thy precious body be transported unto paradise, and thine holy soul shall be in the heavens.' (ed. cit., p. 207). *ORIEL and his SONG*: Oriel is perhaps coined as a name for Christ on the model of the title 'Oriens' used of Christ in the Great Advent Antiphons in the Roman rite (see *ODCC*, s.v. O-Antiphons): these are sung before and after the Magnificat, the song of praise of the Virgin. Oriel's 'Song' may refer to the song of praise which Christ commands in honour of Mary at her ascension (NT apocrypha, ed. cit., p. 208).

143 The *Phœnix* is a traditional Christian symbol of resurrection and the triumph of eternal life over death. Smart uses it of the resurrection of Christ in *Hymns* 6. 79, and of Gratitude in *Hymns* (1771), 22. 21.

144 *The first degree*: probably alluding to 'degrees' in Masonic ritual, symbolizing rank and corresponding stage of spiritual development (cf. *JA*, B217, and *On Gratitude*, 19). In modern Masonic practice the First Degree ('Entered Apprentice') is the lowest, but the three-degree system developed only gradually in England and may not have been established at this date (Carr, 58–62). Smart evidently means the highest stage.

145 *MAMMON and his leav'n*: love of worldly riches, and other traces of an unregenerate nature (for *leaven* in this sense, see 1 Cor. 5: 6–8).

Female Dignity

Lady Susanna Hussey Delaval was the wife of Sir John Hussey (formerly Blake) Delaval, her cousin. At the time of her marriage in 1750, she was the widow of John Potter, Under-Secretary of State for Ireland. Smart's association with the Delavals began in 1746, when he was John Delaval's tutor at Cambridge (see commentary on *An Occasional Prologue and Epilogue to Othello*).

In theme the poem anticipates Smart's hymns for children, in which he redefines the concepts of beauty, charm, and honour in spiritual terms: see *Hymns* (1771) 13, 14, and 30.

25 Cf. *Hymns* (1771) 14. 13.

32 In *Hymns* (1771) 30. 13, *Honour* in women is defined as (among other things) 'sweet dignity'. For *Applause*, see Introduction, p. xxxv.

Epitaph on Henrietta, Late Dutchess of Cleveland

Henrietta Finch, daughter of the Earl of Winchilsea, married

William Fitzroy, 3rd Duke of Cleveland in 1732. She died in 1742, aged 37. There is no need to suppose that Smart's epitaph was written at the time of her death; the religious tone is more compatible with his later work, and *JA* is full of references to friends and benefactors of his early days, including the Duke of Cleveland (B683).

2 Refers to his great-great-uncle, Peter Smart (1569–1652?), prebendary of Durham, who was imprisoned for preaching a sermon against 'Popish ceremonies' in the cathedral, and published a number of puritan tracts (see *DNB*). The allusion was probably intended as a riposte to the *Critical Rev.* (Apr. 1763) which had questioned the Protestant orthodoxy of *A Song to David*.

3 *HOUSE OF GRACE*: a pun: the Duchess of Cleveland was sister-in-law of Grace Fitzroy, who married Henry Vane, Smart's patron.

5–7 For the Duchess of Cleveland's benefaction to Smart, see *Ode to Lord Barnard*, 36 n. Smart was taken under the protection of the family at Raby Castle after the death of his father in 1733.

8 The Duchess of Cleveland died childless.

Epitaph on Henry Fielding

Fielding died in 1754, but the reference in line 12 shows that Smart's epitaph must have been written after 1758. It may have been prompted by Murphy's edition of Fielding's *Works*, published in 1762.

9–10 Fielding was appointed Justice of the Peace for Westminster in 1748.

11 Refers to Fielding's support for the Foundling Hospital: see *The Champion* (21 Feb. 1740) and *Covent-Garden Journal* no. 44.

12 A confusion between Henry and his half-brother, Sir John Fielding, who published a plan for the reformatory for penitent prostitutes in 1758. The error was pointed out by the *Critical Rev.* (Nov. 1763, pp. 395–6). Smart may have read the account of 'Mr. Fielding's plan for a Preservatory and Reformatory for deserted Girls, and penitent Prostitutes' in *Martin's Mag.* (May 1758, ii. 800–2) and thought it was of Henry Fielding's conception.

14–16 Fielding suffered from tuberculosis, and died an invalid at Lisbon.

The Famous General Epitaph of Demosthenes

Demosthenes, *De Cor.* 29, commemorating the Athenians and Thebans killed in the battle of Chaeronea, 338 BC. Their defeat resulted in the subjection of Athens and Thebes to Macedonia.

Ode to the Earl of Northumberland

Hugh Percy, originally Smithson (1714–86), son-in-law of the 17th Earl of Northumberland, succeeded to the title in 1750. He was related by marriage to Smart's patron, the Duchess of Cleveland. His appointment as Lord Lieutenant of Ireland was announced on 20 Apr. 1763.

The ode received favourable notices in the *Public Advertiser* (24 July 1764) which commented that 'Mr. Smart appears plainly to have written for his own feelings, and to have avoided the beaten track of undistinguishing adulation', and in the *Monthly Rev.* (Sept. 1764, p. 231) which praised Smart for his anti-Romanist sentiments: 'he merits the thanks of every true Protestant, for he fights with a truely British spirit against the Whore of Babylon.' The omission of the anti-Catholic stanzas (85–114) from *1791* was probably the responsibility of Smart's wife and daughter, both devout Catholics, who were the printers of the edition: see Mahony and Rizzo, pp. 84–5.

Motto. Horace, *Ep.* I. i. 11: 'I study what is right and seemly' (*quid verum* in original).

13   Lord Warkworth, son of the Earl of Northumberland, was born on 25 Aug. 1764 (*DNB*).

19   Elizabeth Seymour, heiress of the Percy property, married Hugh Smithson in 1740. She subscribed to Smart's *Psalms*.

25–7   Northumberland was president of the Lying-in Hospital: see *Epilogue* to *The Conscious Lovers*.

43–8   Refers to the 'beautifying' of Westminster Guild-Hall: see *GM* (1761), pp. 330–1.

55–60   Lord Warkworth entered the army in 1759 and served under Prince Ferdinand of Brunswick in the Seven Years war, taking part in the battles of Bergen and Minden.

59   *GRANBY:* see *Munificence and Modesty*, 60 n.

61–6   He was elected MP for Westminster on 15 Mar. 1763, during his absence.

85–90   Refers to the proroguing of parliament by James II in 1685.

91–102   Charles Seymour, 6th Duke of Somerset (grandfather of the Countess of Northumberland) refused to introduce the Papal Nuncio at St James's Palace in 1687, and was consequently deprived of his offices at court.

103–14   Smart was not alone in celebrating Northumberland as a guardian of the Protestant church: cf. John Lockman's *Poem on the Return of the Earl of Northumberland from his Government of Ireland* (1764), 65–8:

> Religion, chief did his attention share,
> And *Charter-Schools* were his particular care;
> Where children, out of Popish darkness brought,
> Beneath the GOSPEL's radiant light are taught.

117   Northumberland was noted for his 'constant encouragement of literature and the polite arts' (obituary notice, *GM* 1786, p. 529). In 1761 he commissioned Robert Adam to Remodel Syon House on a lavish scale, with a magnificent sculpture gallery which was the talk of the time.

124   William STANHOPE, Earl of Harrington, and George Montague Dunk, Earl of Halifax, were Northumberland's predecessors in Ireland in 1746–51 and 1761–3, respectively.

To the Honourable Mrs. Draper

Caroline, daughter of Lord William Beauclerk, married William Draper in 1756; she died in 1769.

8   *applause*: see Introduction, p. xxxv.

23   *young DRAPER* was in fact forty-three in 1764, a year older than Smart himself.

On being asked by Colonel Hall

Col. Hall was presumably the Col. Thomas Hall who subscribed to Smart's *Psalms*. Major-General William Kingsley (1698?–1769) commanded a brigade of infantry at the battle of Minden (1759), when a French force of over 50,000 was defeated by an allied army of only 36,000.

23–4   See Introduction, p. xxxv.

Epitaph on the late Duke of Argyle

John Campbell, 2nd Duke of Argyll (1680–1743), Marlborough's general in the wars of the Spanish Succession, won the approval of Tories and opposition Whigs in 1738 by his fierce opposition to Walpole. See Pope, *Epilogue to the Satires*, Dia. ii. 86–7. Mahony and Rizzo (Item 153) suggest that Smart's epitaph was a reply to the couplet on the death of the Duke of Argyll published in *GM* (1743), p. 660: 'Truth, valour, wisdom, gave a dubious light: / Great *Argyle* dies, and all is wrapt in night.'

Epigram of Epictetus

A free rendering of the epitaph in the Greek Anthology (*Pal. Anth.* vii. 676), translated by Johnson, 'Epictetus, who lies here, was a Slave and a Cripple, poor as the Begger in the Proverb, and the Favourite of Heaven.' Johnson comments: 'In this distich is comprised the noblest panegyric, and the most important instruction. We may learn from it that virtue is impracticable in no condition. .... And we may be likewise admonished by it, not to lay stress on man's outward circumstances in making an estimate of his real value.' *GM* (Dec. 1740), pp. 595–6. A request for a translation was published in *CM* in Aug. 1760; three were printed in the following month, none by Smart.

Epigramma Sannazarii

As Mahony and Rizzo note (item 153), this second translation of Sannazaro's epigram (cf. *The Famous Epigram of Sannazarius on Venice*) is very similar to a translation by John Banks printed alongside Smart's first version in *GM* in 1754. Banks's version reads:

> In Adriatic waves when Neptune saw
> Fair Venice stand, and to the sea give law;
> Boast thy Tarpeian towers, thy martial reign,
> O Jove, he said; thy Tiber to the Maine
> Prefer: each city view, and own the odds;
> That seems the work of men, and this of Gods.

The Sweets of Evening

14 *Asterie*: the quail, from the legendary daughter of Coeus, 'on whom Jupiter begat Hercules in the form of an eagle, but being afterwards angry with her, the gods in pity turned her into a quail' (Ainsworth).

21–5 Cf. *Hymns* 1. 29–32.

The Prize Carnation

Discovered by Betty Rizzo: see 'A New Secular Hymn by Christopher Smart: "The Prize Carnation" ', *RES*, NS. 26 (1975), 317–9. A note on the songsheet refers to the composer, Edmund Ayrton, as 'Of the Chapel Royal', which dates it 1764 or later. Ayrton (1734–1808) was appointed to the Chapel Royal in 1764 after studying with Dr Nares. He too contributed to the *Collection of Melodies* for Smart's *Psalms* (see Mahony and Rizzo, Item 157). Rizzo suggests that the subject of the poem was Miss Sheeles, the 'sublime transcendent maid' of *Epistle to John Sherratt*, 25 n.

9 *approbation*: for the special significance Smart attaches to this concept, see *Munificence and Modesty*, 1.

14 *Juba*: the hero of Addison's *Cato*, who marries Cato's daughter.

Epistle to Dr Nares

The card with Smart's holograph is pasted into Nares's own copy of *1791*, now in Pembroke College Library, Cambridge, with a heading by Nares, 'An original card, from Chr. Smart to Dr Nares', and footnote, 'This must have been written about 1764 or 5.'

James Nares (1715–83) received his Mus.D. from Cambridge in 1756, and was organist and composer to the Chapel Royal, and Master of the Children (1757–80). He contributed to the *Collection of Melodies* for Smart's *Psalms* (see Mahony and Rizzo, Item 157).

Song ('A MASON is great and respected')

Headed 'Song by Brother C. Smart, A.M. in *A Defence of Free-Masonry* (1765). Smart declares himself a Freemason in *JA*, B109. Although an unidentified 'Mason's Song' was in the programme of Mrs Midnight's Concert and Oratory on 14 Apr. 1853 (*London Stage*, Pt. 4, p. 365), affinities between the present poem and Smart's later religious poetry suggest that it was written in 1764–5. His concern seems to be to vindicate freemasonry against contemporary charges that it was irreconcilable with Christianity (see *JA*, B109 n.).

3 Cf. *A Song to David*, 177: 'His wisdom drew the plan': see Wisdom 9:8, 'Thou hast commanded me to build a temple'. Freemasons trace the origin of their craft from the building of Solomon's temple.

4 *built on a rock*: i.e. founded in Christ ('upon this rock I will build my Church', Matt. 16:18).

9–12 Smart attached peculiar importance to *good-nature* from his early days (see his ode *On Good-Nature*), claiming it in his later writings as a peculiarly Christian and English virtue: 'Good-nature is the grace of God in grain, and . . . the characteristic of an *Englishman*' (Preface to *The Works of Horace, Translated into Verse*, 1767, I, p. xxx); cf. *Hymns* 21. 44–5, *Hymns* (1771) 14. 1–2. The *corner-stone*, a symbol for Christ and the foundation of true faith (Eph. 2: 20), is frequently used in Smart's religious poems (see esp. *Parables* 64). Thus line 11 asserts the specifically Christian quality of a Mason's 'good-nature'.

15–16 A Masonic 'Charge' of 1735 claimed that 'the greatest

Monarchs in all ages ... have been Encouragers of the *Royal Art*; and many of them have presided as *Grand Masters* over the *Masons* in their respective Territories' (Carr, p. 244). One of the Ptolemys of Egypt and Augustus Caesar are among those said to have encouraged or practised the craft (Carr, pp. 245–6); Frederick the Great was one of the notable Masons in the 18th c.

19–20   The beehive has been an emblem of industry in Masonic symbolism since the early 18th c. (Carr, pp. 100–1).

Madam and the Magpie

36   *deards*: perhaps a nonce-word for precious things; as such, it would make better sense than *dear* in *1791*.

60   *citron*: a drink made of brandy distilled with lemon-rind. *clary*: a mixture of wine, honey and spices.

64   *Roubilliac*: see *Epistle to John Sherratt*, 43–6, and n.

87   *verjuice*: the acid juice of crab-apples, etc. hence 'sour'.

Verses to the Author

Discovered by Roger Lonsdale: see 'New Verses by Christopher Smart', *RES*, NS 33 (1982), 184–7. Sidney Swinney (1721–83), author of *The Battle of Minden*, was educated at Eton and Jesus College, Cambridge, where he matriculated in 1741 and where his acquaintance with Smart probably began. His father, Major Swiney [*sic*], was a subscriber to Smart's *Poems on Several Occasions* (1752), and Sidney Swinney himself subscribed to Smart's *Psalms*. He was ordained in 1745 and became rector of Barton-le-Street, Yorkshire. During the Seven Years' War he seems to have been a chaplain to the forces and to have been present at the battle of Minden (1759) itself (see Lonsdale, art. cit.).

The poem is dated from Spring-Gardens, Sept. 26, 1769.

7   Prince *Ferdinand* of Brunswick was commander of the German forces at Minden.

8   John Manners, Marquis of *Granby*, commanded a line of cavalry at Minden. See *Munificence and Modesty*, 60 and *n*. Lonsdale suggests that a particular motive for Smart's poem was to defend Granby against the attacks on him by 'Junius' which had begun in Jan. 1769. General Draper, another hero of Smart's, championed Granby against 'Junius' (art. cit., p. 187).

Epigram on John Wilkes

Written extempore, according to the 'Anecdote of the late Mr.

Christopher Smart' in which the epigram appears in the *London Chronicle* and other contemporary sources:

> The late Mr. Christopher Smart, with some poetical friends, were, one night, on a party at Vauxhall. They had not been long in the box, before it was proposed to write some humorous descriptive verses of a person who squinted—we believe it was Mr. Wilkes, and, too, that he was one among them . . . Every man was to write two or more lines; but not one of them, when it came to the eyes, could write anything drolly depicturative of the party's squinting—at last Kit Smart jumps up, darts out of the box, runs quite round the garden, returns out of breath with "Give me the pen, I have got it," and immediately writes down the following truly whimsical couplet.

If the distich was genuinely coined for the occasion, it must date from 1750 or earlier, since Smart uses the same conceit in *Horatian Canons*, 91, and (of himself) in *ST*, i. 249; but the earliest direct evidence of his connection with Wilkes dates from 1765, when Wilkes subscribed to Smart's *Psalms*. However, see Sherbo, pp. 250–1. For Smart's lost ode on Wilkes's birthday (1769), see Mahony & Rizzo, Item 19.

The Herald and Husband-Man

Motto. Juvenal, *Sat.* viii. 20: 'Nobility is the one and only virtue.'

6 *Or . . . Fez . . . Gules*: heraldic terms. *Or* is gold, *Fez* (fesse) a horizontal band across the shield, *Gules* red.

8 *blaze on*: i.e. *blazon*, depict according to the rules of heraldry.

25–6 'That Sage was by our ancestors esteemed a very wholesome herb, and much conducing to longevity appears by that verse in *Schola Salernitana, Cur moriatur homo cui Salvia crescit in horto?*' John Ray's *Collection of English Proverbs* (2nd edn., 1678), 36.

47 *The visible diurnal sphere*: Milton, *PL* vii. 22.

Epistle to Mrs Tyler

See note on *An Invitation to Mrs Tyler*.

Lines with a pocket book

Published in George Dyer's 'Cantabrigiana' column in *MM* with a note saying it had been contributed by Smart's daughter (Elizabeth Le Noir) and confessing that 'some liberty' had been taken with the final couplet. Presumably the other variants are also editorial. In her letter to Barker, Mrs Le Noir says the poem was addressed to one of Smart's sisters.

To Mrs Dacosta

The date of composition is problematic. The poem was published in *GM* in a letter from 'A.S.N.' dated 7 June 1770, saying that it had not previously been printed: 'It was addressed, in 1758, to the wife of Mr. Emmanuel Mendez Dacosta, then clerk and librarian to the Royal Society' (Aug. 1818, p. 157); but Da Costa did not become Clerk of the Royal Society until Jan. 1763 (J. Nichols, *Illustrations of the Literary History of the 18th Century*, 1817–58, iv. 750–1). In 1767 he was convicted of defrauding the society and served five years in the King's Bench prison, where he was Smart's fellow-inmate. Da Costa, a naturalist of some note, and a longstanding friend of Smart's old enemy, John Hill, was elected a member of the Royal Society in 1747. For his association with Hill, see G. S. Rousseau (ed.), *The Letters and Papers of Sir John Hill* (New York, 1982).

3–4 For the association of *Virtues* and *Flowers*, cf. *The Prize Carnation*, 9–12.

On Gratitude

Thomas Seaton (1684–1741), fellow of Clare College, Cambridge, and vicar of Ravenstone, Northants, bequeathed part of his estate to the University of Cambridge as endowment for the prize for poetry which was named after him (see Introduction). He himself published hymns and other religious works.

17–18 'If a man say, I love God, and hateth his brother, he is a liar: for he that loveth not his brother whom he hath seen, how can he love God whom he hath not seen?' 1 John 4:20.

19 *the first degree*: i.e. redemption. For Smart's special notion of *degree*, see *Munificence and Modesty*, 144–6 n.

37 Spenser eulogizes his patron Sidney on several occasions, but Smart may have been thinking particularly of the dedication to *The Ruine of Time*, which was written, Spenser says, to show his 'thankefull remembrance' of Sidney (*Spenser's Minor Poems*, ed. E. de Sélincourt, Oxford, 1960, p. 126).

38 Matthew Prior wrote a lavish encomium to the Earl of Dorset, his patron, in the dedication to *Poems on Several Occasions* (1708), published after Dorset's death: it is in this sense, perhaps, that Dorset was *hail'd to heav'n* by Prior.

40 *all the Nine and all the Sev'n*: i.e. the Muses and the Sciences; cf. *ST*, ii. 389, where Smart couples 'the seven sciences' and 'the nine muses' as conventional resources of panegyrical poetry.

47–8 Cf. *Hymns* (1771), 22. 19–20.

INDEX OF TITLES

(An asterisk indicates a poem of uncertain authorship)

INDEX OF TITLES

INDEX OF TITLES

INDEX OF TITLES

INDEX OF TITLES

INDEX OF FIRST LINES

INDEX OF FIRST LINES

INDEX OF FIRST LINES

GENERAL INDEX TO THE TEXT

(Translations from other poets into Latin have not been indexed)

495